VISION

PHILOSOPHICAL ISSUES IN SCIENCE
Edited by W. H. Newton-Smith
Balliol College, Oxford

COLOUR VISION

A study in cognitive science
and the philosophy of perception

Evan Thompson

London and New York

First published 1995
by Routledge
11 New Fetter Lane, London EC4P 4EE

Simultaneously published in the USA and Canada
by Routledge
29 West 35th Street, New York, NY 10001

© 1995 Evan Thompson

Typeset in Palatino by Solidus (Bristol) Limited
Printed and bound in Great Britain by
T J Press Ltd, Padstow, Cornwall

British Library Cataloguing in Publication Data
A catalogue record for this book is available from
the British Library

Library of Congress Cataloging in Publication Data
Thompson, Evan.
Colour vision: a study in cognitive science and the philosophy
of perception/Evan Thompson.
p. cm. – (Philosophical issues in science)
Includes bibliographical references and index.
1. Color vision. 2. Cognitive science. 3. Perception
(Philosophy) I. Title. II. Title: Color vision. III. Series.
QP483.T48 1994
152.14'5–dc20
94–13588
CIP

ISBN 0–415–07717–6 (hbk)
ISBN 0–415–11796–8 (pbk)

for
FRANCISCO J. VARELA
friend and teacher

CONTENTS

CONTENTS

FIGURES

PREFACE

In an essay written shortly before his death, Maurice Merleau-Ponty quotes Paul Cézanne as saying that colour is the 'place where our brain and the universe meet' (Merleau-Ponty 1964: 180). In this remark the painter elegantly expresses why philosophers since Aristotle have been fascinated by colour – colour lies at the intersection of mind and matter, perception and the world, metaphysics and epistemology. Our time is no exception, for within the past seven years there has been a remarkable renewal of philosophical interest in colour, provoking one philosopher to comment on the 'chromatic zeitgeist' at work in contemporary philosophy (Hardin 1989). Yet with one exception (Westphal 1987), this renewed interest has not given birth to a philosophical treatment worthy of Cézanne's remark. Instead, recent philosophers have staked out extreme positions on the nature of colour. Some hold that colours are just the reflective properties of surfaces and so do not depend at all on the perceiver (Hilbert 1987; Matthen 1988); they are willing to identify colours with properties of the physical world even though there is a profound mismatch between such properties and the essential properties of colour. Others hold that there are no colours but only brain-based experiences of colour (Hardin 1988; Landesman 1989); they are willing to eliminate colour altogether as a property of the world, thus convicting colour perception of being in its very nature metaphysically mistaken.

The main aim of this book is to correct this imbalance by articulating a philosophically sensitive treatment of the world-dependence of the mind and the mind-dependence of the world evident in the perception of colour. Thus, in contrast to the extreme views currently favoured, I argue for a relational account: colours are properties constituted jointly by the perceiver and the world. But the arguments that I advance in support of this position are predominantly naturalistic, not a priori. They lean heavily on comparative and evolutionary studies of colour vision, neuroethology, computational vision, and the ecological approach in perceptual psychology pioneered by J. J. Gibson (1979). The relational account of colour that I develop is thus an 'ecological' one: on one side, the world is considered as an animal-inhabited environment, rather than a neutral material universe where the living creatures have been removed; and on the other side, the perceiver is treated as an active exploring animal, rather than a disembodied spectator who serves as little more than a repository for colour sensations.

The naturalistic approach taken here is in keeping with a certain trend in the philosophy of mind and perception – the pursuit of philosophical concerns within the context of what is known as cognitive science. I understand cognitive science in a broad sense to be an interdisciplinary field devoted to the scientific study of the mind. It includes neuroscience, psychology, linguistics, computer science and artificial intelligence, and philosophy. The study of colour vision provides a microcosm of the field, for each of these disciplines has contributed to our understanding of colour. Neuroscientists have uncovered some of the anatomical structures and physiological processes that subserve colour vision in the visual system, particularly in primates; cellular biologists have characterized the light-sensitive cells in the retina; and molecular biologists have isolated and sequenced the genes for the three different types of colour-sensitive cone visual pigments in the human eye. Psychophysicists have contributed quantitative models for human visual performance, and cognitive psychologists have provided models of the structure of human colour categories. Linguists have shown that human languages contain a limited number of basic colour terms and have provided various models to account for these semantic universals. Researchers in artificial intelligence, particularly computational vision, have devised computational models and algorithms for various aspects of colour perception. And finally, philosophers have discussed the nature of colour properties in relation to philosophical issues about the mind and perception.

Although the main aim of this book is a philosophical one, the book is intended also as a contribution to this continuing interdisciplinary effort. When studying topics such as colour and visual perception cognitive science without philosophy is blind, but philosophy without cognitive science is empty. Thus I believe that philosophy has an important role to play in the field, but it can fulfil this role only by immersing itself in the empirical investigations. To this end I have drawn extensively on research from each of the disciplines in cognitive science, but I have also tried to present the main theories and findings in a manner accessible to those not familiar with them.

Evan Thompson

ACKNOWLEDGEMENTS

The dedication of this book expresses my greatest obligation, for it is no exaggeration to say that, were it not for Francisco Varela, the book would never have been written. The study owes its origin to a conversation the two of us had in the summer of 1986 in Paris. Varela suggested that comparative colour vision would provide a novel perspective from which to examine issues about the mind and perception in cognitive science and philosophy. This work is the outcome of that suggestion and is deeply indebted to my continued collaboration with Varela.

Since that conversation in 1986 the work has developed through two stages. A first draft of certain portions was submitted as my doctoral dissertation in Philosophy at the University of Toronto in 1989; Lynd Forguson, who supervised this stage, deserves special thanks. Then, in 1992, an expanded and more technical version of certain sections of the dissertation was published as the target article (co-authored with Francisco J. Varela and Adrian Palacios) 'Ways of coloring: comparative color vision as a case study in cognitive science', *Behavioral and Brain Sciences* 1 (1992): 1–74. Thirty-three commentaries by visual scientists and philosophers were published with the article, as well as our response. I am grateful to many of the commentators for teaching me more about colour vision. Because of the limits to the length of that forum we were not able to discuss in detail all of the important points they raised, but I have tried to take them into greater consideration in this book.

I am deeply grateful to my family – my father, William, my mother, Gail, and my sister, Hilary; as well as my wife, Rebecca

Todd, and our children, Maximilian and Gareth – for their interest, encouragement, and loving support during the writing of this book.

Other people have given their support in numerous ways. Daniel C. Dennett, with whom I worked as a Postdoctoral Fellow in 1990–1, was generous in his encouragement of the project and provided very helpful criticism on some early versions of certain sections of the book. And by being able to read the draft versions of Dennett's book, *Consciousness Explained*, and by participating in the seminar based on them in the autumn of 1990 at Dennett's Center for Cognitive Studies at Tufts University, I was able to clarify many of my own thoughts about consciousness and visual perception. Justin Broackes read an earlier draft of the entire typescript and made many helpful suggestions. For remarks made in conversation or in letters that have been helpful I also wish to thank Valerie Bonnardel, Louis Charland, Don Dedrick, Danny Goldstick, Ronald de Sousa, Larry Hardin, Stevan Harnad, Jim McGilvray, Adrian Palacios, Eleanor Rosch, John Russon, William Seager, Sonia Sedivy, Mark Thornton, and Arthur Zajonc.

Two institutions deserve special acknowledgement for their gracious hospitality – CREA at the Ecole Polytechnique in Paris, where I pursued my research and writing in 1988–9, and the Center for Cognitive Studies at Tufts University, where I was a Visiting Postdoctoral Fellow in 1990–1.

For financial support I am grateful to the Social Sciences and Humanities Research Council of Canada for Doctoral Fellowships during the dissertation stage, and for a Postdoctoral Fellowship immediately thereafter, and to the Program for Biology, Cognition and Ethics of the Lindisfarne Association at the Cathedral Church of St John the Divine in New York City.

Finally, I wish to thank Kluwer Academic Publishers and the editors of *Philosophical Studies* and *Synthese* for permission to use material from my articles 'Novel colours', *Philosophical Studies* 68 (1992): 321–47 and 'Colour vision, evolution, and perceptual content', *Synthese*, in press (1995). The author and publishers have made every effort to determine who controls the copyright for Figure 2. If you do, or if you know who does, please contact us.

1

THE RECEIVED VIEW

Newton's laws and their later scientific corrections were used to impose on the disputed and heterogeneous phenomenon of the scattering of light, observed since the Greek physicists, the authority of the new sciences, which showed the possibility of reducing to analysis and measurement a multiple variable like the emission of light, and this with the most simple instrument in the world: a glass prism. Consequently, the individuality and the materiality of colour no longer belong to painting, or to the literature about colouring and chiaroscuro ... Colours are no longer a 'figure' of pictorial production, but a transmission of light.

(Manlio Brusatin 1986: 68–9. My translation)

Since the time of Newton and Locke, the received view among philosophers has been that colours are not found among the fundamental properties of things. Things as they are in themselves do not have colours; they have colours only by virtue of how they appear to us. Thus being coloured consists simply in being the kind of thing that looks or would look coloured to us in normal perceptual circumstances. In other words, things do not look coloured because they really are coloured; they are coloured only because they look to be so.

This view can be stated with a good deal more philosophical precision. According to Locke (1690/1975) and those who have developed his analysis (for example, Jackson 1968), colour consists in a power or disposition of something to produce sensory experiences of colour in a perceiver. The fundamental or so-called primary qualities of things, on the other hand, do not consist merely in dispositions to produce sensory experiences. According to this view, colour corresponds to a type of property that is both *dispositional* and *subjective*: being coloured consists solely in having the disposition to look coloured. Colour is therefore a relational property in two distinct ways. First and most generally, since dispositional properties typically involve relations between at least two things (for example, salt has the dispositional property of being soluble in water), colour is a relational property simply because it is dispositional. Second and more specifically, colour is a relational property because it can be specified only in relation to the visual experiences of a perceiver. Since the dispositional property in which colour consists is that of having the power to look coloured, and since something can look a certain way only in relation to the visual experiences of a perceiver, it follows that colour must be specified in relation to the colour experiences of a perceiver.

There are philosophers who hold that this conception of colour – indeed, this conception of so-called secondary qualities in general – represents an a priori philosophical discovery, rather than an empirical scientific one (McGinn 1983; Nagel 1986: 75). I disagree. The conception of colour as dispositional and subjective is intimately tied to early modern science and natural philosophy, especially to Newton's theory of light and colour. Of course, one can advocate the dispositional and subjectivist account of colour on purely philosophical grounds. Indeed, most philosophers who defend versions of the received view (for example, McGinn 1983; Peacocke 1983, 1984; Nagel 1986) do not bother to concern themselves with the scientific study of colour and colour vision. Nevertheless, the received view and Newton's theory of light and colour grew up together. As a matter of historical fact this point would not be denied by those who defend the received view on conceptual grounds. Yet these philosophers appear to believe that conceptual considerations alone are sufficient to establish that colour must be dispositional and subjective; empirical considerations can inform us of only the contingent details. I do not accept this attempted segregation of the conceptual and the empirical, the philosophical and the scientific.[1] On the contrary, in the case at hand, I believe that the received view is deeply

2

linked both conceptually and empirically to the Newtonian conception of colour, and furthermore that it is the Newtonian conception that actually gives rise to the modern form of the philosophical debate between subjectivism and objectivism about colour.

My intention in this chapter is to explicate and defend these remarks by examining Newton's theory of colour in relation to the empirical and conceptual features of the received view. There are several reasons for this undertaking. First, by revealing the connection between Newton's treatment of colour and the received view we provide the historical background and some of the conceptual basis for the discussion in the chapters to follow. Second, those contemporary philosophers who do concern themselves with the scientific study of colour vision all abandon, in one way or another, the received view: David R. Hilbert (1987) employs computational colour vision to defend objectivism; C. L. Hardin (1988) employs neurophysiology and psychophysics to defend a nondispositionalist version of subjectivism; and Jonathan Westphal (1987) employs colorimetry (the science of colour specification and measurement) and a Goethean conception of phenomenal colour science to establish real definitions of colour that are simultaneously physical and phenomenal. Finally, in the contemporary debate over the status of colour, the scientific and the philosophical, the empirical and the conceptual are inextricably linked. On the one hand, science is relevant to philosophy because the issue of the ontological status of colour cannot be separated from the issue of levels of explanation for vision (neurophysiological, psychophysical, and computational). On the other hand, philosophy is relevant to science because there are considerable conceptual issues involved in how these various levels of explanation might be related and in how they are to be applied to a specific case like colour vision. Since purely a priori treatments are unsatisfactory, and since the received view has been challenged on empirical as well as conceptual grounds, we must examine both the empirical and the conceptual features of the received view.

3

THE NEWTONIAN HERITAGE

Newton's *experimentum crucis*

Modern colour theory owes its origin to a series of experiments performed by Newton in 1666. Newton reported these experiments in his first scientific paper, a letter written to the Royal Society of London and printed in its *Philosophical Transactions*, 19 February 1671/2, under the title 'The new theory about light and colors' (Newton 1671/1953). He also described the experiments in his *Opticks* (Newton 1730/1952), the first edition of which appeared in 1704.

The purpose of Newton's letter was to establish the differential 'refrangibility' of light according to colour. Light, Newton argued in the first part of his paper, is not simple, but consists of rays that differ in their 'refrangibility' – in the degree to which they are bent, or as we would say today, 'refracted', when they pass from one medium into another. In the second part of his paper, Newton set forth his 'doctrine' of the 'origin of colors' in thirteen numbered paragraphs. The first sentence of the first paragraph conveys the essence of Newton's theory: 'As the rays of light differ in degrees of refrangibility, so they also differ in their disposition to exhibit this or that particular color' (Newton 1671/1953: 74). This relation between colour and degree of refrangibility is, Newton went on to say, 'very precise and strict, the rays always either agreeing in both or proportionally disagreeing in both'.

To appreciate Newton's idea we need to have some familiarity with the experiments he performed. Newton first used a prism to observe 'the celebrated phenomena of colors', i.e., the spectrum that can be generated by a prism and a light source, such as sunlight. He darkened his room, but made a small hole in the window shutters to let in a beam of sunlight. He then placed his prism in front of the aperture so that the light would be dispersed by the prism on to the opposite wall. Newton marked seven divisions within this spectrum – violet, indigo, blue, green, yellow, orange, and red. This sevenfold division actually appears to have been based on an analogy with the seven tones of the musical scale (Wasserman 1978: 19). Most observers fail to distinguish indigo, and so would mark only six divisions.

4

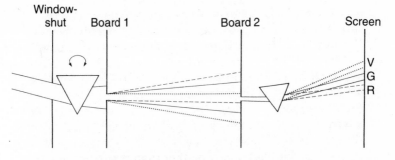

Figure 1 Newton's *experimentum crucis*
Rotating the first prism (left) while keeping the second prism
and the two boards stationary makes the complete spectrum cast on
the second board move up and down, so that different portions of the
spectrum fall on its aperture and pass through, where they are
refracted again by the second prism. Violet is refracted the most (to V),
red the least (to R), and the other colours intermediately.
Source: Sepper (1988: 11)

Newton states in his letter that his research on colour was
provoked by a surprise when he first used the prism. The
received laws of optics at the time led him to expect that the
image of the aperture on the wall would be circular, yet the
image was oblong.[2] He then devised several experiments to
explore this peculiar disproportion and its possible causes.
After ruling out various possibilities, such as the thickness of
the prism, irregularities in the glass, differences in the incidence of the rays coming from the sun, and curved movement
of the rays after they left the prism, Newton was led to perform
what he called his *experimentum crucis* or 'crucial experiment'
(see Figure 1).

> I took two boards and placed one of them close behind the
> prism at the window, so that the light might pass through
> a small hole, made in it for the purpose, and fall on the
> other board, which I placed at about 12 feet distance,
> having first made a small hole in it also for some of that
> incident light to pass through. Then I placed another
> prism behind this second board, so that the light, trajected
> through both the boards, might pass through that also and
> be again refracted before it arrived at the wall. This done,
> I took the first prism in my hand and turned it to and fro

5

slowly about its axis, so much as to make the several parts of the image cast on the second board successively pass through the hole in it, that I might observe to what places on the wall the second prism would refract them. And I saw by the variation of those places that the light, tending to that end of the image toward which the refraction of the first prism was made, did in the second prism suffer a refraction considerably greater than the light tending to the other end. And so the true cause of the length of that image was detected to be no other than that *light* consists of *rays differently refrangible*, which, without any respect to a difference in their incidence were, according to their degrees of refrangibility, transmitted to divers parts of the wall.

(1671/1953: 71–2)

The reader might have noticed that there is no mention of *colour* in the description of this experiment; instead, Newton has presented an experiment and a conclusion about the nature of *light*. What, then, is the connection between colour and the differential refrangibility of light?

By rotating the prism at the window, Newton was able to move the oblong image of the spectrum up and down on the second board, so that different portions of the spectrum would fall on its aperture and pass through, where they would be refracted again by the second prism. Since both boards and the second prism were fixed in place, the angle of incidence was constant for any beam of light striking the second prism. What Newton discovered was that despite this equality, different portions of the spectrum were refracted to different degrees by the second prism. Light that came from the violet end of the spectrum was refracted the most, whereas light that came from the red end of the spectrum was refracted the least. Furthermore, the colours of the beams remained unchanged when they were passed through the second prism. Newton's conclusion, therefore, was not merely that light 'consists of rays differently refrangible', but that the colours we experience correspond to different degrees of refrangibility. In his words: 'To the same degree of refrangibility ever belongs the same color, and to the same color ever belongs the same degree of refrangibility' (1671/1953: 74).

Before Newton no one had held that colours correspond to the component rays of a colourless beam of light, or that these rays are specified by their differential refrangibility (Sepper 1988: 109). Instead, the dominant theories of the time held that colours are produced as a result of the contact of light with some reflecting or refracting body (Sabra 1967/1981: 294–5; Guerlac 1986). This type of theory is called *modificationism* by historians: colours are thought to arise because of some modification of colourless light. When light passes through a prism, for example, it becomes coloured on account of refraction. But the colours do not exist in the light prior to refraction; they are instead produced by the prism. For example, Sabra describes Hooke as having held that

> the pulse of white light could be imagined as the resultant of a large number of 'vibrations' each of which when differentiated would produce a given colour. This would imply that white light is compounded only in a mathematical sense, and prismatic analysis would be understood as a process in which colours are manufactured out of the physically simple and undifferentiated white pulse.
>
> (Sabra 1967/1981: 233–4)

As Sepper notes, these modificationist theories 'could separate the geometric from the chromatic problem: The refraction might be calculated according to the sine law, and the colors explained according to some notion of modification' (Sepper 1988: 124). In other words, for these theories there was no intrinsic connection between the refraction of light and colours. The refraction of light through a prism was to be calculated according to the laws of optics, in particular those based on Snell's law of sines. Colours, however, were to be explained by the ways in which the prism changes the light that passes through it. For such theories there is no intrinsic correspondence, pre-existing in the light, between the degrees to which light can be refracted and dispositions to exhibit colours. Geometry and colour have not yet been united.

Newton's *experimentum crucis* linked these two problems. At the outset of his 'New theory about light and colors', Newton presented himself as concerned with the *chromatic* problem, i.e., with 'the celebrated phenomena of colors'. But despite this claim, he quickly turned to the *geometrical* problem of refraction: why, for a given position of the prism (minimum deviation), and assuming that the light from the sun is everywhere equally refrangible, is the image of the spectrum elongated? The *experimentum crucis* led Newton to conclude that the rays from the sun are not equally, but differentially refrangible: the rays preserve their respective degrees of refrangibility upon being refracted through the second prism. Newton then concluded, apparently on geometrical grounds alone, that sunlight consists of differentially refrangible rays, and so is not homogeneous. (The qualification 'apparently' is added because, as we shall see later, chromatic considerations in fact enter into the specification of what seems purely geometrical.) But the *experimentum crucis* also showed that the rays preserve their *colour* upon being refracted a second time; therefore, the same colour is always attached to the same index of refrangibility. Newton thus drew the further conclusion that colours are not modifications or *'qualifications of light ...* but *original* and *connate properties*, which in divers rays are divers' (1671/1953: 74). These differentially refrangible rays with their colour-producing properties exist unseen in the white light of the sun; the refractive properties of the prism merely render this fact visible.

Here geometry and colour are united, or better yet, inter-twined. For perhaps the first time there is held to be an intrinsic correspondence between properties of light and colour, one that is specified mathematically according to a geometrical index of refraction. In Sepper's words: 'Newton's theory combined the geometric and chromatic problems to explain both refraction and color according to a single principle, differential refrangibility, executed as rigorously as geometry allowed' (Sepper 1988: 110).

This combination of the mathematical and the chromatic was to have decisive and profound consequences for both the science and philosophy of colour. To appreciate these consequences, however, we must realize that Newton's argument is not conclusive. Its basic structure is easy to summarize.[3]

1   There are two and only two possibilities: either it is the case
    that

> (a) the colours of the spectrum are manufactured by the prism
>
> or
>
> (b) the colours have been with the rays from their origin.

2 If (a), then

> (c) white light is homogeneous and colours are modifications, etc.

3 The crucial experiment shows that an isolated beam of coloured light, when refracted through a second prism, does not undergo any modification in colour or degree of refrangibility.

4 Therefore (c) is false.

5 Therefore (a) is false.

---

6 Therefore (b) is true.

It should be apparent that (4) does not follow from (3), i.e., that the crucial experiment is not sufficient to establish the falsity of (c) and hence the truth of (b). What (3) demonstrates is that light which emerges from the first prism behaves differently from direct sunlight: light from the sun is altered in its refraction by the first prism, but is not altered again in its refraction through the second prism. This demonstration leaves open several possibilities: for example, it still remains possible that the *first prism* has manufactured the coloured rays and that the second prism simply preserves them without alteration (Sabra 1967/1981: 295). This hypothesis might not be correct, but there is nothing in the crucial experiment to rule it out.

Newton's argument, though not conclusive, is not, however, implausible. As Justin Broackes has pointed out (personal communication), (3) shows both that refrangibility at the second prism is instrinsic to the light arriving at that prism (i.e., to the light that emerges from the first prism) and that prisms do not have the tendency to modify such light. It is therefore plausible to suppose that the refrangibility of the light arriving at the first prism is intrinsic and that the first prism also cannot modify this light. The tacit general principle would be that if a prism cannot modify the rays emerging from a prism, then it cannot modify any rays at all. The principle is debatable, but certainly plausible.

In any case, my intention in analysing Newton's argument has not been to downplay the genius of his experiments or his contributions to colour science. Rather it has been simply to make apparent the nature of these contributions and their consequences for the science and philosophy of colour. The point is that Newton's genius consisted largely in devising a *hypothesis* about the differential refrangibility of light rays, not in discovering or demonstrating that differential refrangibility is a *fact*, despite Newton's insistence to the contrary.[4] My point here is hardly original: it was made by many of Newton's contemporaries, and Goethe was to insist over and over again that differential refrangibility according to colour is a hypothesis, not a fact (Sepper 1988). Nonetheless the point bears repeating, since there are historians, philosophers, and scientists who persist in describing Newton's achievement as the demonstration or discovery of a fact.[5] Now that this warning has been issued, we can turn to examine the conception of colour that Newton elaborated on the basis of his experiments.

The Newtonian conception of colour

What exactly did Newton mean by referring to colours as 'original and connate properties' of light rays? We have seen that Newton spoke of the correspondence between degrees of refrangibility and dispositions to exhibit colours. We might ask, then, whether the original and connate properties of light are *colours* or *dispositions* to exhibit colours.

In 'The new theory about light and colors', Newton did not express himself clearly on this issue. He often wrote as if colours themselves are properties of the rays. For example, he stated that 'The species of color and degree of refrangibility proper to any particular sort of rays is not mutable by refraction, nor by reflection from natural bodies, nor by any other cause that I could yet observe' (1671/1953: 74). Since colours do change when rays are mixed together, however, and the component colours reappear when they are separated through refraction, Newton held that, 'There are, therefore, two sorts of colors: The one original and simple, the other compounded of these' (1671/1953: 75). The original colours are the seven hues mentioned above, as well as 'an indefinite variety of intermediate gradations'. White is the most compounded of the colours, for no ray ever exhibits this colour, and it requires proportions of all the primary colours. 'Hence therefore it comes to pass that whiteness is the usual color of light; for light is a confused aggregate of rays endowed with all sorts of colors, as they are promiscuously darted from the various parts of luminous bodies' (1671/1953: 76).

In his *Opticks*, however, Newton added an unnumbered definition that clarified his position:

> The homogeneal Light and Rays which appear red, or rather make Objects appear so, I call Rubrifick or Red-making; those which make Objects appear yellow, green, blue, and violet, I call Yellow-making, Green-making, Blue-making, Violet-making, and so of the rest. And if at any time I speak of Light and rays as coloured or endued with Colours, I would be understood to speak not philo-sophically and properly, but grossly, and accordingly to such Conceptions as vulgar People in seeing all these Experiments would be apt to frame. For the Rays to speak properly are not coloured. In them there is nothing else than a certain Power and Disposition to stir up a Sensa-tion of this or that Colour. For as Sound in a Bell or musical String, or other sounding Body, is nothing but a trembling Motion, and in the Air nothing but that Motion propagated from the Object, and in the Sensorium 'tis a Sense of that Motion under the Form of Sound; so Colours in the Object are nothing but a Disposition to reflect this or that sort of Rays more copiously than the rest; in the Rays they are nothing but their Dispositions to propagate this or that Motion into the Sensorium, and in the Sensorium they are Sensations of those Motions under the Forms of Colours.
>
> (1730/1952: 124–5)

This paragraph is often quoted, especially by philosophers, and with good reason, for it encapsulates Newton's theory and implies several fundamental consequences for the science of colour.[6]

1. Newton attempted to distinguish clearly between phy-sical and perceptual phenomena, between stimulus and

11

sensation. This distinction remains foundational in the field of psychophysics.

2. Given this distinction, Newton held that the stimuli involved in colour vision – both proximal (light) and distal (surfaces of objects, etc.) – are not themselves coloured, or have colour only derivatively by virtue of their disposition to cause sensations of colour. Thus things do not look to be coloured because they are coloured; rather, things are coloured only because they look to be so. Although strictly speaking this view locates object colour in the physically grounded, dispositional properties of objects, the temptation is nonetheless to identify colour with – or eliminate object colour in favour of – a type of *sensation*. It is difficult to overestimate the force of this temptation. As James Clerk Maxwell (1890/1970: 75) almost two centuries later would remark: 'It seems almost a truism to say that colour is a sensation; and yet Young, by honestly recognizing this elementary truth, established the first consistent theory of colour.' Although philosophers continue to debate the ontological status of colour, most introductory psychology textbooks today begin with a remark to the effect that 'color is a psychological phenomenon, an entirely subjective experience' (Sekuler and Blake 1985: 181). This indecision between treating colours as physically grounded, dispositional properties of objects or as subjective 'projections' is one of the central features of the Newtonian heritage.

3. Newton referred to the homogeneal rays of light as colour-producing – red-making, yellow-making, green-making, etc. In other words, despite the temptation to identify colours with types of sensations, Newton held that the property of being colour-producing inheres primarily not in the eye or visual system, or in bodies or their surfaces, but in rays of light. As a result, spectral or 'homogeneal' colours were given priority over other forms of colour; they are the basic colours in terms of which others must be explained. This result can still be felt today, for we continue to refer to light of a single wavelength as 'monochromatic', even though the perceived hue of such a light varies with a host of factors such as intensity.[7]

4. The colour that an object is perceived to have (assuming that the visual system is functioning properly) depends on

the characteristics of the light that is being locally reflected from the surface of that object to the eye.

5. If we know the exact composition of the light being reflected from the surface of a given object, we shall be able to predict the colour that the object is perceived to have (again assuming a properly functioning visual system), even though we may not know how the visual system accomplishes this perceptual task.

6. We can make a body appear any colour by illuminating it with the homogeneal light that produces that colour. As Newton himself remarked:

> the colors of all natural bodies have no other origin than this that they are variously qualified to reflect one sort of light in greater plenty than another. And this I have experimented in a dark room by illuminating those bodies with uncompounded light of divers colors. For by that means any body can be made to appear of any color. They have there no appropriate color, but ever appear of the color of the light cast upon them; but yet with this difference that they are most brisk and vivid in the light of their own daylight color.
>
> (1671/1953: 77–8)

It will be useful to summarize these consequences in more contemporary terms. First of all, we have three important empirical claims:

(a) The proximal cause of colour perception is light.

(b) There is a one-to-one correspondence between the colour an object is perceived to have and the composition of the light that is reflected from that object.

(c) The so-called colour of an object corresponds to the character of the light reflected by the surface of that object. Therefore, to the extent that we speak of an object or surface as coloured, its colour will correspond to its disposition to reflect light of a given character.

What are the relations among these three claims? Let us construe (a) and (b) as constituting an argument for (c).[8] Thus if it is true both that light is the proximal cause of colour perception and that there is a one-to-one correspondence between locally reflected light and perceived colour, then what is to prevent us from drawing the further conclusion that colours in objects are merely the dispositions of those objects to reflect light of various characteristics? Newton held that these characteristics are reducible first to the types of rays of which the light is composed, and then to the minute corpuscles which make up the rays. Today we analyse light in terms of wavelength and intensity, and so we would express (c) by saying that colours correspond to the various wavelengths and intensities of the light that objects reflect.

One might claim, however, that this argument is invalid: (a) and (b) do not entail (c). Premises (a) and (b) still leave open the possibility that colours are intrinsic, spatially located features of the surfaces of objects, and that information about these features is carried by locally reflected light. Thus one might argue that a surface reflects, for example, predominantly 'red-making' (long-wave) light because the surface is red; the light merely carries this information (see Mundle 1971: 15). Perhaps Newton himself need not have abandoned this view, for he wrote in his *Opticks*:

> These Colours arise from hence, that some natural Bodies reflect some sorts of Rays, others other sorts more copiously than the rest ... Every Body reflects the Rays of *its own Colour* [my italics] more copiously than the rest, and from their excess and predominance in the reflected Light has its Colour.
>
> (1730/1952: 179)

It is important to realize that this counterargument does not abandon one of the central features of the Newtonian view, namely, the idea that we see colours as a result of the light that is reflected locally by objects. In other words, the argument does not contest the claim that there is a one-to-one correspondence between perceived colour and locally reflected light: it merely asserts that the reason why a surface reflects light which causes us to see the surface as having a given colour is that the surface actually has that colour.[9]

Newton's reply to the above counterargument (and Locke's,

as we shall see) would have been his empirical claim that he could make a body appear to have any colour depending on the homogeneal colour-producing light that he cast upon it. (This claim, if true, would still not provide a decisive refutation of the claim that colour is an intrinsic property of objects, but it would shift the burden of proof and make the claim much more difficult to establish.) The assertion that any body can be made to appear of any colour encapsulates a central feature of the Newtonian conception of colour, namely, that colour is almost entirely illumination-dependent. Since the light that an object reflects depends on the illumination and on the surface spectral reflectance of the object (the percentage of the illumination that the object reflects throughout the spectrum), it follows from (b) that the colour an object is perceived to have should vary with changes in the illumination.

In the next chapter we shall see in some detail, particularly when we discuss computational colour vision, that perceived colour does not in fact vary with changes in the illumination in the way that the Newtonian conception predicts. This relative independence of perceived colour from illumination is known as *approximate colour constancy*. The fact that this phenomenon requires a special name when it is one of the most basic characteristics of our colour perception and the fact that introductory texts still often treat it as a secondary phenomenon indicate that the Newtonian conception continues to serve as something of a 'received view'. By this I mean that the Newtonian conception, in its modern guise as the 'wavelength conception' (Hilbert 1987), still holds a grip on the way people think and write about colour, especially in introductory texts and popular science books, despite the fact that visual science has largely departed from this view. Textbooks, for example, often begin by discussing how the visual system responds to monochromatic lights and mixtures of such lights. Only later are there discussions of the 'puzzling' phenomenon of colour constancy in situations of broad-band illumination. Yet these latter situations are the most common or typical and are those in which the visual system has evolved.

To take one more example, a recent popular science book, cowritten by a noted physicist, contains a chapter on colour in which the thesis is propounded that we are all colour-blind because we cannot see the 'continuous infinity of possible pure colors' present in the light (Wilczek and Devine 1988: 6–11). The authors distinguish between what they call 'physical color', which is 'defined by the amount of each of the pure or elementary colors' a bundle of light contains, and 'sensory color', which is 'what we actually see'. What we see depends, of course, on our eyes, which, since they contain only three types of cone photoreceptors, provide us with merely three averages 'from an infinite manifold of physical colors'. These authors thus not only ignore Newton's stricture that 'the rays are not coloured', but assume that the visual system is simply a deficient wavelength detector: we see 'sensory colors' because we detect 'physical colors' poorly.

This view is quite similar to some philosophical versions of objectivism about colour (see Armstrong 1968a). Although I shall criticize such views in detail in Chapter 3, the fundamental inadequacy of the basic idea can be easily demonstrated here. If we regard the eye as an imperfect detector, then we are committed to the idea that improved detectors would respond with increasing accuracy to the wavelengths and intensities of light. In the limit case, we would have the perfect detector of the spectral composition of light. Such a device, however, would be totally useless for visual perception: illumination varies constantly from moment to moment and place to place. Since the light reflected from objects is a function of the illumination, it too varies constantly. If we were sensitive to these variations, our visual experience would have no stability whatsoever, for there would be no basis for generating a set of perceptual colour categories which would remain relatively constant through such variations.

Of course, contemporary visual science does not imply such a crude and simplistic view, as we shall see in some detail in the next chapter. Yet its espousal by a leading physicist serves to indicate the continuing influence of the Newtonian conception, even when Newton's own words are forgotten.

Newton himself was certainly more rigorous and precise. According to Sabra, 'it would not be a correct description of Newton's position to say that he was completely satisfied with replacing colours by their measurable degrees of refrangibility; that colours were sufficiently *explained* by substituting the difference in refrangibility for the difference in colour' (Sabra 1967/1981: 293).

The issue about what constitutes an explanation of colour had arisen in an exchange between Newton and Christian Huygens. Huygens had expressed doubts about Newton's theory as an explanation of colour in a letter to Henry Oldenburg, the secretary of the Royal Society: 'Besides, if it were true that the rays of light were, from their origin, some red, others blue, etc., there would still remain the great difficulty of explaining by the mechanical physics in what this diversity of colours consists' (Huygens 1897: 228–30. My translation from the French).

Newton's reply was that the differences in colour do not consist in the differences in refrangibility. As he was to say later, 'the rays are not coloured'. The differences in refrangibility explain only the position of various hues within the spectrum: violet-producing light is most refracted; red-producing light is least refracted, etc. (Sabra 1967/1981: 293). But the differentially refrangible rays do have dispositions to produce colour sensations. Thus by referring to their degrees of refrangibility, one can sort types of rays in a way that will correspond to their dispositions to cause various types of colour sensations.

As Sabra (1967/1981) notes, this reply does not really answer Huygens's question. Huygens had asked for a physical and mechanical explanation of colour, and so he could still demand that such an explanation be given of the dispositions of the rays to produce experiences of colour. Already in 'The new theory about light and colors', Newton had avoided this issue: 'But to determine more absolutely what light is, after what manner refracted, and by what modes or actions it produces in our minds the phantasms of colors, is not easy. And I shall not mingle conjectures with certainties' (1671/1953: 78).

In retrospect, however, it seems that Huygens had put his finger on a fundamental inadequacy in Newton's theory. Newton claims that colour is primarily a type of sensation; consequently, for his theory to be complete as a theory of *colour* it must face the problem of how light rays are able to cause colour sensations. (We must not forget that Newton held the property of being colour-producing to inhere primarily in rays of light.) In his *Opticks*, Queries 12–14, Newton suggested an answer to this question: 'Do not several sorts of Rays make Vibrations of several bignesses, which according to their

17

bignesses excite Sensations of several Colours ...?' (1730/1952: 345–6). This reply, however, raises a deeper problem: what is the relation between physiological vibrations ('motions in the sensorium') and colour experience ('sensations of these motions under the forms of colours')?[10] This latter question Newton did not address, for he preferred – at least in his letter to the Royal Society – 'not to mingle conjectures with certainties'.

Philosophers, however, although they profess a passion for certainty, are not so timid when it comes to conjecture. Today philosophers continue to ponder such questions under the heading of the status of the so-called secondary qualities. This distinction between primary and secondary qualities is of the same age as Newton. It was formulated first by Robert Boyle (1666/1979) and then given its mature, classical formulation by John Locke (1690/1975). Just as the influence of the Newtonian conception as the received view of colour can still be felt today, so some version of Locke's distinction continues to be accepted by a majority of English-speaking philosophers, especially those who discuss colour. We must turn, then, to examine the classical formulation of this distinction, especially as it concerns our theme of colour.

PRIMARY AND SECONDARY QUALITIES

Although Boyle is usually given credit for formulating the distinction between primary and secondary qualities, several of its features were anticipated by Galileo and Descartes. Galileo attempted to draw a clear distinction between the properties that a body actually has in itself and those it is merely perceived as having owing to its interaction with the senses. This distinction is most evident in a frequently cited passage from Galileo's *The Assayer*:

Now I say that whenever I conceive any material or corporeal substance, I immediately feel the need to think of it as bounded, and as having this or that shape; as being large or small in relation to other things, and in some specific place at any given time; as being in motion or at rest; as touching or not touching some other body; and as being one in a number, or few, or many. From these conditions I cannot separate such a substance by any stretch of the imagination. But that it must be white or red, bitter or sweet, noisy or silent, and of sweet or foul odor, my mind does not feel compelled to bring in as necessary accompaniments. Without the senses as our guides, reason or imagination unaided would probably never arrive at qualities like these. Hence I think that tastes, odors, colors and so on are no more than mere names so far as the object in which we place them is concerned, and that they reside only in the consciousness. Hence if the living creatures were removed, all these qualities would be wiped away and annihilated. But since we have imposed upon them special names, distinct from those of the other and real qualities mentioned previously, we wish to believe that they really exist as actually different from those.

(Galileo 1623/1957: 274)

This passage exemplifies what Edmund Husserl (1954/1970) described as the 'Galilean style' in science. Science is mathematical natural science; its task is to explain nature as it is in itself, which, for Galileo, meant nature as it is independently of the ways in which it appears to perceiving beings. Our experience is of a world that has colours, tastes, smells, and sounds, but nature in itself has none of these qualities. For Galileo, such qualitative distinctions are not merely mind-dependent; they are, like illusions, entirely subjective – 'they reside only in the consciousness'.

One might think that these sensible qualities, though illusory, are nonetheless constitutive of the way we human beings understand and reason about the world. It seems that Galileo would have denied even this idea: unaided by the senses, reason would never arrive at qualities like these. That reason is typically aided by the senses does not mean that it must be. The language of mathematics enables us to 'resolve' the sensible into the geometrical and mechanical, and thereby free reason from its everyday reliance on merely apparent, qualitative distinctions (Burt 1954: 74–83).

With Galileo we have a distinction between what like-minded philosophers today would call the 'intrinsic properties' of nature and mere 'projections'.[11] This distinction is closely related to, but is not, strictly speaking, the same as that between primary and secondary qualities. According to Boyle and Locke, secondary qualities are not mere projections: they are the powers or dispositions of bodies to produce sensations in us (or other perceiving creatures). This idea appears to have been formulated earlier by Descartes in his *Principles of Philosophy* IV: CXCVIII:

> We must therefore on all counts conclude that the objective external realities that we designate by the words *light, colour, odour, flavour, sound,* or by the names of tactile qualities such as *heat* and *cold,* and even the so-called *substantial forms,* are not recognisably anything other than the powers that objects have to set our nerves in motion in various ways, according to their own varied disposition.
>
> (Descartes 1644/1985: 234)

In this view, at least as worked out later by Boyle and Locke, to attribute a secondary quality to something is equivalent to claiming that if that thing were to stand in a certain relation to a perceiver, then the perceiver would have a certain type of sensory experience. Since only one term of the relation involved in this subjunctive conditional claim is subjective (the sensory experience), secondary qualities are not exhausted by their subjective components.

This notion of a power or disposition was missing from Galileo's account. It was added by Boyle, who agreed with Galileo that 'if we should conceive all the rest of the universe to be annihilated, save one such body – suppose a metal or a stone – it were hard to show that there is physically anything more in it than matter and the accidents we have already named [figure, shape, motion, and texture]' (Boyle 1666/1979: 30). Unlike Galileo, however, Boyle seems to have wished to accord a greater degree of reality to the sensible qualities. Thus he continued by observing 'that there are *de facto* in the world certain sensible and rational beings that we call men ... [whose] sensories may be wrought upon by the figure, shape, motion and texture of bodies without them after several ways, some of those external bodies being fitted to affect the eye, others the ear, others the nostril, &c' (30–1). Boyle seems to have held, at least in some passages, that this 'fitness' or power of the external bodies to affect the 'sensories' is as objective as the existence of the primary qualities on which it depends. Thus several pages later he wrote:

> I do not deny but that bodies may be said in a very favourable sense to have those qualities we call *sensible*, though there were no animals in the world. For a body in that case may differ from those bodies which are now quite devoid of quality, in its having such a disposition of its constituent corpuscles that, in case it were duly applied to the sensory of an animal, it would produce such a sensible quality which a body of another texture would not ... And thus snow, though, if there were no lucid body nor organ of sight in the world, it would exhibit no colour (for I could not find it had any in places exactly darkened), yet it hath a greater disposition than a coal or soot to reflect store of light outwards, when the sun shines upon them all three ... so, if there were no sensitive beings, those bodies that are now the objects our senses would be but *dispositively*, if I may so speak, endowed with colours, tastes, and the like, and *actually* but only with those more catholic affections of bodies – figure, motion, texture, &c.
>
> (1666/1979: 35)

This view of the secondary qualities was given its mature form by Locke. The basic features of Locke's views are relatively easy to state, but the details are somewhat perplexing, for his form of expression is far from clear. In Chapter VIII, §8 of Book II of his *An Essay Concerning Human Understanding,* Locke first distinguishes between *ideas* and *qualities*: 'Whatsoever the Mind perceives in itself, or is the immediate object of Perception, Thought, or Understanding, that I call *Idea*; and the Power to produce any *Idea* in our mind, I call *Quality* of the Subject wherein that power is.' Unfortunately, Locke often mixes his terms: he usually speaks of a quality not as a power, but as the basis or ground of a power, and he sometimes speaks of ideas as if they were qualities of things, an inconsistency to which he admits in advance.

In §9–10 Locke distinguishes between what appear to be two types of qualities, the primary and the secondary:

Qualities thus considered in Bodies are, First such as are utterly inseparable from the Body, in what estate soever it be; such as in all the alterations and changes it suffers, all the force can be used upon it, it constantly keeps; and such as Sense constantly finds in every particle of Matter, which has bulk enough to be perceived, and the Mind finds inseparable from every particle of Matter, though less than to make itself singly be perceived by our Senses ... These I call *original* or *primary Qualities* of Body, which I think we may observe to produce simple ideas in us, *viz.* Solidity, Extension, Figure, Motion, or Rest, and Number.

2dly, Such *Qualities,* which in truth are nothing in the Objects themselves, but Powers to produce various Sensations in us by their *primary qualities, i.e.* by the Bulk, Figure, Texture, and Motion of their insensible parts, as Colours, Sounds, Tastes, *etc.* These I call *secondary Qualities.*

This passage is Locke's first major statement of his distinction between primary and secondary qualities, but the intended contrast is not easy to elaborate. First of all, the passage gives the impression that by 'primary qualities' Locke does not mean the *specific* or *determinate* extension, figure, motion-or-rest, and number of a body, for these are continually undergoing changes and alterations. Instead, he seems to take the primary qualities to be those *determinable* qualities that a body cannot lose in any of its alterations: no matter how it changes, a body or physical thing must always be solid, extended, etc. (For this reason, some philosophers have taken Locke to be making a conceptual point here about the concept of a body: for something to fall under the concept 'body' it must be solid, extended, etc. (Bennett 1971: 90).) But the difference between primary and secondary qualities cannot be the same as that between those qualities that a body cannot lose and those it can, for as we have seen, a body can lose its *determinate* solidity, extension, figure, etc. Since these are not secondary qualities, we must count them among the primary qualities. Indeed, despite the above passage, it is usually such determinate qualities that Locke intends by 'primary qualities' (Bennett 1971: 89–90).[12]

As we have seen, Locke says that qualities are powers to produce ideas in us. To have a power is to be such as to cause a type of effect. The cause of the effect is not the power per se, but rather those properties of a thing that constitute the basis or ground of that power (Mackie 1976: 9–10). What defines the secondary qualities is that they are a particular species of power. Secondary qualities are, first of all, powers to produce sensations, but second and more importantly they are powers that have the primary qualities as their ground or basis. Whereas primary qualities obviously have the power to produce sensations, as Locke indicates in the above passage, they are also real qualities of bodies. Secondary qualities, however, are not real qualities: they are merely powers of those real, primary qualities. The term 'secondary quality' is thus something of a misnomer, for strictly speaking the only real qualities of a body are its primary qualities. Secondary qualities do qualify bodies, but only indirectly: they require primary qualities as their ground, and as powers to cause sensations they must be individuated in relation to a perceiver. Locke's distinction is therefore really between *qualities* and a particular species of *power* (see Jackson 1968). His substantive claim is that what we commonly take to be qualities – colours, sounds, tastes, odours, etc. – are merely dispositions.

Let us now examine in more detail how this claim proceeds in the case of colour. According to the Newtonian conception, with which Locke was familiar, objects are not intrinsically coloured: they have their colours only by being disposed to reflect various types of light rays. But these rays too are not coloured: they are merely disposed to cause types of colour sensations. Locke states this view in his own words (and in the misleading terminology of 'ideas') in Book II, Chapter VIII, §19:

Let us consider the red and white colours in *Porphyre*: Hinder light but from striking on it, and its Colours Vanish; it no longer produces any such *Ideas* in us: Upon the return of Light, it produces these appearances on us again. Can any one think any real alterations are made in the *Porphyre*, by the presence or absence of Light; and that those *Ideas* of whiteness and redness, are really in *Porphyre* in the light, when 'tis plain *it has no colour in the dark*? It has, indeed, such a Configuration of Particles, both Night and Day, as are apt by the Rays of Light rebounding from some parts of that hard Stone, to produce in us the *Idea* of redness, and from others the *Idea* of whiteness: But whiteness or redness are not in it at any time, but such a texture, that hath the power to produce such a sensation in us.

In this passage, we see the same indecision or lack of clarity over whether colour is to be treated primarily as a type of sensory experience or as a highly complex physical property of objects. In fact, this lack of clarity pervades both Boyle's and Locke's discussions of the secondary qualities in general. Sometimes secondary qualities are identified with ideas of secondary qualities, i.e., with the sensations or experiences to which those qualities give rise, as when Locke says that porphyry has no colour in the dark because 'it no longer produces any such *Ideas* in us' (see Bennett 1971: 109; Jackson 1968: 70). At other times, the claim seems to be that secondary qualities are those modifications of texture in bodies that have the power to cause sensations, as when Locke says in §15 that 'what is Sweet, Blue, or Warm in *Idea*, is but the certain Bulk, Figure, and Motion of the insensible Parts in the Bodies themselves, which we call so'.[13]

This last idea seems to be based in what Jonathan Bennett calls the 'Causal Thesis', which is Locke's view that 'in a perfected and completed science, all our secondary quality perceptions would be causally explained in terms of the primary qualities of the things we perceive. For example, our colour-discriminations would be explained by a theory relating the colour aspects of visual sense-data to the sub-microscopic *textures* of seen surfaces' (Bennett 1971: 102). The Causal Thesis is only one component of Locke's theory of secondary qualities. The other component Bennett calls the 'Analytic Thesis'. It is the view, with which we are already familiar, that secondary qualities are *dispositional, relational,* and involve something *subjective.* (Secondary qualities are powers to produce in suitable sentient beings types of sensory experience.) The link between the two theses is the assumption that dispositions are to be explained through the nondispositional properties that constitute their bases or grounds. Since for Locke the only nondispositional properties are the primary qualities, all dispositions are eventually to be explained in terms of their primary-quality bases. This is the Causal Thesis.

If we combine the Analytic and the Causal Theses, and apply them to colour, we have essentially the same account that Newton gave in the unnumbered Definition from his *Opticks*:

(a) The physical constitution of an object (i.e., the primary qualities of the object's 'insensible parts') explains how the object has a disposition to reflect selectively various types of light rays.

(b) The physical constitution of light explains how its rays have dispositions to excite various types of processes in the perceiver ('motions in the sensorium').

(c) These processes explain how we have various types of colour sensations ('sensations of these motions under the forms of colours').

As we can see, the scientific and the philosophical, the empirical and the conceptual are thoroughly intertwined in these three claims. The empirical component consists in the claim that our experience of objects as coloured can ultimately be causally explained in terms of primary qualities: objects look a certain way because the primary qualities of their minute constituents cause them to look that way. For example, an object is red because its primary-quality constitution causes it to reflect light of predominantly small degrees of refrangibility, and light of this composition has the disposition to cause sensations of red. (In contemporary terms, light from the long-wave end of the spectrum causes sensations of red.) The conceptual component consists in the claim that since things can look a certain way only in relation to a perceiver, there is an ineliminable subjective element in the analysis of colour. These two empirical and conceptual components constitute the received view of colour.

THE PROBLEM-SPACE OF THE RECEIVED VIEW

We have now reached the point where we can formulate what I shall call the 'problem-space' of the received view. Although the received view is typically considered to be a form of subjectivism (because of its claim that an ineliminable subjective element enters into the analysis of colour), I shall argue that the received view actually generates both the issue of subjectivism versus objectivism and a particular form of the mind–body problem in the case of perceptual experience. The entanglement of these two issues constitutes the problem-space of the received view.

Recall the account presented above in (a)–(c). This form of explanation is so familiar to us today that we imagine only the empirical details remain to be provided. But there is a funda-mental problem lurking in this explanation, at least in the case of colour. The problem is the one raised by Newton's account, but which Newton did not address: what is the connection between the causal chain responsible for colour and colour as perceived? The problem has two sides. There is first of all the issue of whether colour should be identified with the proper-ties of objects that cause colour experience (secondary qualities *qua* the modifications of texture in bodies) or rather with a type of sensory experience (secondary qualities *qua* the sensations or 'ideas' that are caused by these modifications). This is the problem of objectivism versus subjectivism. Second, there is the issue of how the physiological processes in the causal chain ('motions in the sensorium') are related to colour sensations ('sensations of these motions under the forms of colours'). This is the sensationalist version of the mind–body problem for perceptual experience.

The source of these two problems, I believe, is to be found in the model of perception embedded in (a)–(c).[14] According to this model, the processes that eventuate in perceptual experi-ence are not all of the same kind, and so do not belong to the same scientific domain. There is, first of all, the physics of light and surfaces; second, there is the physiology of motions in the sensorium; and third, there is the psychology of conscious experience, which is considered to be constituted by colour sensations. Among these processes there is in particular a sharp break between (b) and (c), that is, between the physiological impression and the conscious sensation. Thus this model of perception stands in sharp contrast to, say, the earlier Aristote-lian view that there is a formal identity between visual perception and its objects and that the processes involved in perception therefore do fall into the same scientific domain. As Meyering notes in his discussion of the rise of the 'mechanicist program' in optics:

within the mechanicist program the 'chain of perception' is no longer considered as formally homogeneous and continuous. On the contrary, there is a sudden hitch, or a qualitative break, between the physiological impression on the one hand (i.e., either the peripheral or central response) and on the other the sensation as an element of consciousness. This ontological 'leap' provokes and defines the psycho-physiological problematic which has dominated Western thought up to the present day. Indeed, the history of psychology can be described, in part, as a process of progressive differentiation of the various elements of the perceptual chain.

(1989: 86–7)

As I noted earlier when discussing the Newtonian conception of colour, this qualitative differentiation of the 'chain of perception' was the main conceptual and empirical innovation that enabled the received view of colour to be formulated. (It was also one of the master-strokes that helped to create modern psychophysics.) The point for which I wish to argue now, however, is that this innovation did not simply support or give rise to subjectivism: rather, it set the conceptual stage on which the modern debate between subjectivism and objectivism would take place.[15] To put the point in as clear and as forceful a way as possible: the conviction that colours must be either 'out there' or 'in the head' is derived from the model of perception underlying (a)–(c). To demonstrate this point, then, we need to consider this model of perception in more detail.

Embedded in (a)–(c) are the rudiments of what I shall call the *representationist model of perception*. Let me make clear at the outset that I intend to use the term 'representationist' in a wide sense to encompass any theory that considers perception to involve some internal medium in which features of the external world are re-presented to the perceiver. The medium could consist of 'ideas' à la Locke, unconscious physiologically based inferences à la von Helmholtz, or computational operations à la contemporary cognitivism. To be sure, these theories differ from each other in numerous ways, but they are nonetheless all representationist, for according to each perception involves fundamentally a medium of representation.

For the moment, I wish to highlight two general features of

the representationist model of perception. First, the model involves a certain *causal-explanatory order*; second, this causal-explanatory order involves a *principled subjective/objective distinction*. According to the representationist model, in perception one receives sensory impressions or stimulations from the external, objective world; these impressions or stimulations in some way cause, trigger, or select items in an internal, subjective medium; and these subjective items stand for, correspond to, or in some way re-present the properties of the external world.

What I am calling the 'causal-explanatory order' is, then, straightforward: physical → physiological → psychological. Today we take this idea for granted, but it was at one time not obvious at all (see Meyering 1989). Only when it is in place can the distinction between stimulus and sensation be drawn. Furthermore, it is only when this distinction is in place that stimuli can in turn be analysed as having dispositional properties in relation to a perceiver.[16]

In the representationist model, perception is considered to be the penultimate link in a causal chain of events leading to action. Most introductory treatments of perception today begin with a statement to this effect: 'perception represents the final product in a chain of events stretching from events in the physical world external to the perceiver, through the translation of those events into patterns of activity within the perceiver's nervous system, culminating in the perceiver's experiential and behavioral reactions to those events' (Sekuler and Blake 1985: 2). Accompanying such statements there is also usually some diagram that presents the causal-explanatory order for perception: stimulus → sensory transduction → neural processing → perception/experience → action.

The basic elements of this model are clearly present in (a)–(c). In Locke's account, properties of the external world have the power to cause various types of sensory experience. Newton's theory of colour provides an example: an object whose surface reflects light of, say, predominantly small degrees of refrangibility (long-wave light) should appear to be red because light of that composition has the disposition to cause sensations of red.

The causal-explanatory order and dispositionalist analysis clearly involve a principled subjective/objective distinction for perception. We have already seen that for Locke the sensations

28

that result from physical stimulation are a kind of mental item or 'idea'. In Locke's view, such 'ideas' not only provide the sensory content for perceptual representation; they are also the immediate objects of perception. (This version of representationism is known as the 'representative' theory of perception.) This view provides Locke with another way of expressing his thesis about primary and secondary qualities: ideas of primary qualities *resemble* the bases of the powers that produce them, whereas ideas of secondary qualities do not. As Locke writes: 'the *Ideas of primary Qualities* of Bodies *are Resemblances* of them, and their Patterns do really exist in the Bodies themselves; but the *Ideas, produced* in us *by* these *Secondary Qualities, have no resemblance* of them at all' (VIII: §15). How this notion of resemblance is to be elaborated is something of a mystery, for as Berkeley later noted, 'an idea can be like nothing but an idea' (1710/1965: 64). In any case, Locke's claim must at least be something like this: in the case of sensations of primary qualities, the resulting perceptual contents represent the world as it is independently of us, whereas in the case of sensations of secondary qualities, they do not.[17]

Our discussion so far shows how Locke's representationism supports his subjectivist account of colour. I suggested earlier, however, that the representationist view of perception to which Newton and Locke adhered actually set the conceptual stage for the modern debate between objectivism and subjectivism about colour. We can appreciate this point by recalling that neither Newton nor Locke was consistent in his treatment of the status of colour. Newton sometimes wrote as if colours were 'original and connate properties' of light; at other times, he was careful to observe that light is coloured only to the extent that it gives rise to sensations of colour. Similarly, Locke sometimes identified the colours of objects with the primary-quality constitutions of objects that cause them to look coloured; at other times, he identified colours with sensations of colour. This indecision about the status of colour might be thought to be merely the result of careless exposition. In fact, it results from a tension between the dispositionalist and the subjectivist components of the received view.

According to the *dispositionalist* component of the received view, being coloured is *ontologically prior* to looking coloured, for being coloured is identified with having the disposition to look to be coloured. Now, although something can look coloured only relative to a perceiver, whether something possesses the disposition to look coloured depends on its physical constitution, which is not relative to a perceiver. This claim of ontological priority is based in that part of the received view which Bennett (1971) calls Locke's 'Causal Thesis', which states that all dispositional properties should be explained through the nondispositional, primary qualities that constitute their physical bases. It follows from this thesis that something by virtue of its primary-quality constitution can be coloured (in the sense of possessing the disposition to look to be coloured) without actually looking coloured. For example, things do not look coloured in the dark, but they are nonetheless coloured because they possess the disposition to look to be so. To take another example, even if there were no perceivers, something could still possess the disposition to look to be coloured; there would simply be no circumstance in which the disposition could be manifested. Being coloured (having the disposition to look to be coloured) is therefore ontologically prior to looking coloured (the manifestation of the disposition).

Given this ontological claim, it is not surprising that philosophers with objectivist inclinations have fastened on to the dispositionalist component of the received view. These philosophers have attempted to recast the received view so that colour as a dispositional property of objects becomes identified with, or at least supervenient upon, the physical basis of the disposition (Armstrong 1968a; Vision 1982; Jackson and Pargetter 1987). Consider, for example, the following passage from Armstrong (1968a: 283–4):

> the colour of a surface or the colour of an object such as a piece of amber may be identified with a certain physical constitution of the surface or object such that, when acted upon by sunlight, surfaces or objects having that constitution emit light-waves having certain frequencies ... It is therefore a *disposition* of surfaces to emit certain sorts of light-waves under certain conditions. And so, like all dispositions, colour, in this way of talking, can be identified with the state that underlies the manifestation of the disposition: certain physical properties of the surface.

The problem with this objectivist revision arises when we remember that according to the *subjectivist* component of the received view, looking coloured is *conceptually and epistemologically prior* to being coloured: something does not have the disposition to look to be coloured because it is (occurrently) coloured; it is coloured only because it has the disposition to look to be so. This claim is based in that part of the received view which Bennett (1971) calls Locke's 'Analytic Thesis', which states that there is an ineliminable subjective element in the analysis of colour. According to this idea, the dispositions to produce sensations of colour in a perceiver are not themselves colours; they indicate only that an object would look to be coloured in certain circumstances to a perceiver. Furthermore, this kind of disposition is fundamentally different from other dispositions like solubility or fragility, for the former kind has to be specified in relation to perceptual experience, whereas the latter kind does not. It is not surprising, then, that subjectivists continue to resist objectivism by insisting upon the conceptual priority of the subjectivist component in the received view (see Thornton 1972; McGinn 1983; Peacocke 1983, 1984).

Given the tension between the dispositionalist and the subjectivist components of the received view, it is hardly surprising that Newton's and Locke's treatments of colour are indecisive and unclear. In fact, this tension within the received view continues to generate debate in contemporary philosophy. For example, it would appear that there are at least two rival interpretations of the dispositionalist component among philosophers today. Following Boghossian and Velleman (1989), we can call these 'content-dispositionalism' and 'projectivism'. According to the first interpretation, the dispositionalist component specifies the content of visual experience. On this view, when we see an object as coloured we see it as having a disposition to look coloured. According to the second interpretation, the dispositionalist component specifies the property that an object actually has when we see it as coloured. On this view, we see objects as occurrently and intrinsically coloured, but the property they actually have is merely the disposition to look coloured.

The content-dispositionalist account strikes me as false – both as a phenomenological claim and as an interpretation of Locke. It seems undeniable that we typically see objects as occurrently and intrinsically coloured. Of course, it may be possible to devise viewing conditions that would push, if not our colour experience, at least our colour judgements, in the direction of content dispositionalism.[18] A thorough phenomenological investigation would have to take account of such contexts. Nonetheless, the fact that we typically see colours as occurrent properties would seem enough to rule out content-dispositionalism. Furthermore, content-dispositionalism is clearly different from Locke's view that 'what is Sweet, Blue, or Warm in *Idea*, is but the certain Bulk, Figure, and Motion of the Insensible Parts in the Bodies themselves, which we call so'. Locke's view corresponds, rather, to the projectivist account of the dispositionalist component (Boghossian and Velleman 1989: 97, n. 16).

In any case, we can now appreciate how the tension between the dispositionalist and the subjectivist components of the received view sets the stage for the modern debate over where to locate colour. The most remarkable aspect of this debate, however, appears to have been overlooked: *each of the possible moves within the logical geography of the received view actually leads to the disappearance of colour.* Objectivism (as displayed in the above passage from Armstrong) identifies colour with the physical basis of the disposition to look coloured – that is, with the microstates underlying the disposition. This attempt to put colours 'out there', however, simply makes colour recede in favour of physical states that have at best a causal relation to colour perception, but whose properties bear no resemblance to the properties of colours. (The lack of resemblance will be demonstrated at length in Chapter 3.) Subjectivism, on the other hand, denies the straightforward identification of colours with (nonphysiological) physical states. Yet by putting colours 'in the head' subjectivism retains colour only by convicting colour experience of global error. Thus on the projectivist or Lockian account, the lack of resemblance between the properties of physical states and the properties of colour is taken to show that our colour experience is systematically mistaken: the concept of colour supplied to us by our visual experience is that of an occurrent property of objects, but objectively there is no such property. Finally, content-dispositionalism tries to rectify this situation by claiming that when we see objects as coloured we see them as having merely the disposition to look coloured; since they do really have this disposition, our colour experience is not in error. This view attempts to save colour by establishing a resemblance or match between colours as they are 'out there' and as they are 'in the head'. It does so, however, only by getting the phenomenology wrong. As mentioned above, we do not typically see colours as though they were merely dispositional properties: we see them, rather, as occurrent properties of things in the world.

The irony does not cease here, however. The disappearance of colour canvassed in these three moves becomes all the more ironic when we realize that colour is precisely what the received view cannot explain. The inability is due to the representationist model of perception upon which the received view is based. According to the received view, objects are coloured only because they have the disposition to look to be so. Now, whether and how something looks coloured depends on the content of one's perceptual states. But the representationist model as articulated by Newton and Locke provides no account of the perceptual content of colour vision (see Stroud 1989: 228–9). One might be tempted to say that the physical → physiological → psychological causal-explanatory sequence just is the explanation for perceptual content: the content of a perceptual state is the sensation that results from some causal chain of physical-physiological processes. But what kind of explanation is this? All it tells us is that perceptual content is the causal terminus of a three-stage sequence. Furthermore, in the Newtonian and Lockian model, sensations are treated as simple or internally unstructured. But if sensations are simple and hence unanalysable, then how are they to be tied to that which is not simple, but complex, namely, physical-physiological processes? What exactly is the relation here? This problem is the sensationalist version of the mind–body problem for perceptual experience. To explain colour the problem cannot be left hanging, for in the Newtonian and Lockian model it is the content of perceptual states to which we must ultimately refer in specifying the colours of things.

The problem-space of the received view arises precisely because these questions are left hanging. In fact, there really is no way to answer them given the Newtonian and Lockian model of perception. As Jonathan Westphal incisively remarks:

the one thing the Newton Model cannot explain ... is why

a particular type of physical cause should be associated with a particular colour. The Newton Model cannot explain the content or qualitative character of sensations – *colours* – and nothing else could, because they are simple, beyond explanation. There *could* be no explanation of the fact that shortwave or small corpuscle light should finally cause violet-blue ... rather than some other colour. Thus the one thing the Newton Model cannot explain is *colour*. This is not because of a metaphysical limit to explanation or because colour is identical with something which is not colour – some aspect of a brain process – but *because of the structure of the Newton Model.*

(Westphal 1987: 111)

Newton's theory involves the fundamental insight that there is a difference between physical stimuli and perceptual experience. To keep these two things distinct, Newton divested the physical world of colour and assimilated colour to a type of dispositional property of light rays. The specification of colour thereby comes to depend ultimately on the content of perceptual states, which for Newton and Locke corresponds to the sensing of regions in one's subjective visual field as having certain unanalysable qualities. This account not only leaves unexplained but does not even have the resources to explain what these qualities actually are, and therefore how visual experience is constituted. Since sensations are considered to be simple, they can have only an external and contingent relation to each other. The only thing that can be said of visual experience, then, is that it consists of simple sensations pieced together. Thus we arrive at what Westphal calls the 'Mosaic Conception' of colour: 'visual experience ... is composed, like a mosaic, of uniform interchangeable *pieces* of colour' (1987: 104). The colours of these 'pieces' are 'explained' only by deferring back to the physical-physiological chain by which they supposedly came about. But this causal sequence does not explain colour; it simply defers to the unaccountable mosaic of subjective experience. The causal chain ends by putting colours back 'in the head', which turns out to be little more than a repository for simple, unexplained, sensory elements that are somehow pieced together to constitute one's visual field.

The roots of this situation can in fact be traced to the very formulation of Newton's theory of colour in his letter to the Royal Society. Although Newton claimed to provide there a new theory of colour, his concern was really mostly with light.[19] Colour entered largely because it served as a vivid and *necessary* indicator of the behaviour of light. From the narrative structure of Newton's letter, however, it would appear that the conclusions about the complexity of light were established first and independently of colour, and then an analysis of colour was carried out on this basis. Yet as we already know, the full conclusion is really that light consists of rays that are differentially refrangible *according to colour*. It is the order of the colours within the visible spectrum that provides the phenomenal basis for concluding that light is originally complex. The crucial experiment never presents these rays as visible and observable phenomena: it presents only *beams* of light and *images*. 'Beam' and 'image' are terms that have a clear phenomenal application; the term 'ray', however, is theoretical. Newton *inferred* that light consists of rays, and he was able to do so only on the basis of the observed phenomenon of the coloured spectrum. Sepper's Goethean assessment of the situation is worth quoting at some length:

> If color is disregarded, there is no criterion by which to determine that certain rays go to particular parts of the image. Only because there are regular color differences and because these different colors maintain the same order in the spectrum while the prism is rotated can Newton draw the conclusion that this degree of change in the angle of incidence has no material effect on the outcome ... As he rotates the prism, violet remains at one extreme, red at the other, and the rest of the colors retain their positions as well; consequently he can say, on the assumption that there are such constant entities as violet-producing rays, red-producing rays, and so forth, that there is no material effect because the colors were not sensibly translated. But if he did not take the colors as indexes of where these entities go, he would not be able to rule out the possibility that the overall appearance is unchanged although the behavior of the individual rays changes drastically (yet lawfully).

(Sepper 1988: 128)

This, then, is the contortion in Newton's account: colour is 'an ineludible perceptual criterion' (Sepper 1988: 145) for drawing conclusions about light. Using this criterion, Newton supposed that light has a certain structure. He then without warrant took colour to be nothing more than a phenomenal indication of this structure. As a result, the visible and experiential is reduced to the merely subjective, while the hypothetical is taken to be the objectively real. Furthermore, the phenomenal – to which Newton had to continue to appeal – is simply pushed into the mind of the perceiving subject, where it is left entirely unexplained.

It is not surprising, then, that the effect of the Newtonian heritage upon philosophy has been a tangle of issues in metaphysics and epistemology, especially those branches concerned with the mind and perception. Philosophers have continued to be unsure over whether to treat colour as 'out there' or 'in the head' – as a complex physical property or merely as a projection of subjective experience. Given this uncertainty, it is also not surprising that the general trend among those aware of the fundamental empirical inadequacies in the received view (which will become evident in Chapter 2) is to abandon this view and embrace more extreme versions of either objectivism (Hilbert 1987) or subjectivism (Hardin 1988).

My intention in this chapter has not been to impugn Newton's contributions to colour science, or to cast doubt on the philosophical originality of the received view. I have been concerned, rather, to lay out the problem-space that has been inherited from Newton and Locke. This glance back at origins has been necessary, for it enables us to appreciate just how the modern debate between subjectivism and objectivism has come about, how this debate is deeply tied to the metaphysics of sensation and the corresponding version of the mind–body problem, and how this entire problem-space actually leads to the disappearance of colour.

Today most philosophers assume that objectivism and subjectivism exhaust the possibilities for the ontology of colour. They thus succumb to the impulse that tries to locate colours either 'out there' or 'in the head'. As we shall see, this impulse, combined with a knowledge of contemporary visual science, leads inevitably to the modern counterpart of the disappearance of colour within the received view: on the part of subjectivists, it leads to eliminativism (Hardin 1988) or scepticism (Landesman 1989) about colour; on the part of objectivists (Hilbert 1987; Matthen 1988), it leads to an unacceptable replacement of colour with physical states (surface spectral reflectances) that are indeed involved in colour perception, but whose properties do not match the properties of colour.

Throughout this book I shall resist the impulse that tries to locate colours either 'out there' or 'in the head'. The view for which I shall argue later in this book will take from Locke the insight that colours are relational, but will develop a fundamentally different relational account from the received view. The next task, however, is to examine recent theories of colour vision, for the contemporary philosophical debates about colour are inextricable, both conceptually and empirically, from issues about levels of explanation for visual perception. Examining the theories of colour vision will also reveal the empirical inadequacies in the foundation of the received view.

2

COLOUR VISION: RECENT THEORIES AND RESULTS

For the subject of vision, there *is* no single equation or view that explains everything. Each problem has to be addressed from several points of view.

(David Marr 1982: 5)

APPROACHES TO COLOUR VISION

Philosophical issues about colour must be addressed in relation to issues about levels of explanation for vision. This chapter will demonstrate this point by considering recent physiological, psychophysical, and computational theories of colour vision.

It has now been more than three decades since Leo M. Hurvich and Dorothea Jameson proposed a quantitative, psychophysical formulation of the opponent process theory of colour vision (Hurvich and Jameson 1957), and Gunnar Svaetichin and Edward F. MacNichol Jr discovered wavelength-dependent opponent responses in the horizontal cells of fish retinas (Svaetichin and MacNichol 1958). In comparison, the computational study of colour vision is quite young: Edwin Land's 'retinex theory' (Land and McCann 1971; Land 1977) was until recently the only computational model available. Despite its youth, however, computational colour vision has now become a distinct area of research in visual science, one which also has a share in the larger cooperative research programme known as cognitive science. The results and prospects of this new interdisciplinary style of research on colour vision provide one of the topics of this chapter.

To appreciate these results it will prove helpful to begin by emphasizing the contrast between, on the one hand, traditional physiological and psychophysical research and on the other hand, recent computational research. Two basic differences bring out the contrast: first, each approach proposes a different type of explanation for colour vision; second, each approach tends to focus on different types of colour phenomena. As we shall see, these two differences are in fact closely related.

Psychophysics and physiology

In general, research in psychophysics and visual physiology either takes as its point of departure or is ultimately constrained by what I shall call the *phenomenal structure of colour*. By this term I mean to refer primarily to the three dimensions of colour known as hue, saturation, and lightness, as well as to the relations that colours exhibit among themselves, such as the opponent or antagonistic relation between red and green, and yellow and blue. Textbooks often classify these properties of colour as 'subjective colour phenomena' (Boynton 1979) or describe them as features of 'colour experience' (Hurvich 1981). I prefer to use the term 'phenomenal' to describe them because they are first and foremost features of how colours *appear*. I thus intend to use the term 'phenomenal' in its older sense of *pertaining to appearances*, not in its more current sense of *subjective*. The ontological status of the phenomenal features of colour (how colours look) is a topic that will recur throughout this book. Since I do not wish to prejudge the issue, I have tried to avoid using philosophically loaded terminology as much as possible in this chapter.

Such philosophical caveats aside, both psychophysics and physiology take the features of colour appearance to be indicative of the structure of our colour experience. Psychophysics then investigates colour experience by studying behavioural responses to well-defined physical stimuli, whereas physiology attempts to establish precise correlations between these types of behavioural response and neural structures. The reason why the phenomenal structure of colour serves as the point of departure for both kinds of investigation is well put by Hurvich:

the first thing we must establish is the number and variety
of the colors that we experience. It must be first because, to
explain how the nervous system (the visual aspect) interacts with light rays and certain object properties (such as
reflectance) to generate color experiences, it is critical that
we know how many basic colors to account for.

(Hurvich 1981: 11)

This claim is clearly based on the assumption that there exist
lawful relations between experiential states and events, and
physiological states and events. Because of these lawful relations, data about colour experience provide constraints on
models of how neural processes 'encode' the various features of
colour experience. Consequently, although the task of specifying the 'neural code' for colour ultimately belongs to the
explanatory domain of neurophysiology, this task cannot
proceed without psychological and psychophysical data.

Most psychophysical data continue to be gathered by studying perceptual responses in what is known as the 'aperture
mode' of colour perception. In the aperture mode, 'the color is
presented in such a way as to make its localization impossible
with respect to an object' (Boynton 1979: 28). In a laboratory
setting, this mode of perception is devised by having the subject
view coloured lights in small, circular fields of view. A 'reduction
screen', such as a sheet of construction paper with a small square
hole cut in its centre, can also be used. Looking through the hole
provides a mode of perception in which one's entire visual field
consists of a small region of colour. Such 'aperture colours' or
'film colours', as they are typically called, provide an example of
a mode of colour appearance, but one which we almost never
encounter in everyday life. Instead, colours usually appear to us
in the 'surface' (plane object), 'volume' (tridimensional object),
and 'illumination' (filled space) modes (Beck 1972: 17–22). These
latter modes of appearance, especially surface colours, typically
depend on global features of light in the scene. Aperture colours,
however, can be more closely correlated with the spectral power
distribution (energy per second at each wavelength) of the light
coming from the restricted viewing area. By varying the light in
the aperture one can therefore study how the visual system
responds to various combinations of light wavelengths and
intensities.

Such responses provide an example of the type of psychophysical data that constrain models of the neural coding of colour. When we shift to a purely physiological level of explanation, however, what are important are those patterns of neural activity that are correlated with our experience of seeing colours. The origin of this idea can be traced to the nineteenth-century physiologist Johannes Müller and his 'doctrine of specific nerve energies'. Müller pointed out that the brain operates only on the basis of the nerve impulses it receives, not on the physical stimuli responsible for them. He then argued that qualitative differences among sensations (colours, tastes, smells, sounds, etc.) correspond not to features of the physical stimuli, but to the types of nerves that are stimulated. Today it is generally held that if the relevant neural patterns are activated, we shall have the experience of seeing colours, regardless of the type of stimulus – light rays, magnetic fields, electrical stimulation, etc. – that actually occurred (Hurvich 1981: 15). Furthermore, most visual scientists seem to hold that there exists some specific neural pattern of activity that immediately underlies our experience of colour, such that if this neural structure could be activated directly, i.e., without the usual stimulation of retinal or other 'peripheral' areas, we would have the experience of seeing colours.[1] The basic idea here seems acceptable, but it should not be taken too strictly, for the neural processes that underly colour experience are probably nonlocalized in the sense of being distributed across many neural structures. In any case, the present point is simply that physiological explanations are constructed to state generalizations over patterns of neural activity. Since stimuli with many different physical characteristics can trigger or lead to the activation of the same neural structures, the specific physical characteristics of stimuli are relevant largely via their correlation with neural activity, not in themselves.

Computational vision

Computational research, on the other hand, is based on the idea that to understand vision we require yet another level of explanation, distinct from those of psychophysics and physiology, in which visual processes are considered to provide representations of the external world. In this approach, either a 'bottom-up' or a 'top-down' research strategy can be emphasized. In the 'bottom-up' approach, the physiological and psychophysical structure of the visual system is taken as the point of reference and the research problem is then to determine the abstract or design rationale for this structure. In the top-down approach, the research problem is first to specify the form of the visual input and of the desired representational output, and then to discover how one is transformed into the other in a given visual system. Of course, these two approaches are not mutually exclusive.

The top-down approach in computational vision research has been most forcefully stated by David Marr (1982). Marr argues that vision must be explained at three different levels: (1) the level of 'computational theory'; (2) the level of 'algorithm'; and (3) the level of 'implementation'. For Marr, the computational theory of vision is the most important (Marr 1982: 27). This level explains vision as an information-processing activity whose 'underlying task is to derive properties of the world from images of it' (1982: 23). The images are the patterns of light reflected on to the retinal array and the properties of the world are distal features of the environment, such as shape, texture, colour, etc. To derive or 'recover' such features the visual system must rely on internal representations. In Marr's words: 'The purpose of these representations is to provide useful descriptions of aspects of the real world. The structure of the real world therefore plays an important role in determining both the nature of the representations that are used and the nature of the processes that derive and maintain them' (1982: 43). The task of computational theories is to specify which aspects of the real world need to be represented by the visual system and to define the computational operations that derive these representations from the information present in the retinal array.[2] Given these operations, the task of the second level is to determine the specific algorithms that carry out the computations. The third level determines how these algorithms are implemented or physically realized. In Marr's view, the level of algorithm corresponds to psychophysics and to parts of neurophysiology, whereas the level of implementation corresponds to most of neurophysiology and to neuroanatomy (1982: 26).

Computational studies of colour vision provide a perfect

example of the level of computational theory in visual science. At this level, the explicit concern is the abstract nature of the task that the visual system must perform. What might this task be for colour vision? Think for a moment of what would happen if, on a sunny day, you took an apple out of the bright light of an open field and viewed it in the shade of a low, leafy tree. In the shade, the ambient light would look somewhat green, and yet the apple would continue to look red.[3] Or to take another example, if you placed a white sheet of paper in the shade and a black sheet of paper in the sunlight, the black sheet would continue to look black, even though it would now be reflecting considerably more light than the white sheet. In each of these situations, the spectral power distribution of the light reaching the eye changes dramatically, and yet the colours that we perceive are relatively constant. This phenomenon is known as *approximate colour constancy*.[4] How is this type of constancy possible for the visual system? What must the visual system do so that the colours we see do not generally vary with the considerable changes in the light that perturbs the eye?

At the level of computational theory these questions provide the central information-processing problem for colour vision. Stated in the most general terms the problem is to assign colours to a scene that are insensitive to changes in the ambient light (Maloney 1985: 2). The ambient light in the scene is the product of the spectral power distribution of the incident illumination and surface spectral reflectance (the percentage of light at each wavelength throughout the spectrum that a given surface reflects). Consequently, as the illumination varies, so too does the light that reaches the eye. But the percentage of the incident light that a surface reflects, which depends on the physical structure of the surface, does not change. These two variables of illumination and surface reflectance are confounded in the light that is actually reflected to the eye. Nevertheless, within certain limits, the colours that we perceive objects to have are typically correlated with the spectral reflectances of their surfaces. The understanding of colour vision would therefore seem to require a solution to the following information-processing problem: how is it possible to evaluate and then to discount the illuminant, and so recover information about surface spectral reflectance? When stated in these terms the problem is general, and so holds for both

43

artificial and biological visual systems. Thus this formulation of colour vision as an information-processing problem exemplifies Marr's general claim that, 'There must exist an additional level of understanding [that of computational theory] at which the character of the information-processing tasks carried out during perception are analyzed and understood in a way that is independent of the particular mechanisms and structures that implement them in our heads' (Marr 1982: 19).

Since computational theories usually assume that the function of colour vision is to recover information about surface spectral reflectance, they focus considerably on the phenomenon of colour constancy. Other aspects of colour, such as the phenomenal dimensions of hue, saturation, and lightness, or hue-opponency, have not been explored in as much detail from a computational viewpoint.[5] On the other hand, whereas physiology and psychophysics have offered largely successful models for explaining colour appearance, they have not been able to propose comparable models for colour constancy.[6] Thus the issue naturally arises of how these various kinds of colour phenomena and levels of explanation for colour vision might be related. The issue might seem to be purely a matter for visual scientists that need not concern philosophers. As we shall see at the end of this chapter, however, one's stance on this issue has decisive consequences for the philosophical treatment of colour.

THE PHENOMENAL STRUCTURE OF COLOUR

In the previous section I mentioned that the phenomenal structure of colour (how colours look) constrains models of colour vision. For this reason our first task must be to examine some of the basic features of colour appearance. Before beginning, however, I wish to note that discussing how colours look requires that one make claims about colour experience and so unavoidably involves one in at least a minimal kind of phenomenology. Although I do not intend to argue the matter here, I believe that even such a minimal 'descriptive' phenomenology cannot be entirely neutral or uncommitted about various theoretical and methodological issues. Such issues deserve treatment in their own right, but to do full justice to them here would detract from the flow of the discussion.

When discussing the basic features of colour appearance, many introductory psychology textbooks rely on colours perceived in the aperture mode as examples of supposedly 'pure' colour percepts. This idea of a pure colour percept – one that is of colour yet uncontaminated by other visual qualities – reflects the sensationalist view that the colour sensation is the basic unit of colour perception (Davidoff 1991: 2–3). Given my discussion in Chapter 1, it should come as no surprise that I do not accept this sensationalist phenomenology. On the contrary, I agree with those who argue that we typically do not see colours without seeing something as coloured and that consequently the fundamental element of colour perception is the seeing of a coloured thing, not the colour sensation.[7] This point is no less true for the supposedly 'pure' aperture colour percept, for even here we still perceive colours as situated in some visual context and as partaking of other visual qualities, such as being luminous (glowing) and as filling spatially extended areas. In the everyday three-dimensional world, however, colour appears primarily as a quality of the surfaces of objects, with notable exceptions such as the colour of the sky. In any case, colour is a quality that is always perceived as situated in some visual context.

In the previous paragraph the term 'colour' was being used in the most general sense as naming a *kind* of (visually perceived) object quality or alternatively as naming the (determinable) property of *being coloured.* Something can be coloured, however, only if it is coloured *a colour.* We thus arrive at another sense of the term 'colour' as naming *particular determinate colours* or *shades.* Finally, we can talk about shades being 'of the same colour'. Here the term 'colour' denotes a *class* or *category* of shades or particular determinate colours. (The English colour terms 'red', 'yellow', 'white', 'blue', etc. have this categorical sense and are also used to refer to particular shades.) Hence for something (a) to be coloured is for it (b) to exemplify a determinate colour (shade), which (c) belongs to a colour category.[8]

The movement from talking about things being coloured to talking about shades of colour and colour categories takes one from the perceptually concrete to the progressively more abstract. At the most abstract level, we can consider colours in terms of the dimensions in which they are typically scaled. There are many colour-scaling systems (Kuehni 1983), but the most common is based on Albert H. Munsell's 'color notation' (Munsell 1905). Munsell took colour experts as his subjects and asked them to rate the perceptual differences among colour samples. Based on these judgements he devised a system in which perceptually equal intervals occur along three dimensions called hue, chroma, and value in the Munsell system, but more commonly known as *hue, saturation,* and *lightness.*[9] 'Hue' refers to the degree of red, green, blue, yellow, purple, etc. in a given colour. 'Saturation' refers to the proportion of hue in a given colour in relation to a neutral achromatic point. Saturated colours have a comparatively greater degree of hue, whereas desaturated colours are comparatively closer to grey. 'Lightness' refers to the achromatic dimension of white through grey to black. This dimension is primarily an attribute of colours in the surface mode of appearance (Beck 1972: 25–9). In the aperture mode, the corresponding dimension is known as *brightness,* along which colours vary from dim or barely visible at one end to dazzling at the other.[10]

These three dimensions are typically represented geometrically in the form of a colour solid, also known as *phenomenal colour space* (Figure 2). Lightness provides the vertical axis of the solid with white at one end and black at the other. Saturation provides the horizontal axis with the centre of the solid corresponding to the neutral achromatic point. The hues at maximal saturation are arranged around the central circumference, called the 'hue circle', so that movement away from the circumference towards the neutral achromatic point corresponds to progressive desaturation.

This colour solid also emphasizes in its construction the antagonistic or opponent structure of colour relations. Certain hues mutually exclude each other and so are said to be antagonistically or opponently related: red and green are mutually exclusive (there are no reddish-greens and greenish-reds), as are yellow and blue (there are no yellowish-blues and bluish-yellows). Each member of these two opponent hue pairs can, however, combine with either hue of the other pair: red can combine with yellow (orange) and with blue (purple); and green too can combine with yellow (green–yellow) and with blue (green–blue). Such combinations are called *binary hues.*

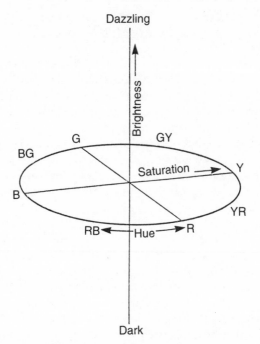

Figure 2 The phenomenal colour space of hue, saturation,
and lightness
Source: Burnham, Hanes, and Bartelson (1963: 13)

The pure examples of red, green, yellow, and blue – that is, a
red or green containing neither yellow nor blue, and a yellow
or blue containing neither red nor green – are called *unitary
hues* or *unique hues*. In the colour solid, the unitary hues are
arranged at 90-degree-angle intervals on the hue circuit, with
opponent hues on opposite sides of the circuit at 180 degrees.
Thus hues that are opponent never overlap, and so moving
from one member of an opponent hue pair to the other always
requires travelling through another hue that differs from each
of them. (For example, to pass from red to green requires
moving through either blue or yellow, and to pass from blue to
yellow requires moving through either red or green.)

The achromatic colours black and white also deserve comment. Being coloured black or white depends on contrasts in
the light intensity between adjacent areas. For example, in the

aperture mode one can make a white spot in a white surround take on a variety of achromatic appearances by varying the brightness of the surround. If the surround is made bright enough, the central spot will look black. Black and white are not the only colours that depend on this kind of brightness (or lightness) contrast. In the aperture mode, the colour brown arises as an effect of surrounding a yellow or orange area with a brighter area of white light. Just as an increase in the brightness of the surround can drive a white area towards grey or black, so a similar increase can drive a yellow or orange area towards brown (Boynton 1979: 32–3). Browns are accordingly often described as blackish-oranges or blackish-yellows (Hurvich 1981: 7–9).[11]

It is often said that human beings can distinguish more than a million different colours. This statement is actually rather misleading, but we can see what it intends by referring to the dimensions of hue, saturation, and lightness as displayed in the colour solid. Along the hue dimension we can distinguish approximately two hundred steps from yellow through green and blue, and finally to red. Along the saturation dimension we can distinguish at least twenty steps for any hue. Finally, we can distinguish about five hundred steps along the lightness dimension. Combining these figures gives us more than a million possible distinctions (Gouras 1985). In this sense we can discriminate more than a million particular determinate colours or shades. These colours, however, can all be described in terms of the drastically more limited number of colour categories to which they belong – the hue categories red, green, yellow, and blue, and the achromatic categories white and black (Gouras 1985; Hurvich 1981).

I intend to take the three dimensions of hue, saturation, and lightness, and the six colour categories, red, green, yellow, blue, white, and black, as providing a minimal skeleton for the phenomenal structure of colour. By making use of this skeletal structure, we can make informative statements about colour that do not depend on our knowledge of physics or optics. The hue circle, for example, displays how the hues are interrelated, but does not tell us anything about the physics of light, the chemistry of dyes, or the rules for mixing coloured paints (Hurvich 1981: 5). Instead, the circle displays certain features of the phenomenal structure of the hues by providing a

Table 1 Rules for the unique hues

Name of hue	Cannot coexist with	Also is devoid of hues shown, with which it can potentially coexist
Red	Green	Yellow or blue
Yellow	Blue	Green or red
Green	Red	Blue or yellow
Blue	Yellow	Red or green

Source: Boynton (1979: 31)

geometrical representation of the rules for how they are related. Consider, for example, the rules for the unitary or unique hues in Table 1 (Boynton 1979: 31). These rules are easily translated into the geometry of the hue circuit. Hues that are adjacent, for example, green and yellow, or green and blue, are those that can potentially be combined to form a binary hue. Hues that are opposite each other – red and green, and yellow and blue – are those that cannot be combined to form a binary hue.

These rules refer only to the (opponent) phenomenal structure of the hues. By adding the saturation and lightness dimensions, however, we shall be able to make informative statements about the full range of colours. In such a three-dimensional colour space, the colour categories red, green, yellow, and blue would correspond to volumes within the solid. Particular determinate colours or shades, on the other hand, would correspond to subvolumes or points that represent hues with specific degrees of saturation at specific levels of lightness.

The colour solid represents colour at a phenomenal level without implying specific claims about how the phenomenal structure of colour is generated – that is, whether the mechanisms and processes responsible for its generation are primarily physical, physiological, psychological, etc. The colour solid thus provides a natural constraint on various scientific and philosophical treatments of colour, and so I shall often appeal to it in this book. Two important qualifications, however, must be added here.

First, when considering colours in abstraction from coloured things, and in terms of the dimensions in which they are scaled, one might be led to suppose that colour perception is based on an independent unit or module in the operation of the visual system. Whether colour perception is modular, however, is very much an open empirical question that should not be prejudged. Hence in referring to the phenomenal structure of colour, I do not intend to imply that hue, saturation, and lightness constitute a modular component of visual perception. In fact, a strong case can be made for thinking that colour perception is *not* modular in the technical sense of being either 'informationally encapsulated' (Fodor 1983) in relation to other processes or 'cognitively impenetrable' (Pylyshyn 1984) with respect to belief, desire, expectation, attention, etc. For example, perceived shape can affect colour matching (Egeth and Pachellea 1969; Overmeyer and Simon 1985; Williams 1974; as reported by Davidoff 1991, 1992), suggesting that colour perception is not informationally encapsulated in relation to shape perception; colour matching can also be somewhat affected by the meaning of the colour-containing boundaries (for example, what objects they are perceived as being) (Menaud-Buteau and Cavanagh 1984; as reported by Davidoff 1991, 1992), suggesting that colour perception is not cognitively impenetrable with respect to beliefs about objects in the scene.[12]

The second qualification is simply a reminder that hue, saturation, and lightness should not be considered as dimensions for scaling simple sensations in the Lockian sense. Three reasons based on psychophysics can be given here. First, the dimensions in which colours are appropriately scaled involve the modes in which colours appear. For example, as I noted above, the achromatic lightness dimension of black to white is primarily an attribute of colours in the surface mode of appearance, whereas brightness (dim to dazzling) is primarily an attribute of colours in the aperture mode. Second, hue, saturation, and lightness are not perceptually isolated, but interact. It is well known, for example, that the hue perceived varies with the intensity of the illumination (the Bezold-Brücke effect); so too does the saturation perceived (the Abney effect). Hue, saturation, and lightness also interact in categorization tasks (Garner and Felfoldy 1970; Felfoldy and Garner 1971; as reported by Davidoff 1991). These various interactions have led some scientists to call these scaling dimensions (as well as others such as loudness, pitch, and timbre) 'integral' in relation to one another (Garner 1974; Lockhead 1992). Third, there is considerable evidence for the hypothesis that perceptual attributes are not judged independently of their environment, but rather in relation to their spatial and temporal contexts (Davidoff 1991; Lockhead 1992).

These two qualifications are meant to reinforce the point made above that we typically perceive colours as properties of things in some visual context. The same point deserves stating in relation to hue, saturation, and lightness: even though it is very useful to consider these attributes as scalar dimensions in abstraction from coloured things, they are not perceived floating freely, as it were. Rather, as attributes of the colours exemplified by coloured things, hue, saturation, and lightness – as well as other attributes such as the unitariness and binariness of hue – are best construed as second-order properties of coloured things.

PHYSIOLOGY AND PSYCHOPHYSICS

Visual pigments, photoreceptors, and additive colour mixture

I noted above that different kinds of stimulation can trigger the experience of seeing colours. Nevertheless, the appropriate stimulus for vision is obviously light. Visible light comprises a small portion of the spectrum of electromagnetic energy. It can be considered either as being composed of individual particles called *photons*, or as a *wave* phenomenon that has various frequencies. In vision research, light is generally treated in the wave framework, but most often is measured not in terms of frequency but rather in terms of wavelength, which is reciprocally related to frequency. The unit of measurement for wavelength is the nanometre (nm), which is equal to 1 millimicron or a billionth of a metre. Sunlight comprises wavelengths ranging from approximately 300 nm in the ultraviolet through 800 nm in the near-infrared. For humans visible light ranges from approximately 400 nm to 700 nm. Other animals have different visible ranges. For example, the visible range for the honeybee is 300 nm–650 nm (Menzel 1979; Menzel and Backhaus 1991); for many diurnal birds it is approximately 350 nm–720 nm (Bowmaker 1980b).

One of the central themes in the history of colour science is known as *additive colour mixture*, or the study of which light wavelengths can be substituted for each other without changing the colour that one sees. For example, at an average light level, a spectral stimulus of 580 nm will appear to have a yellow hue. This hue can be matched by combinations of 590 nm and 570 nm, 550 nm and 610 nm, 540 nm and 630 nm, 540 nm and 670 nm, or many other stimulus combinations. In fact, to match all the hues throughout the spectrum just three appropriately chosen lights of fixed spectral composition are required. (Each light must be such that it cannot be matched by a mixture of the other two.) To achieve a complete colour match for spectral stimuli, not only hue, but also brightness and saturation must be matched. Brightness is matched by adjusting the intensities of the matching lights. Saturation is more difficult. In general, narrow-band stimuli (those comprising only a few wavelengths) appear more saturated than broad-band stimuli (those comprising many wavelengths). To match saturation it is therefore often necessary to add one of the matching lights to the test-light. Depending on the test-light, a complete match can sometimes be achieved by a single primary, sometimes by a mixture of two or three, or sometimes by adding one primary to the test-light to match a mixture of the other two primaries. Three primary lights are therefore necessary and sufficient to match all the colours that we see throughout the spectrum.[13]

This property of normal human colour vision is called *trichromacy*. According to the standard history, the trichromacy of human colour vision was first recognized by Thomas Young in 1801, although George Palmer had suggested a similar idea some 27 years earlier (Wasserman 1978: 25). Young argued that it cannot be assumed that the eye contains distinct components that are sensitive to each noticeably different hue in the spectrum. Instead, the eye must contain a limited number of components that are selectively sensitive to various regions of the spectrum. Young suggested that the number of components was limited to three and that the colours we see are determined by the relative proportions of the responses among the three components. This theory was later elaborated and supported first by James Maxwell, and then by Hermann von Helmholtz.

Although Maxwell developed much of its mathematical and conceptual basis, the trichromatic theory has come to be known as the Young–Helmholtz theory of colour vision.[14]

It was not until the 1960s, however, that the physiological basis for trichromacy was confirmed. It had been known for some time that the retina contains photoreceptor (light-sensitive) cells called *rods* and *cones* because of their shape. (The rods are active mainly during scotopic or night vision, when only achromatic discriminations can be made; the cones are active mainly during photopic or daytime vision, when both achromatic and chromatic discriminations can be made. Colour vision is thus primarily subserved by the cone photoreceptors, though there is evidence of rod–cone interaction in colour vision (Reitner et al. 1992).) These cells contain high concentrations of molecules known as *visual pigments* because they bleach while selectively absorbing light (Bowmaker 1991). In 1964 P. K. Brown and G. Wald showed that within the human retina each cone cell contains one out of three different types of visual pigment that collectively are sensitive from approximately 400 nm to 700 nm (Brown and Wald 1964; see also Marks et al. 1964). They measured the absorption spectra of the pigments of single cones (the probability of the pigment's absorbing a given quantum of light at each wavelength) and found that each type of pigment has its own spectral absorption curve. One type of pigment was found to absorb maximally at 445 nm, another at 535 nm, and the third at 570 nm. The cone cells accordingly fall into three classes depending on which type of visual pigment is embedded in their membranes; these three classes form at the retinal level the physiological basis for trichromacy.

There is unfortunately no standard terminology for referring to the different cone visual pigments. They are often referred to as the 'blue' (419 nm), 'green' (531 nm), and 'red' (559 nm) pigments. These designations are unsatisfactory for several reasons. First, although the hues associated with wavelengths at 419 nm and 531 nm are blue and green respectively, the hue associated with 559 nm is greenish-yellow, not red. Second, the three visual pigments are not individually responsible for our seeing spectral stimuli as blue, green, red, or yellow. Collectively the pigments respond throughout the spectrum, but the visual system responds only to the differences in their relative levels of activity. Third, our hue experiences – even those associated with narrow-band stimuli at 419 nm, 531 nm, and 559 nm – are the result of considerably more neural activity than occurs simply at the photoreceptor level. Since we still do not fully understand how patterns of neural activity generate the experience of colour, it seems at best misleading to describe pigment responses using colour terms. I shall therefore follow the convention that designates the three cone types as 'S' (short wave), 'M' (middle wave), and 'L' (long wave).

Since 1964 considerable progress has been made in biological studies of colour vision at the receptor level (Bowmaker 1991). The most remarkable discoveries are enabling visual scientists to sketch a path from the molecular biology and genetics of the visual pigments to the anatomy and physiology of the photo-receptor cells, and even to psychophysical differences in colour vision (Mollon 1992). At the molecular level, the structure of the visual pigment molecules consists of a large protein called *opsin* that is bound to a derivative of vitamin A called *retinal*. Small variations in the amino acid sequence of the protein produce visual pigments with different peak sensitivities. In 1986 a team of researchers determined the nucleotide base sequences for the opsin component of the human visual pigments, thereby isolating the opsin genes in humans (Nathans et al. 1986a; Nathans 1989). In a related study published at the same time, it was noted that the normal gene for the pigment maximally sensitive in the long-wave region is polymorphic (Nathans et al. 1986b). These genetic data support slightly earlier studies of the human retina that not only provided new data on the visual pigment absorption spectra (Dartnall et al. 1983), but also indicated that there are two alternative types of maximally long-wave sensitive pigments (Dartnall et al. 1983; Neitz and Jacobs 1986).[15] Still more recently, the absorption spectra have been determined by using tissue culture to express the opsin genes; this study also demonstrates that there are two alter-native long-wave pigments (Merbs and Nathans 1992).[16] Finally, the polymorphism in the long-wave visual pigment has been shown in psychophysical colour-mixture experiments to be associated with varying sensitivities to long-wave light (Dartnall et al. 1983; Neitz and Jacobs 1986; Winderickx et al. 1992).

I shall discuss these findings in more detail in Chapter 4. For the moment we can return to the general features of tri-chromacy. What does the visual system achieve by having three classes of photoreceptors (excluding the scotopic rods) that it would not achieve by having only one or two? Consider first a visual system that has only one type of receptor. Although this receptor might be more sensitive to certain light wavelengths than to others, it will nevertheless not be able to distinguish changes in intensity from changes in wavelength. For example, suppose that the receptor is twice as sensitive to light at 500 nm than it is to light at 550 nm, i.e., that it absorbs light quanta at 500 nm twice as much as light quanta at 550 nm. If we double the intensity of the 550 nm light in relation to that of the 500 nm light, however, the receptor will no longer be able to tell the difference between them: it will generate the same neural signal in response. This fact exemplifies the so-called *principle of univariance*, which states that the signal generated by a receptor has only one dimension of response resulting from its state of excitation, not from the wavelengths of the exciting stimulus. For this reason the neural signals that a single type of receptor generates in the presence of light of a given wavelength can always be duplicated by a stimulus of a different wavelength at the appropriate intensity. A single-receptor system is thus *monochromatic*: it needs only one light to match all other lights (the match is achieved simply by varying the intensity of the light). Since a single-receptor system cannot discriminate on the basis of wavelength, it is unable to detect differences between an object and its back-ground that depend on wavelength; it can detect an object only if it reflects more or less light energy than its background.

This inability can be considerably reduced by adding another type of photoreceptor with a different but overlapping spectral sensitivity. A visual system that has two types of photoreceptor is *dichromatic*: it requires two primary lights of different and fixed spectral composition to match all other lights. Stimuli that have the same wavelength composition will often affect the two types of photoreceptor differently. Although the principle of univariance still holds for each receptor, differences in wavelength can be preserved in the differences in the relative responses of the two types of receptor. For the differences in wavelength to be visually significant, however, there must also exist postreceptoral neurons that can compare receptor responses. The minimum requirement for wavelength discrimination, upon which colour vision depends, is consequently two types of photoreceptor cross-connected to postreceptoral neurons that can compare the receptor responses (Bowmaker 1991: 111).

Even for a two-receptor system there are still different spectral stimuli that will produce the same relative responses from its two receptor types. Such stimuli will be undetectable for a dichromatic system. A visual system that contains another third type of photoreceptor whose senstivity overlaps those of the other two types, yet responds maximally in a different region of the spectrum, will typically be able to distinguish between stimuli that are identical for a dichromatic system. Such a system is *trichromatic* and, as we saw above, requires three appropriately chosen primary lights to match any testlight.

These features of wavelength discrimination and additive colour mixture can be stated in more abstract terms. Since a monochromat possesses one receptor type, it requires only one light to match any test-light, and so its discriminatory abilities can be represented in one dimension. Similarly, the discriminatory abilities of a dichromat require two dimensions for their representation, whereas those of a trichromat require three. The terms 'monochromatic', 'dichromatic', and 'trichromatic' thus indicate what is known as the *dimensionality* or *type* of colour vision that an individual possesses.

Postreceptoral mechanisms and opponent processes

Since discriminating hue requires being able to discriminate light mixtures on the basis of wavelength, colour vision is usually behaviourally defined in visual science as the ability to discriminate wavelengths independently of their relative intensities.[17] Care must be taken here, however, for if by 'colour vision' we mean, as we usually do, the perception of determinate colours belonging to hue categories such as red, green, yellow, blue, etc., then although wavelength discrimination at the receptor level is necessary for colour vision, it is not sufficient. As Gouras notes:

the honeybee and other animals detect objects using three

photoreceptor systems but may never see the colors of these objects if the input from these receptors is not mixed to allow for color contrast, the essential feature of color perception in higher animals ... A color detector must be able to distinguish how much each of the three cone mechanisms is activated by the object.

(Gouras 1985: 386)[18]

Two important ideas are condensed in these remarks. The first is that colours are always seen in some visual context; in particular, the colours we see are always relative to their surround. The relation between colours and their surround is a central feature of colour perception. As Gouras notes in another article: 'The brain forms colors by comparing objects to their background and not by analyzing their local spectral reflectance. An object is bright or dark, and of a particular color, only in relationship to its background' (Gouras and Zrenner 1981: 142).

The kind of contrast being referred to here is known as *simultaneous colour contrast.* For example, a yellow patch on a green background appears more reddish than it does on a grey background. On a blue background, the yellow appears more saturated, whereas on a yellow background it appears desaturated. The other main type of contrast is *successive colour contrast,* or afterimages. For example, if one stares at a yellow patch in a bright light for about 30 seconds, and then averts one's gaze to a neutral white patch, one will see a bluish afterimage. Staring at a red patch induces a greenish afterimage. We usually notice these kinds of phenomena only when we devise artificial displays, but in fact both types of contrast effects are continually operative in our visual field (Hurvich 1981: 152). Furthermore, as we shall see later, perceived colour depends not only on local contrast, but also on global comparisons that extend throughout the visual field. These global comparisons are especially important for understanding the phenomenon of colour constancy.

The second important idea contained in the remark by Gouras is that to explain these kinds of perceptual phenomena we cannot refer simply to the signals generated by the photoreceptors in response to lights of various wavelengths. First, triplets of cone responses do not uniquely or efficiently specify the colours we see (Hurlbert 1991). Simultaneous colour contrast indicates that the colours we see at one place in a scene depend not only on the cone responses there, but also on surrounding cone triplet responses; successive colour contrast indicates that the colours we see at one time depend not only on cone responses at that time, but also on cone triplet responses moments before. Moreover, the cone responses overlap considerably throughout the spectrum (especially the L and M cones), and so their responses are highly correlated. Therefore, for a colour detector to be able to distinguish how much each of the three cones is activated by an object the cone reponses must be decorrelated (Lennie 1984).

Research in sensory physiology indicates that the decorrelation is achieved by neurons that in effect pit the cone responses against each other in an antagonistic or opponent fashion by responding to *differences* in the cone absorption spectra. This idea is best understood by first considering certain cells in the retina known as 'on' and 'off' visual neurons.[19] Each on- and off-cell has its own *receptive field*, which is the area of the retina that when stimulated by light triggers an excitation or inhibition of the cell's base firing rate. The receptive fields have what is called a *centre-surround* organization: on-cells are excited by a light stimulus in the centre of their receptive field, but are inhibited by the same stimulus in an annulus immediately surrounding the central area. The situation is reversed for off-cells: they are inhibited by the presence of light and excited by its removal in the centre of their receptive field, but are excited by the same stimulus in their receptive field's surround. These two types of cell subserve each unit area of visual space on the retinal array in parallel and so together form an antagonistic 'push-pull' system responding to increments and decrements of light. Furthermore, like most visual neurons, including the photoreceptors themselves, each on- and off-cell also receives antagonistic signals indirectly from neighbouring photoreceptors through the neural networks of which it is a member. The antagonistic influence is usually strongest in the area of the receptive field immediately surrounding the photoreceptors the cell subserves, and so is known as *surround* or *spatial antagonism.*

Spatial antagonism is fundamental in the operation of the visual system and implies that the visual system reponds primarily to contrasts rather than absolute magnitudes. In particular, it responds to contrasts across the boundaries of objects rather than the overall light reflected from their surfaces. For this reason, spatial antagonism is thought to play a considerable role in achromatic perception, for whether an area is perceived as black, grey, or white depends on contrasts in the light intensity between it and adjacent areas.

Spectral antagonism arises as a complication of spatial antagonism. Certain visual neurons have the additional property of responding not simply to signals from one type of cone, but to signals from at least two types: they are excited (or inhibited) by signals from one type in the centre of their receptive field and inhibited (or excited) by signals from the other type in the surround of their receptive field. Although the signals from the different cone types are thus mixed in the same neuron, they can nonetheless still be distinguished because they are treated as carrying, in effect, opposite signs. Consequently, the neurons enhance the difference between the cone absorption spectra, discounting the redundancies inherent in the highly correlated cone signals (Lennie 1984).

This type of visual cell is often called a *single opponent* neuron because it responds to the difference in cone signals in one unit area of visual space. Single opponent neurons were first found in the horizontal cells of the fish retina by Gunnar Svaetichin and others in the 1950s (Svaetichin and MacNichol 1958). They were subsequently found in the retinal ganglion cells and geniculate neurons of monkeys (Hubel and Wiesel 1960; DeValois and Jacobs 1968), and have now been found in all organisms that are known to possess colour vision (Jacobs 1981).

To perceive colour contrast requires being able to detect not simply the wavelengths in a unit area of visual space, but also the spectral contrasts across space, particularly between adjacent areas. Cells known as *double opponent* neurons appear to play an important role in this process. The receptive fields of these cells have opposite opponent responses: for example, one type is excited by signals from L cones and inhibited by signals from M cones in the centre of its receptive field, and excited by signals from M cones and inhibited by signals from L cones in the surround of its receptive field. A double opponent cell can thus compare the responses from single opponent neurons subserving neighbouring areas of visual space and will

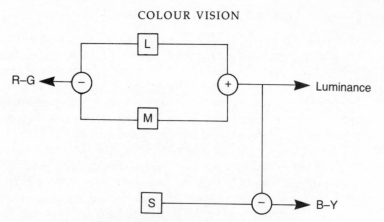

Figure 3 The opponent process model
Contributions of the various classes of receptor to the
postreceptoral opponent processes in colour vision. The 'red–green'
process (R–G) receives opposed signals from L and M receptors; the
'blue–yellow' process (B–Y) receives signals from S receptors
oppposed to a combined signal from L and M receptors; and the
achromatic mechanism (Luminance) receives a combined signal from
L and M receptors.
Source: After Lennie (1984)

respond maximally when there is maximum spectral contrast
between the areas (Gouras 1991a: 176). Double opponent neurons were first found in the ganglion cells of the goldfish retina
(Daw 1968), but in primates are found in the visual cortex,
specifically within the so-called 'blobs' of the primary visual
area (V1) and the 'thin stripes' of the second visual area (V2)
(Livingstone and Hubel 1984, 1988).

At this point it will be useful to present the postreceptoral
opponent processes involved in colour vision in more abstract
terms. Figure 3 provides the standard model of the so-called
'channels' formed by the excitatory and inhibitory combinations of the receptor signals in postreceptoral neural
networks.[20] There are three receptor types, L, M, and S,
corresponding to the L, M, and S cones. The receptor signals are
added (corresponding to excitation) and/or subtracted (corresponding to inhibition) to form three postreceptoral channels,
one achromatic and two chromatic. The first is the achromatic
L + M channel. Because it simply combines the L and M signals
it is not spectrally opponent, and so signals only differences in
luminance, not wavelength. The second is the L – M channel,

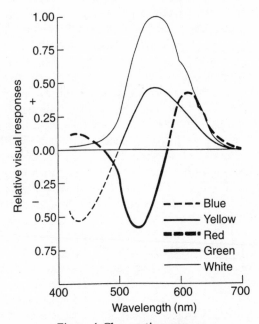

Figure 4 Chromatic response
Chromatic (red–green and yellow–blue) and achromatic responses
(whiteness) throughout the visible spectrum. One observer.
Arithmetic representation.
Source: Hurvich (1981: 64)

which pits the L and M signals against each other. The third is
the S – (L + M) channel, which pits the S signals against the L
and M signals combined. These are the two spectrally opponent
and hence chromatic channels. It should be emphasized that
although the channels in this model are presumed to be
physiologically realized in populations of spectrally opponent
cells, they are nonetheless functionally characterized and
typically specified in psychophysical terms, and so do not
necessarily correspond to unique neuronal pathways (Boynton
1988: 77).

The traditional method for specifying the channels in psychophysics involves determining their sensitivities with an
experimental procedure known as *hue-cancellation* devised by
Leo Hurvich and Dorothea Jameson (Jameson and Hurvich
1955; Hurvich and Jameson 1957; Hurvich 1981). The sensitivity
of each channel is given in terms of its *chromatic response*, and

the hue-cancellation technique measures this response 'by determining how much of the antagonistic response is necessary to "zero" or "null" the system' (Hurvich 1981: 53).[21]

Figure 4 presents three visual response curves. One is the achromatic response curve and the other two are the red–green and yellow–blue chromatic response curves as determined by the hue-cancellation technique. The achromatic response curve is given by the *photopic luminosity function*, which specifies the amount of energy necessary at each wavelength for a given observer to first detect the stimulus. When the stimulus is first detected it is not seen as having a hue but as achromatic; the assumption therefore is that the achromatic channel has been stimulated to the exclusion of the chromatic channels. As can be seen from the figure, the achromatic curve is always positive (it never dips below the zero line); the reason is that black can be produced only by spatial contrast. The achromatic curve is thus often construed as a 'whiteness' response.

The other two curves are the chromatic response curves; they cross the zero line at various points and so have negative as well as positive values.[22] Each zero crossing represents a neutral balance point where the respective chromatic response is zero, presumably because the corresponding chromatic channel is nulled. The first balance point occurs where the red–green response curve crosses the zero line at 475 nm. At this spectral location there is neither 'red' nor 'green' chromatic response. The yellow–blue response curve, however, is negative, indicating that there is 'blue' chromatic response. At this point the subject sees a blue that contains neither red nor green, i.e., a unique blue. The next zero crossing occurs at 500 nm. Here the yellow–blue response is neutral, but the red–green response is negative, indicating that there is 'green' chromatic response. At this point the subject sees a green that contains neither yellow nor blue, i.e., a unique green. The next zero crossing occurs at 577 nm. At this point the subject sees a unique yellow. What about unique red? If one examines Figure 4 closely, one can see that the yellow–blue response curve remains positive into the long-wave end of the spectrum, thus showing that there is no spectral red that does not generate some yellow response. There is consequently no unique red in the spectrum (at moderate energy levels). To obtain unique red one must take a spectral red and add the appropriate amount of short-wave ('blue') light required to cancel the yellow response.

It can also be seen from Figure 4 that there are several points where the response curves cross each other. For example, around 480 nm the green response crosses the blue response. At this point the subject sees a balanced, binary blue–green, i.e., a blue–green that contains equal amounts of blue and green. Another balanced, binary point occurs around 590 nm. Here the subject sees a balanced yellow–red, i.e., a balanced orange.

The discussion so far has been restricted to the achromatic and hue attributes of colour. The saturation at a given spectral location corresponds to the ratio of the responses of both chromatic channels at that location to the sum of the chromatic and achromatic response at that location. This ratio is higher for spectral blues than yellows, and so the most vivid blues are more saturated than the most vivid yellows. Similarly, the most vivid reds are more saturated than the most vivid greens.

It is worth pausing to consider the visual response curves in relation to the received view of colour discussed in the previous chapter. Recall that the received view gives a dispositional account of colour: objects have the disposition to reflect lights of various wavelengths, and these in turn have the disposition to cause colour sensations. Colours are thus identified with dispositional properties of lights at specific wavelengths. (For example, red is a dispositional property of long-wave light.) What the response curves enable us to appreciate, however, is that although lightwaves certainly provide the proximal stimuli for colour vision, lights at specific wavelengths do not in any straightforward way determine perceived colour. Rather, there is a only a complex many-to-one relation between the two.

Take, for example, the perception of white. Although Newton knew from his own colour-mixture experiments that a combination of only three appropriately chosen spectral lights suffices to create perceived white, he also claimed that perceived white was the most compounded of all the colours because no ray ever exhibits it and it requires proportions of all the primary colours: 'Hence therefore it comes to pass that whiteness is the usual color of light; for light is a confused aggregrate of rays endowed with all sorts of colors' (Newton 1671/1953: 7). Figure 4 shows, however, that perceived white will result whenever both of the chromatic responses are neutrally balanced and that this can be accomplished in numerous ways with as few as two wavelengths of light. For example, given a bluish-green light, the blue is cancelled by adding the appropriate amount of 'yellow' light and the green is cancelled by adding the appropriate amount of 'red' light. Both chromatic responses will then be neutrally balanced, leaving an achromatic perception whose amount of whiteness depends on the degree of achromatic response.

Those partial to the received view might seek to defend a revised version of the dispositionalist thesis that acknowledges that there is no one-to-one correlation between specific light wavelengths and particular determinate colours. It might be held, for example, that colours are dispositions of *lightwaves*, though not of *specific light wavelengths*. Or it might be held that although particular determinate colours (shades) should not be identified with dispositional properties of specific light wavelengths, nonetheless colour, as a kind of visual quality, can be identified with a type of dispositional property of light. These revisions, however, amount to little more than the claim that lightwaves have the dispositional property of causing colour experience. Although it is true, the claim is rather uninteresting because so many of the factors responsible for our experience of colour reside in the visual system, not in the physical stimulus per se. Consider, for example, the six primaries red, green, yellow, blue, black, and white and the phenomenal structure that colour exhibits in virtue of their relations. There is nothing in the lightwaves themselves that accounts for this sixfold structure: the spectrum is rather a physical continuum. But opponent process theories of colour vision do provide a model of this sixfold structure. Hence if colours are to be assigned as dispositional properties to whatever occurrent processes bear the brunt of the causal responsibility for colour experience, then it would seem that the visual system provides a better candidate than lightwaves.

On the phenomenological side, the received view holds that the basic component of colour experience is the colour sensation and that these are simple and hence unanalysable. Setting the issue about sensations being the units of perception aside, we already know from considering the phenomenal structure of colour that colours are not simple but have dimensional components. The visual response curves enable us to appreciate quantitatively these components for spectral aperture colours: the achromatic response curve displays the whiteness component; the chromatic response curves indicate the four basic hue components in various combinations (unique, binary, balanced, and unbalanced); and the ratio of the chromatic response in relation to the sum of the chromatic and achromatic responses indicates the saturation component. There is therefore a clear and quantitative sense in which colours have perceptual components, and so, contrary to the received view, are complex, not simple (Hardin 1988: 42–4).

Psychophysical issues about the postreceptoral channels

Visual scientists agree unanimously that spectral opponency of the sort presented in Figure 3 plays a major role in colour vision, but there are numerous specific issues, both empirical and methodological, that remain unresolved. The main debates concern the specific psychophysical and physiological features of the postreceptoral channels, and the extent to which there are other distinct levels of operation in the visual system devoted to colour.

The issues can be approached by considering the postreceptoral treatment of the cone signals as a transformation from one three-dimensional space to another. The first space has as its coordinate axes the cone sensitivities and is spanned by all possible cone triplets. It can accordingly be termed a *receptoral colour space*. The second space has three mutually orthogonal coordinate axes corresponding to the postreceptoral channels (Ingling and Tsou 1977) and can accordingly be termed a *postreceptoral colour space*.

In principle, a postreceptoral colour space could be formed from any three mutually orthogonal axes used to recode the cone triplets. We already know, however, that the spectrally antagonistic responses in postreceptoral neurons have the effect of enhancing the difference between the overlapping cone absorption spectra. In a more abstract analysis, Buchsbaum and Gottschalk (1983) have shown formally that, given a set of three receptor types and a class of spectral signals, there is 'a unique transformation that has the property of most efficiently transmitting the visual information to higher stages of perception' (Buchsbaum and Gottschalk 1983: 91). The basic idea is to obtain the weighted combination of mutual excitation and inhibition that maximally decorrelates the receptor responses. Applying this procedure to psychophysically derived data about the receptor responses in humans, Buchsbaum and Gottschalk derive two chromatically opponent channels that match rather closely the channel sensitivities as determined by Hurvich and Jameson's hue-cancellation technique. Hence the optimum transformation from the receptoral space to the postreceptoral space in humans is shown to require two opponent antagonistic channels (1983: 94). Buchsbaum and Gottschalk's overall conclusion is that 'Opponent type processing in the visual system can be deduced as the next logical step after the three initial cone mechanisms' (1983: 109).

This result is of considerable importance because it provides an abstract rationale for the linkage between trichromacy (three receptor types) and the postreceptoral opponent channels. In colour science, the trichromacy of normal human colour vision has traditionally been taken to be due to the three types of receptor in the human eye. We can now appreciate, however, that the dimensionality of normal human colour vision results not simply from trichromacy, but from the more extensive *trivariance* of having three receptor types cross-connected to three postreceptoral channels (Lennie 1984: 244). From now on, when I use the term 'trivariance' I shall be referring to this receptor–channel linkage.[23]

Let us turn now to the relation between the postreceptoral colour space and the phenomenal colour solid. One of the main research tasks in psychophysics involves determining the directions the axes in the postreceptoral space take in relation to the colours as arrayed in the colour solid. The standard view, which owes its origin to the nineteenth-century physiologist and psychologist Ewald Hering (1920/1964), but was given its first quantitative formulation by Hurvich and Jameson using the hue-cancellation technique, is that the directions correspond to the grey scale of black to white and to the unique opponent hues. Thus the $L + M$ axis links black and white, the $L - M$ axis links unique red and green, and the $S - (L + M)$ axis links unique blue and yellow. The three channels are accordingly also known as the white–black, red–green, and blue–yellow channels. Different accounts of the relation between the chromatic channels and phenomenal colour space, however, emerge from several more recent lines of experimental work in psychophysics.

One line, pursued by Finkelstein and Hood, implies that the chromatic channels can change their spectral tuning in relation to changes in the stimulus parameters, with the consequence that there is no one-to-one correspondence between the chromatic response in a given channel and the appearance of a given hue (Hood and Finkelstein 1983; Finkelstein and Hood 1984; Finkelstein 1992). Whereas the hue-cancellation experiments measured chromatic response for the appearances of large, long-duration, foveal lights presented under specific states of adaptation, Finkelstein and Hood examined the detection and discrimination of small, brief lights. Contrary to the standard assumption that small light flashes are detected primarily by the achromatic channel, Finkelstein and Hood's data indicate that the detection and discrimination of such stimuli involve multiple mechanisms at least some of which are spectrally opponent. Furthermore, the data cannot fit the same spectrally opponent mechanisms that fit the data for large light flashes. To account for these findings, Finkelstein and Hood propose what they call the 'variable tuning hypothesis' according to which a channel can increase or decrease its degree of opponency with changes in stimulus parameters. In their words: 'The hypothesis discards the notion of discrete red–green and yellow–blue pathways that represent some fixed weighted difference of receptor absorption spectra. Instead the tuning to the relevant dimension, wavelength, is drastically changed by presumably irrelevant dimensions, size and duration' (Hood and Finkelstein 1983: 391).

The variable tuning framework has implications for the assumption that the chromatic channels are aligned to the red–green and blue–yellow axes in phenomenal colour space. According to the traditional 'appearance assumptions',[24] hue is coded in the overall polarity of response in the chromatic channels, as depicted in Figure 4. For example, a positive response from the red–green channel implies that the colour perceived contains some red, whereas a negative response implies that it contains some green. To abandon the hypothesis of discrete red–green and blue–yellow pathways, however, implies discarding the assumption that there is 'a fixed link between positive and negative responses in a given channel and a given pair of hues' (Hood and Finkelstein 1983: 392). Instead, a more complicated theory about the relations between patterns of activity across channels and colour appearance is required.

Another line of psychophysical research employs methods for delineating the chromatic channels that are different from hue-cancellation. Krauskopf et al. (1982) used what they call a 'selective habituation' method by having observers adapt to fields whose colours were modulated sinusoidally in time and then measuring their sensitivity to brief flashes of coloured light. (The modulations do not change the average chromaticity and luminance of the adapting field over time, and so there is little adaptation on the part of the cones. Thus the method habituates or densensitizes the postreceptoral channels without significantly altering the cone sensitivities.) They found that the detection thresholds for the colour flashes were raised (i.e., sensitivity was reduced) in a highly selective fashion in relation to the modulated colour fields: the thresholds for detecting reddish and greenish changes from white were raised after viewing a field modulated chromatically along the reddish–greenish axis, but were not raised after viewing a field modulated along the bluish–yellowish axis. Similarly, the detection thresholds for bluish and yellowish changes from white were raised after viewing a field modulated chromatically along the bluish–yellowish axis, but were not raised after viewing a field modulated along the reddish–greenish axis. When the adapting field was intermediate between the two axes the detection thresholds were uniformly raised for all test stimuli. Krauskopf et al. conclude that the reddish–greenish and bluish–yellowish axes constitute what they call 'cardinal directions' in the postreceptoral colour space, i.e., mutually orthogonal directions corresponding to separate channels that can be selectively habituated or fatigued. (The study also specified a third cardinal direction corresponding to the achromatic luminance channel.)

The existence of such cardinal directions conforms to the predictions of the opponent process theory. The actual directions as determined by Krauskopf et al.'s procedure, however, do not correspond entirely to the unique opponent hue axes in phenomenal colour space as traditionally predicted by Hering and as determined by the hue-cancellation technique. One cardinal direction corresponds to the L – M channel and is aligned with the unique red–green axis in the colour solid. The other cardinal direction, however, corresponds to an axis along which the ratio of the L and M cone activities remains constant and only the S cone activity changes in the S – (L + M) channel. This direction deviates considerably from the unique blue–yellow axis in phenomenal colour space, corresponding instead to a purple–chartreuse (greenish-yellow) axis.[25]

Other psychophysical experiments support this delineation of the chromatic channels. Flanagan et al. (1990) have shown that there are orientation-selective mechanisms that respond independently to colour contours along the cardinal directions proposed by Krauskopf et al. Another intriguing line of support comes from a study by Krauskopf and Farrell (1990) on the influence of colour on motion perception (see also Albright 1991). Their hypothesis was that motion signals arising from different chromatic channels would be less likely to yield the perception of coherent motion than motion signals arising from the same chromatic channel. They used drifting spatial grating patterns (plaids) that were modulated along either different or the same chromatic axes. Patterns that were designed to stimulate the L – M and S – (L + M) channels independently appeared to slip with respect to one another, whereas patterns that were designed to stimulate only one of the channels appeared to cohere. These results are significant not only because they reinforce the significance of the cardinal directions, but also because they indicate that visual attributes such as colour that are unrelated to motion per se can profoundly affect how we see things move (Albright 1991: 268).

In a more recent study, Webster and Mollon (1991) used a technique similar to Krauskopf et al.'s but arrived at different results (see also Hurlbert 1991). They had observers adapt to temporally modulating colour fields, but then performed colour-matching experiments for suprathreshold test-lights rather than measuring detection thresholds for brief light flashes. They found that when observers adapted to colour modulations along one of the cardinal directions, the greatest change in the colour appearance of test-lights occurred along that direction and the least change occurred for test-lights along the orthogonal direction. This finding conforms to what one would predict on the basis of Krauskopf et al.'s results. But Webster and Mollon found in addition that for some observers adaptation to colour modulations along intermediate directions also resulted in the colour appearance of test-lights changing most along that direction and least along the orthogonal direction. Furthermore, in all cases the colour appearance changes involved hue shifts corresponding to rotations away from the direction to which the observer had adapted towards an orthogonal direction.

These results bear on several issues and support various interpretations (Hurlbert 1991). First, there is the methodological question of what adaptation or habituation reveals about the visual system. Adaptation is usually interpreted as revealing distinct channels by selectively desensitizing or fatiguing them. On the basis of this view, the highly selective adaptation effects found by Webster and Mollon not only in the cardinal but also intermediate directions would imply that there are many channels each tuned to a different chromatic direction. Furthermore, if the only effect of adaptation is to densensitize the channels, and if there are stimuli that change the activity in only one chromatic channel, then it should be the same channel that responds to the stimulus after adaptation; consequently, the perceived hue of the stimulus should not change as a result of adaptation. But in all cases the changes in colour appearance did involve hue shifts. This result suggests that there are no chromatic directions for which only a single chromatic channel is responsible.

Some visual scientists, however, have argued that adaptation may enable the visual system to reduce its sensitivity to frequently occurring contingencies in the environment, enabling it to be more sensitive to the unexpected and so to respond more flexibly in a dynamic environment (Barlow and Foldiak 1989). This view suggests the hypothesis that there are only a small number of chromatic channels and that these are not only densensitized by adaptation, but also caused to rotate away from their natural alignment to the cardinal directions. Thus adapting the visual system to chromatic modulations along intermediate directions would cause the channels to realign along those directions to match the environmental changes in the ambient light (Hurlbert 1991).

Second, there is the question of the level at which the

selective adaptation effects occur in the operation of the visual system. In their original study defining the cardinal directions, Krauskopf et al. found a hint of the selective habituation effects for intermediate directions revealed by Webster and Mollon. One explanation that they proposed to account for this 'residual selective habituation' – an explanation for which they also provided additional evidence in a subsequent paper (Krauskopf et al. 1986) – is that there is a third level of operation in colour vision distinct from the receptors and the post-receptoral chromatic channels. This third level would comprise adaptable mechanisms that would respond to specific propor-tions of activation among the postreceptoral channels and so be tuned to many directions in colour space.

To summarize, then, the selective desensitization effects reported by Webster and Mollon might reflect a third level of operation in the visual system comprising mechanisms that respond to combinations of activities in the $L - M$ and $S - (L + M)$ opponent channels. The mechanisms might be 'multiple, adaptable channels, each tuned to a different direc-tion in colour space' (Webster and Mollon 1991: 238); or they might be composed of a small number of channels whose tuning can be altered through adaptation.

Physiological issues about the postreceptoral channels

Another set of issues centres on determining the neural substrates of the postreceptoral channels and their specific physiological characteristics. To appreciate these issues a sketch of the relevant anatomy is required.

As the optic nerve leaves the retina, the nerve fibres divide at the *optic chiasma* so that the signals originating from the left half of the visual fields of both eyes are sent to the right side of the visual cortex, and the signals originating from the right half of both visual fields are sent to the left side of the visual cortex. Between the retina and the visual cortex is a part of the thalamus called the *lateral geniculate nucleus* (LGN). In primates, the LGN is a six-layered structure that has two major subdivi-sions, the four dorsal *parvocellular* (small-cell) layers and the two ventral *magnocellular* (large-cell) layers. The LGN inter-digitates the signals from the eyes in alternating layers: each half of the visual field is mapped twice to the parvocellular layers and once to the magnocellular layers, giving a total of six topographic maps of the visual field.

The two subdivisions of the LGN receive projections from two anatomically distinct types of ganglion cell in the retina whose properties are similar to cells in the LGN: the larger, so-called type P-alpha ganglion cells project to the magnocellular division, and the smaller, so-called type P-beta cells project to the parvocellular division. These retino-geniculate connections form two parallel but distinct pathways, known accordingly as the M (magnocellular) and P (parvocellular) pathways.

In addition to being anatomically segregated, the cells of the P and M pathways have different response characteristics. The P-beta ganglion cells and the P cells are mostly wavelength selective (cone opponent), have small receptive fields, and respond in a slow, sustained fashion to visual stimulation. The P-alpha ganglion cells and the M cells are not wavelength selective, are more sensitive to luminance contrast, have large receptive fields, respond in a rapid, transient fashion to visual stimulation, and have faster conduction velocities.

Recordings from single cells in the P pathway in the macaque monkey, an animal that has colour vision similar to ours, show that the cell sensitivities cluster along the cardinal directions discussed above (Derrington et al. 1984). The cells are single opponent neurons, and each responds best to stimuli modulated along one of the cardinal directions, but fails to respond to stimuli modulated along the directions orthogonal to the cardinal directions. Two classes of cells were found, corresponding to those that responded best to chromatic modulation along one cardinal direction and those that responded best along the other direction. Furthermore, the cells show no signs of adaptation in their responses to the type of stimuli used in the psychophysical experiments reviewed above, which supports the hypothesis that the selective habituation effects reported in Webster and Mollon's experiment involve mechanisms in the visual cortex (Krauskopf et al. 1986: 31; Webster and Mollon 1991: 238).

The physiological differences between the P-beta and P-alpha cells combined with the anatomical segregation of the P and M pathways have been taken as indicating that the pathways comprise parallel physiological channels or 'processing streams' (Livingstone and Hubel 1988; DeYoe and Van Essen 1988). There are numerous disagreements about how the channels should be conceived, however, and about their specific physiological characteristics.[26]

One difference involves labelling the pathways and is terminological. The P pathway is often called the 'colour opponent' channel because 90 per cent of its cells are wavelength selective; whereas the M pathway, whose cells are not wavelength selective, is often called the 'broad-band' or 'luminance' channel. These terms are rather misleading, however, because both pathways are involved in the perception of many attributes such as colour, shape, texture, movement, and depth (DeYoe and Van Essen 1988).

In psychophysics the use of these terms appears to have been reinforced by experiments based on using so-called *equiluminant* stimuli. These are stimuli whose luminance levels have been equated so that all luminance contrast is eliminated and only contrasts in wavelength remain. Livingstone and Hubel (1987, 1988) found that in such equiluminant conditions both motion and depth perception are impaired, and they ascribed the deficits to the presumed unresponsiveness of the M pathway in the absence of luminance cues. On the basis of these and other results, Livingstone and Hubel propose that the M pathway mediates motion and depth perception, and the P pathway mediates colour vision and high-resolution form perception.

This proposal has been challenged, however, on several grounds. First, there are results that suggest equiluminant stimuli are unsatisfactory for determining the roles of the pathways (Schiller and Logothetis 1990: 393; Davidoff 1991: Chapter 4). For example, fine-pattern and texture perception, which are thought to be handled by the P pathway, are also impaired at equiluminance (Logothetis et al. 1990); and some studies have shown that chromatic information can be used in the perception of form, motion, and depth at equiluminance (see Schiller and Logothetis 1990 for a review). Evidence has also been reported that neurons in the M pathway respond to equiluminant borders (DeYoe and Van Essen 1988: 225).

Second, lesion experiments indicate a more complex assignment of visual capacities to the M and P pathways than Livingstone and Hubel's proposal (Schiller et al. 1990; Schiller and Logothetis 1990). For example, although lesions to the P pathway leave luminance detection and discrimination unimpaired at low spatial frequencies, so too do lesions to the M pathway, indicating that the M pathway should not be considered as a unique luminance channel. Lesion experiments also indicate that the P pathway is essential not only for chromatic discrimination, but also for form and depth perception at high (but not low) spatial frequencies.

Third, it is problematic to suppose that separate anatomical pathways and the distinctive properties of single cells reflect separate perceptual mechanisms, especially given the evidence from psychophysics and the lesion studies just mentioned. Indeed, although there are separate pathways at the anatomical level, there are also numerous cross-connections among them at many levels, making the pathways highly intertwined (DeYoe and Van Essen 1988; Zeki and Shipp 1988). It seems likely that colour, form, movement, and depth perception are mediated considerably by these cross-connections, thereby precluding any one-to-one correlation between perceptual attributes and neuronal pathways (DeYoe and Van Essen 1988).

Earlier in my discussion of the phenomenal structure of colour, I argued that we typically perceive colours as properties of things in some visual context, and I suggested that colour perception is probably not modular in the traditional sense (neither 'informationally encapsulated' nor 'cognitively impenetrable'). These two features are just what one would expect if there is significant overlapping of perceptual attributes across neuronal pathways. In DeYoe and Van Essen's (1988) framework for the visual pathways, for example, each low-level sensory cue, such as luminance and spectral contrast, binocular disparity, two-dimensional orientation, etc., provides a basis for perceiving many distinct attributes, such as colour, form, movement, and three-dimensional relationships; conversely, most perceptual attributes are tied to many sensory cues. Given this 'patchwork' architecture it is not surprising that there is no such thing as a 'pure colour percept' that reflects a modular colour channel or processing stream (Davidoff 1991). In the next section, we shall see that this point continues to hold for 'higher' or more 'central' levels of operation in colour vision.

Cortical connections[27]

The cerebral cortex, the most complex structure known in the universe, is a highly convoluted sheet of nervous tissue organized into layers of intricately connecting neurons. The visual cortex, located at the back of our head, comprises a third of the cerebral cortex and is a mosaic of many so-called visual areas. The areas are identified cytoarchitecturally by the grouping of cells into different layers. There are two major distinctive regions: the *striate cortex*, so called because of its laminated appearance, is the most posteriorly situated and is also known as visual area 1 (V1) because it is the first to receive projections from the retino-geniculate pathways. In front lies the *prestriate cortex*, which is divided into the distinct areas V2, V3, V4, and V5 (also called the middle temporal area or MT).

V1 and V2 have a distinctive organization whose cytoarchitecture is revealed by staining for the metabolic enzyme, cytochrome oxidase. In V1 the cytochrome oxidase-rich patches appear as columns that lie perpendicular to the cortical surface and intersect the cortical layers. In layers 2 and 3 of V1 the columns form 'blobs' that are separated from each other by the more lightly stained regions called 'interblobs'. In V2 the patches appear as alternating thick and thin dark stripes, separated from each other by light interstripes. Both blobs and thin stripes contain high proportions of double opponent, wavelength-selective cells.

The M and P pathways project to different areas of the visual cortex, remaining segregated in both V1 and in the prestriate cortex. The M pathway includes several subpathways linking layers in V1, the thick stripes in V2, and areas V3 and V5. The P pathway projects to V1, where it splits into two pathways: the parvo-interblob (P-I) pathway includes the interblobs of V1 and the interstripes of V2; the parvo-blob (P-B) pathway includes the blobs of V1 and the thin stripes of V2. Both pathways then project to V4.

There is also evidence that these pathways remain segregated through the still higher so-called visual association areas, which comprise two major divisions, the parieto-occipital region and the temporal-occipital region. The former seems to be concerned primarily with the position of objects, the latter with identifying objects (Ungerleider and Mishkin 1982). V5 (MT) projects heavily to the parietal lobe, whereas V4 projects heavily to the temporal lobe. Thus there appear to be two major visual pathways, one dominated by the M pathway that projects to V5 and on to the parietal lobe, and the other dominated by the P pathway that projects to V4 and on to the temporal lobe.

The most prevalent hypothesis is that these two pathways constitute two functionally distinct processing streams, known as the 'where' and 'what' streams, concerned with, on the one hand, movement, position, navigation, etc., and on the other hand, with object identification on the basis of colour, shape, texture, etc. (Ungerleider and Miskin 1982; Mishkin et al. 1983; Livingstone and Hubel 1988). It must immediately be added, however, that the details of this hypothesis are contested, with many of the issues again having to do with the cross-connections between the pathways and subpathways, and the physiological properties of the cortical areas (DeYoe and Van Essen 1988; Schiller and Logothetis 1990).

One issue that bears directly on our concerns is the role played by cortical area V4 in the 'what' pathway. On the basis of electrophysiological recordings of single cells in the monkey visual cortex, Semir Zeki has proposed that V4 is an area devoted specifically to colour (Zeki 1980, 1983a, 1983b, 1985). Zeki recorded from the cells while flashing a multicoloured pattern (a so-called colour 'Mondrian' made up of about a hundred coloured papers randomly arranged) with one col-oured patch centred on the cell's receptive field. The cell responses could not be correlated with the wavelength compo-sition of the light reflected from the patch, but could be correlated with the colour of the patch as perceived by a human observer (Zeki 1983a). Thus the cells seem not only to respond preferentially to particular hues, but also to exhibit colour constancy, a finding Zeki takes as indicating that V4 is specialized for colour.

There are a number of problems with this proposal, however. With regard to the supposedly special connection between V4 and colour selectivity, other studies have not confirmed Zeki's results (Krüger and Gouras 1980; Schein et al. 1982; Krüger and Fischer 1983), and Gouras (1991b: 189) argues that the cell responses Zeki recorded may be due to simultaneous colour contrast (in which the colour appearance of an object depends not simply on its spectral reflectance but also on the spectral reflectance of its background), noting that there have been very specific responses to simultaneous colour contrast demonstrated in other visual areas, specifically V1 (Michael 1987a, 1987b, 1987c) and V2 (Gouras and Krüger 1979).

Nonetheless, there do seem to be close connections between V4 and the cortical levels of operation involved in colour vision. Other studies have found that some cells in V4 have a broad spectral response curve and respond well to white light (Desimone et al. 1985; Desimone and Schein 1987). This type of cell response seems analogous to a photocell covered with a broad-band colour filter, such as a piece of coloured glass, which would respond not only to white light, but also preferentially to certain coloured lights. The same studies also found, however, that V4 cells are highly sensitive to stimulus form, with selective responses to length, width, orientation, and spatial frequency. Lesion studies too support this linking of colour and form: in the macaque monkey, lesions to V4 impair not only hue and saturation discrimination, but also the discrimination of pattern and orientation (Heywood and Cowey 1987). These results indicate that rather than being solely devoted to colour, 'V4 is both a "color area" and a "form area"' (Desimone and Schein 1987: 861).

There is a methodological problem, however, with assigning stimulus attributes such as colour and form to specific cortical areas on the basis of the kind of experiment performed by Zeki and Desimone et al.: the experiments are performed with anaesthetized monkeys who are consequently not seeing any colours (in one sense of 'seeing') (Boynton 1988: 93). Moreover, studies in alert, unparalysed monkeys reveal that both attention and the relevance of a stimulus for the performance of a behavioural task can considerably modulate the responses of cells in V4 (Moran and Desimone 1985; Haenny et al. 1988). As Haenny et al. (1988: 245) note: 'These findings suggest that signals arising from sources other than the retina may represent an important aspect of neuronal activity in visual cortex.'

This last point dovetails with more theoretical issues about levels of operation in the visual system. My discussion has reflected the standard procedure of ordering the levels hierarchically from 'lower' or more 'peripheral' (retina and LGN) to 'higher' or more 'central' (visual cortex), measured in terms of synaptic distance from sensory stimulation. This procedure is convenient as long as it is not taken to imply that visual processes must proceed sequentially and hierarchically. It is well known that there are not only 'forward' projections from 'lower' to 'higher' areas, but also numerous 'backward' projections in the reverse direction, as well as reciprocal 'sideways' or 'lateral' connections between pairs of areas (Zeki and Shipp 1988). Take, for example, the LGN, which is typically described as a 'relay station' on the 'retina-to-cortex route'. There are massive backward projections from all areas of the cortex to the thalamic nuclei (Steriade and Deschenes 1985), however, and in the case of the visual system, there are actually more nerve fibres that go down from the visual cortex to the LGN than go in the reverse direction (Robson 1983). This organization suggests that neuronal activity in central areas may considerably modulate the activity at peripheral layers, an idea that is also supported by some experiments on cortico-thalamic inter-actions and binocular rivalry (Varela and Singer 1987). (Unfortunately, there are to my knowledge no comparable experiments for colour vision.)

Given the dense connectivity of the nervous system it is not surprising that extraretinal (for example, somatosensory or task-specific) signals should contribute to neuronal activity in the visual cortex, particularly when the animal studied is awake and not unduly immobilized. Indeed, other experiments have shown that when animals are alert and behaving in more normal sensory surroundings many kinds of neuronal response in visual cells become highly dependent on behavioural factors such as the bodily tilt of the animal (Horn and Hill 1969), its posture (Abeles 1984), and auditory stimulation (Morell 1972; Fishman and Michael 1973).

These findings suggest that the response characteristics of single cells do not provide sufficient ground for making inferences about the roles played by anatomically distinct areas such as V4 in the operation of the visual system. On this point some remarks from a recent review by Martin are worth quoting at length:

> The concept that areas are specialized for different functions dominates our thinking because it is the most convenient explanation for the plethora of cortical visual areas. Given this *Weltanschauung* it makes perfect sense to

highlight a single property, as has been done for motion coding in MT and colour processing in V4. Such debate that has arisen about the function of areas has been about whether the proportion of a particular functional class of cell is high enough to justify calling the area 'specialized' for that function. This debate is irrelevant since no area has cells that are selective for only one feature; all cells can be characterized by an envelope of multiple tuning curves. The tuning of single cortical cells is generally broader or coarser than our behavioural performance. It would thus help to know how finely tuned neurones need to be to a particular stimulus property (e.g. wavelength) in order for them to be used in processes relevant to that property (e.g. colour perception). It would also be useful to establish, at least theoretically, what kind of physiological types ought to be present if a particular process (e.g. colour constancy) is hypothesized. Some progress is being made in this direction, but neural models have as yet made little impact on the direction of physiological research.

(Martin 1988: 383–4)

The neural models to which Martin is referring (Lehky and Sejnowski 1988; Land 1983) are actually abstract, task-level analyses that are computational in Marr's sense. How these models are to be related to the physiology and hence what kind of impact they should have on physiological research is a substantive empirical and methodological issue, but the working assumption is that the models characterize the abstract properties of large populations of neurons – neuronal ensembles, networks, maps, systems, etc. – and so are related to the physiology at a much higher level or scale than that of the single cell (Churchland and Sejnowski 1988). With these kinds of models we move from psychophysics and physiology to the younger research endeavours of cognitive neuroscience and computational vision.

COMPUTATIONAL COLOUR VISION[28]

Colour constancy and the 'natural image'

Our discussion so far has concentrated on light signals and colour appearance in the aperture mode. Given a knowledge of the three cone absorption profiles and of the chromatic and achromatic responses of the postreceptoral channels, accurate predictions can be made for colour appearances in the aperture mode. The results presented so far do not, however, enable us to predict the colours seen in what Edwin Land calls the 'natural image', a complex, multicoloured scene or image (Land 1959, 1983). In such an image, the colours one sees are due both to local comparisons across the boundaries of coloured areas and to the global interactions of different areas throughout the visual field (see Brou et al. 1986 for a colourful demonstration). These local–global interactions cannot be studied in a restricted aperture context. The aperture mode is invaluable for studying certain aspects of colour appearance and for investigating the psychophysical properties of the visual channels. A complete explanation of colour vision, however, requires an understanding of how colour appearances remain relatively stable or constant in more natural visual environments. Given Marr's delineation of the computational level of explanation as being concerned with deriving properties of the actual visual environment from retinal images, it is not surprising that the study of colour vision in the 'natural image' has been especially pursued in computational colour vision, with considerable attention given to the phenomenon of colour constancy.

We can begin by recalling how computational vision treats colour constancy abstractly as a 'problem' that must be solved for any colour vision system, biological or artificial. The initial stage in colour vision is the absorption of light by the photoreceptors. The receptor surface can be considered as a two-dimensional sensor array that receives light from different locations in the scene. The light arriving from the scene at any location on the array is the *intensity signal*; it is the product of the spectral power distribution of the illuminant and the surface spectral reflectance of the location in the scene. The two illuminant and reflectance variables are thus confounded within the intensity signal. Measurements of the intensity signal are taken by the receptors for each point in the scene; they are a function of the number and sensitivities of the receptor types, and they exhaust the information about the scene available to the visual system (Maloney 1985: 12). The problem, then, is given only the measurements of the intensity signal by the receptors, how is it possible to derive indicators of object colour that depend not on the varying spectral power distribution of the ambient light, but on the invariant surface spectral reflectances?

This approach to colour constancy is a prime example of computational vision as 'inverse optics', the recovery of what are taken to be objective, perceiver-independent properties of three-dimensional scenes from ambiguous two-dimensional projections (Poggio et al. 1985). In the case of colour vision, the problem consists in discarding the source illuminant and thereby recovering spectral reflectance given only the retinal activity. The problem shares a common structure with other problems in early vision, such as edge detection and the computation of motion, for they are all underconstrained or 'ill-posed' (Poggio et al. 1985). A problem is said to be ill-posed when it has no unique solution. (See Poggio et al. 1985 for a more formal definition.) To solve an ill-posed problem, the class of admissible solutions must be restricted by introducing constraints; these are said to 'regularize'the problem.

Most current computational models of colour vision can be described as attempts to solve the ill-posed problem of colour constancy with the appropriate regularization constraints. For this problem, a combination of empirical evidence and task-level analysis has shown that the necessary regularization constraints are basically of three kinds: (1) global computations; (2) low-dimensional, linear models of lights and reflectances; and (3) spatial segmentation.

Global computations and lightness

One might assume that, since colours are perceived to be spatially located, the colour a surface is perceived as having can be correlated with the light reflected locally from that surface. Suppose, for example, that the surface is perceived to be green. Surfaces that look green typically reflect a high percentage of middle-wave light and a low percentage of long-wave and short-wave light. It might be supposed, then, that the surface looks green because it reflects more middle-wave light to the eye. This would be true when the surface is viewed in isolation, i.e., if everything else is excluded from the field of view. But when the surface is viewed as part of a complex scene, it will continue to look green even if it reflects more long-wave and short-wave light than middle-wave light. In other words, when the surface is viewed as part of a complex scene, the light that it locally reflects is not sufficient to predict its perceived colour. Thus we encounter another major flaw in the received view: contrary to the received view, there is no one-to-one correspondence between the perceived colour of an area in a scene and the light reflected by that area to the eye.

This fact has been known for some time by colour scientists. The most dramatically convincing demonstrations, however, are due to Edwin Land (1977, 1983). Land uses a display of about 100 different coloured papers arranged arbitrarily called 'colour Mondrians' because they resemble the paintings of Piet Mondrian. The display is illuminated by three projectors, which project bands of short-wave, middle-wave, and long-wave light respectively. An observer picks one of the coloured areas in the display – a yellow patch, for example. The experimenter then measures separately the short-, middle-, and long-wave radiances that are reflected from that yellow area. The observer then picks another coloured area, one that is white. The experimenter then independently adjusts each projector so that the white paper will reflect the same triplet of short-, middle-, and long-wave radiances that the yellow paper previously reflected. The question is: when all three projectors are turned on simultaneously, what colour will the white paper appear to be? Will it appear yellow, since it will reflect the same radiance triplet that the yellow paper reflected? In fact, when the projectors are turned on, the white paper continues to look white, even though the light it reflects has the same composition as the light that previously produced the appearance of yellow. Land continues this demonstration by going from paper to paper in the display and arranging the projectors so that each paper sends the same radiance triplet to the eye. In each case, however, the perceived colours of the papers change very little. On the basis of these experiments, Land concludes that *the composition of the light from an area in an image does not specify the colour of that area* (Land 1985: 7).

Land reached this conclusion first in the late 1950s on the basis of somewhat different experiments involving 'two-filter' colour projections (Land 1959). In these experiments, Land found that he could produce a full range of colours in an image by superimposing on a screen two black and white negatives. The negatives were taken with different filters and were illuminated by projectors with filters that passed different bands of wavelengths. Land undertook a systematic investigation of such 'two-filter' projections and came to the conclusion that the perceived colours of areas in the images could not be correlated with the wavelength composition of the light reflected from the areas. This conclusion of the lack of a one-to-one correspondence between colour in an image and light wavelengths had been reached by others before Land. But Land insisted that the existing theories of colour vision could not explain his findings. Many colour scientists disagreed (for example, Walls 1960) and saw in Land's work merely a sophisticated example of simultaneous colour contrast or the phenomenon of 'coloured shadows', the same phenomenon that long before had provided the basis for Goethe's critique of Newton's physical colour theory (Creutzfeldt et al. 1987).[29]

In the course of refining his experiments, however, and devising new ones, such as the 'colour Mondrians', Land developed an approach to colour vision that was quite novel. As Land remarks in a more recent paper:

the high degree of independence [of perceived colour in an image from the light reflected at a point] cannot be accounted for on the basis of visual phenomena such as adaptation, pigment bleaching, wandering of the eye, and so on. Rather, one must search for *a precise computational process extending over large areas of the field of view and possibly over the whole field of view.*

(Land 1983: 5164. My italics)

The novelty of Land's approach is to be found in this attempt to devise a computational explanation of colour vision. Indeed, as Marr (1982: 17) notes, Land's theory of colour vision was one of the first attempts to formulate 'a clear computational question' about perception (the first attempt in the case of colour vision is probably Yilmaz (1962)). Therefore, even though the first of Land's assertions in the above quotation can be debated, the theoretical importance of his research remains.

Land calls his computational model the 'retinex theory' of colour vision. (The term 'retinex' is derived from combining 'retina' and 'cortex'; it is meant to leave open the exact physiological location of the mechanisms that implement the computational process. Land et al. (1983) have argued, however, that the cortex is required for long-range colour computations.) This theory is now only one of many computational models of colour vision. It is nonetheless worth examining for several reasons: (1) it was one of the first computational models to be proposed; (2) it has inspired new psychophysical and physiological experiments;[30] and (3) it has been the subject of considerable attention in philosophical discussions of colour.[31]

Land's retinex theory falls into the class of models that attempt to compute colour by computing *lightness* (Hurlbert 1986).[32] The term 'lightness' as Land uses it refers to a perceptual attribute that is related to the psychosensorial value for scaling colours along the achromatic dimension, but is differently defined. In colour science, lightness is normally defined as 'the attribute of a visual sensation according to which the area in which the visual stimulus is presented appears to emit more or less light in proportion to that emitted by a similarly illuminated area perceived as a "white" stimulus'(Wyszecki and Stiles 1982: 494). In Land's usage, however, lightness refers to a perceptual attribute that results from comparing luminance values throughout the entire visual field. It is thus an internally computed visual attribute rather than a raw sensorial value. The psychophysical correlate of lightness, according to Land, is 'average relative reflectance', the surface reflectance of an area relative to the average reflectance of its surround (Land 1983).[33]

What is the connection between lightness and colour in Land's theory? When a scene is illuminated by a restricted waveband of light, for example, middle-wave light, and the intensity of the light is varied, light objects will stay light and dark objects will stay dark. For example, red peppers will always look almost black and green peppers will always look light grey–green (Land 1985). This situation will be reversed, however, in long-wave illumination: red peppers will always look light and green peppers will always look dark. On the basis of these kinds of observations, Land argues that

> it is reasonable to venture the hypothesis that an object which always looks light with middle-wave illumination on the scene and always looks dark with long-wave illumination on the scene will look green when the scene is illuminated with both illuminators and *will continue to look green* as we change the relative brightness of the long- and short-wave illuminators and hence the relative fluxes from the object to the eye.

(Land 1985: 7)

Land suggests that perceived colour in an image can therefore be predicted on the basis of lightness values for this image within each of three short-, middle-, and long-wave bands. The wavebands are taken to correspond to the spectral sensitivities of the three types of cone receptor. Each receptor type generates a separate lightness image, and the comparison of lightness values among these three images specifies the colours that are perceived. The computational problem thus becomes the derivation of three independent lightness images using only the information provided by the intensity signal.

Land's algorithms are devised for the restricted visual environment of colour Mondrians. Given this environment, several physical assumptions can be made. Indeed, in the absence of these independent physical constraints, the computational problem involved in deriving lightness is underconstrained, and so cannot be solved (Hurlbert 1986). The physical assumptions thus serve to regularize the ill-posed problem of lightness computation.

The first assumption is that each patch within the scene has a uniform spectral reflectance. The second assumption is that the illumination varies slowly and smoothly across the scene. Given these two constraints, it can be assumed that gradual changes in the intensity signal are due to variations in the illumination, whereas discontinuous, step changes correspond to boundaries or edges between patches of different reflectance. In other words, step changes in intensity can be used to *segment* the scene into different regions each with its own uniform reflectance. Once the visual field has been segmented in this way, the lightnesses (average relative reflectances) of the unit areas can be calculated. Here we begin to see the interdependence in colour vision among global computations, a finite number of channels, and spatial segmentation.

Land has proposed several algorithms for the computation of lightness (Land 1983, 1985, 1986). In general, though, all lightness algorithms proceed by (1) differentiating the intensity signal over space; (2) applying a threshold operation that eliminates small values due to smooth changes in the illumination and retains large values due to abrupt changes in reflectance at the borders between patches; and (3) integrating the result of this threshold operation over space to recover surface reflectance (Hulbert 1986). In Land's retinex algorithms, the computations are carried out three times, once for each of the three (short-, middle-, and long-) wavebands. A given patch will thus have associated with it three independent lightness values called a lightness triplet. The lightness triplets serve as indicators of perceived colour and so are called by Land 'colour designators'.

The colour designators can be represented in a way that reflects the trivariance of normal human colour vision. Each colour designator corresponds to a triplet of lightness values and so can be represented as a point in a three-dimensional colour space that has the short-, middle-, and long-waveband lightness values as its three axes. Retinex theory thus treats the trivariance of human colour vision as consisting in three independent lightness channels that define the axes of a three-dimensional *lightness colour space*.

Since I have mentioned that computational models of colour vision are largely concerned with recovering the invariant surface spectral reflectances in a scene, it should be noted that Land's lightness values do not provide absolute measures of surface reflectance (Hurlbert 1986). Lightness corresponds to surface reflectance relative to the average reflectance of the surround as determined within a given waveband. If, within each of the three wavebands, the average surface reflectance in the scene is grey (i.e., the average of the lightest and darkest naturally occurring reflectances), then the computed lightness of a patch will correspond to its average relative reflectance. But if this constraint does not hold, then the lightness algorithms will be unable to tell the difference between a change in the spectral power distribution of the illuminant and a change in the background colours (Hurlbert 1986). Consequently, lightness algorithms do not exhibit perfect constancy. In Hurlbert's words:

> Lightness algorithms recover lightness values that have an arbitrary relationship to the physically correct surface-spectral-reflectance function and therefore recover only a weak form of color constancy. This fact does not disqualify lightness algorithms as models for the computation of color by humans, because humans also display weak color constancy. The limitation of lightness algorithms as models for color computation arises from the fact that they are designed for the restricted world of two-dimensional Mondrians. They do not address a task essential to color constancy in the natural three-dimensional world: to distinguish shading and shadows resulting from object contours and the spatial distribution of the illuminant from true reflectance changes. As Land (1985) has recently demonstrated using still-life scenes, lightness algorithms may, nevertheless, approximate human perception even in the three-dimensional world.
>
> (Hurlbert 1986: 1687)

Criticisms of the retinex theory

A number of criticisms have been made of Land's retinex theory. First, although the retinex algorithm, like human colour vision, does not display perfect colour constancy, one can still ask whether the chromatic values it assigns to patches in a scene match those of human vision (Hardin 1988: 191). According to Brainard and Wandell (1986), for certain types of simple Mondrian images in 'daylight' illumination (as defined by the Commission Internationale de l'Eclairage), Land's 1983 algorithm predicts changes in the appearance of the patches as their backgrounds are varied. The changes are not seen by human observers, however, who in this situation exhibit complete colour constancy. On the other hand, according to Worthey (1985), if the Mondrian image is illuminated by monochromatic light sources, instead of the three waveband sources Land employs, the retinex algorithm will predict a higher degree of colour constancy than is displayed by human vision.

Second, similar questions can be raised about the achromatic values that the retinex algorithm assigns: do the assigned lightness values match those of human vision? With respect to earlier versions of Land's algorithms, Marr (1982: 257) noted that there are aspects of lightness perception due to simultaneous contrast that are not predicted by Land's approach. More recently, Shapley (1986) reports that in achromatic Mondrians there are widespread departures in lightness perception from the values assigned by the retinex algorithm (see also Shapley et al. 1990: 436–8). Whereas Land proposes that the lightness of an area is correlated with the area's average relative reflectance, Shapley argues that 'the brain seems to assign brightnesses to areas in complex scenes that correlate with their average border contrasts', thereby suggesting that 'the computation of brightness is much more localized in fact than in Retinex theory' (Shapley 1986: 59, 56). In another study, Creutzfeldt et al. (1987) began by attempting to test the retinex model of lightness perception but found that it did not take into account several important variables. In particular, they report that the retinex theory does not take into account what they call the 'shunting effect' whereby two adjacent fields attenuate each other's effect (Creutzfeldt et al. 1987: 281–2).

These results all emphasize the importance of local contrasts and not simply the relative reflectances of patches in the scene. It should be noted, however, that Land (1986) has proposed another algorithm in which the light signal from an area is compared with an average of the signals from all areas *weighted for distance*. The weighting of values on the basis of distance provides for the importance of more local contrast effects. As Jameson and Hurvich note: 'This alternative algorithm for the first time in retinex computations relaxes the strict coupling between computed lightness at a point on a surface and surface reflectance at that location' (Jameson and Hurvich 1989: 180).

These criticisms all occur at what Marr would call the 'algorithm' level of explanation for vision, for they are concerned with how well the retinex algorithms match the performance of human colour vision as determined by psychophysics. Other critical points have been made about the neurophysiological plausibility of the retinex algorithms. First, retinex calculations are made separately in each of the short-, medium-, and long-wavebands before being compared to generate colour designators, but it is known from physiology that the cone signals are mixed and compared at early post-receptoral levels. Second, no role is given to opponent processes in retinex theory, whereas the neurophysiological evidence indicates that they occur at many levels in the visual system.

The significance of these two points is difficult to assess, however, because it is not clear what the proper level of comparison is for relating retinex theory to neurophysiology (Daw 1984: 334). The most plausible view is that retinex computations might correspond to higher, cortical levels of operation in colour vision (Land et al. 1983; but see Pöppel 1986). Livingstone and Hubel (1984) suggest that the visual system might perform a transformation from the axes of the lightness colour space to a set of axes within this space corresponding to the responses of the double opponent cells in V1. Zeki (1985) suggests, on the other hand, that the lightness-generating system could be based on the double opponent cells, whereas the colour constancy designators might correspond to cell responses in V4. Desimone et al. (1985) advance a similar proposal based on their view that many V4 cell responses are comparable to photocells covered with a broad-band colour filter, which, they note, resemble the colour filters predicted by retinex theory (Desimone et al. 1985: 448). Desimone et al. also found that V4 cells have large suppressive surrounds that extend beyond their excitatory receptive fields. Stimuli placed outside the cell's excitatory receptive field have no effect themselves, yet they do suppress the cell's response to a stimulus placed inside the excitatory receptive field. The suppression was found to be almost complete when the surround stimulus and the receptive field stimulus had the same wavelength; furthermore, the cell responded best if there was a spectral difference between the receptive field stimulus and its surround. According to Desimone et al., the larger receptive field sizes and spectral interactions could reflect a mechanism for colour constancy of the type predicted by retinex theory (Desimone et al. 1985: 447).

Finally, there are computational-level criticisms of retinex theory. Two related points can be made about the physical constraints assumed in Land's model. The first concerns access to the constraints; the second concerns the problem of spatial segmentation. Only the first will be reviewed here, for it serves to introduce another type of computational model. The second will be considered below in the section on spatial segmentation.

The main computational criticism to be made of retinex theory is that although it depends on assumptions about the physical world as one would expect from the computational level of explanation (Marr 1982: 18), the assumptions are based on independent physical measurements within the Mondrian environment, measurements that the visual system on its own is not capable of performing. Recall that lightness algorithms depend on being able to use step changes in the intensity signal to separate the two confounded variables of illumination and reflectance. This procedure works because given the Mondrian environment, we – that is, the computational theorists – know that the illumination varies slowly and continuously across the scene and that patches have uniform spectral reflectances. But how could the visual system have access to such knowledge of the scene? How, for example, could it know in advance or determine for itself that patches in the scene always have uniform spectral reflectances? We should not expect to find such knowledge implicit in natural visual systems, for although it might be fruitful to describe the visual system as embodying 'expectations' or 'assumptions' about its environment (Snyder and Barlow 1988), Land's Mondrian displays are hardly 'natural images' in comparison to the three-dimensional world of texture, shape, orientation, shadows, etc. in which natural visual systems have evolved.[34] The problem that remains, then, is to find regularization constraints that are plausible for the three-dimensional world and that do not need to be spoon-fed to the visual system.

The linear models framework (LMF)

Another family of computational models relies on a different kind of physical constraint to regularize the problem of recovering surface reflectance. The basic idea is to show how the range of possible lights and reflectances can be limited to a model with a small number of parameters. Consider first that any function of wavelength ranging between 0 and 1 is potentially a surface reflectance and that to describe all such functions would require an infinite number of parameters (Maloney 1986: 1674). Visual systems have at their disposal only small numbers of receptor types, however, and so can achieve colour constancy only across limited ranges of possible lights and reflectances. Consequently, any visual system that achieves colour constancy must be relying on constraints on the possible lights and reflectances in the scenes it encounters (Maloney 1986: 1673).

In the family of computational theories belonging to what is known as the *linear models framework* (LMF) (Maloney 1992), the constraints take the form of specifying the lights and reflectances in a linear model with a small number of parameters. Actual lights and reflectances are described by representing them as the weighted sums of a small number of illuminant and reflectance basis functions. Colour designators correspond to weighted sums of the reflectance basis functions, and recovering reflectance consists in estimating the weights used to describe a particular reflectance (Maloney 1986: 1673). The class of surface spectral reflectances within a given model can thus be considered as a *reflectance colour space* (see D'Zmura and Lennie 1986). For example, in a linear model with three parameters, the reflectance colour space will have three orthogonal, reflectance basis functions as its axes, and object colours (spectral reflectances) will correspond to points in this three-dimensional space.

The empirical justification for this approach comes from a body of work indicating that many naturally occurring illuminants and surface reflectances can be described as lying within a low-dimensional space: only a few illuminant and reflectance basis functions are needed as axes for the space spanned by the totality of actual lights and reflectances (Maloney 1985, 1986). For example, Judd et al. (1964) showed that various phases of daylight can be described with only two to three parameters, and more recently Maloney (1986) has shown that a linear model with five to seven parameters suffices to describe the variance in two large sets of empirical surface reflectances, with six parameters providing an almost perfect fit.[35] Moreover, when the human spectral sensitivity curve is taken into account, Maloney found that the fit between surface reflectance and the linear model is enhanced so that only three to four parameters are needed.

The basic physical constraints in LMF thus consist in specifying the classes of lights and surfaces within a given model's domain of application. Specific algorithms for colour constancy then build on these constraints in various ways. For example, Maloney and Wandell (1986) provide an algorithm that can achieve perfect colour constancy provided that two major conditions hold: (1) the number of parameters in the model of lights must be less than or equal to the number of surfaces of distinct spectral reflectance in the scene; and (2) the number of receptor types must be greater than the number of parameters in the model of surface reflectance. There are also algorithms that extend the framework to deal with other factors such as specular reflectance (D'Zmura and Lennie 1986), nonuniform illumination (Funt and Drew 1988, as reported by Maloney 1992), and even ontogenetic considerations about the development of colour vision (Dannemiller 1989).

LMF also serves to generate predictions about the relationship between any visual system and its environment (Maloney 1992). When the constraints built into the LMF algorithms are satisfied, then the algorithms provide virtually perfect colour constancy. Thus LMF predicts that there are *privileged spaces* of lights and reflectances for a given visual system where colour constancy is near perfect. When the constraints built into the algorithms are not satisfied, however, LMF predicts that colour constancy will be only approximate, and relative to a given choice of linear model and algorithm, LMF predicts the direction and degree of nonconstancy.

Spatial segmentation

The discussion so far has focused on the recovery of surface reflectance as the main computational problem of colour vision. If the scene has already been segmented into regions of distinct surface reflectance, then given the constraints and algorithms outlined above, colour designators for the regions that depend on reflectance alone can be computed. To assume that the scene has been segmented prior to the deployment of the algorithms for colour constancy, however, misses in part the role that colour vision plays in object discrimination and identification. As D'Zmura and Lennie note: 'to find the loci of responses that correspond to different objects, one must already have segmented the scene to establish which lights come from which objects. This begs the question of the purpose of color vision, which we believe plays an important role in the discrimination among objects and in their identification' (D'Zmura and Lennie 1986: 1666).

To appreciate this point consider the two-dimensional Mondrian displays introduced by Land. With uniform or slowly varying illumination, step changes in the intensity signal will correspond to the boundaries or edges between patches of different but uniform reflectance in the scene. If a threshold operation is applied that eliminates small variations in intensity, but retains step changes, the scene can be segmented into different regions, each of which then receives a colour designator (lightness triplet) that depends on its average relative reflectance. This procedure works for Mondrian scenes, but these scenes are highly simplified in comparison with our three-dimensional world: 'The real visual world contains surfaces that are not planar, edges that are not sharp, and changes in albedo [reflectance] that are not abrupt (for example, gradual changes in pigment density). A complete theory of color vision ought to encompass all the natural events described above' (Rubin and Richards 1982: 216).

To encompass these factors computational theories often rely explicitly on chromatic information. Thus spectral information and information about colour as hue have been used in the tasks of edge detection, in determining material changes in a scene, in recovering shape from shading, and in segmentation (Gershon 1982: 45–7; 1987: 5–7). For example, Rubin and Richards (1982, 1984) propose that one goal of biological colour vision is to determine where material changes occur in a scene using only spectral information in the image on the sensor array. In the image the effects of material changes are confounded with the effects of other processes, such as shadows, surface orientation changes, highlights, and variations in pigment density. Rubin and Richards argue that the confounding processes must be rejected in order to conclude that the effects are due to material changes. They show that the confounding processes cannot be rejected by sampling regions in the image at just one wavelength. Two spectral samples are adequate, however, for the rejection. They propose two conditions that indicate material changes, *spectral crosspoints* and *opposite slope signs* (Rubin and Richards 1982, 1984). The conditions are defined by the relations between the two spectral samples. A spectral crosspoint occurs if the graphs of image intensity versus wavelength for two regions X and Y intersect (i.e., have a crosspoint). The opposite slope sign occurs when the graphs of the two regions have different signs: one goes up and the other goes down. (The two conditions are completely independent: they can occur together, or each can occur alone, or neither can occur.) Since it is generally accepted that the spectral sensitivities of visual pigments in biological receptors often serve to maximize contrast in various photic environments (Lythgoe 1979; Levine and MacNichol 1982), Rubin and Richards suggest that a study of the reflectances of natural objects might reveal whether biological visual pigments have also evolved to maximize the detection of spectral crosspoints and opposite slope signs.

This study makes use of low-level spectral information, but does not employ chromatic information in the form of hue, which depends on postreceptoral processes. D'Zmura and Lennie (1986), however, provide a finite dimensional linear model of colour constancy in which the colour designators are computed without relying on information about the shape or position of an object. In this model, mechanisms of light adaptation ('a multiplicative change in sensitivity in the independent cone mechanisms followed by an adaptive linear transformation of scaled cone signals at color-opponent sites' (D'Zmura and Lennie 1986: 1670)), combined with eye movements that expose the eyes to the average light reflected from the field of view, are used to evaluate and discount the illuminant, thereby recovering reflectance designators. The scheme does not rely on a prior segmentation of the scene. Instead, the designators are transformed to yield estimates of hue, which is, compared to saturation and lightness, relatively independent of object shape and viewing geometry. The hue estimates can then be used in the task of segmentation. In D'Zmura and Lennie's words: 'Our scheme does not require that the scene be segmented before chromatic designators are extracted; indeed the geometric stability of hue permits its use in segmenting a scene, and the variations in specular and diffuse components of reflection carried along the dimensions of lightness and saturation permit their use in establishing an object's shape and position' (D'Zmura and Lennie 1986: 1670).[36]

These two examples, one making use of low-level chromatic information and the other making use of higher-level processes, give computational support to the already accepted view that natural colour vision is involved not just in compensating for the illumination and recovering reflectance, but also in object discrimination and identification. Nonetheless, it might seem that the problems involved in spatial segmentation should be solved first; then, once the scene has been segmented, colour designators should be computed for the materially distinct regions. Logically, this proposal is reasonable. Thus algorithms for spatial segmentation could rely on other non-chromatic features, such as texture, motion, stereo, or nonvisual tactile information (Rubin and Richards 1982: 215). If recourse is had to chromatic information, however, the task of segmentation is much easier. Consequently, the processes involved in colour constancy and in spatial segmentation are likely to be intertwined, not just biologically, but also computationally (Gershon et al. 1986; Gershon 1987; Brill 1990).

Summary

In this section I have sketched only the basic outline and overall orientation of computational models of colour vision. It has been shown (1) that perceived colour depends on computations that extend throughout the entire visual field; (2) that naturally occurring lights and surface spectral reflectances do not vary arbitrarily, but can be described in a linear model with a small number of parameters; and (3) that to recover colour constant designators the visual scene must be spatially segmented and colour vision has a role to play in this task.

In comparison with investigating colour appearance in the aperture mode, computational research emphasizes a larger perceptual context for colour vision, including the entire visual field, high-level physical constraints, and visual phenomena such as constancy and object discrimination and identification. Traditional psychophysics and physiology, on the other hand, study colour appearance and the perceptual channels and neural processes that sustain our experience of colour. How might these various sides of colour vision be related? How, for example, might the computational processes involved in colour vision be related to the phenomenal structure of colour, or to the psychophysical and physiological processes that are responsible for colour experience?

LEVELS OF EXPLANATION AND COLOUR SPACE

To provide a framework for addressing the issues raised above, which will occupy us in various ways throughout the rest of this book, I wish to delve more deeply, first into the levels of explanation at work in visual science, and then into the 'colour spaces' that have been presented in this chapter. I shall then apply this framework to the specific case of colour constancy.

Levels of explanation

The relation among various levels of generalization and explanation is a central concern in contemporary visual science, indeed throughout all cognitive science. Following Churchland and Sejnowski (1988), several notions of 'level' at work in cognitive science can be distinguished: levels of *analysis*, of *organization*, and of *operation* ('processing' in Churchland and Sejnowski's terms).

The notion of levels of analysis is already familiar to us from Marr's framework, in which vision requires analysis and explanation at three different levels – the level of computational theory, the level of algorithm, and the level of implementation. To review the levels quickly, the computational level is an abstract analysis of the problem or task, which for early vision, according to Marr, is the recovery of three-dimensional scenes from ambiguous two-dimensional projections, otherwise known as 'inverse optics'. For colour vision, the inverse optics problem is to recover the invariant surface spectral reflectances in a scene. The algorithmic level is concerned with the specific formal procedures required to perform a given computational task. Finally, the level of implementation is concerned with how the algorithms are physically realized in biological or artificial systems.

In contrast to the notion of levels of analysis, the notion of levels of organization is relatively straightforward. In the nervous system, we find highly organized structures at many scales from molecules to synapses, neurons, neuronal ensembles, neural networks, maps, systems, and so on. Each level has properties specific to it, which in turn require different techniques for their investigation. Organizational complexity is certainly evident in colour vision, ranging from the chemical properties of receptor visual pigments to the electrophysiological properties of single cells, and the network properties of retinal, geniculate, and cortical cells.

Finally, in addition to the levels of organization, there are many levels of operation in the nervous system. How these levels are to be assigned, however, is considerably less clear than it is for the levels of organization. The typical procedure, which the presentation in this chapter reflects, is to order the levels hierarchically from peripheral (lower) to central (higher), thereby suggesting that operations in the nervous system proceed sequentially. The notion of levels of operation should be dissociated, however, from the idea that processes in the nervous system proceed sequentially, for the anatomical connections in the visual system suggest that there are not only serial and hierarchical circuits, but also parallel, lateral, and distributed circuits. However the relations among levels of operation must ultimately be conceptualized, it is clear that there are various levels to be distinguished. For example, in primate colour vision, we need to understand at the very least the reciprocally interconnected operations in the retina, thalamus, striate (V1) and prestriate visual cortex.

Colour vision has been treated at each of these three levels in this chapter. We can appreciate this by reviewing the colour spaces that have been presented to model various aspects of colour vision.

Colour space: a résumé

We began with the phenomenal colour space or colour solid defined by the three scalar dimensions of hue, saturation, and lightness. As a colour appearance space that presents colour at a phenomenal level without implying anything about lights, reflectances, visual pigments, perceptual channels, etc., the colour solid deserves the title of colour space *simpliciter*.

The other colour spaces that have been presented are all defined by new coordinates and model various associated aspects of colour vision at different levels of analysis, organization, and operation.

1   *Receptoral colour space.* The colour space that is specified at the retinal level of organization and operation. It is defined by the three L, M, and S cone receptor types and is spanned by all possible triplets of cone responses. It models the trichromacy of normal human colour vision and corresponds to a trichromatic sensor array at the algorithmic and computational levels.

2   *Postreceptoral colour space.* The colour space in which the cone triplets are recoded by three mutually orthogonal axes corresponding to the three postreceptoral channels of the opponent process theory. This colour space models the more extensive trivariance of normal human colour vision and corresponds to the so-called 'second-stage' decorrelation channels at the algorithmic and computational levels. It can be further subdivided into:
2a *Psychophysical channels space.* The colour space defined by the three psychophysically specified L + M, L – M, and S – (L + M) postreceptoral channels.
2b *Physiological channels space.* The colour space defined at the retino-geniculate levels of organization and operation whose axes correspond to the postreceptoral neurons that sum and difference the cone response signals.

3   *'Third-level' colour space.* The hypothesized higher-level colour space defined by adaptable mechanisms that respond to specific proportions of activation among the postreceptoral channels and so are tuned to many directions in phenomenal colour space. It too can be subdivided into a psychophysical channels space and a physiological, presumably cortical-level, channels space.

4   *Lightness colour space.* The computational-level colour space based on lightness algorithms whose axes correspond to three independent lightness channels and in which lightness triplets serve as constant surface colour designators.

5   *Reflectance colour space.* The LMF, computational-level colour space defined by reflectance basis functions and in which weighted sums of the basis functions designate (illumination-independent) object colours.

The order in which I have listed these colour spaces is simply the order in which they have been presented in this chapter: no hierarchical arrangement is implied. It should also be kept in mind that the colour spaces are not only models that have some degree of overlap (for example, lightness colour space might also be an instance of a third-level colour space), but also models of processes that are likely to be far more intertwined than the above sequential presentation suggests.

We can now return to the questions raised at the end of the section on computational colour vision. The computational level of explanation for colour vision is largely concerned with the inverse optics problem of recovering surface spectral reflectance. Hence the two computational colour spaces presented above – the lightness colour space and the reflectance colour space – are ones that comprise surface reflectance designators. The other colour spaces are in comparison more closely tied to the phenomenal colour space and its properties, such as the relations that colours bear to one another in virtue of hue-opponency. The questions raised above can thus be considered collectively under the umbrella issue of how the colour spaces are related to each other, in particular how the more psychologically constrained colour spaces (receptoral and postreceptoral colour spaces) are related to the more environmentally constrained colour spaces (lightness and reflectance colour spaces).

The case of colour constancy

To simplify the discussion I shall focus specifically on colour constancy. It is well known that human colour vision exhibits only approximate colour constancy. The best-known and now classic studies of nonconstancy were undertaken by Helson (1938; Helson and Jeffers 1940) and by Judd (1940); the results of the studies are now known as the 'Helson–Judd effect'. Helson and Judd found that spectrally nonselective surfaces seen against a spectrally nonselective background all appear achromatic in white light. When these surfaces are illuminated by chromatic light, surfaces whose reflectances are near the background level appear grey; those whose reflectances are above the background level take on the hue of the illuminant; and those whose reflectances are below the background level take on the hue complementary to that of the illuminant. Spectrally selective (coloured) surfaces in chromatic illumination exhibit similar hue shifts: their hues shift towards that of the illuminant or its complementary. As Jameson and Hurvich note in a recent review on colour constancy: 'Such departures from perfect color constancy with changes in spectral quality of illumination ... imply that perceived contrast between objects of different surface reflectance varies with the level and kind of illumination in which they are seen and to which the visual system is adapted' (Jameson and Hurvich 1989: 7).

From the standpoint of the computational level of explanation, the approximate constancy of human colour vision is not surprising. Lightness algorithms do not exhibit perfect colour constancy and so, taken as models of human colour vision, they would predict that our vision displays similar departures from colour constancy. (The departures from colour constancy appear to be different, however, for lightness algorithms and human colour vision. See the section 'Criticisms of the retinex theory' above.) In Maloney and Wandell's (1986) LMF algorithm, one of the constraints is that the number of receptor types be greater than the number of parameters in the linear model of surface reflectance. This constraint does not appear to be satisfied for human colour vision: Maloney (1986) found that five to seven parameters are needed to capture the variance in many naturally occurring reflectances; the number of parameters drops to three when the human spectral sensitivity curve is taken into account. A trichromatic system, however, can completely recover reflectances from a model of at most two parameters. LMF thus predicts that there are differences among naturally occurring surface reflectances that cannot be detected by a trichromatic system (assuming that no other kind of disambiguation is available) and, given a choice of linear model and algorithm, can predict the direction and degree of nonconstancy.

In psychophysics, two stimuli that differ in their physical characteristics, but are perceived by the observer to be the same colour, are said to be *metamers* for that observer. Thus, for surface colour perception, two surfaces that have different spectral reflectance profiles, but are perceived to be the same colour by an observer, are metamers for that observer. It should be noted that surfaces are metameric only in relation to the illumination. Since their spectral reflectance profiles are different, there will always be some illuminant under which the surfaces will no longer match in colour and so no longer constitute a metameric pair.

The discussion so far suggests an overall agreement between psychophysics and computational vision about colour constancy. The problems arise when it is asked how the approximate colour constancy of human colour vision is to be *explained*. For example, if one assumes that the function of colour vision is the achievement of colour constancy, defined as the recovery of the invariant surface spectral reflectances in a scene, then one will naturally be led to explain approximate colour constancy as a departure from perfect colour constancy, the implication being that the departure constitutes a visual shortcoming or error. Maloney and Wandell provide an example of this line of thought when they write: 'With three classes of photoreceptors, we can exactly recover surface reflectances drawn from a fixed model of surface reflectance with at most two degrees of freedom. Additional degrees of freedom in the surface reflectance will, in general, introduce error into the estimates of surface reflectance obtained, precluding perfect color constancy' (Maloney and Wandell 1986: 32).

One might wonder, however, whether this 'top-down' computational approach, although consistent with the approximate constancy of natural colour vision, should be accorded the status of an explanation. If one wishes to design a visual system that exhibits complete constancy, and the system exhibits only approximate constancy, then one is justified in saying that the system does not perform optimally, that it fails to achieve the task *for which it was designed*. Appealing to such a strong, engineering notion of optimality might be out of place, however, in explanations of natural colour vision. Perhaps biological colour vision has been evolutionarily formed by trade-offs and compromises among many factors, and consequently does not exhibit what, from an engineering standpoint, would be a clean and optimal design (Ramachandran 1985).

The issue is not limited to colour vision. Marr's computational theory is in general an optimizing theory. In Marr's (1982: 19) words: 'It becomes possible, by separating explanations into different levels, to make explicit statements about what is being computed and why and to construct theories stating that what is being computed is optimal in some sense or is guaranteed to function correctly.' This optimality assumption as applied to biological vision could very well turn out to be wrong. One prominent visual scientist has described the visual system as a 'bag of tricks' composed of specialized and unrelated strategies for various visual tasks (Ramachandran 1985; but see Snyder and Barlow 1988). The point at issue is well summarized by the philosopher of science Patricia Kitcher:

> Insofar as Marr and his co-workers can devise experiments that reveal vision as an 'elegant contrivance', then the Computational approach of functional decomposition into optimally designed stages will seem attractive. If they are wrong in this very substantial assumption, however, then the unified theory of vision that Marr dreamt of will be impossible. The passages from global Computational theories to local theories, and to algorithms, and to biological hardware will not be at all smooth, or perhaps even possible. Computational theories will not suggest lower level theories, nor will they constrain them, if the assumption of optimality is badly wrong. Indeed, a Computational theory might reject actual implementation as impossible for the task. Except in a loose and approximate way, the Computational theory will not explain how the mechanism carries out the task of vision.
>
> (Kitcher 1988: 23)

Returning now to the issue about colour constancy, even if biological colour vision should turn out to be in some sense optimal (relative to a given species and its niche), it might nonetheless exhibit approximate constancy for biological and ecological reasons that preclude designating this kind of constancy as being simply a visual shortcoming or error. For example, many computational approaches seem to rest on the assumption that colour vision is concerned primarily with the reflecting properties of surfaces. As a result, estimates of the illuminant are often treated largely as something to be 'discounted' in the task of recovering reflectance. This 'surface fixated compuational viewpoint' (Reeves 1992) neglects the point that natural colour vision might be concerned with illumination conditions in their own right, for these provide indications about weather conditions, time of day, and so forth (Jameson and Hurvich 1989: 2; Reeves 1992). To emphasize colour constancy at the expense of sensitivity to the illumination in its own right would therefore seriously prejudge the behaviours that natural colour vision serves.

Philosophers might suppose that these issues should be left to the scientists. Consider, then, what happens if the computational level of explanation with its optimality assumption is taken as the reference point for understanding colour. At this explanatory level, colour vision is defined as that visual process that recovers information about the invariant surface spectral reflectances in a scene. Once again, given this conception it is natural to explain approximate colour constancy as involving visual error. Surface colour metamers would therefore constitute a species of visual illusion. Consider, for example, the following remark by Maloney:

> The analyses of Chapter 2 [those presenting finite dimensional linear models of lights and reflectances] used data appropriate to human environments and suggested that what we call color corresponds to an objective property of physical surfaces. Depending on the light and the surfaces present in a scene, we succeed or fail in estimating these properties. Failures of color constancy, from this viewpoint, can be considered as visual illusions. We misestimate true color as we might misestimate true height in an Ames room.
>
> (Maloney 1985: 199)

The point in citing this remark is not that the computational level of explanation commits one to an objectivist view about colour – Land, for example, holds distinctly nonobjectivist views (see Land 1978, 1983). Rather, it is that the computational conception of colour vision as concerned primarily with the task of recovering surface spectral reflectance suggests a particular form of objectivism. Notice, for example, that the computational characterization of colour vision makes no explicit mention of the phenomenal colour space, the emphasis being placed instead on the reflectance colour space. Consequently, one is led to wonder how the two colour spaces are related, in particular how the features of hue might be related to surface spectral reflectance.

Consider now what happens if one proceeds in a more 'bottom-up' direction by taking the performance of natural colour vision and its biological embodiment as the reference point. Here the concern is primarily with colour appearance and the colour spaces constituted by the psychophysical and physiological channels. That colour constancy is only approximate provides an example of how colour appearance can shift depending on the state of the perceiver and the conditions of viewing. Hence more attention is given to the local, context-dependent features of perception than to high-level, physically invariant properties of the distal environment. Moreover, because the point of departure is colour construed phenomenally, it is less likely that one will play favourites among the different ways that colours can be encountered. For example, afterimage colours as well as surface colours require explanation. These both count as colour phenomena because they exhibit the phenomenal dimensions of hue, saturation, and lightness (or brightness). Consequently, it becomes natural to identify colour with this phenomenal structure. Because this structure does not reduce to properties of either lightwaves or surface reflectance, one will probably be led to embrace a subjectivist view about colour. Thus, consider the following passage from the conclusion of Zeki's pioneering study of cortical cell responses to both surface colours and afterimage colours in a Mondrian display:

> The results described here ... suggest that *the nervous system, rather than analyze colours, takes what information there is in the external environment, namely, the reflectance of different surfaces for different wavelengths of light, and transforms that information to construct colours,* using its own algorithms to do so. In other words, it constructs something which is a property of the brain, not the world outside.
>
> (Zeki 1983a: 764)

Similar statements can be found in the works of many visual scientists, especially physiologists. To quote one more:

Our cerebral cortex essentially creates and interprets conscious reality, establishing an order and logic to our thoughts and actions. Colour vision is just one manifestation of the abstractions it creates, in this case out of the colourless physical world.

(Gouras 1991b: 179)

If one compares the above remarks by Zeki and by Gouras with the quotation from Maloney, it becomes evident that despite the remarkable advance made in the study of colour vision in this century, the issue of the ontology of colour is not only undecided, but remains basically within the problem-space of objectivism versus subjectivism inherited from Newton and Locke. In fact, the two positions just outlined, with their links respectively to computational vision, and to psychophysics and neurophysiology, correspond precisely to recent discussions by philosophers: David R. Hilbert (1987) and Mohan Matthen (1988) have defended objectivism largely on the basis of computational colour vision (LMF and Land's retinex theory); and C. L. Hardin (1988) has defended subjectivism largely on the basis of neurophysiology and psychophysics (opponent process theory). The two different views espoused can hence be called *computational objectivism* and *neurophysiological subjectivism*.

The claim made at the outset of this chapter, that philosophical issues about colour must be addressed in relation to issues about levels of explanation for vision, has now been demonstrated. We are therefore ready to address the distinctly philosophical issues head-on.

3

NATURALISTIC
ONTOLOGIES

It cannot be required that the philosopher should be a naturalist,
and yet his co-operation in physical researches is as necessary as
it is desirable. He needs not an acquaintance with details for this,
but only a clear view of those conclusions where insulated facts
meet.

(Johann Wolfgang von Goethe 1840/1970: 283, §717)

Philosophical discussions about the ontology of colour typically proceed by attempting to determine whether colours can
be identified with some set of perceiver-independent physical
properties. Thus philosophers have argued that the colours of
objects can be identified with the wavelengths of light that
objects reflect (Armstrong 1968a), or with the surface spectral
reflectances of objects (Hilbert 1987). This kind of view about
colour is known as *objectivism*. The position I am calling
computational objectivism results when objectivism is defended
by appealing to the computational level of explanation for
vision. Most philosophers since Newton's time have found
objectivism to be unsatisfactory, and so have argued for some
version of *subjectivism*. The traditional version was explored in
Chapter 1; it is the view that things are coloured only in so far
as they have the disposition to cause sensations of colour in a
perceiver.[1] There is another version of subjectivism, however.
According to this view, nothing is strictly speaking coloured at
all, not even dispositionally. Rather, colours are entirely 'in the
head'; they are nothing but sensations of a certain type. Colours
are 'projected' on to the world, but there is no further sense in
which the world is coloured (see the quotations from Gouras

and Zeki at the end of the last chapter). In philosophical terms, this extreme version of subjectivism can be termed *eliminativism* about colour as a property (whether dispositional or intrinsic) of objects (Hardin 1988: 112; Landesman 1989). Combining this view with a reductionist, neurological treatment of colour experience yields the view I am calling *neurophysiological subjectivism.*[2]

The main task of this chapter is to evaluate computational objectivism and neurophysiological subjectivism about colour. Because these positions draw expressly on types of explanation in visual science, I shall begin with some methodological considerations about explanation and descriptive vocabularies for colour.

EXPLANATION AND DESCRIPTIVE VOCABULARIES

What counts as an explanation is a complicated and much-discussed issue in the philosophy of science, but it is agreed that one of the basic features of an explanation is the vocabulary it employs to capture the revelant features of the phenomena. As Hilary Putnam notes: 'whatever the pragmatic constraints on explanation may or may not be, one constraint is surely this: The relevant features of a situation should be brought out by an explanation and not buried in a mass of irrelevant information' (Putnam 1973: 206). Whether the relevant features of a situation are brought out depends on the descriptive vocabulary that is employed. To use Putnam's example, given a vocabulary for macroscopic and geometric properties of objects, one can not only describe but explain why a square peg will not go into a round hole. Given the vocabulary of particle physics, however, one might in principle be able to describe the same situation, but the description would not count as an explanation. In the particle physics description, the relevant features of the situation (that the peg and board are approximately rigid under transportation, that the hole in the board is too small, etc.) would be buried in a mass of irrelevant information (the microstructure of the board and the peg). The relevant features of the situation are macroscopic and geometric, not microphysical. A description that succeeds in bringing out these features will therefore have more chance of being an explanation than one that does not. The general point, then, is that since vocabularies describe phenomena in different ways, one must choose the appropriate descriptive vocabulary – the one that brings out the relevant features – if one is to explain the phenomena (for further discussion see Putnam 1975).

What descriptive vocabulary is appropriate when explaining colour phenomena? We have already seen that colour vision can be treated at various explanatory levels. Each level typically employs terms that refer to perceiver-independent physical properties, such as 'luminance', 'wavelength', 'spectral power distribution', 'spectral reflectance', etc., and terms that refer to properties of the perceiver, such as 'trichromacy', 'chromatic channels', 'chromatic response', etc. The colour space models also cover both physical and perceptual features, from the reflectance colour space of computational vision to the receptoral and postreceptoral colour spaces of physiology and psychophysics. It seems, then, that which descriptive vocabulary is appropriate is an interest-relative matter that depends on which features are relevant to the description and explanation of the particular situation.

To drive home this point it will be helpful to examine the so-called *tristimulus* method for specifying colours used in psychophysics and colorimetry. The task for which this method is designed is the precise matching of samples for colour. Two samples match in colour if they have the same *tristimulus values*. The tristimulus values have both physical and perceptual components. They are computed by first determining the spectral tristimulus values of a so-called *standard observer*, which are the relative amounts of three arbitrarily chosen lights that a standard observer needs to match the perceived colour of each chosen wavelength interval in an equal-energy spectrum. The tristimulus values for a given colour sample are then computed by taking the products at each wavelength of the surface reflectance (or transmittance) of the sample and the spectral energy distribution of the illumination, multiplying these products by each of the three spectral tristimulus values of the Commission Internationale de l'Eclairage (CIE) standard observer, and adding the values within each of the three sets of products. The summed values are the tristimulus values of the sample (see Hurvich 1981: Chapter 20).

Although the tristimulus values uniquely specify colours for certain purposes of colour matching, they do not enable one to specify the particular determinate colour that a given observer will see. In fact, two colour samples that have the same tristimulus values will probably not look the same to any given individual, for at least two reasons. First, the 'standard observer' is not any actual individual; it is an average based on the visual responses of a large number of normal human observers. The visual sensitivity of any actual individual observer will usually diverge from that of the standard observer. Second, the averaged visual responses are determined only for the restricted and highly artificial aperture viewing condition of a small field in a dark surround. When these conditions are changed the original tristimulus colour specification will no longer hold. The cumulative result is that a sample having a given colour in tristimulus terms can vary in hue, saturation, and brightness, depending on the individual observer, his or her adaptive state, memory, and attention, as well as the illumination conditions, the surrounding objects, and their relative sizes and positions (see Hardin 1988: 67–82 for further discussion).

These variations are neither problematic nor surprising given the task for which the tristimulus specification is designed. The point to be made is simply that the descriptive vocabulary provided by the tristimulus values, although quite useful in precise colour-matching situations, is not useful in situations where the relevant features have to do with colour appearance. In these situations what is needed is a descriptive vocabulary closer to hue, saturation, and lightness (or brightness).

The actual practice of visual science thus suggests that no exclusively physical or exclusively perceptual descriptive vocabulary would be adequate to cover the totality of colour phenomena. Visual scientists have in fact developed a number of technical terms to avoid the ambiguities inherent in the everyday use of the term 'colour'. The fact that both physical terms and perceptual terms are indispensable suggests that the concept of colour is inherently double-sided, with one side facing the world and the other facing the perceiver.

This double-sidedness is apparent in the received view, especially when Locke is read as attempting to develop a relational ontology in which colours have both physical and perceptual components. Yet contemporary philosophers have gravitated towards more extreme, nonrelational ontologies, arguing either that colours are really 'out there' (computational objectivism) or really only 'in the head' (neurophysiological subjectivism). Such gravitation is not especially surprising when viewed in the light of the tension between the dispositional and subjective components of the received view (see Chapter 1). It is surprising, however, when viewed in the light of contemporary visual science, for although most philosophers today would agree with Hardin that 'discussions about color proceeding in ignorance of visual science are intellectually irresponsible' (Hardin 1988: xvi), they do not seem to have appreciated the implications that the indispensability of both physical and perceptual descriptive vocabularies in visual science might have for the ontology of colour.

My approach in the rest of this chapter will be to show that neither computational objectivism nor neurophysiological subjectivism is able to provide a satisfactory naturalistic colour ontology. The upshot of the investigation will be to suggest that the physical and perceptual components of colour cannot be prised apart with the ontological privilege going to one over the other as both computational objectivism and neurophysiological subjectivism imply.

COMPUTATIONAL OBJECTIVISM

Objectivism is distinguished by its attempt to provide a purely physical, nonperceptual specification of colour. Ideally the objectivist would like to be able to identify colours with properties that can be specified purely in the vocabulary of physics. Some objectivists allow, however, that the properties could be arbitrary in the sense that they would not figure in the statement of physical laws. Although physical, the properties would be of scientific interest only because there exist perceivers that are sensitive to them. In any case, objectivism is committed to the view that the existence of the properties to be identified with colours does not depend in any way upon perceptual experience (Smart 1975; Jackson and Pargetter 1987; Hilbert 1987).

The central problem that objectivism faces is how to link physical or objective colours with the colours that we perceive objects to have, i.e., with particular determinate colours or shades belonging to the hue categories red, green, yellow, and blue, as well as the achromatic categories black and white (Hardin 1988: 7). The minimum requirement for establishing such a link is that the candidate physical properties be distal ones that the visual system can at least approximately track or detect. The reasoning behind this requirement is simply that if the properties were merely proximal ones (for example, patterns of irradiation on the retina), then although they would certainly participate in the processes that culminate in our seeing colours, they would nevertheless not qualify as properties that we *see*. Colours, on the other hand, are clearly properties that we see; consequently, if they are to be identified with physical properties, these too should be ones that we are at least in part capable of seeing.

Colour and wavelength

The point just made can be illustrated with an example. Consider D. M. Armstrong's (1968a, 1969) attempt to identify colours with the wavelengths of light that objects emit or reflect:

> In one way of talking, the colour of a surface is determined by, and so can be contingently identified with, the actual nature of the light-waves currently emitted at the surface. In this way of talking, the colour of the surface is constantly changing, really changing, as changes in condition of illumination occur ...
>
> But in another, more usual way of talking, colour is determined by the nature of the light-waves emitted under *normal illumination*: ordinary sunlight. It is therefore a *disposition* of surfaces to emit certain sorts of light-waves under certain conditions.
>
> (Armstrong 1968a: 284)

Armstrong considers the first of these two 'ways of talking' about colour to be the logically more fundamental: colour in the second sense is simply colour in the first sense given 'normal illumination'.[3] Hence Armstrong's basic claim seems to be that object colours are identical with the wavelengths of light the objects emit or reflect. Armstrong's view thus provides a good example of an attempt to revise the received view along objectivist lines.

In the passage just cited, Armstrong does not distinguish between *colour* and *perceived colour*, but since he is arguing on behalf of objectivism he would certainly accept the distinction. Indeed, Armstrong's intention is to identify an object's *being coloured*, though not necessarily (or only secondarily) an object's *looking coloured*, with the wavelengths of light the object emits or reflects (Armstrong 1968a: 272). Nonetheless, care must be taken in interpreting his claim that 'the colour of a surface is determined by the ... actual nature of the light-waves currently emitted at the surface'. If the claim here is that perceived colour is determined by locally reflected lightwaves, then the claim is false. As we saw in Chapter 2, particularly in our discussion of global computations and lightness, the composition of the light from an area in a scene does not specify the perceived colour of the area. Contrary to the received New-tonian view, there is in general no one-to-one correspondence between perceived colour and the spectral power distribution of light. This fact should be evident both from the discussion of the psychophysical opponent process theory (see the discussion of chromatic response in Chapter 2) and from the discussion of colour constancy. Moreover, that perceived colour is approximately constant indicates the falsity of the claim that the perceived colour of a surface continually changes with changes in the illumination.

Suppose, then, that Armstrong's claim is that perceived colour aside, the 'real' or 'objective' colours of things are identical with the wavelengths of light emitted or reflected. The plausibility of this view depends on whether colour vision is concerned with tracking or detecting the spectral power distribution of the light emitted or reflected by objects.[4] That this is in fact not the case should be evident from Chapter 2. From a computational perspective colour vision is certainly not concerned with tracking the spectral power distribution of the light reflected locally from an area. In both LMF and retinex theory, the colour designators correspond to estimates of surface reflectance – in the former to weighted sums of the basis reflectance functions and in the latter to triplets of lightness or average relative reflectance (the surface reflectance of an area relative to the average reflectance of its surround). Nor from a biological perspective is colour vision concerned with tracking the spectral power distribution of locally reflected light. As Gouras and Zrenner observe:

> Color vision has evolved to enhance wavelength differences between the reflectance of an object and its background in an environment where gradients of energy are often minimal. Color vision is not concerned with analyzing the wavelength composition of light reflected from an object's surface but with exposing an object in its background. That is why totally different wavelength combinations can produce identical colors (red and green mixtures match a spectrally different yellow) or why different colors can be produced by identical combinations of wavelengths (white objects can appear pink, pale green, or as other contrasting colors in the proper background). The colors we see in objects are those that best set them off from their backgrounds under the prevailing light conditions.
> (Gouras and Zrenner 1981: 139–40)[5]

The futility of trying to link the colours of objects with the wavelengths of light that objects emit or reflect becomes even more apparent when we consider what would happen if colour vision *were* concerned with tracking the spectral power distribution of locally reflected light. Even in the so-called 'normal illumination' of sunlight, the spectral power distribution of the light that strikes and is reflected from objects varies considerably with changes in the time of day, weather, viewing angle, etc. Suppose, then, not only as Armstrong does that the 'real' surface colours change with variations in the illumination, but that the visual system could track these changes so that visual sensitivity would be directly tied to the wavelength composition of the light reflected from objects. If one were visually acute in this way, one would not be able to *identify* objects by their colours, for these would be constantly changing with changes in the illumination and angle of viewing. How could something be identified as, for example, an orange, if its colour could appear to be orange, red, yellow, green, blue, etc., depending on the illumination and viewing conditions? Given such sensitivity, colour vision as we know it would become totally useless – it would 'lose its significance as a biological signalling mechanism' (Zeki 1983a: 742). Land's statement of this point is worth quoting at length:

> If, as has long been thought, the color name characterizing the surface of an object were determined essentially by the wavelength composition of the light reaching the retina from the object, then a simplistic mechanism in which rays of light tie the object point by point to related points on the retina would suffice conceptually for the first step in seeing objects as coloured. Such a scheme would be an evolutionary failure because the moment-to-moment and place-to-place variations in the composition of illumination in the world around us would change the moment-to-moment wavelength composition of the radiation reaching the retina from the object – and hence would lead to complete unpredictability of the color names characterizing the surfaces of the objects around us.
>
> (Land 1978: 24)

Armstrong actually considers the possibility that there is no one-to-one correspondence between colour and light wavelengths, but suggests that the

> different combinations of wavelengths may be instances that fall under some general formula. Such a formula would have to be one that did not achieve its generality simply by the use of disjunctions to weld together artificially the diverse cases falling under the formula. Provided such faking were avoided, the formula could be as complicated as we please.
>
> (Armstrong 1968a: 288)

Armstrong is certainly right that 'no physical considerations about colour rule out such a possibility'. Nevertheless, no such formula has yet been stated, and there is no evidence that there is any such formula to state. There is therefore no reason to believe Armstrong's proposal.

I mentioned above that the central problem objectivism faces

114

is how to link physical or objective colours with the colours that we perceive objects to have. There is no way to establish this link on the basis of identifying colours with light wavelengths. Colour vision is not concerned with tracking the wavelength composition of reflected or emitted light; consequently, identifying colours with light wavelengths renders the relation between colour and colour vision inexplicable. It is one thing to argue for a principled distinction between being coloured and looking coloured, but if it cannot be shown how the two are related, then there is no reason to believe that the properties in which being coloured supposedly consists have been successfully identified. The identification of colours with light wavelengths must therefore be rejected.

Colour and surface reflectance: anthropocentric realism

A much more plausible physical candidate for colour is surface spectral reflectance. The most extensive arguments for identifying colour with surface reflectance are due to David R. Hilbert (1987), though arguments have been proposed by others (Averill 1985; Matthen 1988). Two basic claims make up Hilbert's position. The first is the defining objectivist claim that there is a principled distinction between objective, physical colour (being coloured) and colour as it is perceived (looking coloured). It is the former that is in the first instance to be identified with surface spectral reflectance. In Hilbert's view, each distinct spectral reflectance profile is a particular determinate colour. Thus two objects whose surfaces have the same spectral reflectance profile have the same colour (in the sense of being objectively coloured the same colour); whereas two objects whose surfaces have different spectral reflectance profiles have different colours. Second, Hilbert claims that because not every difference in spectral reflectance corresponds to a difference in perceived colour, 'color perception and color language give us anthropocentrically defined colors and not colors themselves' (Hilbert 1987: 27). Anthropocentric colours, like colours themselves (surface spectral reflectances), are specifiable in purely physical terms, and so too are objective. Their specification is arbitrary from a purely physical standpoint, however, being of interest only in relation to the structure of the human visual system. To quote from Hilbert's own description of his position:

> Perception does not reveal the whole truth about colors and the truth it does reveal is delimited by the characteristics of our perceptual systems ... The nature of our experience only influences which of the many possible kinds of color our color terms and perceptions refer to. The kinds themselves exist independently of our color experience and are fully objective. One way of describing anthropocentric realism with respect to color is that the colors we perceive and talk about are objective although scientifically uninteresting kinds.
>
> (Hilbert 1987: 27)

Hilbert's position is the prime example of the position I have called computational objectivism. A number of the arguments he advances rely on the computational models of colour vision discussed in the previous chapter. He uses LMF to support his claim that objective colour is surface spectral reflectance and Land's retinex theory to argue that anthropocentric colours correspond to triplets of average relative reflectance. (See P. M. Churchland (1985, 1986) and P. S. Churchland (1986) for a similar use of retinex theory.) Hilbert does believe that philosophical arguments are needed to establish the identities, however (1987: 17–18, 129). He writes that 'the question of the objectivity of color is in the end a conceptual one. To settle the question, we need to discover which way of conceptualizing color allows us to account for both pre-theoretic intuitions regarding color and the wide range of known color phenomena' (1987: 16).

Many of the arguments that Hilbert offers are directed against previous subjectivist analyses of colour, especially those based on the mistaken view that the perceived colour of a surface can be correlated with the light that the surface locally reflects. (Hilbert refers to this view as the 'wavelength conception of colour'.) These critical arguments need not concern us here. We can focus rather on Hilbert's own positive views, beginning with the claim that nonanthropocentric physical colour is identical with surface spectral reflectance and then moving on to the claim that perceived colour is objective yet physically arbitrary and hence anthropocentric.

The main problem that arises for the surface reflectance view Hilbert actually discusses at length: it is the status of colour metamers. Two surfaces can differ in their spectral reflectance profiles and yet be perceived as having the same colour. The surfaces are known as metamers and are said to form a metameric pair. Given the existence of surface colour metamers one might wonder why each distinct surface spectral reflectance should be considered as a distinct, particular determinate colour. If two surfaces of distinct reflectance can be perceived to have the same colour, then why should differences in spectral reflectance be counted as differences in colour?

This type of objection to the surface reflectance view has been independently advanced by C. L. Hardin (1988).[6] In Hardin's view, the phenomena of metamerism prevent identifying surface colours with spectral reflectances, the colours of emitting lights with relative spectral energy, and the colours of transparent and translucent objects with relative spectral transmittance (Hardin 1988: 63–4). His argument is that there is 'little *physical* justification for putting … [metamers] into the same color class … Assimilating these to each other could, it appears, be motivated only by the similar effect they have upon organisms constructed like ourselves' (1988: 64).

Hilbert's answer to this type of objection takes advantage of the fact that metameric stimuli are always defined relative to a given illumination and a given observer. Thus two surfaces having different spectral reflectances will constitute a metameric pair only relative to a certain set of illumination conditions. Because they reflect light differently there will always be some illumination condition in which the surfaces no longer match in colour (for a given observer). How are these situations to be described? Are the 'true'or 'real' colours those perceived when the surfaces constitute a metameric pair? Or are they the colours perceived under the illuminant that makes apparent the difference in reflectance? Hilbert canvasses three possible answers to these questions and argues in favour of the third.

The first two answers are based on the received view according to which object colours consist in physically based dispositions of objects to produce sensations of colour in a perceiver. On this view, to say that an object is coloured is equivalent to saying that it would look to be coloured in certain circumstances to a suitable perceiver. Looking coloured is thus held to be conceptually and epistemologically prior to being coloured: objects do not look to be coloured because they are objectively coloured; they are objectively coloured only in so far as they have the disposition to look to be so.

The first answer is the simplest. One might claim that, because being coloured amounts to the disposition to look to be coloured, when the surfaces look to be the same colour they really are the same colour, and when they no longer look to be the same colour they really are different colours. There is no inconsistency here, for according to this proposal a given object can look to be one colour relative to one set of illumination conditions and look to be another colour relative to a different set of illumination conditions. The colours of the surfaces simply change from one situation to the other.

Hilbert argues that the problem with this proposal is that it makes colour an entirely illumination-dependent property. The reason why the perceived colours of the surfaces have changed in the present example is that the illumination conditions have been altered, making apparent the differences in spectral reflectance. But, Hilbert argues, colours are usually perceived as relatively stable properties of objects: they do not vary as the illumination-dependent proposal would seem to predict.

This argument does not strike me as particularly compelling because it holds only against the most simplistic versions of the thesis that object colours are circumstance-dependent. A more sophisticated view according to which there is no context-independent ascription of colour could be defended, however, without relying on a dispositionalist analysis and without presupposing an unduly simple (and hence false) conception of the illumination-dependence of colour (see, for example, Hardin 1990b). Because my present concern is the surface reflectance view, however, I shall not explore this possibility here.

The second answer to the question about metamers is also based on the received view and arises from trying to accommodate the relative stability of perceived colour. Dispositionalist accounts often attempt to draw a distinction between real and apparent colour by specifying a set of 'standard conditions' for viewing and a type of 'normal observer' whose colour experiences are taken to be authoritative. Surface reflectances that are colour metamers within the standard conditions and for the normal observers are to be counted as having the same colour. If two surface reflectances no longer form a metameric pair in some nonstandard illumination, then their colour difference counts as merely apparent or as an illusion.

This route has two basic problems. First, it is much harder to specify 'standard conditions' and 'normal observers' than most philosophers have imagined (Hardin 1983, 1988: 67–82, 1990b). I have already discussed how the 'normal observer' in the tristimulus specification of colour is a statistical average of many actual observers, and so cannot be used to predict how colours will appear to any given individual. Moreover, the 'standard conditions' used to specify this 'normal observer' are the aperture conditions of a 2-degree field in a dark surround (Hurvich 1981: 282). Seen in an aperture or through a reduction screen a colour loses its object and surface characteristics. How, then, are 'standard conditions' for viewing surface colours to be specified? Consider the following suggestion by Boynton:

> Illumination is provided by a hemisphere of uniform luminance. The object whose surface color is to be described is placed in the center of a horizontal circular plane lying below the luminous hemisphere as if lying on flat ground illuminated by cloudy sky. An observer peeks through a hole in the hemisphere, located at an angle of 45° with respect to the plane, and through this hole he sees most of the plane, but none of the 'sky'. The plane is free to rotate, doing so at a rate of 12rpm. The plane is covered by a 40% neutral reflecting surface, one that diffusely reflects all wavelengths equally. The hemispherical source emits an equal-energy spectrum sufficient to cause a luminance of 100cd/m2 of the neutral reflecting surface.
>
> (Boynton 1978: 176–7)

Here is a set of rigorously specified conditions for viewing the colours of surfaces. Yet the conditions eliminate all contextual effects due to the interaction of different coloured areas. To eliminate such effects is hardly standard, however, if by 'standard conditions' one means natural, everyday viewing conditions. Nor are the conditions 'standard' in the sense that philosophers have wished to give to this term. Philosophers typically use the term as a way of gesturing towards some set of conditions, usually taken as 'ordinary sunlight' (Armstrong 1968a: 284), in which the supposedly 'true' or 'real' colours of things are displayed. But even viewing conditions in ordinary sunlight can vary significantly depending on the time of day, direction (consider the northern light preferred by painters), the kinds of reflecting and emitting objects present in the scene, etc.

The point here is not that it is impossible to specify 'normal' viewing conditions. Rather, it is that too many can be specified, all of which are legitimate. Visual science is in fact replete with very precise ways of specifying viewing conditions. The problem in the present context is that the specifications are all interest-relative: they are suited to the pragmatic demands of specific types of colour-matching tasks, but not to the philosophical demand for a principled determination of the 'real' colours of things (Hardin 1983, 1988, 1990b).

The second problem is the one that Hilbert chooses to emphasize. If one claims that differences in colour, as revealed in nonstandard illumination conditions, are merely apparent, then one seems committed to the implausible view that underlying differences in surface spectral reflectance can be visually detected only by suffering from a colour difference illusion. Because the spectral reflectances of the two surfaces are different, the surfaces reflect different percentages of the incident light at certain wavelengths. It is this difference in spectral reflectance between the two surfaces that becomes apparent in the illumination conditions in which the surfaces are no longer metameric. The simplest explanation would accordingly seem to be that the surfaces are perceived as not matching in colour because the new illumination conditions enable the observer to perceive the difference in reflectance. The received view, on the other hand, seems to be committed to the odd claim that, because the viewing conditions are no longer 'standard', the underlying difference in reflectance is perceived through a colour difference illusion.

We thus come to the third possibility, the objectivist account. Hilbert argues that in the illumination conditions where the surfaces no longer match in colour, differences in objective, physical colour are what is perceived. Hilbert thus holds that there is no illusion of a colour difference; rather the difference in spectral reflectance is correctly perceived as a difference in colour. This view implies that each distinct surface spectral reflectance is to be identified with a distinct particular determinate colour. Differences in the perceived colour of two surfaces will usually correspond to differences in spectral reflectance. Sameness of perceived colour, however, does not always correspond to sameness of spectral reflectance. Our perceptual capacities are limited: they do not provide us with a complete view of surface spectral reflectance. Hilbert thus takes the existence of surface colour metamers as indicating that human colour vision is limited and indeterminate with respect to objective, physical colour. Our colour perception sorts surface spectral reflectances into metameric equivalance classes that are anthropocentric because they are determined by the structure of the human visual system.

Hardin too considers this type of approach to the phenomena of metamerism. He writes that we could 'decide to settle for such properties as relative spectral reflectance, illumination, etc. as constituting "physical color", and drop the requirement that objects that match metamerically over a wide range of illuminants are to be denominated as having the same color' (1988: 64–5). But he argues that '[h]owever attractive this strategy may seem on other grounds, one must realize that the concept of "color" it yields is one in which two matching yellow spots will usually not have the same color. If one wants an account of the ontological locus of red, green, yellow, and blue – what features they share, and in what ways they differ – one must look elsewhere' (1988: 65).

Hardin's argument can be rephrased in a way that brings out its implicit connection with the points I made in the previous section about descriptive vocabularies for colour. Settling for surface spectral reflectance as constituting physical colour is tantamount to adopting the descriptive vocabulary of physical optics for talking about colour. Hardin's point is that this descriptive vocabulary is too fine-grained in relation to colour in the sense of red, green, yellow, and blue. Colours in this latter and arguably primary sense correspond to metameric equivalence classes of physically distinct surface reflectances and so cannot be brought out by the descriptive vocabulary of physical optics. In other words, the fact that two surfaces having different spectral reflectances can nonetheless be seen as coloured the same red, orange, yellow, green, blue, purple, etc.

cannot be captured simply by the descriptive resources of physical optics.

This argument is on the right track, but as it stands it is not sufficient to counter Hilbert's objectivist position. In Hilbert's view, red, green, yellow, and blue are *anthropocentric colour kinds* – anthropocentric because they are arbitrary from the perspective of physics, and kinds because they are indeterminate with respect to surface reflectance. Once again, two surfaces that match in perceived colour will not necessarily have the same spectral reflectance, and so will not necessarily have the same particular determinate physical colour. But they will share the same indeterminate anthropocentric colour (Hilbert 1987: 112).

There is another, related line of argument, also developed by Hardin (1984b, 1988: 66–7, 1990b), that can be brought to bear on Hilbert's position. Recall Hilbert's claim that 'the question of the objectivity of color is in the end a conceptual one. To settle the question, we need to discover which way of conceptualizing color allows us to account for both pre-theoretic intuitions regarding color and the wide range of known color phenomena' (1987: 16). Whatever may turn out to be the proper ontology of colour, our pretheoretic intuitions regarding colour are certainly about colour in the sense of red, green, yellow, and blue. Moreover, the wide range of known colour phenomena presumably qualify as *colour* phenomena because they are describable in terms of red, green, yellow, blue, black, and white. The appropriate descriptive vocabulary for colour in this sense is provided at the phenomenal and psychophysical levels by the scalar dimensions of hue, saturation, and lightness. Are these scalar attributes, as well as the features that colours possess in virtue of them as displayed in the phenomenal colour space, brought out by the objectivist conception of colour as surface spectral reflectance?

The question can be refined by focusing on hue and holding constant the saturation and lightness dimensions. The phenomenal and psychophysical colour spaces show that hues themselves have certain features, such as being organized into opponent pairs, being unique or binary, and being balanced or unbalanced. Can these features be brought out by the descriptive vocabulary supplied by the objectivist's physical account of colour?

The force of this question can be seen by observing that it amounts to adding a constraint on the objectivist position. At the beginning of this section I noted that the minimum constraint on objectivism is that the candidate physical properties for colour be distal ones that the visual system can at least approximately track or detect. To this is now being added the further constraint that objectivism should provide the descriptive resources for making statements about colour as hue.

Hilbert's objectivism certainly satisfies the first constraint. But what about the second? Given only the spectral reflectance profiles for surfaces, one cannot model or make informative statements about hues and their features. Spectral reflectances do not stand in relations to each other that can be described as unique or binary, or for that matter as opponent or non-opponent, balanced or unbalanced, saturated or desaturated, and so on for all the other features of the phenomenal structure of colour as displayed in the colour solid. Thus the second constraint is not satisfied by surface reflectance objectivism.

It is worth presenting this argument more formally. Its main features are due to Hardin (1984b, 1988: 66–7, 1990b), but I have reformulated it and given it the name 'the argument from external irreducibility' (Thompson et al. 1992).

The argument from external irreducibility

1 For something to be a (chromatic) colour it must be a hue.
2 For something to be a hue it must be either unique or binary.
3 Therefore, if hues are to be reductively identified with perceiver-independent, physical properties, these properties must admit of corresponding unique and binary divisions.
4 External, perceiver-independent physical properties, such as lightwaves and spectral reflectances, do not admit of such divisions.

---

5 Therefore, colour cannot be reductively identified with such perceiver-independent physical properties.

This argument brings out the features that distinguish the phenomenal from the physical description of colour. The former focuses on the features of colour in the central sense of red, green, yellow, and blue, whereas the latter focuses on the features of the environment that are perceived as being coloured. What the argument from external irreducibility indicates is that *there is no robust, perceiver-independent mapping from the physical to the phenomenal aspects of colour.* To make the point in relation to the colour spaces presented in the previous chapter: *there is no mapping from the reflectance colour space to the phenomenal colour space that is structure-preserving in a robust sense and that does not proceed through one of the perceiver-dependent, physiological or psychophysical colour spaces.*[7]

Hilbert acknowledges the difficulties involved in attempting to provide an objectivist account of the phenomenal structure of colour, but arrives at a different assessment:

> There is no immediately clear sense in which one kind of reflectance is darker than another, and it is at least disputable that the kinds of reflectances associated with various color names actually stand in the relationships that we commonly suppose the colors do. It is, in fact, possible to account for many of these truths, but in doing so it will be important to keep in mind the anthropocentric nature of our color language.
>
> (1987: 116)

According to this assessment, not only does the phenomenal structure of colour reflect our limited and anthropocentric perspective on objective physical colour, but the main phenomenal features of anthropocentric colour *are* specifiable in purely physical terms (*pace* the argument from external irreducibility). If this is true, then there must be some perceiver-independent, physical property that is common to the otherwise physically distinct surface spectral reflectances that are perceived as the same colour. In other words, there must be physical properties with which anthropocentric colour kinds can be identified.

Hilbert's proposal for physically identifying anthropocentric colours relies on a series of psychophysical experiments designed to test Land's retinex theory (McCann et al. 1976; Land 1977). As we saw in Chapter 2, Land's retinex theory computes colour by computing lightness. To determine the colour of areas in the scene lightness values are independently calculated in three wavebands. The result is lightness triplets that serve as designators for the colours in the scene. The experiments performed in a psychophysical study of retinex theory showed that lightness could be correlated with a property called *scaled integrated reflectance* (McCann et al. 1976). This property corresponds to the reflectance of a surface integrated over a given waveband and then scaled so that equal increments in reflectance correspond to equal increments in lightness. Since perceived colours are designated by lightness triplets, the integration and scaling of reflectances must be carried out over each of the three wavebands that correspond to the spectral sensitivities of the cone photoreceptors. The resulting reflectance triplets provide the psychophysical correlates of the perceived colours in Land's Mondrian displays. Hence surfaces that have the same triplet of scaled integrated reflectances will generally be perceived as the same in colour, and surfaces that have different triplets of scaled integrated reflectances will generally be perceived as different in colour.

On the basis of these experiments, Hilbert claims that anthropocentric colours correspond to triplets of scaled integrated reflectances (P. M. Churchland (1985, 1986) and P. S. Churchland (1986) put forward a similar proposal). He proposes that the phenomenal structure of colour can be modelled by representing the reflectance triplets as located in a three-dimensional space whose axes are the reflectance values integrated over each of the three wavebands. Colours will thus correspond to volumes within this reflectance colour space, and the relations among colours will be modelled by the relations among the locations in the space.

This account of anthropocentric colour relies heavily on an objectivist interpretation of retinex theory.[8] Two important features of Land's retinex theory are overlooked by this interpretation. First, Hilbert takes the retinex colour space to be composed by axes of integrated reflectance, whereas Land usually specifies them as axes of lightness. The distinction is important because integrated reflectance is a psychophysical property that can be measured by a meter, whereas lightness is strictly speaking a psychosensorial or perceptual property that can be measured only by the visual system (McCann et al. 1976: 454). Second, the retinex colour space models only certain aspects of the phenomenal structure of colour. In particular, because retinex theory does not make use of opponent processes, the lightness colour space does not succeed in modelling the opponent relations among the colours and the phenomenal structure that colours exhibit in virtue of these relations, such as the unique/binary structure of hue.

These two points, taken together and in combination with the foregoing arguments, provide a strong case against Hilbert's objectivist account of anthropocentric colour. For this reason, I wish to explore them at greater length.

Although it is certainly possible to construct a colour space with axes corresponding to values of integrated reflectance within a given waveband, the retinex colour space is typically presented as a lightness colour space (Land 1977, 1983). The distinction between reflectance and lightness is not merely a technical nicety, for there are important differences between the two properties. Surface spectral reflectance is an illuminant-invariant property of objects, whereas lightness is not (Dannemiller 1990). Hence McCann et al. state that one of the fundamental assumptions of the retinex model is that it 'must have the ability to arrive at lightness in situations in which lightness does not correlate with reflectance' (McCann et al. 1976: 454).

One case where two patches of identical spectral reflectance can have different lightnesses happens when the patches are placed in markedly different surrounds (see Brou et al. 1986 for a vivid demonstration). Hilbert dismisses such shifts in lightness and colour in a footnote by claiming that they 'involve the creation of color illusions' (Hilbert 1987: 87). This treatment would perhaps be justified if colour vision were concerned with detecting *local* spectral reflectance, which, because it is an intrinsic physical property of surfaces, cannot vary with changes in the surround. But colour vision seems more concerned with detecting and tracking objects in relation to their backgrounds. As Gouras and Zrenner observe:

> both the background within which an object is seen and the object itself contribute to its color, and the color an object assumes will always tend to be the one that contrasts most with its background. Objects may assume different colors, even though their local spectral reflec-

tances are identical [Land 1977], if the backgrounds of these objects bring out different spatial color and luminance contrast detectors.

(Gouras and Zrenner 1981: 172)

Because the surround always contributes to the perceived colour of an object, appealing merely to changes in the surround is not sufficient to establish that the resulting lightness and colour shifts are illusions.

Another case where two areas of identical reflectance do not match in lightness happens when the intensities of the illuminants under which they are viewed are very different. Retinex theory tries to handle both cases by having lightness computations correspond to computations of the average relative reflectance – the surface reflectance relative to the average reflectance of the surround. As I discussed in Chapter 2, however, lightness will correspond to average relative reflectance only if within each of the three wavebands the average reflectance in the scene is grey. If this constraint does not hold, then the lightness algorithms will be unable to tell the difference between a change in the spectral power distribution of the illuminant and a change in the background colours (Hurlbert 1986). Furthermore, other experiments show lightness to be much more closely correlated with the average border contrasts in a scene than with reflectance (Shapley 1986; Shapley et al. 1990). The upshot would seem to be that lightness values are context-dependent in ways that prevent their being straightforwardly correlated with values of reflectance.

Because triplets of lightness rather than triplets of reflectance are the colour designators in retinex theory, Mohan Matthen, who also uses retinex theory to defend objectivism, is mistaken when he asserts that 'Land type-identifies perceptual states by the external property they present, not by their quale or any other internal characteristic' (Matthen 1988: 9). On the contrary, Land actually type-identifies perceptual states by specifying their location within a colour space defined by axes of lightness. Since lightness is a psychosensorial or perceptual attribute, it does not count as an 'external property' in Matthen's sense (which is not to say that it should be treated as a quale, 'raw feel', or sensation in the sensationalist sense). Within retinex theory lightness triplets do serve as *designators* of the external property of (average relative) reflectance. Nevertheless, it is lightness as a perceptual attribute that Land uses to type-identify the chromatic content of perceptual states:

> Color can be arranged in the lightness solid with long-, middle- and short-wave axes of lightness. All visible colors reside in this solid independent of flux, each color having a unique position given by the three axial values of lightness. It should be remembered that the reality of color lies in this solid. When the color Mondrian is nonuniformly illuminated, photographed and measured, reflectance in the photograph no longer correlates with the color but the lightness does.
>
> (Land 1977: 128)

Since triplets of lightness specify colours, and since lightness cannot always be correlated with reflectance, it is not surprising to find that Land himself considers colour to be an attribute that is internally generated from lightness computations and then treated as if it were an independent, external property (Land 1978, 1983).

One might of course argue that Land's interpretation of his own theory is misguided (Hilbert 1987: 17). The point being made now, though, is that because Hilbert's concern is anthropocentric colour – that is, colours as we actually see them – the lightness type-identification of the chromatic content of perceptual states cannot be replaced by a reflectance type-identification. The reason is that lightness perceptions depend not just on reflectance but also on the surround and overall level and quality of the ambient light (McCann et al. 1976: 454; Jameson and Hurvich 1989). If the chromatic content of perceptual states is type-identified simply in terms of reflectance, then it will not be possible to capture all of the generalizations that need to be stated about colours as we actually see them (for example, that they depend on the level and quality of the illumination).

We come now to the second problem with the objectivist use of retinex theory as an account of anthropocentric colour. The retinex lightness colour space does not provide a satisfactory model of the phenomenal structure of colour. Because the lightness algorithms do not make use of opponent processes, lightness colour space does not bring out the opponent relations among the colours and the phenomenal structure that colours exhibit in virtue of these relations (for example, the unique/binary structure of hue). This is not to say that retinex theory is incompatible with opponent process theories. For example, Livingstone and Hubel (1984) have suggested that the visual system might perform a transformation from the long-, middle-, and short-wave axes of the lightness colour space to a set of axes that would correspond to the double opponent cell responses in the striate cortex. Alternatively, one might suppose that the retinex processes correspond to a post-opponent, third level of operation in the visual system (Zeki 1985). These proposals do not affect the present point, however, which is simply that the opponent relations among the colours are not modelled in the lightness colour space. Instead, this space must either be transformed into or be a transformation of a colour space that does have two chromatically opponent axes.

Another problem is that in identifying colours with lightness triplets, retinex theory and lightness algorithms in general provide no indication of how different values of the *achromatic* quality of lightness can combine to form single *chromatic* perceptions (Campbell 1982; McGilvray 1983). Land says only that colours result from the comparison of lightness values in three wavebands, but as McGilvray notes, 'the notion of "comparing" remains inarticulate except as a mapping into this [lightness-colour] solid' (McGilvray 1983: 47). A natural place to look for articulation of the comparison processes is neurophysiology, but as we have already seen, it is conceptually rather difficult to relate retinex theory to neurophysiology (Daw 1984), and there is a lack of detailed neurophysiological models and evidence about how the activity in multiple cortical areas is organized so as to generate chromatic perception, as well as about the mechanisms that subserve colour constancy (Boynton 1988: 92). The upshot is that at the present time it is not understood how the phenomenal structure of colour could arise out of lightness comparisons.

Contrary to Hilbert's assessment, the foregoing points imply that retinex theory does not provide either the resources for a perceiver-independent, physical specification of anthropocentric colour or an adequate model of the phenomenal structure of colour. Anthropocentric colours – that is, particular determinate colours belonging to the colour categories red, green, yellow, blue, black, and white – cannot be adequately described without making statements about hue, saturation, and lightness. Consequently, any ontology of anthropocentric colour must account for these properties. The fact that these properties have no perceiver-independent, physical specification shows objectivism about anthropocentric colour to be a failure.

There is still one more response available to the objectivist that needs to be considered. Implicit in Hilbert's treatment of red, green, yellow, and blue as anthropocentric colour kinds is the view that the specification of objective physical colour need not be bound by the constraint of having to provide the descriptive resources for making statements about colour as hue. Since, as we have just seen, anthropocentric colours are also not physically specifiable, the objectivist could go one step further and claim that they amount simply to the subjective content of chromatic visual experience. Colour proper would be held to be perceiver-independent and physical, and would be identified with surface spectral reflectance, whereas red, green, yellow, and blue, as well as the features they share and the ways they differ, would be held to be entirely subjective visual qualities. In relation to the argument from external irreducibility, this view would imply that the correspondence requirements in premise 3 are too strong (Mausfeld et al. 1992) because objectivism need not be committed to there being any smooth mapping from phenomenal to physical colour (Matthen 1992).

The first thing to be noticed about this proposal is that it involves a major concession. Recall again Hilbert's point that settling the question about the objectivity of colour requires accounting for our 'pre-theoretic intuitions regarding color'. Surely one of these intuitions is that red, green, yellow, and blue are properties of things in the world, not subjective visual qualities. Indeed, the objectivist proposal for trying to ground this intuition is to identify colours with perceiver-independent, physical properties. But in arguing that the anthropocentric colour kinds red, green, yellow, and blue are actually only subjective visual qualities, objectivism could no longer claim to follow faithfully our pretheoretic intuitions and moreover would give colour in its central pretheoretic sense over to the subjectivist.

The main problem with this proposal should spring immediately to mind. If there were a successful, perceiver-independent physical account of red, green, yellow, and blue, then there would be an alternative, nonperceptual theory of colour and hence reason to conceptualize colour in purely physical terms. But given that there is no such account, in particular no perceiver-independent account of red, green, yellow, and blue as physical properties of surfaces, what reasons could there be for conceptualizing colour as surface spectral reflectance?

The main route leading to this view comes from computational objectivism, specifically from its approach to perceptual content, and was developed first by Matthen (1988) and subsequently by Hilbert (1992b). They argue that the contents of perceptual states are to be type-identified in terms of the (perceiver-independent) distal properties that it is the biological function of the states to track or detect. Applied to colour perception, the proposal is that the content of chromatic perceptual states is to be type-identified in terms of the distal property that it is the biological function of colour vision to track or detect. To establish that this property is surface spectral reflectance, Matthen (1988) appeals to the retinex theory and Hilbert (1992b) appeals to LMF.

Matthen's and Hilbert's accounts thus have three main components, one functionalist (perceptual states are functionally characterized), one evolutionary and adaptationist (the functions are adaptive), and one externalist (content is distal). The view that colour should be conceptualized as surface reflectance is thus supported by assuming that colour is whatever distal property it is the biological function of colour vision to detect; and it is the computational level of explanation that suggests this property is surface spectral reflectance.

Because this line of argument for computational objectivism relies explicitly on considerations about the biological function of colour vision, I shall postpone considering it in detail until the next chapter, which is devoted to comparative and evolutionary considerations about colour vision, and shall focus here only on the problems that arise for it in present context.

In his 1988 article Matthen supposed that retinex theory supplied a successful physical account of colour in the sense of red, green, yellow, and blue. Faced with the fact to the contrary,

Matthen has recently suggested that the computational objectivist should distinguish between two quality spaces for colour, one a phenomenal colour space which contains red, green, yellow, and blue, and the other a distal quality space containing spectral reflectances (Matthen 1992). He then allows that the phenomenal colour space might contain structure that completely fails to match anything in the structure of the distal quality space, yet nonetheless continues to maintain, on the basis of the idea that it is the biological function of colour vision to detect surface reflectance, that it is the distal quality space that determines perceptual content.

It is important to be clear about the issue before us. I make no objection to the distinction that Matthen draws between the two types of quality space; they in fact correspond to the phenomenal colour space and the reflectance colour space models I presented in Chapter 2. Moreover, in counting the reflectance space as a *colour* space, I am acknowledging that there is in visual science a perfectly legitimate, pragmatic sense in which being coloured as a property of surfaces can be treated as spectral reflectance. Rather, the issue before us is whether there is some further perceiver-independent, metaphysical sense in which colour is to be conceptualized as surface reflectance.

This issue is largely conceptual and strikes me as being of no foreseeable consequence to visual science. Be that as it may, what 'evidence' there is here in the way of philosophical intuitions about the application of colour concepts strikes me as not favouring the objectivist conceptualization. In its first and foremost sense 'colour' applies to what is seen in colour vision, namely, objects having particular determinate qualities that belong to the hue categories red, green, yellow, blue. Now if, despite there being no perceiver-independent, physical account of colour in this sense, it is nonetheless held that the content of colour perception is distal in the way that Matthen and Hilbert suppose, then it follows that red, green, yellow, and blue do not provide the perceptual content of colour vision. This consequence is simply unacceptable.

The conclusion to be drawn, then, is that colour should not be conceptualized as surface spectral reflectance in the absence of colour perceivers. The concept of colour applies to surface spectral reflectance only because there are perceivers for whom reflectances fall into metameric equivalence classes corresponding to red, green, yellow, and blue (Hardin 1992b; Hatfield 1992). This fact, combined with the fact that there is no perceiver-independent, physical specification of red, green, yellow, and blue, implies that objectivism about colour must be rejected.

NEUROPHYSIOLOGICAL SUBJECTIVISM

Does the failure of objectivism indicate that subjectivism is the proper ontology of colour? Many philosophers have believed that objectivism and subjectivism exhaust the possibilities for the ontology of colour. Their assumption has been that colours must be either 'out there' or 'in the head', and so they have supposed that subjectivism follows as a matter of course from the denial of objectivism.

It is easy to show, however, that establishing subjectivism takes positive arguments in addition to those that disprove objectivism and consequently that subjectivism does not follow simply from denying objectivism. Consider the reasons why objectivism cannot be maintained. First, there is no context-independent and noninterest-relative method of assigning colours to objects. Visual science contains numerous, precise specifications of viewing conditions, but they are all interest-relative, suited to the pragmatic demands of various colour-matching tasks, but not to the philosophical demand for a principled determination of the 'real' colours of things (Hardin 1983, 1988, 1990b). Second, there is no perceiver-independent, physical specification of red, green, yellow, and blue, and given this fact the consequences of identifying colour with surface spectral reflectance are unacceptable.

Are these two reasons, taken either individually or in conjunction, sufficient to establish subjectivism? It is hard to see how they could be. That there is no all-purpose, context-independent method of specifying the colours of things does not entail that colours are located 'in the head' as subjectivism claims. Colours are certainly not perceived as being located in the subject, and so additional arguments are required to establish the subjectivist claim. Nor does the lack of a perceiver-independent, physical specification of red, green, yellow, and blue entail that these are subjective visual qualities (sensations, sense-data, qualia, etc.). Another possibility that still remains open is that colours are *relational* properties and so are not intrinsic to any item, whether 'out there' or 'in the head'. Hence additional arguments are again needed to establish the subjectivist claim.

The most recent and extensive arguments for subjectivism are due to C. L. Hardin (1988). In his view, 'We are to be eliminativists with respect to color as a property of objects, but reductivists with respect to color experiences' (1988: 112). To be an eliminativist about object colour is to claim that there is no such property as being coloured, but only chromatic visual states, in other words that colours do not exist 'out there' but only 'in the head'. To be a reductivist about colour experience is to claim that chromatic visual states are to be reductively identified with neural states.[9] Thus Hardin's position corresponds to the view I am calling neurophysiological subjectivism.

Hardin believes that the failure of objectivism *does* imply subjectivism: 'a physicalist who is not prepared to reject our colour attributes *tout court* must embrace subjectivism, warts and all. Since objectivism is false, it's the only game in town' (Hardin 1984b: 500). Hardin does not offer any explicit argument for this assertion, but it is not hard to see what the implicit argument is. Hardin shows quite persuasively that there is no context-independent and noninterest-relative method of assigning colours to objects, but then infers on that basis that colours are not properties of objects and so must be 'in the head'. The supposition, then, is that eliminativism about object colour follows from the context-dependence and interest-relativity of colour ascriptions.

The conclusion does not follow, however. What follows from the fact that colours can be assigned to objects only relative to the conditions of viewing and to some pragmatic concern (for example, colour-matching tasks) is simply that colour specification is context-dependent and interest-relative. And this, combined with the fact that there is no perceiver-independent account of red, green, yellow, and blue, would seem to suggest that colours, rather than being intrinsic properties of either objects or perceivers, are relational properties, where one term of the relation is the object and the other term is the perceiver in a specific viewing condition. To establish the eliminativist subjectivist view against the relational view would require further arguments to show, first, that context-dependence and interest-relativity imply subjectivity, which is not obvious at all, and second, that the levels of generalization in which colours figure as properties of objects can be replaced by other levels that capture the same or comparable generalizations, and thus are cognitively satisfying, but in which colours do not figure as properties of objects at all.

Hardin does have another, more programmatic set of arguments for subjectivism. Building on the fact that there is no perceiver-independent, physical account of colour, as demonstrated by the argument from external irreducibility, Hardin argues that the phenomenal structure of colour can be explained by identifying experiences of objects as coloured with neural states and by using the structural relations among these states to model the phenomenal structure of colour. His main strategy can be presented as what I shall call the 'argument from internal reducibility':

The argument from internal reducibility

1 For something to be a (chromatic) colour it must be a hue.
2 For something to be a hue it must be either unique or binary.
3 Therefore, if hues are to be reductively identified with physical properties, these physical properties must admit of corresponding unique and binary divisions.
4 External, perceiver-independent physical properties, such as lightwaves and spectral reflectances, do not admit of such divisions.
5 Internal, psychophysical and neurophysiological states and processes (for example, the psychophysical and physiological chromatic channels) do admit of such divisions.

---

6 Therefore, object colour can be eliminated in favour of the reductive identification of perceptions of objects as coloured with psychophysical and neurophysiological states and processes.

It is this argument, combined with considerations about the

context-dependence and interest-relativity of colour ascription, upon which Hardin bases his neurophysiological version of eliminativist subjectivism. As he puts it:

> we may resolve the problem of the ontological status of color in the following way: Since physical objects are not colored, and we have no good reason to believe that there are nonphysical bearers of color phenomena, and colored objects would have to be physical or nonphysical, we have no good reason to believe that there are colored objects. Colored objects are illusions, but not unfounded illusions. We are normally in chromatic visual states, and these are neural states.
>
> (Hardin 1988: 111)

When Hardin says that physical objects are not coloured he means that 'they are neither reddish nor yellowish nor blueish nor greenish' (1988: 201, n. 35). Colour as a property of the world – being coloured – thus disappears in favour of chromatic visual states, which are held to be reducible to neural states.

Before evaluating Hardin's position, it is worth pausing to observe that neurophysiological subjectivism and computational objectivism have something in common: both positions lead to what in Chapter 1 I called the disappearance of colour. Eliminativist subjectivism holds that red, green, yellow, and blue are not genuine object properties, but rather entirely subjective visual qualities, which, in Hardin's neurophysiological version of the position, are to be reductively identified with neural states. Eliminativist subjectivism thus either convicts colour perception of global error (Boghossian and Velleman 1989; Landesman 1989) or holds that what is presented in colour perception is a 'natural illusion' (Hardin 1988: 81). In contrast, computational objectivism holds that colour perception provides only a limited perspective on 'real', objective colour, and so does not convict colour perception of global error. But in holding that 'real' colour is to be conceptualized as the distal quality space of surface spectral reflectance, whereas red, green, yellow, and blue constitute merely the subjective quality space of colour vision, computational objectivism inadvertently accepts the subjectivist assessment of phenomenal colour.

Let us return now to the argument from internal reducibility. The main empirical work in the argument is clearly accomplished by premises 4 and 5. Premise 4 has already been discussed in the context of the argument from external irreducibility. Readers who wish to review the kind of evidence used by Hardin to support premise 5 should consult the section on physiology and psychophysics in Chapter 2. The material covered there shows that there is still considerable controversy about the psychophysics and neurophysiology of colour vision; consequently, premise 5 has to be taken as programmatic. Hardin scrupulously admits this point:

> The tactic that suggests itself is to show how phenomena of the visual field are represented in the visual cortex and then to show how descriptions of the visual field may be replaced by descriptions of neural processes ... we have no good reasons for thinking that such a replacement of the one description by the other would leave anything out, with a consequent loss of information. On the contrary, we have reason to expect that a proper neural description would be richer, more complete, and, in principle, more penetrable by the intellect. Problems that are intractable at the extradermal physical level or at the phenomenal level promise to yield to analysis in neurological terms. Of course, at the present rudimentary state of our knowledge of the visual system, most of this is promise, program, and principle.
>
> (Hardin 1988: 111)

There are at least three different questions that can be raised about Hardin's neurophysiological subjectivism. The first is methodological and concerns Hardin's advocacy of the neurophysiological level of description for colour perception. How much can the explanatory levels and descriptive vocabularies of neuroscience accomplish in the explanation of colour perception? The next two questions are more philosophical. The second also concerns neuroscientific levels of explanation, but now in relation to the mind–body issue in philosophy rather than methodological issues in visual science. Is it possible to give a neuroscientific account of colour perception along the reductive lines that Hardin proposes that answers philosophical questions about visual experience? The final question concerns the argument from internal reducibility proper. Is this a sound argument? In particular, do premises 1–5 entail the conclusion that we are to be eliminativists about being coloured as a property of objects? It is the third question that will occupy us now; the others will occupy us in later chapters.

Let us accept premise 5 of the argument from internal reducibility, taking it as a promissory note that will be redeemed as psychophysics and neuroscience progress. We are consequently committed to holding, first, that there is no perceiver-independent account of red, green, yellow, and blue (the argument from external irreducibility), and second, that the distinctive features of these hues – their opponent and unique/binary structure – can be explained in terms of the psychophysics and neurophysiology of colour vision (premise 5). Does it follow that object colours do not exist and that there are only chromatic visual states?

Contrary to Hardin, I think that it does not follow and consequently that the argument from internal reducibility is invalid. It is quite possible to assert premises 1–5 and to deny 6, the conclusion. Once again it can be held that being coloured is a relational property where one term in the relation is the object and the other term is the perceiver in a specific viewing condition. This view would acknowledge both that there is no perceiver-independent account of red, green, yellow, and blue, and that the structure of the visual system is responsible for the opponent and unique/binary structure of hue. The conclusion drawn, however, would not be that there is no such property as being coloured, but rather that there is no *intrinsic*, that is, nonrelational, property of being coloured, only a relational one.

These considerations indicate that there is a missing premise that would make the argument from internal reducibility valid. The premise is that colours are intrinsic properties of either the world or the perceiver. The remarks by Hardin quoted above suggest that he has actually incorporated this premise into the claim that colours have to be physical, for by 'physical' Hardin seems to mean either an intrinsic physical property of the extradermal world or an intrinsic physiological property of the perceiver. Whether colours are physical or nonphysical, however, is clearly a distinct issue that should not be conflated with the issue of whether they are intrinsic or relational properties, for something can be both physical and relational.

Amending the argument from internal reducibility by adding the premise that colours are intrinsic properties of either the world or the perceiver would still not establish Hardin's position. The reason is that the premise clearly begs the question against the relational view. From the perspective of the relational view, the assumption that colours must be either 'out there' as perceiver-independent distal properties or 'in the head' as the subjective qualia of visual states is precisely the mistake to be avoided. To borrow a term from Whitehead, the assumption provides an example of 'the fallacy of simple location' in the case of perceptual qualities.

Hardin interestingly advertises his position as something of a middle way: 'it is the biological perspective which is the *via media* between the way that would place colors in the extra-dermal physical world and the way that would have it that colors are properties of sense-data' (1988: 58). But Hardin's middle way actually turns out to be eliminativist subjectivism, which is hardly a middle way in comparison with a relational ontology that would not succumb to the Scylla of placing colours 'out there' apart from perceivers or the Charybdis of placing them 'inside the head' of perceivers.

BEYOND OBJECTIVISM AND SUBJECTIVISM

In Chapter 2 it was shown how the positions of computational objectivism and neurophysiological subjectivism arise within visual science as a result of favouring either the computational or the psychophysical and physiological levels of explanation for vision. This chapter has focused on the philosophical articulation of these two positions and has shown that neither provides a satisfactory approach to the ontology of colour.

Computational objectivism and neurophysiological subjectivism are positions that privilege for the purposes of ontology one or the other of the physical and perceptual poles essential to colour vision. It is this leaning to one or the other extreme that makes both positions unacceptable. Consider that colours are visual qualities that (1) are seen to be exemplified in a relatively stable fashion by things in the world and (2) have certain distinctive properties such as hue opponency. By concentrating on the connection between (surface) colour perception and surface spectral reflectance, computational objectivism rightly attends to (1), but does so only at the expense of (2), for it refuses to acknowledge that spectral reflectances correspond to colours only because there are perceivers for whom reflectances fall into metameric equivalence classes. In contrast, neurophysiological subjectivism, by concentrating on the phenomenal structure of colour, rightly attends to (2), but does so only at the expense of (1), for it holds that object colour is an illusion.

At this point it is worth reconsidering the point made at the beginning of this chapter about the necessity for both physical and perceptual descriptive vocabularies in visual science. Given the unsatisfactoriness of the objectivist and subjectivist ontologies, one might think to acknowledge right from the start the 'inherent Janus-facedness of the concept of color ... as *the* essential ingredient of research on color perception' (Mausfeld et al. 1992: 47). One could then take this feature as the inspiration for working out a more adequate relational ontology of colour.

Such a relational view has so far been merely announced as a possibility. Considerably more work needs to be done to present the view on its own terms and to show how it differs from the received view. Whereas Hardin appeals to the 'biological perspective' to support his 'via media', I shall appeal in the next two chapters to the ecological perspective that can be discerned from comparative and evolutionary studies of colour vision, and I shall use this perspective to develop a relational ontology that provides a more genuine middle way.

4

THE COMPARATIVE ARGUMENT

He who understands baboon would do more for metaphysics
than Locke.

(Charles Darwin (Barrett 1974: 281))

INTRODUCING COMPARATIVE COLOUR VISION

'Colour' in the first and foremost sense means red, green,
yellow, blue, black, and white, and to study colour in this sense
visual scientists must rely on the reports of human subjects.
Therefore, the assumption that human colour vision provides
the reference point for understanding colour, both in philosophy and in visual science, is justified. Care must be taken in
applying the assumption, however, because certain distinctive
features of colour (for example, hue opponency) appear to be
traceable to our psychophysical and biological makeup, and
from the psychobiological perspective many of the discriminative behaviours and physiological structures involved in
human colour vision are not unique. Moreover, from the
perspective of evolutionary biology, human colour vision –
indeed primate colour vision in general – is not the norm.
These psychobiological and evolutionary dimensions indicate
that, although it may be impossible not to take colours as we
see them as the standard, a fuller understanding of colour can
be had only by situating human colour vision within a wider
comparative context.

Questions immediately arise, however, when the attempt is
made to enlarge our perspective to a comparative one. We

141

know what colour vision is from our own perceptual experience – it is the ability to see colours, or to use the terminology employed here, the ability to see particular determinate qualities belonging to the hue and achromatic categories. Yet how is this conception of colour vision to be applied to other animals? A number of philosophical issues arise with this question. Some will be addressed in the course of this chapter; others will be postponed until Chapter 6. All are best set to one side, however, until we have examined the visual capacities related to colour that are distinguished by visual scientists.

First, there is *wavelength discrimination*, which provides the standard operational definition of colour vision in visual science. Colour vision, specifically hue discrimination, requires being able to discriminate stimuli on the basis of their wavelength composition independent of relative intensity. The presence of colour vision in an animal is accordingly demonstrated by showing that the animal can treat wavelength and intensity as independent variables, and so can discriminate stimuli on the basis of chromatic differences regardless of their relative brightnesses or when matched for equal brightness. ('Equal brightness' here means as perceived to be equal by the animal; consequently the brightness response of the animal must first be determined. See Jacobs (1981).) Wavelength discrimination has been shown to exist in insects, fishes, birds, and mammals (for reviews see Jacobs 1981; Nuboer 1986; Menzel and Backhaus 1991; Thompson et al. 1992; Varela et al. 1993).

Operant conditioning is the technique typically used to train animals in wavelength-discrimination experiments. The animal is presented with various light stimuli and is rewarded for, say, pushing a bar or pecking at a spot, when it sees the 'correct' stimulus. Because the stimuli have been equalized for brightness (according to the animal), to identify the stimulus the animal must be capable of detecting in it some generalizable quality associated with wavelength. For these experiments to work the animal must be capable of learning. This fact does not demonstrate that learning is a prerequisite for colour vision, however; without additional considerations all that can be concluded is that learning is needed to probe the animal's visual capacities (Goldsmith 1990: 302).

Second, there is what is known as *wavelength-dependent*

behaviour (also called 'wavelength-selective' or 'wavelength-specific behaviour'), which is often considered to be an evolutionary precursor to colour vision as wavelength discrimination. Many animals, primarily among the invertebrates, are sensitive to lights of different wavelengths, but their photoreceptor responses trigger highly specific behavioural routines, such as escape, feeding, egg-laying, etc. (Menzel 1979). Wavelength-dependent behaviour is not usually taken to imply colour vision, for several reasons. First, the behavioural routines often depend considerably on the light intensity within the relevant spectral range; and second, it is unlikely that postreceptoral neurons compare the receptor signals before these affect the initiation of motor responses (Menzel and Backhaus 1991). Finally, there is no learning involved in the behaviours in the sense that the relation between wavelength and motor response cannot be altered by training; hence there is no evidence for colour vision of the sort found in the wavelength-discrimination experiments, which rely on the operant conditioning paradigm (Goldsmith 1990: 302).

Wavelength-dependent behaviour and wavelength discrimination are sometimes found in the same animal, and so they need to be distinguished not only according to the particular animal species, but also according to the particular behaviour (Menzel 1979; Menzel and Backhaus 1991). For example, the forager honeybee has trichromatic colour vision, but seems to employ it only in feeding and in recognition at the hive; in other visually guided activities, such as celestial orientation and navigation, it relies on a rich repertoire of wavelength-dependent behaviours (Menzel 1985).

Although there is a relatively principled distinction between wavelength-dependent behaviour and wavelength discrimination, there is as yet no comparable way of distinguishing between discriminating wavelengths and seeing colours (Hardin 1988: 148). It is certainly possible to imagine visual creatures being able to discriminate wavelengths without being able to see colours. Moreover, two examples of wavelength discrimination without colour vision can be given, which, because they are drawn from human vision, do not involve speculations about nonhuman creatures (the following two examples are taken from Stoerig and Cowey (1992a)).

The first example is wavelength discrimination in the

phenomenon known as blindsight. Subjects who have suffered damage to the striate cortex are often both partially blind and in a certain sense sighted. They are experientially blind within particular regions of their visual fields, yet within the very same regions they display residual visual abilities, such as being able to locate by pointing to stimuli presented there, and being able to detect and discriminate movement (Weiskrantz 1986; Cowey and Stoerig 1991). It should be emphasized that these abilities are not spontaneously displayed, but are revealed only when the subject is forced to guess in a so-called 'forced-choice' behavioural experiment. Using the forced-choice method in conditions meant to favour the chromatically opponent channels, Stoerig and Cowey have shown not only that blindsight subjects may have normal (though reduced) spectral sensitivity in their blind visual fields (Stoerig and Cowey 1989), but also that they may be able to discriminate targets of different colours whose luminances have been matched on the basis of the subjects' spectral sensitivity curves (Cowey and Stoerig 1991; Stoerig and Cowey 1992a, 1992b). In their words: 'As the blindsight patients do not experience any visual sensation when their blind field is stimulated, these results demonstrate discrimination of wavelength independent of their relative intensities that does not entail the experience of colour, or indeed of seeing' (Stoerig and Cowey 1992a: 53).

The second example is the phenomenon known as acquired cortical colour blindness or cerebral achromatopsia (see Davidoff 1991: Chapter 3 for discussion). This condition results from cortical damage and in its most extreme form leaves the subject able to perceive only various shades of grey (see Sacks and Wasserman 1987 for a popular description of such an extreme case). Even in such extreme cases, however, wavelength discrimination can be preserved; for example, subjects may still be able to detect the borders between adjacent colour patches regardless of their luminances and despite the fact that the patches look the same shade of grey (Stoerig and Cowey 1992a).

These two examples clearly demonstrate that wavelength discrimination does not necessarily imply colour vision in the usual sense. Nevertheless, the operational definition of colour vision as wavelength discrimination need not be abandoned for two reasons. First, wavelength discrimination remains the minimal behavioural requirement for colour vision; and second, it is not unreasonable to conjecture on biological and evolutionary grounds that creatures exhibiting wavelength discrimination will also exhibit other chromatic phenomena, such as colour contrast and colour constancy. For example, the honeybee, which as just mentioned exhibits both wavelength-dependent behaviours and wavelength discrimination, exhibits as well both simultaneous and successive colour contrast (Neumeyer 1980, 1981) and colour constancy (Neumeyer 1981; Werner et al. 1988).

These considerations suggest that one build on the operational definition of colour vision as wavelength discrimination by holding that colour vision involves at the very least three important and visually intertwined phenomena, all of which depend upon wavelength discrimination: (1) additive colour mixture, i.e., chromatic and achromatic matches for spectral stimuli; (2) simultaneous and successive colour contrast; and (3) colour constancy.[1] This proposal is meant to specify the minimal behavioural requirements for applying the term 'colour vision' to other species; it is not meant to solve philosophical problems about the perceptual experience of colour. Once again, the distinctively philosophical issues are being postponed until the comparative evidence has been reviewed.

COMPARATIVE COLOUR SPACES

The most general approach in comparative colour vision involves determining the type or *dimensionality* of the colour vision of a given animal (Jacobs 1981: 21). Human colour vision, as we have seen, is trichromatic. The human eye contains three different kinds of cone visual pigments, which are responsible for the fact that three appropriately chosen primary lights are necessary and sufficient to match all the colours that we see throughout the spectrum. Trichromacy is not unique to humans: indeed, it seems that virtually every animal class has some species with trichromatic vision (Jacobs 1981: 153). Trichromacy is not the norm, however. Many animals are dichromats – squirrels, rabbits, tree shrews, some fishes, possibly cats and dogs, male and some female New World monkeys; others appear to be tetrachromats – goldfish, the Japanese dace, turtles, pigeons, ducks, with pigeons and ducks being perhaps

even pentachromats; and it is even possible that some proportion of the female human population is tetrachromatic (see
below).

Before examining some of these differences, it is useful to
consider how colour vision also varies considerably in its
amount or *sensitivity*. In general the spectral range available for
vision is approximately 300 nm–800 nm. The 'visible window'
(extent of spectral sensitivity) differs, however, according to
the animal. For example, the visible range available to most
primates is approximately 400 nm–700 nm; in the honeybee it
shifts down to 300 nm–650 nm (Menzel 1979; Menzel and
Backhaus 1991); and in diurnal birds it broadens to approximately 350 nm–720 nm (Bowmaker 1980b). The broadest
spectral range appears to be found in cyprinid and salmonid
fishes; their spectral sensitivity extends from below 350 nm up
to around 800 nm (Bowmaker 1991: 117).

Within a given visible range, colour vision sensitivity is
specified more precisely in terms of the spectral sensitivity,
wavelength discrimination, and colorimetric purity functions.
These functions specify respectively the sensitivity to brightness, hue, and saturation throughout the spectrum. Hence by
measuring the functions for various animals, one can compare
their overall sensitivities to spectral stimuli, their abilities to
discriminate on the basis of wavelength, and whether spectral
stimuli appear relatively saturated or desaturated.

Each of the three functions will differ for colour vision of
different dimensionalities. Take, for example, the wavelength-
discrimination function, which is determined by measuring
the just-noticeable differences in wavelength necessary for
wavelength discrimination throughout the spectrum. This
function is generally understood by appealing to the spectrally
different types of photoreceptors at the first stage of the colour-
vision system.[2] As discussed in Chapter 2, a single-receptor
system cannot discriminate on the basis of wavelength, for
such discrimination requires a comparison of the relative
responses from at least two spectrally different types of
receptor. Hence, on the one hand, if, in a given spectral range,
different wavelengths excite only one receptor type, they will
always generate the same receptor response ratio, and so will
not be discriminable. On the other hand, wavelength discrimination will be best in the ranges where the spectral sensitivity

functions of the receptors are steep and cross each other. Thus in such ranges a minimum in the wavelength-discrimination curve can be expected. For example, a dichromatic system has two spectrally different receptor types, leading one to expect one minimum in the wavelength-discrimination curve; a trichromatic system has three spectrally different receptor types, leading one to expect two minima; and a tetrachromatic system has four spectrally different receptor types, leading one to expect three minima, etc. Thus the goldfish, a tetrachromat, has three minima in its wavelength-discrimination curve around 610 nm, 500 nm, and 400 nm (Neumeyer 1985, 1986; Crawford et al. 1990). The pigeon, a tetrachromat but perhaps even a pentachromat, has four minima around 390 nm, 450 nm, 540 nm, and 600 nm (Wright 1979; Delius and Emmerton 1979; Emmerton and Delius 1980; Palacios et al. 1990a). Unfortunately the relationship between the wavelength-discrimination minima and colour vision dimensionality is not really so straightforward, because there can be more than one range of greatest steepness in the spectral sensitivity functions of the receptors. For example, although the wavelength-discrimination curve for normal human trichromats does have two prominent minima around 580 nm and 470 nm, many measurements show another minimum around 460 nm (Wright and Pitt 1934). For this reason, the inference in the reverse direction from the number of minima in the wavelength-discrimination curve to the dimensionality of the colour vision system, though suggestive, is not strictly speaking valid. Rather, behavioural experiments such as additive colour mixture must be performed to determine definitively colour vision dimensionality, as they were for the goldfish (Neumeyer 1985, 1992b), and are currently being done for the pigeon (Palacios et al. 1990b; Palacios and Varela 1992).

The spectral sensitivity, wavelength-discrimination, and colorimetric purity functions can also differ among animals that have colour vision of the same dimensionality, among 'normal' and 'anomalous' individuals, and even among 'normal' individuals. To cite examples of each kind of variation: (1) Humans and honeybees are both trichromats, but the visible window of the honeybee is shifted towards the ultraviolet (300 nm–650 nm), with the regions of best hue discrimination at 400 nm and 490 nm (von Helverson 1972; Menzel 1979).

(2) For normal human trichromats, spectral sensitivity peaks at about 555 nm; the spectral sensitivity of deuteranomalous trichromats, however, is shifted towards longer wavelengths, whereas that of protanomalous trichromats is shifted towards shorter wavelengths (see Hurvich 1981). Finally, each of the three functions can differ slightly among 'normal' individuals. For example, men and women appear to differ in their colour mixtures (more on this later) (Neitz and Jacobs 1986; Mollon 1992; Jordan and Mollon 1993).

Now that the idea of variations in the dimensionality and sensitivity of colour vision has been introduced, the comparative phenomena can be considered in more detail. Of particular interest is the relationship between the comparative phenomena and the colour space models presented in Chapter 2. I turn now to explore this issue, focusing on the specific example of colour vision in birds.

A bird's-eye view

Earlier I remarked that from the perspective of evolutionary biology primate colour vision is not the norm. As J. K. Bowmaker noted in a short review some years ago: 'The true culmination of the evolution of colour vision in vertebrates is probably to be found in the highly evolved diurnal animals, perhaps best represented by diurnal birds, and it is within these species that we should look for colour vision significantly more complex than our own and utilizing more of the available spectrum' (Bowmaker 1980b: 196).

The evidence that is now being accumulated indicates that diurnal birds such as the pigeon and the duck are at least tetrachromats, perhaps even pentachromats (Chen et al. 1984; Jane and Bowmaker 1988; Burkhardt 1989; Goldsmith 1990; Palacios et al. 1990a, 1990b; Palacios 1991; Palacios and Varela 1992; Thompson et al. 1992). The evidence is derived from a variety of experiments with species ranging over various families within each order. The evidence also pertains to several levels of analysis and organization, from the photoreceptor and retinal levels to the neurophysiological and psychophysical or behavioural levels.

To begin at the retinal level, the cones in the avian retina, unlike those in mammals and insects, contain oil droplets located in their ellipsoid inner segments; the droplets are thus placed between the visual pigment and the light that strikes the retina. (Oil droplets are also found in the retinas of some fishes, amphibians, and reptiles.) Seen under a light microscope the droplets range in colour from transparent, to clear, yellow, orange, and red. The colours are due to concentrations of carotenoids; the concentrations are often so high that the droplets act as cut-off filters that transmit only the longer wavelengths (Bowmaker 1980b, 1991). In retinas containing oil droplets it is therefore the oil droplet–visual pigment combination that has functional significance, rather than the visual pigment alone.

In the retinas of birds such as the pigeon and the duck, five different types of cone–oil droplet combinations have been described (Bowmaker 1977; Jane and Bowmaker 1988); passerine birds have at least four such combinations (Chen and Goldsmith 1986). In the pigeon retina, for example, there are up to four types of coloured oil droplets in combination with three types of cone visual pigment for the long-wave region alone (Bowmaker 1977). Moreover, this information about retinal organization is regional, because in birds such as the pigeon there are two foveal regions. The evidence indicates that sensitivity and discrimination differ in the two regions (Nuboer and Wortel 1987; Remy and Emmerton 1989; Hahmann and Güntürkün 1993), and that the two visual fields mediate different behaviours (Block and Martinoya 1983; Maldonado et al. 1988). These regional differences increase even more the complexity of pigeon colour vision, for the colour that is seen will depend on the visual field being attended.

As mentioned above, the visible spectral range available to diurnal birds includes that available to humans, but also extends considerably further into the short-wave region. It is now generally agreed that many birds have colour vision in the near-ultraviolet region. For example, Wright (1972) found that the removal of an ultraviolet component changes the colour of certain stimuli for the pigeon; and Goldsmith (1980) found that hummingbirds can distinguish near-ultraviolet light (370 nm) from darkness, and from white light lacking wavelengths below 400 nm. Humans cannot perform either of these tasks. Recently, additive colour mixtures in the near-ultraviolet have also been demonstrated in pigeons (Palacios and Varela 1992).[3]

Turning now to psychophysics, the wavelength-discrimination curve for the pigeon shows four distinct minima, suggesting that pigeon colour vision might be pentachromatic (Emmerton and Delius 1980; Palacios et al. 1990a). As noted earlier, additive colour-mixture experiments provide the most straightforward evidence about the dimensionality of colour vision. Such experiments for the pigeon provide direct evidence for tetrachromacy (Palacios and Varela 1988, 1992; Palacios et al. 1990b). A definitive proof of pentachromacy would require five-way additive colour-mixture experiments, which have yet to be performed.

There is unfortunately little evidence at present about the neural basis for avian chromatic channels in general (see Maturana and Varela 1982; Varela et al. 1983; Palacios et al. 1991). It is nevertheless possible to form an educated guess about the possible shape of the pigeon's chromatic channels by using the formal procedure introduced by Buchsbaum and Gottschalk (1983), which was discussed in Chapter 2 in the section on psychophysical issues about the postreceptoral channels. The basic idea is to obtain the weighted combination of mutual excitation and inhibition that maximally *decorrelates* the receptor responses (see Thompson et al. 1992 for a technical presentation). In their original calculations, Buchsbaum and Gottschalk used psychophysically derived data about the human receptor responses. In contrast, the animal data are incomplete; the best available are raw microspectrophotometric data and physiological data. The channels predicted by applying Buchsbaum and Gottschalk's formal methods to the animal data can be validated, however, by their capacity to predict the known behavioural evidence on sensitivity, wavelength discrimination, and colour mixture in the animal. Applying the procedure to the honeybee, the goldfish, and the pigeon does predict adequately the known behavioural data for these animals (Palacios 1991; Thompson et al. 1992). For the pigeon at least four but most probably five postreceptoral channels are needed to account for the available data – one achromatic channel and either three or four chromatically opponent channels (Palacios 1991; Thompson et al. 1992).

The increased dimensionality of pigeon colour vision relative to ours should not be taken to mean that pigeons have greater sensitivity to the spectral hues that we see. For example, it should not be supposed that, because the pigeon's wavelength discrimination is best around 600 nm and we see a 600-nm light as orange, pigeons are better at discriminating spectral orange than we are. Indeed, there is reason to believe that such a mapping of our hue terms on to the pigeon would be mistaken. In an experiment designed to determine whether and how pigeons group spectral stimuli into hue categories, Wright and Cummings (1971) found that pigeons treat wavelengths to either side of 540 nm as falling into different hue categories, whereas humans do not. As Jacobs notes in his discussion of this experiment: 'Among other things, this result strongly emphasizes how misleading it may be to use human hue designations to describe color vision in non-human species' (Jacobs 1981: 118).

This point can be made even more forcefully, however, when it is a difference in the *dimensionality* of colour vision that is being considered. Such an increase clearly implies a corresponding increase in the number of independent variables in the colour space model. Consider the human receptoral and postreceptoral colour spaces. The former trichromatic space has as its three axes the three types of receptor response; the latter trivariant space has as its axes the three postreceptoral channels (one achromatic and two chromatic). In comparison, a tetrachromatic or tetravariant colour space needs four independent axes, corresponding respectively to the four types of receptor response or to the four postreceptoral channels, whereas a pentachromatic or pentavariant colour space needs five. Since the number of dimensions for these spaces is greater than three, tetrachromatic and pentachromatic colour spaces provide examples of what can be called *colour hyperspaces*.

The difference between, say, a tetrachromatic and a trichromatic colour space is therefore not like the difference between two trichromatic spaces. Considered as dimensional types, tetrachromatic and trichromatic colour spaces are *incommensurable* in a precise sense because there is no way to map the *kinds* of distinctions available in four dimensions into the kinds of distinctions available in three dimensions without remainder. This point can clearly be generalized: any two colour spaces of dimensionalities n and $n+1$ respectively will be incommensurable in the precise sense just indicated.

If pigeon colour vision is indeed at least tetrachromatic,

perhaps pentachromatic, then the colour space models for the pigeon and for the human will be incommensurable in the above sense. How, then, *is* pigeon colour vision to be understood in relation to ours? Furthermore, given the evidence that other animals, such as the goldfish (Neumeyer 1988, 1992b) and the turtle *Pseudemys scripta* (Arnold and Neumeyer 1987), are tetrachromats, what more generally do colour hyperspace models imply for our understanding of colour as red, green, yellow, blue, black, and white?

Colour hyperspaces and novel colours

Most people when they hear of the evidence for tetrachromatic or pentachromatic colour vision respond by asking what extra colours such vision affords. This question is a fascinating one, and its many facets will occupy us here and later in Chapter 6.

I mentioned above when discussing pigeon colour vision that it cannot be assumed that tetrachromats and pentachromats would simply see more shades of our colours, that is, simply see more particular determinate colours belonging to our colour categories. Although such an ability would certainly be an increase in the *sensitivity* of colour vision, it is not so clear that it would amount to an increase in the *dimensionality* of colour vision. Consider that to model the metameric equivalence classes of a tetrachromat requires four degrees of freedom, whereas only three are needed for a trichromat. To have four degrees of freedom at one's discriminatory disposal, however, is not reducible to being able to discriminate more finely with only three degrees of freedom. To put the point more succinctly and less precisely: seeing in four dimensions is not a better way of seeing in three dimensions; it is simply different. Hence if the issue is what tetrachromacy and pentachromacy imply for understanding colour, then the question to be asked is what the possession of additional degrees of freedom for making chromatic distinctions might mean in perceptual terms.

The colour space models presented in Chapter 2 provide the best way to approach this question.[4] Consider the receptoral-level colour space, which for humans is defined by the three L, M, and S cones and is spanned by all possible cone response triplets. At this level there is a traditional representation of the

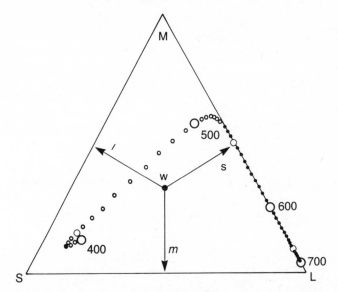

Figure 5a Comparative colour spaces at the receptoral level (a)
For any light, the relative long/medium/short wavelength
absorptions (L, M, S) can be plotted as relative activity on a Maxwell
triangle with orthogonal axes *l, m, s* of unit length. The loci of pure
spectral colours are shown calculated by normalizing the pigment
spectra for equal areas and computing the quantum catch. Equal
absorption for all three areas is labelled as *w*.
Source: Goldsmith (1990: 311)

trichromacy of human colour vision known as the Maxwell
colour triangle (Figure 5a). Intensity (brightness) is held constant and so the triangle is presented in two dimensions. Each
vertex represents one of the L, M, and S human cone visual
pigments, with points in the space corresponding to relative
pigment absorptions. Thus any spectral test-light can be represented in the space in terms of how it affects differentially the
three cones (see figure for details).

Similar visual pigment colour spaces can be constructed for
other animals (Menzel 1979; Neumeyer 1988; Burkhardt 1989;
Goldsmith 1990). In Figure 5b, the pigment colour space for the
tetrachromatic goldfish is presented (Neumeyer 1988, 1992b). In
relation to the human pigment space, this colour space requires
an additional dimension to accommodate the four visual
pigments present in the goldfish retina. In this representation,

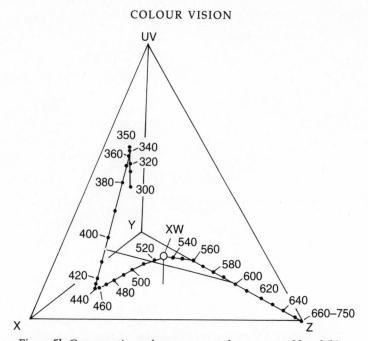

Figure 5b Comparative colour spaces at the receptoral level (b) Colour tetrahedron of the goldfish based on photoreceptor sensitivity functions. In contrast to 5a, the representation requires an extra dimension. It can be seen as a three-sided pyramid with a ground plane 'xyz' and an apex 'uv'. The line inside the tetrahedron from 300 nm–750 nm represents the loci of the spectral colours. The point XW is the locus of xenon-white light. The loci of all spectral colours between 660 nm and 800 nm are located at the 'z' corner, indicating that light of these wavelengths stimulates only the long-wavelength type of cone receptor. Between 660 nm and 560 nm the loci of spectral colours are along the line 'yz', indicating that light of these wavelengths stimulates the long- and middle-wavelength receptor types. Between 450 nm and 660 nm the loci of the spectral colours lie inside the plane 'xyz', indicating stimulation of three receptor types. Finally, between 440 nm and 300 nm the loci of spectral colours move towards the 'uv' corner and are located in a plane inside the tetrahedron roughly parallel to the 'x–y–uv' plane.
Source: Neumeyer (1992b: 646)

the additional coordinate is provided by adding a third dimension, thus giving a colour space in the form of a tetrahedron (see figure for details). A similar idea was advanced independently by Burkhardt (1989) to model tetrachromacy in birds. Figure 5c presents Goldsmith's (1990) rendering of the same idea for an 'imaginary' tetrachromatic turtle whose photoreceptors have

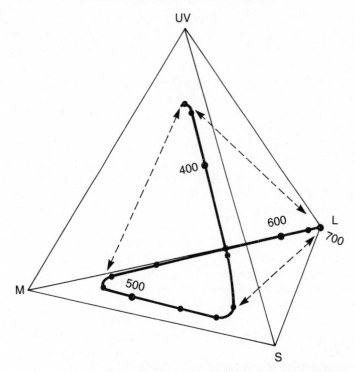

Figure 5c Comparative colour spaces at the receptoral level (c)
Pigment tetrahedron for an 'imaginary' turtle with no oil droplets in
its cones, having visual pigment maxima at 370 nm, 450 nm, 520 nm,
and 620 nm. The spectral locus is shown with wavelength intervals
marked at 20-nm intervals. This format suggests that an animal with
tetrachromatic colour vision is likely to see three nonspectral colour
classes rather than the single nonspectral class of purples that is
characteristic of human trichromatic vision. The nonspectral colour
classes would fall along the dashed lines. All colours for this animal lie
within the smaller tetrahedron defined by the spectral locus and the
double-headed arrows.
Source: Goldsmith (1990: 313)

no oil droplets. The dashed lines in the space correspond to
novel nonspectral colours that, like the purples of human
colour vision, do not occur in the daylight spectrum. As both
Burkhardt and Goldsmith observe, whereas there is a single
nonspectral colour class (purple) for normal human trichromats, tetrachromats are likely to have *three* nonspectral colour
classes. In Burkhardt's words: 'While in man's chromaticity

diagram there is only one intermediate colour which does not occur in the daylight spectrum, namely purple, in tetrachromatic vision there would be three intermediate colors which are not present in the daylight spectrum, namely, mixtures of red and blue (purple), of green and UV [ultraviolet], and of red and UV' (Burkhardt 1989: 794–5).

This difference in the nonspectral colour classes available to trichromats and tetrachromats supports the claim made above that two colour spaces of dimensionalities n and $n+1$ will be incommensurable in the sense that there is no way to map the kinds of distinctions available in the higher-dimensional space into the kinds of distinctions available in the lower-dimensional space without remainder. The three nonspectral colour classes available to a tetrachromat clearly cannot be mapped into the single nonspectral colour class available to a trichromat without remainder.

Consider in comparison two different trichromatic colour spaces, such as the human's and the bee's. The main difference between human colour vision and bee colour vision is that our visible window comprises 400 nm–700 nm, whereas in bees it shifts down by 100 nm to the shorter wavelengths, comprising 300 nm–650 nm (Menzel 1979: 561). This difference means, however, that the spectral metameric equivalance classes for the human and for the bee are different. For example, the nonspectral colour class for the bee, known as 'bee purple', is produced by mixing (within certain intensity ranges) a light at 588 nm, which we can see, with a light at 360 nm, which we cannot see (Menzel 1979: 561). Thus the complementary colours of wavelengths to which we are also sensitive are for the bee all found outside of the human visible window in the near-ultraviolet (Menzel 1979: 561–2). The consequences of this fact are well put by Hardin: 'Human hues cannot, then, have the same opponents as the bee "hues" to which they are matched by these [additive colour-mixture] type-identity conditions' (Hardin 1988: 152).

These differences, significant though they are, are not ones in dimensionality, and so human colour space and bee colour space are not incommensurable in the restricted sense that I am giving to this term. This can be seen from the fact that the human and bee colour spaces can be compared in a way that two colour spaces of dimensionalities n and $n+1$ cannot. For example, although the nonspectral colour classes in the human and bee colour spaces are different, the *number* of the classes is the same; in comparison, the number of nonspectral colour classes increases to three in a tetrachromatic colour space. The tetrachromatic colour space thus contains a *greater number of colour classes* in relation to colour spaces of lower-order dimensionality. This is one sense in which there are more *kinds* of chromatic distinctions available to a tetrachromat than to a trichromat.

One might still object that the term 'incommensurable' is too strong in this context because the higher-dimensional colour space is 'projectible' into the lower-dimensional space, and so the increase in dimensionality means simply that the higher-dimensional space contains more chromatic content. This interpretation begs the fundamental question of *how* the higher space is to be projected into the lower. Because the spaces are not isomorphic there is no unique projection relation. Moreover, in any given instance to pass from one space to another requires specifying the appropriate axes (pigment absorptions, chromatic channels, etc.), which differ according to the animal (this point holds too for animals having colour vision of the same dimensionality, for example, the human and the bee).

The foregoing comparative discussion of colour space has been confined to the receptoral level, and so two important qualifications are in order. First, we have been applying hue terms at this level by referring to nonspectral stimulus mixtures as nonspectral colours, and by describing these in turn as mixtures of red and blue (purple), green and ultraviolet, and red and ultraviolet. This use of hue terms must be taken as only a useful shorthand for more precise wavelength specifications of light mixtures or visual pigment responses. (It is in this sense that, for example, the L, M, and S human cone visual pigments are also known as the red (R), green (G), and blue (B) receptors, whereas the M, S, and UV visual pigments of the bee are also called the green (G), blue (B), and ultraviolet (UV) receptors.) Strictly speaking, hue terms are not really appropriate at this level, for seeing colours involves much more than simply receptoral-level activity as probed by spectral stimulus mixtures.

Second, the Maxwell triangle-type colour spaces do not provide a quantitative representation of the metrics of colour space as determined psychophysically (Goldsmith 1990: 311). Rather, they are meant primarily to describe colour matches for spectral stimuli and so are best thought of as receptoral-level stimulus spaces. For understanding the perceptual characteristics of colour vision, however, it is the psychophysical metrics (for example, just-noticeable differences in hue) that are more relevant.[5]

To close the gap between the receptoral levels and the perceptual levels would require more psychophysical and physiological knowledge of the postreceptoral processes involved in tetrachromatic colour vision than is currently available. But by considering in tandem the phenomenal and psychophysical levels of human colour space, and by asking how additional dimensions at these levels would transform the space, we can imagine what a tetrachromatic colour hyperspace might be like perceptually and then take what we imagine as a prediction to be tested experimentally. Recall, then, that because our visual system is trivariant at the postreceptoral level, having two chromatically opponent channels and one achromatic channel, we have four basic hue components, red, green, yellow, and blue, that combine to form binary hues such as orange, purple, turquoise, etc. A tetravariant visual system, however, would possess three chromatically opponent channels. One can speculate, then, that these three channels (call them r–g, y–b, and p–q) would provide a tetrachromat with *six* basic hue components (r, g, y, b, p, and q), plus not only their binary combinations (r + y, y + p, etc.), but *ternary* combinations as well (for example, r + y + p, g + y + p, etc.). Thus a tetrachromat's phenomenal colour hyperspace (colour hypersolid) might contain not only colours composed of two novel basic hue components, which would combine to form novel binaries, but also an entirely *new kind of hue* not found in our phenomenal colour space, namely, ternary hues (Hardin 1988: 146; Thompson et al. 1992; Thompson 1992). These ternary hues would correspond to the additional kind of chromatic distinction available to a tetrachromat, but not to a trichromat.

The possibility of novel ternary colours can also be illustrated using the Maxwell triangle-type colour spaces just presented. As Neumeyer writes:

The statement that tetrachromatic color vision systems possess 'ternary' colors cannot be overemphasized. It means that there are colors that are perceived as 'red–green–blue' at the same time! This is impossible for us to imagine. For the goldfish or the turtle *Pseudemys* (Arnold and Neumeyer 1987) we must expect four classes of such colors that are located in the four planes of the tetrahedron: 'red–green–blue', 'red–UV–green', 'green–UV–blue', and 'blue–UV–red'.

(Neumeyer 1992a: 49)

Again it must be emphasized that hue terms in this context have to be taken with a grain of salt. They do not indicate psychophysical quantities that are directly relevant to perceived colour, such as the chromatic response of the postreceptoral channels; rather, they indicate peaks in the spectral sensitivities of the visual pigments. Consequently, it is not necessarily the case that a ternary mixture of 'red–green–blue'pigment responses would be perceived as having a quality that violates the phenomenal opponency of red and green in human colour perception. Adding this clarification, however, makes one wonder just how the four classes of ternary stimulus mixtures indicated by Neumeyer would be recoded in the postreceptoral colour space of a tetrachromat and whether such recoding would subserve the perception of ternary hues in the sense imagined on the basis of the opponent process theory.

One final qualification is in order before closing this section. I have been discussing the dimensionality of an animal's colour space in terms of the number of degrees of freedom needed to map all of the animal's chromatic discriminations throughout the spectrum. It does not follow, however, that the dimensionality of an animal's colour space in this sense is the same as the dimensionality of its discrimination at any one time or in any local spectral region.[6] For example, in the 546 nm–690 nm longwave region normal human trichromats make dichromatic matches because their S receptor response is virtually zero (Jordan and Mollon 1993: 1497). Similarly, it is possible that local retinal regions in the pigeon are no more than trichromatic, so that tetrachromacy requires that the visual scene be scanned over more than one retinal region (Palacios and Varela 1992;

Goldsmith in press). (In fact, the situation with the pigeon is quite complex, for as mentioned earlier the pigeon has two visual fields that have different sensitivities and mediate different behaviours.)

The considerations in the previous two paragraphs point towards issues about tetrachromatic colour vision that need to be investigated experimentally. Do the novel nonspectral and ternary classes in the tetrachromatic pigment space amount to novel colour classes at the psychophysical levels? Would the novel colours include ternary hues in the sense of the opponent process theory? Finally, supposing the existence of such novel colours is demonstrated psychophysically, what kinds of behavioural significance would they have for the specific animal in its natural habitat?

Whereas the first two questions skirt the limits of current psychophysical knowledge, the last question touches on the evolutionary and ecological dimensions of colour vision. I turn now to these dimensions, which are among the most important for understanding colour vision, both in visual science and in philosophy.

THE EVOLUTION AND ECOLOGY OF COLOUR VISION

A comprehensive theory of the evolution of colour vision would require far more data than are currently available. Some general conclusions can be drawn, however, from data about the various levels of operation in colour vision and from considerations about the ecological roles played by colour vision in animal life.

Molecular biology of the visual pigments and psychophysics

In the past decade, a wealth of new data about the visual pigments has been provided by molecular biologists. The structure of the visual pigment molecules consists of a large protein called *opsin* that is bound to a derivative of vitamin A called *retinal*. Small variations in the amino acid sequence of the protein produce visual pigments with different peak sensitivities. The nucleotide base sequences and the inferred amino acid sequences of the opsin components have now been determined for a number of visual pigments (Applebury and Hargrave 1986; Nathans et al. 1986a, 1986b; Nathans 1987). The studies show that the amino acid sequences of all visual pigments are quite similar and that the visual pigment genes of even distantly related organisms have identical DNA segments. The conclusion that has been drawn is that the visual pigments all derive from an ancient ancestor (Applebury and Hargrave 1986; but see Goldsmith 1990: 288).

Although the origins of the three human cone visual pigments are ancient, trichromacy is not the norm, as shown from the discussion above. Many vertebrate animals have more complex retinas possessing not only four or even five visual pigments, but also oil droplet inclusions. Among mammals, oil droplets are absent, retinas with three cone visual pigments are found only in primates, and the primitive condition, still exemplified by most modern mammals, appears to be dichromatic (Jacobs 1981; Goldsmith 1990). The conclusion that is generally drawn is that mammalian colour vision is evolutionarily 'degenerate' (Bowmaker 1980a; Goldsmith 1980, 1990). During much of their evolutionary history, which occurred prior to the extinction of the dinosaurs, mammals were most probably small and had nocturnal habits. As a result, their capacity for photopic vision declined considerably. As Goldsmith writes:

> birds and turtles appear to have a rich capacity for color vision, and in this respect they illustrate what might have been the future of other evolutionary lines. Such was not to be for the mammals, for the adoption of nocturnal habits in the premammalian or early mammalian stock probably reduced the number of cone pigments to two, one absorbing in the blue in the neighborhood of 430 nm and the second absorbing at longer wavelengths, near 540 to 560 nm.
>
> (Goldsmith 1990: 306)

In this context, humans and Old World primates are something of an exception, for they seem to have secondarily evolved trichomatic vision with the adoption of diurnal habits (Bowmaker 1980a). There are two recent sources of data that provide insight into the evolution of primate colour vision (Goldsmith 1990: 306): one is the genetic studies of the cone visual pigments mentioned above; the other is studies of the genetic basis of colour vision polymorphism in humans and other primates.

Studies of the molecular genetics of the cone visual pigments have shown that in humans the genes for the L and M pigments are placed close together on the X chromosome and have DNA sequences that are 96 per cent identical, but only about 40 per cent identical with the DNA sequences of the S pigment and the rod pigment (Nathans et al. 1986a). It is thought that the two loci on the X chromosome represent a duplication of a single locus present in an ancestral primate from which both the Old and New World primates evolved (Bowmaker 1991: 124). Hence the L and M pigments have diverged from each other relatively recently, namely, within the last 65 million years during the adaptive radiation of the mammals (Goldsmith 1990: 292). Primate trichromacy, then, is a recent achievement – certainly within the context of vertebrate colour vision but also among the mammals – that resulted from adding the 'red–green' system formed by the L and M pigments on to the older 'blue–yellow' system formed by the S pigment and the ancestral middle-wave pigment (Mollon 1989). Gouras (1991a) provides a nice summary of the basic idea:

> In mammals the pairing of blue *vs* yellow appears to have been the first stage of colour vision (Ladd-Franklin 1929). In this way, the entire white spectrum was divided into a short-wave (blue) and a long-wave (yellow) region. In more diurnal primates with well developed foveas, the yellow part of the spectrum was again subdivided into a longer-wave side (red) and a shorter-wave side (green) by the introduction of pigments straddling the yellow region of the spectrum. In organisms with trivariant colour vision, two separate pairs of single opponent neurons are found, blue–yellow and red–green opponent channels. In organisms with tetravariant colour vision there must be three such colour opponent pairs.
>
> (Gouras 1991a: 176)

The story becomes even more complex and fascinating when the behavioural and genetic data about colour vision polymorphism are considered. Take first the inherited colour-vision deficiencies in humans, or what is more commonly known as colour-blindness (see Hurvich 1981). Excepting monochromats, true colour-blind individuals are dichromats who are unable to distinguish colours along either the red–green or blue–yellow axis. There are two forms of red–green colour deficiency, *protanopia*, due to the absence of the L pigment, and *deuteranopia*, due to the absence of the M pigment. Blue–yellow deficiency, which is much less common, is known as *tritanopia* and is due to the absence of the S pigment. The other main type of colour-vision deficiency is known as *anomalous trichromacy*. Anomalous trichromats have a visual pigment whose spectral absorption is intermediate between the L and M pigments. The spectral sensitivity of *protanomalous* trichromats is shifted towards shorter wavelengths, whereas that of *deuteranomalous* trichromats is shifted towards longer wavelengths. Anomalous trichomats are also recognized behaviourally because they perform differently in 'Rayleigh-matching' experiments, where one must find the ratio of monochromatic red and green light that matches a monochromatic yellow.

In studies of the molecular genetics of the colour-vision deficiencies, Nathans et al. (1986b) have shown that both red–green dichromats and anomalous trichromats have hybrid pigment genes derived from the L and M pigment genes. The X chromosome normally contains a gene for the L pigment and several copies of the M pigment gene. The hybrid genes are formed as a result of unequal crossover events (Nathans et al. 1986b; see also Goldsmith 1990: 307 for a useful table based on Nathans et al.). If the L pigment gene is absent or rendered nonfunctional, then a male having this genotype will lack the L visual pigment, being a protanope. If the M pigment is absent or rendered nonfunctional, a male having this genotype will lack the M visual pigment, being a deuteranope. If the hybrid gene contains coding segments from both the L and M pigment genes, then the male will be an anomalous trichromat.

It is useful to compare the colour-vision deficiencies in humans and their genetic basis with the colour-vision polymorphism in New World primate species such as the squirrel monkey, the spider monkey, and the marmoset. In these species, the basic condition is dichromacy, yet about one-third of the individuals are trichromats. Moreover, there is significant variation in the character of the colour vision among both the dichromats and the trichromats. In the squirrel monkey population, for example, there appear to be six different forms of colour vision (Mollon et al. 1984; Jacobs 1985, 1986; Bowmaker et al. 1987). This species has one short-wave visual pigment and a polymorphic long-wave pigment that has three variants. All male squirrel monkeys are dichromats, possessing the short-wave pigment plus one of the three long-wave pigments. Females are either dichromats like the males or trichromats having any two of the three long-wave pigments plus the short-wave pigment. Thus within the species there are three different forms of dichromacy plus three different forms of trichromacy. Similar polymorphisms are found in other species, such as the marmoset (Tovée et al. 1992).

A genetic model has been proposed to account for the inheritance of these six forms of colour vision (Mollon et al. 1984; Jacobs and Neitz 1985, 1987). According to the model, there are two gene loci, one for the short-wave pigment and one for the polymorphic long-wave pigment. The locus for the long-wave pigment is on the X chromosome, and there are at least three alleles possible at this locus. Hence male monkeys, who have only a single X chromosome, will inherit only one locus and so can express only one of the three pigments, the result being three different dichromatic male phenotypes. Females who are homozygous at this locus will also express only one of the three long-wave pigments and so will be dichromats like the males. Females who are heterozygous, however, will inherit two different loci and so will be trichromats.

This type of colour-vision polymorphism has been suggested as a possible evolutionary 'stage through which Old World primates passed on their way to routine trichromacy'(Jacobs 1990: 290). It has already been discussed how early mammalian colour vision was most likely dichromatic. In primates, adding a visual pigment allele on the X chromosome would result in variations among the spectral sensitivities of the individuals, with possible advantages and disadvantages. It would also result in heterozygous females who would become capable of trichromatic vision if their nervous systems could take advantage of the additional pigment response. If trichromacy proved to be advantageous for these primates, its frequency would presumably increase. To establish trichromacy as a more permanent feature, however, the locus would have to be duplicated to establish a second pigment gene on the X chromosome. As we have seen, this appears to have happened in the evolution of the Old World primates.

The genetic models and data about colour-vision polymorphism in New World primates have been invoked to make sense of some intriguing data about colour mixture in humans (see Goldsmith 1990: 307–8). People with normal trichomatic vision can differ in their Rayleigh matches (mixtures of monochromatic red and green matched to a monochromatic yellow). In a population of normal trichomatic males, Neitz and Jacobs (1986) found a bimodal distribution of Rayleigh matches and suggested that it resulted from the presence in the population of two L pigments having different spectral sensitivities and produced from two alleles of the L pigment gene. Females, on the other hand, were found to have a trimodal distribution of Rayleigh matches, as would be predicted from the nearly equal frequencies of the two L pigments in the normal population. Roughly half the females display matches intermediate between the two groups of males and hence are presumably heterozygous, having both L pigments, though in different cones.

As mentioned briefly in Chapter 2, Nathans et al. (1986a, 1986b), in their studies of the molecular genetics of the human visual pigments, noted that the L pigment gene is polymorphic. They found that one of the polymorphic sites corresponds to number 180 in the amino acid sequence of the opsin. In a more recent study, the absorption spectra of the visual pigments have been determined using tissue culture to express the opsin genes; this study also demonstrates that there are two alternative L pigments, differing at site 180 (Merbs and Nathans 1992). The two gene products have different spectral absorptions: the pigment with alanine at site 180 has a peak sensitivity at 552.4 nm; the pigment with serine at site 180 has a peak sensitivity at 556.7 nm. Furthermore, in another study published in the same issue of *Nature* as Merbs and Nathans's article, Winderickx et al. (1992) show that the same single amino acid polymorphism at site 180 explains the bimodal distribution of Rayleigh matches found by Neitz and Jacobs (1986). Winderickx et al. also find that in a population of 50 normal trichromatic males, 62 per cent have the code for serine at site

180 and 38 per cent the code for alanine. Subjects in the former group exhibit a greater sensitivity to red light, as would be expected from the spectral absorption curves measured by Merbs and Nathans.

These discoveries have numerous implications for visual science, two of which must be mentioned here. The first is methodological. As J. D. Mollon writes in a short review of these studies:

> The significance of these discoveries for psychologists cannot be exaggerated. Here is a case where a difference of a single nucleotide places people in distinct phenomenal worlds and where we know almost all the steps in the causal chain from gene to molecule to neural signals; only the final steps from cortical activity to sensation elude us. It is the first such case in psychology. It cannot be the last.
>
> (Mollon 1992: 378)

Given the comparative lack of knowledge of the cortical levels of operation in colour vision (see Chapter 2), plus the debates about consciousness currently underway in neuroscience (Edelman 1989; Crick and Koch 1990; Kulli and Koch 1991; Engel et al. 1992) and in the philosophy of cognitive science generally (Dennett 1991; Varela et al. 1991; Humphrey 1984, 1992; Flanagan 1992), one might find Mollon's assertion that 'only the final steps from cortical activity to sensation elude us' to be something of an ironic understatement. But Mollon's main point about the importance of the molecular studies for psychology stands nonetheless. Indeed, the point can be driven home by considering the second implication of the molecular studies that I wish to mention. It is actually less an implication and more a suggestive possibility raised by the molecular and psychophysical findings. Mollon outlines the possibility in the final paragraph of his review:

> given the Ser/Ala [serine/alanine] polymorphism in the male population, there ought to be women who are heterozygous for this substitution and carry different alleles on their two X chromosomes. Because of random X-chromosome inactivation, only one of the two long-wave pigments will be expressed in any individual cone.

In female platyrrhine monkeys, the two corresponding types of cone are able to sustain a colour-opponent signal [Tovée et al. 1992]. Does this mean that a heterozygous woman can be tetrachromatic, experiencing an extra dimension of hue that must forever be forbidden to her male conspecifics?

(Mollon 1992: 379)

The possibility of tetrachromacy in some proportion of the female human population is among the most fascinating known to me in visual science. At present the evidence in our possession does not seem definitive one way or the other. In the most recent study at the time of writing, Jordan and Mollon (1993) performed a series of psychophysical experiments on women known to be carriers for anomalous trichromacy.[7] In what they call 'large-field Rayleigh matches' eight out of fourteen carriers of anomalous trichromacy were unable to find a red–green mixture to match a monochromatic yellow, all reporting 'a residual difference in hue between the two fields' (Jordan and Mollon 1993: 1501). This finding provides preliminary evidence for tetrachromacy in these subjects. On the other hand, Jordan and Mollon also performed what they call a 'ratio-matching' task to determine whether carriers of anomalous trichromacy make unique trichromatic matches in a spectral region (546 nm–690 nm) where normal human trichromats make dichromatic matches. The subjects were asked to find colour matches between two mixture fields, one a mixture of green and orange light (546 nm + 600 nm), the other a mixture of yellow and red light (570 nm + 690 nm). The hypothesis was that carriers of anomalous trichromacy who are strong tetrachromats, having an additional pigment in the middle- to long-wave region, might become trichromats in this region where colour-normal humans are dichromats. They found, however, that the matching ranges of the individual carriers were comparable to those of normal trichromats. Therefore, in the ratio-matching task, there is no evidence for tetrachromacy in carriers of anomalous trichromacy.

Where, then, do these findings leave the hypothesis of tetrachromacy in female humans who are carriers for anomalous trichromacy? Here I can do no better than to quote from the conclusion to Jordan and Mollon's article:

Our hypothesis that carriers of anomalous trichromacy may be tetrachromactic has received only limited support and it does not seem possible simply to translate the New World monkey model to our own species. Although several carriers of anomaly – and no other subject – rejected large-field Rayleigh matches, most carriers of anomaly do not find a unique match in our ratio-matching task and in this respect offer no evidence that they enjoy an extra dimension of discrimination in the particular long-wave spectral region that we have tested.

We did, however, find one woman ... who generated only a very restricted range of match-points in the ratio-matching task and who was the mother of a simple deuteranomalous son. This woman remains in play as a candidate tetrachromat in the strong sense. What are now required are full colour-matching functions for women of this phenotype. It also remains possible that a discrimination task, as opposed to a matching task, would reveal a higher proportion of tetrachromats.

(Jordan and Mollon 1993: 1505)

Visual ecology

We have thus far been considering what studies of the molecular genetics of the visual pigments together with psychophysical studies indicate about the evolution of colour vision. A related question concerns the absorption spectra of the visual pigments – what ultimate evolutionary factors are involved in the pigments absorbing where they do (Goldsmith 1990: 294)?

In addressing this question, ecological considerations become especially relevant, though the details are of course controversial (Lythgoe 1979; Goldsmith 1990; Bowmaker 1991; Kondrashev 1992). The best case to begin with is the ecological link between visual pigment absorption and animal niche in fish colour vision, which has been studied extensively (Lythgoe 1972, 1979; Levine and MacNichol 1979, 1982).

Aquatic settings provide a continuous range of luminous environments where the absorption and scattering of light by the water and ambient particles make the medium itself coloured, ranging from the nearly complete darkness of the deep sea where little light penetrates, to the clear blue water of the tropical oceans, blue-green coastal waters, the dark green water of freshwater lakes and rivers, and the red-brown water of marshes and swamps. Because these media provide coloured backgrounds against which fish have to detect objects, attempts have been made to correlate the distribution of visual pigments and types of colour vision in fishes with the photic characteristics of aquatic environments.

The current hypothesis is that the visual pigments of many fishes have evolved so that their spectral absorptions serve to highlight object contours against the background ambient light (Levine and MacNichol 1979, 1982). Some fishes spot their prey from below, and so must detect dark objects against a brighter background; other fishes spot their prey from above, and so must detect bright objects against a dimmer background. If the peak in the visual pigment spectral absorption curve correlates with the wavelengths of maximum transmission of the water, then a dark object will stand out against a brighter background. On the other hand, if the peak in the spectral absorption is offset from the wavelengths of maximum transmission, then a bright object will stand out against a dimmer background.

For example, deep-sea fishes tend to be monochromats – their retinas normally contain only rods with one (rhodopsin) visual pigment having an absorption maximum around 480 nm (Levine and MacNichol 1979; Loew and Lythgoe 1978; Partridge et al. 1989), which correlates with the wavelength of maximum transmission at this depth (Lythgoe 1972, 1979). According to one interpretation, this absorption maximum would permit maximum contrast sensitivity for movement (Muntz 1975; Crescitelli et al. 1985).

Many deep-sea fishes also possess bioluminescent (light-emitting) organs whose maximum emission is in the blue (short-wave) range, correlating both with the maximum sensitivity of the rod visual pigment and the maximum transmission of the water (Bowmaker 1991: 112). Some genera have not only blue bioluminescent organs, but also ones that emit in the red (long-wave) spectral range, with a maximum emission at about 700 nm (Bowmaker 1991: 112). These emissions will be invisible to the deep-sea monochromatic fishes that have only the one rod visual pigment with maximum sensitivity at 480 nm. The red-emitting bioluminescent fishes, however, do not possess this pigment, but have rather two pigments with maximum sensitivity around 515–20 nm and 545–50 nm (Bowmaker et al. 1988). These two pigments enable the species to be sensitive not only to their own red bioluminescence, but also to their own and other species' blue bioluminescence. Moreover, because these animals possess two types of visual pigment, they have the potential for dichromacy and hence may be able to detect the red and blue light emittances not only by differences in brightness but also by differences in hue (Bowmaker 1991: 113).

As one moves upwards towards more illuminated depths, all species show a greater variety of visual pigments and retinal cell arrangements (Lythgoe 1972, 1979; Levine and MacNichol 1979, 1982). In blue-green coastal waters, many fish are dichromats, having two cone visual pigments. In clear tropical marine environments the water is more blue than green, and the pigment absorption maxima of many species are shifted to shorter wavelengths. In tropical freshwater environments, fishes that live near the surface have three visual pigments that span a broad spectral range from the near-ultraviolet to the red. Other tropical freshwater species live in mid-water but feed on the surface; their visual pigments are shifted to longer wavelengths, but many species, such as the roach, the Japanese dace, the goldfish, and the brown trout, have in addition to the S, M, and L cone visual pigments a UV pigment maximally sensitive in the near-ultraviolet around 350 nm–380 nm (Avery et al. 1983; Harosi and Hashimoto 1983; Neumeyer 1985; Bowmaker and Kunz 1987). These fishes, as we have seen in the case of the goldfish, are tetrachromats.

The link between visual pigments and visual ecology is further complicated by pigment polymorphisms. In some fishes, the ratio of the opsin components can vary depending on a host of factors that are still not fully understood. For example, the ratio of rhodopsin to porphyropsin in the receptors of the rudd varies with seasonal changes (Whitmore and Bowmaker 1989). The receptors in this fish are dominated by porphyropsins during most of the year, but during the summer are replaced by rhodopsins, which has the effect of shifting the animal's sensitivity to shorter wavelengths. In the long-wave visual pigment, the shift is from about 620 nm down to 570 nm, which must change considerably the colours seen by the animal (Bowmaker 1991: 117). The ecological significance of these changes is not known. They may reflect seasonal varia- tions in the light environment, changes in feeding strategies and diet, and/or changes in hormone levels during spawning (Bowmaker 1991: 117). Such polymorphisms are also exhibited by fishes, such as the Pacific salmon, that migrate from freshwater to marine environments, which differ considerably in their photic characteristics. Here the relative amounts of rhodopsin and porphyropsin can change not only according to the season but also according to the time of day (Beatty 1969, 1984; Bridges 1972; Muntz and McFarland 1977; Muntz and Mouat 1984; Whitmore and Bowmaker 1989).

In contrast to mammals, which lived nocturnally through much of their early evolution, the highly diurnal birds possess a variety of oil droplet–visual pigment combinations, includ- ing a pigment sensitive in the near-ultraviolet. The complex avian retina presumably enables birds to take advantage of the solar spectrum in a way that is not available to mammals (Goldsmith 1990: 309). Indeed, the lack of oil droplets in mammalian retinas may be another indication of the evolu- tionary degeneracy of mammalian colour vision. As Goldsmith notes: 'In species of birds that live in ecological conditions where the retina is starved for light, the proportion of cone oil droplets that are pale or colorless increases ... consequently, total loss of oil droplets is a reasonable end point to expect if selection for photopic vision were relaxed for a sufficient time' (Goldsmith 1990: 305).

Among birds, the retinal oil droplets can vary considerably, even for species having similar global living conditions (Bud- nik et al. 1984; Martin and Lett 1985; Martin 1986; Jane and Bowmaker 1988). For example, the common tern, a predator bird, has a significant amount of red and yellow droplets in the dorsal retina, whereas the barn swallow, which catches insects, has a large quantity of translucent droplets (Goldsmith et al. 1984). In fact, Partridge (1989) has shown by means of cluster analysis that the ecological niche (herbivore, fishing, etc.) is more significant in predicting the kinds and distribution of oil droplets than strict phylogenic kinship.

The presence of ultraviolet visual pigments also provides another example of the importance of avian visual ecology. Some have argued that these pigments can be linked to bird–fruit coevolution (Snow 1971; Burkhardt 1982). Fruit plants with ultraviolet reflectances can be detected by birds sensitive in the ultraviolet; the birds, eating the fruit, disseminate the kernels, thereby helping the plants to reproduce. Ultraviolet sensitivity can also be linked to ethological factors involving animal recognition, for bird plumages have been shown to have high frequency content, and so might require higher-dimensional colour vision with ultraviolet sensitivity for their recognition (Weedon 1963; Durrer 1986; Burkhardt 1989; Hudon and Brush 1989; Brush 1990).

Ultraviolet sensitivity might also be used in aerial navigation. Pigeons, we have seen, have excellent short-wave and near-ultraviolet discrimination. Nuboer (1986) observes that it is possible that 'the excellent spectral discrimination within this range ... represents an adaptation to the coloration of an unclouded sky. This property enables pigeons to evaluate short-wave gradients in the sky, ranging from white at the sun's locus to highly saturated (ultra) violet at angles of 90° to the axis between observer and sun.' Furthermore, since pigeon navigation is based on orientation with respect to the sun's azimuth, 'the perception of colour gradients in the sky may control navigation indirectly when the sun is hidden by clouds' (Nuboer 1986: 370–1).

Ultraviolet sensitivity is also found in bees, whose visible window is shifted relative to ours by about 100 nm towards the short-wave end of the spectrum (300 nm–650 nm). It has been argued that the bee's distinctive form of trichromacy coevolved with the colours of flowers, which often have contrasting patterns in ultraviolet light (Lythgoe 1979; Menzel 1979; Barth 1985; Nuboer 1986).[8] Nuboer provides a concise summary of the basic idea:

> These animals rapidly learn to associate nectar or pollen with colour patterns ... Forager honey bees are general pollinators. From the point of view of pollination strategy it is advantageous for a flower to attract pollinators by its food content. It therefore needs to be conspicuous and recognizable as a flower but at the same time it should be different from flowers of competing species so that the animal that successfully visited one flower of the species will tend to visit other flowers of the same species. From the point of

view of efficient food collection, however, it is advantageous for a forager bee to be able to make quick decisions at a distance with regard to the selected flowers ... This mutual advantage for the reproduction of bees and plants will have determined this co-evolution of plant features and of the sensory-neural capacities of the pollinator.

(Nuboer 1986: 362)

Similar types of explanation have been proposed for the evolution of primate trichromacy. Consider first the colour-vision polymorphism in the squirrel monkey, in which approximately three-quarters of the females are trichromats. Several explanations have been proposed for this polymorphism (Snodderly 1979; Mollon et al. 1984; Nuboer 1986). According to one, it has resulted from adaptation to the spatial heterogeneity of the environment: it is possible that phenotypes inhabit different regions of the jungle that differ in the spectral composition of their ambient light. A second proposal appeals to the hypothesis of group selection: it might be advantageous for the animal community to have members with several forms of colour vision. A third proposal appeals to frequency-dependent selection: there may be an ecological balance between the availability of certain fruits and the number of phenotypes that can detect them. Finally, another hypothesis holds that the local coloured fruits coevolved with the differences in colour vision.

The idea that primate trichromacy may have coevolved with coloured fruits dates back to the 1950s (Polyak 1957; as reported by Mollon 1989). Mollon (1989: 32–3) observes that recent studies lend support for the view. He notes that many species of catarrhine monkeys (macaques, patas monkeys, talapoins, and guenons), although varying considerably in their habitat, size, and body colouration, all have in common, on the one hand, a middle-wave pigment with peak sensitivity around 535 nm and a long-wave pigment with peak sensitivity around 565 nm, and on the other hand, a diet that consists largely of fruit. He also cites recent studies of fruit-eating monkeys in tropical rainforests that show that the fruits eaten are predominantly orange or yellow, whereas those eaten by birds are red or purple (Gautier-Hion et al. 1985). The monkeys disperse the plant seeds by filling their cheek-pouches with fruit; large seeds they spit out at some distance from the tree, and small seeds they swallow and then excrete intact. Thus the fruit colours appear to be biological signals targeted for the monkeys; and the monkeys need trichromatic vision to detect them among the green foliage.

The discussion thus far has concentrated on differences in the visual sensitivity and visual ecology of animals. The similarities are also important, however. As just noted, for example, different monkey species have visual pigments with similar peak sensitivities. More generally, visual pigments in widely divergent species can have identical spectral absorption curves (Jacobs 1990: 288). At the psychophysical level, despite the differences in colour-vision dimensionality, there are certain common features in the wavelength-discrimination function (Neumeyer 1991: 288): (1) the ranges of best discrimination are narrow as revealed by the pronounced minima in the wavelength-discrimination curves. (2) The spectral regions of best discrimination cluster around 400 nm, 500 nm, and 600 nm – the main exception to date being the pigeon, whose minima are at 390 nm, 450 nm, 540 nm, and 600 nm. As Neumeyer notes, 'The pigeon seems to be able to discriminate very well in the spectral range which appears to us "green", a range in which other animals are rather impaired' (ibid.). (3) The best performance is always in the range of a just noticeable difference value of 3–4 nm, with only humans able to do better. Finally, at a more global level, similar ecological conditions seem to be correlated with common visual structures in very different animals. Two examples are mentioned by Maier and Burkhardt (1992): the spectral properties of penguin cones more closely resemble those of certain fishes than those of other birds (Bowmaker and Martin 1985); and animals active at twilight tend to be dichromats, even among the highly evolved birds, as shown by the tawny owl (Martin and Gordon 1974).

As a final topic, it is useful to consider in more general terms the perceptual abilities that colour vision affords in relation to the environment. As I mentioned in Chapter 3, colour vision appears to be largely concerned with detecting objects against their backgrounds, rather than with invariant physical properties per se. Many current discussions assume that colour vision facilitates this task by being particularly concerned with differences in chromaticity (hue and saturation) when object and background are equiluminant. But such equiluminant situations hardly ever occur in the natural world (see the section on spatial segmentation in Chapter 2). As Mollon observes: 'it is rare in the natural world for one surface to lie in front of another in such a way that both have the same reflectance, both lie at the same angle to the incident illumination, and the nearer throws no shadow on the farther' (Mollon 1989: 23).

A broader and more satisfying perspective on the benefits afforded by colour vision, one which is particularly suited to the comparative framework, is provided by Mollon (1989). He argues that the biological advantages of colour vision, specifically of primate trichromacy, are revealed by the disabilities experienced by colour-blind (dichromatic) humans. In scenes where the ambient lighting varies randomly – for example, when the background comprises dappled foliage and/or different reflective surfaces lying at varying angles to the illuminant – there are three perceptual abilities that human dichromats find particularly difficult: (1) detecting certain coloured objects; (2) segmenting ('segregating', to use Mollon's term) the visual scene; and (3) identifying particular objects or states. Consequently, Mollon proposes that colour vision has evolved because it affords advantages in each of these tasks.

We have already considered an example where trichromatic colour vision serves object detection – the detection of orange/ yellow fruits against the forest background by trichromatic monkeys. Such fruits are presumably not conspicuous to other dichromatic animals. For example, the dichromatic squirrels seem to feed on fruits that have a dull, reddish-brown colour (Gautier-Hion et al. 1985; as reported by Mollon 1989: 33).

The importance of spatial segmentation was emphasized in Chapter 2. For objects to be recognized the visual scene must be segmented into the elements that belong together. There are many attributes that facilitate this task, such as colour, lightness, shape, texture, etc. Where the ambient light varies unpredictably, hue can be a particularly useful attribute for linking elements that belong together in a scene.

Turning now to object identification, colours can help to identify the state of an object by indicating conditions beneath its surface. For example, colour provides an indication of the state of ripeness in fruits; and variations in the colour of ground vegetation can indicate the presence of water (Mollon 1989: 25–6). Colours also serve to assign already segmented elements in the scene to categories that have perceptual significance (Jacobs 1981: 170–1; Mollon 1989: 25–6). A perceptual colour category can guide behaviour in various ways depending on the things that exemplify it and their significance for the animal. In the case of fruits, it can guide feeding; in the case of animal colouration, it can be used to identify conspecifics, their sex, and their sexual state, and so can guide various social interactions, such as mating. Colour as a category and as an indication of object state can thus be joined; certainly they seem to be so in humans, for as Mollon observes, 'human observers have a finely developed (though little studied) capacity to use skin colour to estimate the health, or emotional state, of conspecifics, and this ability may have biological advantage in the selection of sexual partners or in the care of infants' (Mollon 1989: 27).

The fact that dichromats find object detection, spatial segmentation, and object identification difficult in relation to trichromats makes one wonder what additional facility tetra- or pentachromatic vision might afford for these tasks. Birds are particularly interesting in this regard, for pigeons have been shown to group spectral stimuli into perceptual categories, presumably of hue (Wright and Cummings 1971); and the brightly coloured feathers of birds, which also reflect in the ultraviolet to which diurnal birds are particularly sensitive (Burkhardt 1989), must have perceptual significance for behaviour, especially behaviour involving sexual recognition. The perceptual significance of colour for birds might therefore have an affective dimension (Varela et al. 1983), for as a biological signal involved in social behaviour, colouration and colour vision are likely to be related to the overall hormonal and motivational state of the animal.

Some research has been done on the behavioural significance of perceptual colour categories for nonhuman animals (Hailman 1977; Burtt 1979), but clearly much remains to be done. Of particular importance are the affective aspects of colour just mentioned, for these might provide an index of the extent to which an animal has the capacity for the perceptual experience of colour, in addition to colour vision operationally defined as wavelength discrimination and the associated phenomena of colour contrast and constancy. For example, although it has been convincingly demonstrated that bee colour vision involves both simultaneous and successive colour contrast (Neumeyer 1980, 1981), as well as colour constancy (Neumeyer 1981; Werner et al. 1988), one may doubt that the colours detected by the bee have affective significance. In contrast, the emotional effects of the warm/cool colour polarity, which we know from our own experience and which painters put to good use, have been studied in monkeys. Rhesus monkeys, for example, become agitated when forced to spend long periods in a red environment and show a preference for blue-green when given the choice (Humphrey and Keeble 1978). Red and blue-green are also salient as sexual signals in the colouration of many primates (Mollon 1989: 26–7). These findings suggest that colour perception in primates has an experiential dimension comparable to our own, which is hardly surprising given our close evolutionary relationship. Do comparable affective dimensions exist among the highly visual nonprimate animals, such as fishes, turtles, and birds? In the avian case, I think the hypothesis that they do is not at all extravagant, given the evidence about bird colour vision reviewed above, but clearly experiments need to be designed to test the hypothesis.

THE COMPARATIVE ARGUMENT

The rest of this chapter will be devoted to motivating the ecological view to be presented in the next chapter. The basic thesis of the ecological view is that colours are properties that depend on both colour perceivers and their environments. Colours are not intrinsic to objects in the physical world (computational objectivism) or to neural processes in the visual system (neurophysiological subjectivism); rather, they are properties of the world taken in relation to the perceiver. Thus on the question of whether colours are intrinsic properties or relational properties, I side with the received view that they are relational. But unlike the received view, the relational position that I shall defend is distinctly *ecological* in the sense pioneered by the psychologist J. J. Gibson (1979). On one side, the world is considered as an animal environment, rather than a neutral material universe from which the living creatures have been removed; on the other side, the perceiver is treated as an active exploring animal, rather than a disembodied spectator who serves as little more than a repository for sensations or qualia. To prepare the way for this relational and ecological view the remainder of this chapter will focus on reconsidering computational objectivism and neurophysiological subjectivism in the light of the comparative framework presented above.

Computational objectivism revisited[9]

One of the most interesting features of the computational theory of visual perception is that it offers an answer to the traditional philosophical question about how perception is related to the world. According to the computational theory pioneered by David Marr (1982), Tomaso Poggio (Poggio et al. 1985), and their colleagues (Hurlbert and Poggio 1988), 'vision is the *process* of discovering from images what is present in the world, and where it is' (Marr 1982: 3). The images are patterns of light reflected on to the retinal array, and to discover what is present in the world, and where it is, the visual system relies on internal representations. The computational theory is thus both representationist and objectivist. In Marr's words: 'The purpose of these representations is to provide useful descriptions of aspects of the real world. The structure of the real world therefore plays an important role in determining both the nature of the representations that are used and the nature of the processes that derive and maintain them' (Marr 1982: 43).

The best way to formulate the main difference between the representationism of the computational approach and the older 'representative' theory of perception of Newton and Locke is in relation to the philosophical notion of perceptual content. Perceptual states exhibit *intentionality* – they are about something or have objects, and they present what they are about in a certain manner. In the representative theory, what is seen, the object of a visual state, is a sense-datum, or to use the Lockian terminology, an 'idea', and these are supposed to stand for or represent features of physical objects that are external to the perceiver. In this view, we do not see the world directly; we see the world only in virtue of seeing sense-data or ideas, which are intermediate between us and the world. In contrast, the computational theory holds that perception is indirect only in the sense that it requires operations on internal representations. The representations are not the objects of perception, however; rather, they are what enables the perceptual state to be directed towards its object – they *re*present the object, which is something in the physical world, to the perceiver in a certain manner. Thus one main difference between the representative and the computational theories is that the former holds perceptual content to be internal or proximal, whereas the latter holds it to be external or distal.[10]

Computational models of colour vision provide a paradigm of the new representationist approach to visual perception, and so it is not surprising that they have figured prominently in philosophical defences of the externalist approach to perceptual content (Matthen 1988). As discussed in Chapter 2, computational models focus on the phenomenon of colour constancy and try to show how 'indicators' of surface spectral reflectance can be extracted from the retinal image. Given only the intensity signal, the extraction problem is underconstrained or ill-posed; it admits of no unique solution. Additional constraints must therefore be added to the model to restrict the class of admissible solutions. The constraints typically involve restricting the types of lights and reflectances present in the model; often these restrictions are based on the empirical finding that naturally occurring lights and reflectances do not vary arbitrarily, but can be described in a linear model with a small number of parameters (see the discussion of LMF in Chapter 2). Such constraints in the model are taken to correspond to 'assumptions' or 'expectations' that the visual system has about the environment, the assumption being that, because of evolution by natural selection, expectations about certain pervasive regularities in the physical world have been internalized in a representational form (Snyder and Barlow 1988; Shepard 1987).

In the realm of natural vision (in contrast to engineering and robotics), the representationism and objectivism of the computational theory are based on the assumption that it is evolutionarily advantageous for organisms to represent the distal world. It is also assumed that in vision 'what is being computed is optimal in some sense or is guaranteed to function correctly' (Marr 1982: 19). Applied to colour vision, the assumption is that it is evolutionarily advantageous for organisms to detect surface spectral reflectances and that the internal representations involved are more or less optimal for the task.

In philosophy, a sophisticated externalist account of perceptual content that incorporates this evolutionary assumption and takes colour vision as a paradigm has been developed by Mohan Matthen (1988, 1989, 1992). Matthen distinguishes between two components that together make up the content of a perceptual state. One component he calls 'individual-directedness': a perceptual state has a unique object to which it is directed. The other component he calls the 'mode of presentation': a perceptual state presents its object as having certain characteristics – for example, being coloured red. In Matthen's view, an adequate theory of individual-directedness will be causal and indexical: every perceptual state is directed towards some individual causing that very state itself (see also Searle 1983: 37–78). But an adequate theory of the mode of presentation will not be causal, but rather functionalist. Matthen's specific proposal is that the modes of presentation in perception be type-identified in terms of the distal properties that perceptual states have the biological function to detect:

> A perceptual state is a state that has the function of *detecting* the presence of things of a certain type, where things of that type are sometimes present, sometimes absent, and

> A perceptual state with internal characteristic S is a presentation of property F if and only if its function is to detect the presence of a thing with property F.
>
> (1988: 20)

The key element in this view is that the content of a perceptual state is F not when it does in fact detect F, but when its biological function is to detect F. A perceptual state having this function may nonetheless fail on occasion to detect F. The failure might be due to a malfunction in the visual system or to exposure to conditions to which the visual system is not adapted (maladaptation). But it could also be due to what Matthen calls 'normal misperception', that is, to 'the use of [sensory] indicators that are imperfect, but nonetheless the best available' (1988: 13). In this case, the misperception does not result from malfunction or maladaptation, but rather from the fact that 'the indicator is not perfectly reliable even in the range of situations to which the visual system is adapted' (ibid.).

In the case of colour vision, Matthen enlists computational models of colour constancy, specifically Land's retinex theory, as support for the claim that the biological function of colour vision is to detect surface reflectance and hence that the content of chromatic perceptual states is distal. In addition, he employs the notion of normal misperception to explain certain psychophysical and phenomenological features of human colour vision. One well-known psychophysical phenomenon, discussed in Chapter 3, is surface colour metamerism. Two surfaces that have different spectral reflectances can nonetheless be perceived as having the same colour because the proportion of the incident light they reflect produces the same ratio of activity in the cone photoreceptors. Such surfaces are known as surface colour metamers, and they indicate that human colour perception is indeterminate with respect to surface reflectance. Matthen would hold that metameric matches of coloured surfaces are examples of normal misperception because we do not correctly perceive the difference in reflectance, yet the misperception is not due to malfunction or maladaptation, but rather to the less-than-perfect nature of the indicators involved in colour perception.[11] Turning now to phenomenology, it is a familiar feature of our colour experience that we see the clear daytime sky as blue, yet the sky is not a surface. Matthen suggests that this too is a misperception and appeals to the evolutionary assumption mentioned earlier:

> Maybe the evolutionary advantages of color vision pertain only to the discriminatory resources it affords with respect to surfaces. Perhaps perceiving the sky as blue is just an artifact of this mechanism and it neither increases nor decreases the fitness we get as a result. That would be the sort of case in which we should want to say that the sky is (normally) misperceived as blue.
>
> (1988: 25)

Matthen's theory of perceptual content thus depends on combining three major components. The first is *functionalist*: whether a creature possesses perceptual states of a given type

181

depends on the functional role played by the states, not on the anatomical structures and physiological mechanisms that subserve this function. The second component is *evolutionary* and *adaptationist*: perceptual states have the functions they do because of natural selection. The functions are adaptive biological functions, i.e., the mechanisms subserving them have been selected for because of their contributions to the fitness (reproductive success) of their possessors. The third and final component is *externalist*: the adaptive function of visual perception is to detect things in the world, and so perceptual content is distal – it is external to and independent of the perceiver.

The main problem that comparative colour vision poses for this type of externalist approach to chromatic perceptual content is that both across and within animal species there are fundamental differences in colour vision, and these differences do not appear to converge on the detection of any single type of environmental property. Colour vision varies in both dimensionality and sensitivity across the animal world; and the environmental properties detected in colour vision appear to include not only surface spectral reflectances, but also ambient lighting conditions and gradients in a source of illumination in both aerial and aquatic media. To review the main examples: for fish the hypothesis is that colour vision serves to heighten the contrast between foreground objects (surface colours) and the background aquatic space light (volume colours) (Levine and MacNichol 1979, 1982), and to detect spectral emittances in the case of bioluminescent organs (Bowmaker 1991). For birds the hypothesis is that colour vision serves not only in the detection of surface reflectance, but also in the detection of silhouettes against the background sky (Lythgoe 1979) as well as illumination gradients during aerial navigation (Nuboer 1986; Varela et al. 1993). For the honeybee the hypothesis is that colour vision serves to detect the surface reflectances of flowers (Menzel 1979), but some have claimed that it is also involved in orientation to light-polarization patterns in the sky (van der Glas 1980). For primates the hypothesis is that colour vision facilitates object detection and identification, as well as the segmentation of the visual scene (Mollon 1989); it has also been argued that colour vision facilitates the perception of illumination conditions in their own right (Jameson and Hurvich 1989).

These empirical hypotheses and the evidence that supports them suggest that there is no single type of distal property that it is the biological function of colour vision to detect. The strong likelihood of this possibility raises a problem for any externalist attempt to type-identify the perceptual content of colour vision. The distal properties detected in colour vision form a heterogeneous collection whose type-divisions at the physical level do not match the type-divisions at the perceptual level. The natural move for the externalist to make would be to treat the mismatch as due to normal misperception. But notice that this move is no longer very plausible here because the empirical findings also suggest that the evolutionary advantages colour vision affords do not pertain only to surface detection. For example, rather than being an artifact of a mechanism whose function is to detect surface reflectance, perceiving the sky as coloured might be due to colour vision's being concerned with illumination conditions in their own right, for these provide indications about a range of important environmental properties such as weather conditions and time of day (Jameson and Hurvich 1989). There is therefore only an *ad hoc* philosophical motivation, but no firm empirical basis, for treating all nonsurface colour perception under the heading of normal misperception.

The strong possibility that there is no single property that it is the biological function of colour vision to detect also raises a dilemma for the computational objectivist ontology of colour. As Hilbert notes in a recent article, the objectivist 'must either deny that the possession of color vision entails that the organism has the ability to visually determine the color of a surface or give up his claim that color is an objective property' (Hilbert 1992b: 358). The second alternative is of course equivalent to giving up objectivism, but adopting the first, as Hilbert notes, 'eliminates the motivation for thinking that whatever objective property we have identified with color is color' (ibid.).

Hilbert attempts to escape this dilemma by relying on an extension of the externalist approach to perceptual content. This approach, he insists, is an 'anthropocentric' one. Hilbert originally used this term to describe the view that colours, although objective, are uninteresting from a purely physical standpoint, being of interest only because there are colour perceivers (Hilbert 1987). In relation to the comparative colour vision phenomena, however, the term is meant to describe the view that colour is simply whatever property *human* colour vision has the biological function to detect. The objectivity of this property is not impugned by other species detecting different properties, and so externalism about colour perception and objectivism about colour can still be upheld.

The problem with this line of argument, of course, is that other species of animal – both primate and nonprimate – also possess colour vision. How, then, can the claim that colour is whatever distal property we humans perceive be justified? Hilbert's attempt to deal with this problem is ingenious, but it is also empirically unworkable and in the end philosophically desperate, for it tries to hold on to externalism and objectivism even in the face of some very counterintuitive consequences.

As discussed extensively in Chapter 2, human color vision goes far beyond simply being able to discriminate between lights of different wavelength independent of their relative intensities. Our colour vision also involves colour constancy, colour contrast, categorical perception (the grouping of stimuli into chromatic equivalence classes or hue categories), to say nothing of a whole host of affective associations. Mere wavelength discrimination, which provides the operational definition of colour vision in visual science, is necessary but certainly not sufficient for colour vision in this full-blooded sense. Hilbert exploits this fact to argue that any attempt to provide a criterion for the possession of colour vision that relies on discriminatory behaviour alone is inadequate. Comparative studies of colour vision do largely rely on such a criterion, however. A gap thus appears between, on the one hand, the behavioural and operational use of the term 'colour vision'in visual science, particularly comparative colour vision, and, on the other hand, the anthropocentric use in the philosophy of perception. This gap, Hilbert argues, opens up the possibility of a functionalist and externalist criterion for the possession of colour vision, one which provides a way out of the dilemma facing the computational objectivist and which the comparative study of colour vision no longer seems capable of challenging:

The only way an objectivist can meet the challenge posed

by the apparent fact that color vision functions to detect different properties in different kinds of organisms is to deny that this really [is] the case ... objectivism requires a more restrictive criterion for possession of color vision than the one that is most commonly used in the literature on comparative color vision. To possess color vision on this conception is to possess a visual system one of whose functions is the recovery of information about the reflecting characteristics of surfaces. If this is admitted as the correct criterion for possession of color vision then it is no longer possible that some organisms might possess color vision and use it to detect properties different from the ones human beings do.

(1992b: 365–6)

Hilbert admits that this account may seem circular. The objectivist relies on features of human colour vision to pick out which distal property is colour, but at the same time relies on the visual ability to detect this property as the criterion for possessing colour vision. What is needed is some independent route either to colour or to colour vision. To meet this demand Hilbert appeals to the phenomenology of human colour perception. Reflection on the phenomenology of our visual experience 'reveals an aspect ... that is clearly different from figure, texture, depth, to which we give the name color experience' (Hilbert 1992b: 363). We can then investigate this type of experience at the psychophysical and neurophysiological levels and form hypotheses about the biological function of the system responsible for it. At this point, Hilbert appeals to computational models of colour constancy to support the claim that the biological function of human colour vision is to detect surface spectral reflectance. He thus arrives at his desired objectivist conclusion that colour is this distal physical property.

I agree with Hilbert that we have an independent phenomenological route to colour vision. What this route reveals, however, is that colour vision, whatever else it may be, is the ability to see visual qualities belonging to the hue categories red, green, yellow, and blue. As noted at the beginning of this chapter, to study colour vision in this sense visual scientists cannot avoid relying on the reports that human subjects make about their visual experience, and so anthropocentrism of the sort that takes human colour vision as the main reference point for understanding colour vision, whether in philosophy or visual science, is justified. But this sort of phenomenological anthropocentrism does not sit well with Hilbert's and Matthen's externalism about perceptual content. The main reason is based on the fact, emphasized by C. L. Hardin (1988, 1989, 1990a, 1990b, 1992b) and discussed in Chapter 3, that there is no distal-based scheme that can generate the basic chromatic categories of human colour vision (red, green, yellow, and blue) plus the resemblance and difference relations among the hues that result from the opponent structure of these categories (red–green, yellow–blue).[12]

Hilbert ignores this problem in his most recent article, but Matthen (1992) has tried to accommodate it within the externalist framework. His suggestion, already mentioned in Chapter 3, is that the objectivist should distinguish between two quality spaces for colour, one a phenomenal colour space which contains red, green, yellow, and blue, and the other a distal quality space containing spectral reflectances. Matthen then allows that the phenomenal colour space might contain structure that completely fails to match anything in the structure of the distal quality space, yet he nonetheless continues to maintain, on the basis of the idea that it is the biological function of human colour vision to detect surface reflectance, that it is the distal quality space that determines perceptual content:

> The functional view of content is not committed to [any] smooth mapping from experience to distal property space … Phenomenal space might contain structure that totally fails to correlate with anything in the structure of content [distal quality space] … the objectivist would be well-advised to give visual science its conception of color (especially given that most color concepts are founded on the phenomenal structure of color vision, which is what is directly available to us), and to maintain, paradoxically perhaps, that it is not color that is the content of color vision, but some other physical quantity. For that is the clear consequence of distinguishing between content and experience and allowing each a role of its own.
>
> (Matthen 1992: 46)

The main philosophical problems with Hilbert's and Matthen's externalist theory of chromatic perceptual content can now be stated. The basic problem has already been presented in Chapter 3: in its first and foremost sense 'colour' applies to what is seen in human colour vision, namely, objects that appear to possess qualities belonging to the phenomenal categories red, green, yellow, and blue. Now if, despite there being no perceiver-independent, physical account of colour in this sense, it is nonetheless held that the content of colour perception is distal in the way that Matthen and Hilbert suppose, then it follows that red, green, yellow, and blue do not provide the content of colour vision. This consequence certainly runs counter not only to our pretheoretic intuitions about colour, but also, as Matthen notes, to the concept of colour as it figures in visual science. Moreover, Hilbert's insistence that detecting surface reflectance be the criterion for possessing colour vision engenders two further consequences that are even more counterintuitive: the first is that any creature that sees red, green, yellow, and blue, but does not detect surface reflectance, does not count as a genuine colour perceiver; the second is that any creature that has visual states whose biological function is to detect surface reflectance, but whose perceptual quality space does not involve at least one of the opponent hue-category pairs (red–green or yellow–blue), does count as a genuine colour perceiver.

Consider now what these consequences would mean in a comparative context. Suppose that my earlier speculations about tetrachromatic colour spaces containing ternary hues are right. A fully fledged tetrachromat might then perceive a quality that bears a resemblance relation to red, green, yellow, and blue, yet is neither reddish, nor greenish, nor yellowish, nor bluish. Yet according to Hilbert's and Matthen's externalist criterion, if such a tetrachomat's visual states did not have the biological function of detecting surface reflectance, then the tetrachromat would not count as a genuine colour perceiver, and consequently we mere trichromats would not count as 'colour-deficient' in relation to it, as dichromats are in relation to us.

These consequences are not merely paradoxical; they amount to a *reductio ad absurdum* of the externalist and objectivist view. The argument is partly a priori and partly empirical. The a priori element is the premise that 'colour' in its first and foremost sense applies to the phenomenal categories red, green, yellow, and blue. Notice that it is not open to the objectivist to claim that this premise is question-begging, for, as we have just seen, the objectivist needs the phenomenological route to colour vision to break into the circle that arises from relying on features of human colour vision to pick out which distal property is colour while at the same time relying on the visual ability to detect this property as the criterion for possessing colour vision. Once the premise is in place, the issue becomes whether colour in this sense can be accounted for in distal terms. The empirical element, then, is the fact the distal-based schemes are not sufficient to generate the opponent structure and resemblance and difference relations that constitute red, green, yellow, and blue. It is by clinging to externalism in the face of this fact that one is forced into the position of holding that red, green, yellow, and blue do not provide the perceptual content of colour vision, or as Matthen puts it, 'that it is not color that is the content of color vision'. And this position in turn implies that any creature that sees red, green, yellow, and blue but does not detect surface reflectance does not count as a genuine colour perceiver, whereas any creature whose visual system does detect surface reflectance but whose perceptual quality space does not involve at least one of the opponent hue-category pairs does count as a genuine colour perceiver. Such consequences are simply unacceptable, and so are tantamount to a *reductio ad absurdum* of the externalist and objectivist view.

The problems with Matthen's and Hilbert's theory of perceptual content that I have just discussed derive from its externalist component, not from its functionalist and adaptationist ones. What I now wish to discuss is how colour vision may afford evolutionary advantages in the perceptual domain without being based on representationist objectivism of the computational sort.

To begin let me return to the claim, implicit in many computational models of colour vision and explicit in Matthen's and Hilbert's theory of perceptual content, that the biological function of colour vision is to detect surface reflectance. We have already seen that the comparative evidence presents a strong case against this claim and implies at the very least that detecting surface reflectance cannot be the sole biological function of colour vision. Hilbert tries to rule this evidence out of court by restricting the discussion to the biological function of human colour vision. But even if we set aside the philosophical problems it entails, this restriction will not work on empirical grounds. First, it is not possible to draw conclusions about the biological function of human colour vision apart from some larger comparative and evolutionary picture. In fairness to Hilbert, it must be acknowledged that he does not claim that it is possible to do so. Nevertheless, in replying to the comparative argument by focusing on the biological function of human colour vision, he may have underestimated the extent to which the comparative and evolutionary data not only significantly constrain attributions of biological function to human colour vision, but also constrain such attributions in a way that is not philosophically neutral. Indeed, I shall argue shortly that comparative and evolutionary studies support a different approach to the biological function of colour vision from Hilbert's and Matthen's computational objectivism. Second, although comparative colour vision studies do rely largely on the discriminatory criterion for possessing colour vision, a range of other chromatic phenomena, including colour constancy, colour contrast, and categorical colour perception, have been demonstrated in nonprimate species,[13] and, as I mentioned earlier, there is also a significant body of evidence to suggest that colour vision in these species serves functions other than or in addition to that of detecting surface spectral reflectance. Third, it is not at all empirically obvious that the colour constancy exhibited by humans and some other animals is the result of selection for surface reflectance detection. At least three further questions arise here: first, is colour constancy an adaptation or is it an artifact of a mechanism that was selected because it enhanced the fitness of its possessors in some other way? Second, if colour constancy is an adaptation, is it an adaptation for the detection of surface reflectance or for some other perceptual task? Finally, is there any cogent adaptationist story to be told about human colour vision at all, or is it the result of trade-offs among a host of factors in a meandering and idiosyncratic evolutionary history?

One theory that attempts to answer these questions, which Hilbert enlists in his support, comes from the psychologist

Roger N. Shepard (1990, 1992). His theory builds on the linear models framework (LMF) in computational colour vision discussed in Chapter 2. Recall that the computational problem of recovering surface spectral reflectance requires that the illuminant and reflectance variables be disentangled from the intensity signal. In theory any function of wavelength between 0 and 1 is potentially a surface reflectance, and to describe all such functions would require an infinite number of parameters. Naturally occurring illuminants and reflectances are generally smooth and simple, however, and so can be described in a linear model having only a few degrees of freedom: two to three parameters suffice to describe the various phases of daylight (Judd et al. 1964); five to seven parameters suffice for two large classes of naturally occurring surface reflectances, with six parameters providing an almost perfect fit (the number drops to only three or four when the human spectral sensitivity curve is taken into account) (Maloney 1986). It has also been shown, however, that surface reflectance can be completely recovered only if the degrees of freedom in reflectance are less than the number of receptor types (Maloney and Wandell 1986). Human colour vision is trichromatic – we possess three types of cone photoreceptor – and so, as surface colour metamerism makes evident, there are chromatic differences among naturally occurring reflectances that we cannot detect.

The question that Shepard poses is: 'Why should this reduction [in the number of degrees of freedom of the representation of colours] be to precisely three dimensions – as opposed, say, to two dimensions or to four dimensions?' (1990: 302). His suggestion is that the trichromacy of human colour vision is a reflection of the three degrees of freedom in the phases of natural daylight. These three degrees of freedom correspond to (1) a light–dark variation between the sunlight of midday and evening or deep shade; (2) a red–green variation between the long-wavelength-rich illumination direct from the low sun and the same illumination as it penetrates the atmosphere loaded with water vapour; and (3) a yellow–blue variation between the short-wavelength-poor illumination reaching an object and the short-wavelength-rich illumination scattered back to the object from the clear sky. To achieve colour constancy and thereby to detect objects on the basis of their surface spectral reflectances, the visual system must compensate perceptually for these three types of variation. A trichromatic (or more properly a trivariant) system can meet this demand by analysing the ambient light into three visual channels to correct for the three types of variation and thereby recover reflectance. Hence Shepard's hypothesis is that tri-chromacy was selected for because it enables object detection through colour constancy, a hypothesis that forms part of his general representationist and objectivist theory that perceptual and cognitive capacities are internalizations, achieved through evolution by natural selection, of abstract, enduring regularities in the external world (Shepard 1987).

There is a major weakness in Shepard's theory, one which becomes evident when we consider the theory in the framework of comparative colour vision. Although it is true that virtually every animal class has some species with trichromatic vision, many animals are dichromats, others are tetrachromats, and some may even be pentachromats. These variations alone should cast doubt on Shepard's hypothesis that 'in the terrestrial environment, there has been a consistent selection pressure toward an analysis of the visual input into three chromatic channels in order to achieve a high degree of color constancy' (1990: 307). Shepard attempts to meet this doubt by arguing that species active in less illuminated environments can make do with fewer than three channels, whereas other species may have evolved more than three for basically idiosyncratic reasons (Shepard 1992: 51). The problem with this reply, however, is that primate trichromacy is simply not the norm in the animal world. In contrast, tetrachromacy is common not only among the highly visual diurnal birds, but among vertebrate lineages in general, and is thus evolutionarily more ancient than primate trichromacy (Goldsmith 1990).

Attention to this fact suggests a rather different approach from Shepard's to the question 'Why three dimensional colour vision as opposed to two or four?' Shepard's assumption is that an answer to this question must show 'why the optimum number [of receptors or chromatic channels] is specifically three' (1990: 303). But given the fact that tetrachromacy is evolutionarily more ancient than Old World primate tri-chromacy, it is not at all obvious that the optimum number is three or even that this type of question is a fruitful one to ask.

To see why, recall the data presented earlier about the evolution of colour vision. Molecular biological studies show that the amino acid sequences of all visual pigments are quite similar and that the visual pigment genes of even distantly related organisms have identical DNA segments. The conclusion that has been drawn is that the visual pigments all derive from an ancient ancestor. Yet although the origins of the human cone visual pigments are ancient, trichromacy is not the norm. Many vertebrate animals have more complex retinas possessing not only four or even five visual pigments, but also oil droplet inclusions. Among mammals, however, oil droplets are absent, retinas with three cone visual pigments are found only in primates, and the primitive condition, still exemplified by most modern mammals, is dichromatic. The conclusion that has generally been drawn is that mammalian colour vision is evolutionarily degenerate. During much of their evolutionary history, which occurred prior to the extinction of the dinosaurs, mammals were most probably small and had nocturnal habits. As a result, their capacity for photopic vision declined considerably. In this context, humans and Old World monkeys are something of an exception, for they seem to have secondarily evolved trichromatic vision with the adoption of diurnal habits. In contrast, the evolutionarily more ancient visual systems of fishes, amphibians, reptiles, and birds appear to be largely tetrachromatic (Goldsmith 1990; Neumeyer 1991). The colour vision of these animals has not been evolutionarily compromised by the adoption of nocturnal habits, and so it, not primate trichromacy, provides a better reference point for framing hypotheses about the evolution and biological function of colour vision.

It is worth considering a specific example. Because Shepard takes primate trichromacy as his reference point for understanding the biological function of colour vision, he assumes from the outset the primate perspective on visible light, which excludes the ultraviolet region of the spectrum. Thus he states that 'the visible spectrum ... has a total width of about 300 nm' (Shepard 1990: 303), referring to the human visible window of approximately 400 nm–700 nm. The spectral ranges available to other animals differ considerably, however. In the honeybee (also a trichromat) spectral sensitivity is shifted towards the ultraviolet and has a total width of about 350 nm

(300 nm–650 nm); in many diurnal birds it extends considerably further than ours both into the ultraviolet and the long-wave end of the spectrum, having a total width of about 370 nm (350 nm–720 nm); in cyprinid and salmonid fishes it appears to extend from less than 350 nm to around 800 nm, 'providing perhaps the broadest spectral range amongst the vertebrates' (Bowmaker 1991: 117).

Consider now the question 'Why do these animals have ultraviolet sensitivity?' Because Shepard focuses on primate trichromacy and supposes that there has been a consistent selection pressure towards it, he approaches this question by looking for largely species-specific, idiosyncratic reasons to explain the presence of tetrachromacy and ultraviolet sensitivity (Shepard 1992). But what we know about the evolutionary history of colour vision suggests that this approach might be back to front. What Shepard calls the 'full range of visible solar wavelengths' (1990: 304) includes the ultraviolet. Trichromatic primates such as ourselves and the Old World monkeys are not sensitive to the ultraviolet; whereas many fishes, amphibians, reptiles, and birds are. In making hypotheses about the selection pressures involved in colour-vision dimensionality and sensitivity, it must be remembered that primate trichromacy is recently derived in comparison with tetrachromacy and ultraviolet sensitivity in these other vertebrate lineages. In an adaptationist context, this fact would suggest that in highly visual environments there are selection pressures towards tetrachromacy and/or ultraviolet sensitivity. According to this hypothesis, the comparative lack of both in mammals – the only mammals known to exhibit ultraviolet sensitivity are rodent species (Jacobs et al. 1991), and these have either an ultraviolet or a violet receptor but not both (Jacobs 1992), suggesting that the corresponding genes are alternatives in mammals (Goldsmith in press) – would be due to the absence of such selection pressures with the adoption of nocturnal habits early in mammalian evolutionary history; and the emergence of trichromacy in primates with the adoption of diurnal habits would accordingly represent a half-way point between the nocturnally compromised vision of mammals and the tetrachromacy of other highly visual animals whose vision has not been so compromised.[14]

Although the common occurrence of tetrachromacy casts

serious doubts on Shepard's hypothesis that there has been a consistent selection pressure in the terrestrial environment towards *trichromacy*, it does not directly challenge his claim that colour vision in general has evolved because of selection for object detection through colour constancy. Once the visual spectrum is extended to include the near-ultraviolet, which typically occurs in tetrachromatic species, it seems likely that trichromacy will not be sufficient for good colour constancy. The present point, however, is that whether colour vision has so evolved cannot be determined by focusing on primate trichromacy as Shepard does. The roles played by colour constancy in the evolution of colour vision can be appreciated only by developing and testing theories that span the full range of visual capacities and visual ecologies in di-, tri-, tetra-, and pentachromatic perceivers.

This point bears on Hilbert's externalist position. Although this position is a philosophical one, it rests on empirical theories and has empirical consequences. Hilbert relies on Maloney and Wandell's and Shepard's theories of colour constancy to ground empirically his externalist attribution of biological function to colour vision. In his words: 'The existence of color constancy suggests that the function of color vision is to determine the reflecting properties of distal surfaces' (Hilbert 1992b: 365). Consequently, animals that do not achieve a high degree of colour constancy will not, according to Hilbert's externalist criterion, possess colour vision. Now, according to Maloney and Wandell (1986) and Shepard (1990), at least three photoreceptor types are needed for good colour constancy. Therefore, Hilbert argues, '[t]here will be a strong prima facie case against the possession of color vision by species for which dichromacy is the normal case ... The objectivists [*sic*] attribution of function is clearly a claim with empirical consequences' (ibid.).

We have just seen that Shepard's theory is not sufficient to establish claims about the biological function of colour vision. The empirical support for Hilbert's position is therefore not as strong as he appears to believe. It should also be emphasized how counterintuitive this position is. In the human case, we know that a dichromat perceives colours along either the red–green or yellow–blue opponent hue axes. But according to what follows from Hilbert's criterion, if such a perceiver did not exhibit a high degree of colour constancy, he or she would not count as a genuine colour perceiver; and if a perceiver did exhibit a high degree of reflectance constancy, yet surfaces did not look red, green, yellow, and blue to that perceiver, he or she would count as a genuine colour perceiver.

In the human case at least, Hilbert suggests in a footnote that the conclusion that human dichromats do not possess colour vision can be blocked by 'assess[ing] function in terms of evolutionary history rather than individual characteristics' (1992b: 369, n. 15). But this move raises other problems. As Hilbert himself goes on to admit: 'There may be some difficulties in this area since at least one species of monkey has sex-linked polymorphism between trichromacy and dichromacy. What to say in functional terms about color vision for these monkeys is not at all clear' (ibid.). But this statement underestimates considerably the data we have about colour-vision polymorphism: as we have seen, not only do sex-linked colour-vision polymorphisms appear to be common among New World primates in general (Mollon et al. 1984; Jacobs 1985, 1986; Bowmaker et al. 1987; Tovée et al. 1992), but there may also be a sex-linked polymorphism in human colour vision between trichromacy and tetrachromacy (Mollon 1992; Jordan and Mollon 1993) – a possibility that, contrary to what Shepard and Hilbert appear to assume, makes the evolutionary assessment of function for human trichromacy not at all straightforward.

We can now return to the more general issue about the status of colour constancy. Computational objectivism, whether in visual science or the philosophy of perception, takes colour constancy as indicating that the biological function of colour vision is to detect objects by recovering their surface spectral reflectances. A better and more satisfying perspective on the benefits colour vision affords, which I discussed earlier in this chapter, is provided by Mollon (1989). He argues that the biological advantages of colour vision, in particular of primate trichromacy, are revealed by the disabilities experienced by human dichromats. In scenes where the ambient light varies randomly, there are three perceptual tasks that human dichromats find particularly difficult: (1) detecting certain coloured objects; (2) segmenting the visual scene; and (3) identifying particular objects or states.[15]

Consider how these three tasks can be perceptually and

ecologically combined. In monkeys, trichromatic vision facilitates the detection and identification of orange/yellow fruits
against the green forest background. To detect and identify
these fruits the visual scene must be segmented into the
elements that belong together, and colour and lightness are
particularly useful attributes in linking these elements. The
orange/yellow fruit colour also helps to identify the state of the
object by indicating conditions beneath its surface – for
example, that it is ripe. In addition, colours serve to assign
already segmented elements in the scene to categories that
have perceptual significance. A perceptual colour category can
guide behaviour in various ways depending on the things that
exemplify it and their significance for the animal. In the case of
fruits, it can guide feeding; in the case of animal colouration, it
can be used to identify conspecifics, their sex, and their sexual
state, and so can guide various social interactions, such as
mating.

Like Hardin (1990a, 1992b) and Gary Hatfield (1992), I think
that the key to colour constancy is to be found in this joining of
object identification and categorical colour perception. Rather
than providing constant perceptual indicators of surface reflectance, the primary role of colour vision is probably to generate a
relatively stable set of perceptual categories that can facilitate
object identification and then guide behaviour accordingly. The
detection of surface reflectance is certainly useful for object
identification, but, as Jameson and Hurvich note, 'surface color
recognition ... is adequately accomplished by category matching
and does not require precise matching-to-sample by the three
color variables of hue, brightness, and saturation' (Jameson and
Hurvich 1989: 20). In general, categorical perception involves a
many-to-one mapping from the physical to perceptual dimensions (Bornstein 1987); in the particular case of colour vision, this
means that many physically distinct surface reflectances will be
lumped together into one colour category. It is the approximate
invariance of the categorical colour with variations in the
illumination that is crucial for object identification and subsequent behaviour, not constant hue–saturation–lightness
correlates of surface reflectance.

Having a small set of relatively stable colour categories
(which will be based on an even smaller set of hue categories)
also facilitates object detection without sacrificing visual sensi-

tivity to illumination conditions in their own right. The hue, saturation, and lightness shifts that occur with variations in the illumination will usually not move surface colours from one colour category into another (Jameson and Hurvich 1989: 19); therefore, colour appearances in the surface mode will remain categorically stable. Yet, as noted earlier, categorical colour appearances in the light or illumination mode can also be perceptually significant in their own right, for they can provide indications about a range of important environmental properties such as weather conditions and time of day. Hence there are good reasons for the visual system not to devote all its efforts to recovering the constant surface reflectance properties of objects at the expense of being able to perceive (not just compensate for) the ambient light.

Psychophysical studies of human colour-vision performance lend support to this claim. Arend and Reeves (1986), for example, have shown that colour constancy is very poor when observers are asked to adjust a test-patch in one multicoloured array to match the hue and saturation of a particular patch in another array, but reasonably good when observers are asked to match the patches as if they were 'cut from the same piece of paper'. The former task requires perceptual judgements in the illumination or light mode of colour appearance, whereas the latter requires judgements in the surface mode. Except for this difference, the conditions in Arend and Reeve's experiments were identical, and so their results can be taken to indicate, first, that observers can perceive both surface chromaticity and illumination conditions, and second, that colour constancy is not automatic or modular (in, say, Pylyshyn's (1984) sense of being 'cognitively impenetrable'), but rather strongly task- and judgement-dependent (Reeves 1992).

It is the categorical nature of colour vision that, I suggest, enables this perceptual flexibility. Therefore, if colour constancy is an adaptation, it is better regarded not as an adaptation for object detection via the recovery of surface reflectance, but rather as an adaptation for integrating a physically heterogeneous collection of distal stimuli into a small set of visually salient equivalence classes (Hardin 1992b: 380; Hatfield 1992), ones that can be deployed in a variety of perceptual conditions. What the comparative framework indicates is that both the perceptual equivalence classes and the distal stimuli will differ according to the animal and its visual ecology.

This point is worth illustrating at some length in relation to the second of the three visual tasks emphasized by Mollon, the spatial segmentation of the visual scene. Although spatial segmentation algorithms figure prominently in computational colour vision (see Chapter 2), computational objectivists hold that the function of colour vision is simply to recover surface spectral reflectance given a collection of objects. The unspoken assumption is that the visual scene has already been segmented into areas that correspond to distinct objects and their surfaces. This assumption begs the question of the roles that colour vision may play in perception. As D'Zmura and Lennie note: 'to find the loci of responses that correspond to different objects, one must already have segmented the scene to establish which lights come from which objects. This begs the question of the purpose of color vision, which we believe plays an important role in the discrimination among objects and in their identification' (D'Zmura and Lennie 1986: 1666).

Consider the regularization constraints involved in computational colour vision. Among these constraints is the fact that naturally occurring illuminants and reflectances can be adequately modelled in a low-dimensional space. What, one might ask, constitutes a 'naturally occurring reflectance'? An examination of computational models reveals that so-called natural reflectances correspond to the surface reflectances of typical objects from our human environment, for example, bricks, grass, buildings, as well as less ecological items such as Munsell colour chips. Given a class of such objects, one can measure their surface spectral reflectances and then determine which finite set of basis reflectance functions best models the variance in the class. The visual system, however, is never simply presented with such prespecified objects. On the contrary, the determination of what and where an object is, as well as its surface texture and orientation – and hence the overall context in which colour is perceived – is a complex process that the visual system must achieve.

Colour vision has a role to play in this process. As Mollon (1989) notes, where the ambient light in a scene varies unpredictably, both lightness and hue can be particularly useful attributes for linking the elements that belong together. At the computational level, Rubin and Richards (1982, 1984) propose that one biological goal of the early stages of colour vision is to determine where material changes occur in a scene by relying on spectral crosspoints and opposite slope signs; and D'Zmura and Lennie (1986) propose an algorithm for colour constancy in which the geometric stability of hue contributes to segmentation, while variations in lightness and saturation contribute to establishing an object's shape and position. At the neurophysiological level, although there is considerable disagreement over the properties of the retino-geniculate-cortical pathways involved in colour, form, and motion perception (see Chapter 2), it nonetheless seems safe to say that not only the achromatic processes involving the lightness dimension of surface colour, but also the chromatically opponent processes play a role in spatial segmentation – for example, colour contrasts can be used to determine borders. Moreover, both cell-response and lesion studies of V4 indicate that the treatment of colour and form are combined in this cortical area (Desimone et al. 1985; Desimone and Schein 1987; Heywood and Cowey 1987).

The fact that colour vision plays a role in spatial segmentation has suggestive implications in a comparative setting. Consider the claim that 'it is impossible to separate the object sensed from its color because it is the color contrast itself that forms the object' (Gouras and Zrenner 1981: 172). This claim suggests an intriguing prediction in a comparative context. Recall that the perception of colour contrast requires being able to detect not simply the wavelengths in a unit area of visual space, but also the spectral contrasts across space, particularly between adjacent areas. At the neurophysiological level, spectral contrast detection appears to be subserved by single and double opponent cells; these cells also form at least part of the physiological substrate of the postreceptoral chromatic channels. Both the number and the chromatic response of these channels will differ according to the type of colour-vision system. As Gouras observes: 'In organisms with trivariant colour vision, two separate pairs of single opponent neurons are found, blue–yellow and red–green opponent channels. In organisms with tetravariant colour vision there must be three such colour opponent pairs' (Gouras 1991a: 176). Consequently, there should be significant differences in the perception of colour contrast between trichromats and tetrachromats. But if, as Gouras and Zrenner claim, it is the colour contrast that forms (even if only in part) the perceived object, then other aspects of the perceptual object besides colour – for example, visual shape – should differ for trichromats and tetrachromats. The prediction based on Gouras and Zrenner's claim, then, is that *the relevant object for visual perception may vary depending on the type of colour-vision system involved.*

This prediction can also be formulated within the framework of computational vision. For example, the segmentation algorithm developed by Rubin and Richards (1982, 1984) is based on a trichromatic categorical colour space in which the red–green and yellow–blue axes represent boundaries between different materials:

> Our claim that Hering's color quadrants [bluish + reddish, bluish + greenish, reddish + yellowish, and greenish + yellowish] correspond to material categories is predictive: we expect that shadows, surface orientation changes, and pigment density changes would only rarely cause perceived hue to change from *reddish* to *greenish* (or vice-versa), or from *yellowish* to *bluish* (or vice-versa).
>
> (Rubin and Richards 1984: 205)

Rubin and Richards go on to cite Wright and Cummings's (1971) study that showed pigeons have categorical colour perception, which, they say, 'suggest[s] the computational scheme we propose here is fundamental to color vision across species'. But if pigeons are fully fledged tetrachromats (perhaps even pentachromats), then their colour space involves an additional orthogonal hue axis. The additional hue categories available to the pigeon might correspond in some systematic way to material categories that are significant in the pigeon's visual ecology – for example, the pigmentations underlying ultra-violet reflectances. In any case, a segmentation algorithm based on a tetrachromatic categorical colour space would presumably segment the world differently from the trichromatic-based algorithm developed by Rubin and Richards.

The possibility of such differences suggests that, in relation to the distal stimuli involved in colour vision, there could be significant variations in what counts as a surface for animals having different types of colour vision. The line of argument leading to this speculation can be formulated as follows:

The argument from perceiver-relativity

1 Colour vision plays a role in segmenting the visual scene into regions of distinct surfaces and/or objects.
2 Colour vision varies considerably throughout the animal world.
3 Therefore, spatial segmentation is also likely to vary throughout the animal world.

---

4 Therefore, what counts as a surface for visual perception will vary according to the perceiver.

This argument should be taken as conditional, based on a reasoned hypothesis that requires further empirical investigation in a comparative perceptual and ecological context. Nevertheless, the argument points to a gap in the computational objectivist account of perception.

On the empirical side, computational colour vision has to date focused on our familiar human environment, rather than the considerably different environments of birds, fishes, or insects. For example, the objects in the computational models are typically middle-sized, frontally viewed, 'human' objects, such as bricks, grass, buildings, Munsell colour chips, Mondrian displays, and so forth. They are not, for example, silhouettes against the background sky, as seen frontally and laterally by birds, ultraviolet reflectance patterns of flowers, as seen by birds and bees, aquatic objects that contrast with the illumination colours of the downwelling or background space light as viewed by fishes, and so on. Because of this focus on already specified human objects, the issue of how there can be significant variation in the perceptual segmentation of the world has been largely neglected.

On the philosophical side, computational objectivists such as Hilbert and Matthen assume that surfaces provide a perceiver-independent peg on which to hang objective colour as spectral reflectance. But what exactly is to count as a surface? Although the *spectral reflectance at any point* in the scene can be specified in perceiver-independent physical terms, what counts as a *surface* might be relative to the perceiver. The argument from perceiver-relativity raises this possibility, though it certainly does not entail it. The point of the argument is simply the hypothesis that what actually gets *perceived* as a surface depends on colour vision. Surfaces themselves (unlike colours) may nonetheless be perceiver-independent features of the world. But objectivists cannot simply assume this without argument. Computational objectivism about colour depends on objectivism about surfaces, and so some defence of the latter should be given. And just as objectivism about colour must be defended in the face of wide variations in colour vision throughout the animal world, so objectivism about surfaces must be defended in the face of wide variations in spatial segmentation throughout the animal world.

In this section, I have argued that externalism about perceptual content and the representationist objectivism upon which it is based are unsatisfactory in the case of colour vision. Colour vision and in particular colour constancy need not be representational to be evolutionarily advantageous. The comparative argument implies that the biological function of colour vision is not to *re*present surface spectral reflectance; rather it is to *present* to the animal a set of perceptual colour categories that can apply to the world in a stable way through variations in the ambient light without sacrificing perception of the illumination conditions in their own right. Although computational objectivists do not deny the categorical nature of colour vision, they continue to ignore the fact that colour categories are not found in the world apart from perceivers – once again, there is no distal-based scheme that can generate the basic chromatic categories of human colour vision.

What, philosophically speaking, does the difference between 'representation' and 'presentation' mean in this context? Here it is helpful to recall the distinction that Matthen makes between the 'individual-directedness' and 'mode of presentation' in perceptual content: every perceptual state is directed towards a unique object and presents that object as having certain characteristics. Matthen's claim about the mode of presentation is that a perceptual state presents an object as having certain characteristics if and only if the biological function of the state is to detect the presence of things that have those characteristics. This claim implies that the mode of presentation is (in at least one sense) really a mode of *re*presentation: a perceptual state has the function of *re*presenting what is already present in the physical world. And of course this idea sits well with the computational framework within which Matthen is operating, for according to this framework (at least as articulated by Marr and his followers), there is no direct visual perception of the world because 'vision is the *process* of discovering *from images* [my italics] what is present in the world, and where it is' (Marr 1982: 3). (What this means more precisely is that vision is the internal computational 'recovery' of external properties from patterns of retinal irradiation that underspecify their distal source.) Applied to colour perception, then, the idea is that objects are perceived as being coloured because certain perceptual states have the biological function of detecting their surface spectral reflectances; hence perceived colour, although a mode of presentation in visual perception, is really a *re*presentation of something that is already present in the distal world. Thus the term 'mode of representation', rather than 'mode of presentation', would better convey Matthen's conception of this component of perceptual content.

In contrast, I have argued that the biological function of colour vision is not to detect surface reflectance, but rather to generate a set of colour categories that have significance for the perceptual guidance of activity. In my view, the categories that give structure to colour perception are indeed modes of *presentation* in visual perception, but they are not modes of *representation*, at least not in the typical computationalist sense, because colour perception does not represent something that is already present in the world apart from perceivers; it simply presents the world to the animal in a manner that satisfies the animal's adaptive ecological needs.

Let me make clear that I am not claiming that the distal environment does not enter at all into the account of perceptual content. It is perfectly legitimate, and indeed necessary, to appeal to relatively stable properties of visual ecologies such as spectral reflectance, illuminance, and emittance when discussing colour perception and the advantages it affords to various animals. My objection is rather to the way in which the externalist appeals to such properties. For the externalist, the perceptual content of colour vision is distal because colour is surface reflectance. My view, however, is that surface colour is surface reflectance only because there exist perceivers for whom reflectances fall into metameric equivalence classes corresponding to red, green, yellow, and blue (and other visual qualities that bear the appropriate resemblance and difference relations – see above and Chapter 6). Thus I hold that the perceptual content of colour vision, rather than being distal in the externalist sense, is relational: chromatic perceptual content is jointly constituted by the perceiver and the environment (see also Hatfield 1992: 498). I shall present this relational view in more detail in the next chapter.

What about the other two, functionalist and adaptationist, components of Matthen's and Hilbert's theory of perceptual content? Nothing that I have argued challenges the functionalist criterion for individuating perceptual states or perceptual systems. Externalism is actually just one type of functionalist criterion – one in which the relevant function is to detect a distal property – and so my critique of externalism has no implications for other forms of functionalism. Indeed, there are other functionalist criteria that are perfectly compatible with the argument I have given here. For example, Hilbert himself notes that 'it would not serve the objectivist's purpose if the relevant function were to produce experiences of some characteristic type' (1992b: 363); and he claims that it is 'unlikely that the production of color experience by itself makes the kind of contribution to fitness that would be necessary for it to be selected for' (1992b: 369, n. 14). The argument that I have pursued leads to the opposite conclusion. If colour constancy is an adaptation, then it is one in which the production of a central aspect of colour experience – a small number of stable and salient perceptual categories makes exactly the kind of contribution to fitness that would result in its being selected.

What, now, of the adaptationist component? I have argued that colour vision does not represent the world; rather, it presents the world to the animal by categorizing physically disparate stimuli into perceptual equivalence classes. As we have seen, such categorization is clearly useful for the animal in a variety of biological and ecological ways. Does this mean that colour constancy has been selected for along the lines of what Gould and Lewontin (1979) call the 'adaptationist programme'? The question in this context strikes me as an empirical one, and as far as I can tell it cannot be decided on the basis of the evidence currently available.[16] In any case, whether it is due to natural selection and/or other types of evolutionary factors, colour constancy in the sense discussed here figures largely in human colour vision and probably does so in the visual ecology of other colour-seeing animals. It therefore remains a reasonable strategy to pursue ecologically and evolutionarily based, if not adaptationist, approaches to perceptual content.

Neurophysiological subjectivism revisited

Neurophysiological subjectivism, as defended by C. L. Hardin (1988), is the view that combines eliminativism about being coloured as a property of objects with neuroscientific reductionism about colour experience: there is no such property as being coloured; there are only chromatic visual states, and these are to be reductively identified with neural states.

At the end of Chapter 3, I argued that Hardin's main argument for neurophysiological subjectivism – the argument from internal reducibility – is invalid. One can hold that there is no perceiver-independent account of red, green, yellow, and blue without holding that there is no such property as being coloured: one can hold that although there is no *intrinsic* (nonrelational) property of being coloured, there is a *relational* one. The question I wish to pursue now, however, is the methodological one about Hardin's advocacy of the neurophysiological level of description for colour perception. How much can the explanatory levels and descriptive vocabularies of neuroscience accomplish in the explanation of colour perception?

Hardin writes: 'Problems that are intractable at the extradermal physical level or at the phenomenal level promise to yield to analysis in neurological terms' (1988: 111). The problems to which Hardin is referring have to do with perceptual content and mind–body relations; I shall focus on the former here. Hardin's view is that externalism of the sort I criticized in the previous section cannot give a satisfactory account of the perceptual content of colour vision – that is, of red, green, yellow, and blue – yet any account that is explanatory must move beyond the purely phenomenal level. With these two points I completely agree. Nonetheless, I think that there is an important aspect of the perceptual content of colour vision that does not yield to analysis in purely neurological terms. This aspect is *ecological* in the broadest sense: that is, it encompasses not only the extradermal world as an animal environment, but also animals as perceiving subjects above and beyond their internal visual states, subjects that interact with the extradermal world and in so doing shape that world into an environment.

The aspect that I have in mind is one to which Hardin himself has recently drawn attention (Hardin 1990a, 1992b): it is the perceptual or 'signal' significance that categorical colours have for perceiving animals in their behavioural interactions (Jacobs 1981: 170–1). Specific colours often serve as biological signals that can guide behaviour in various ways: for example, in the case of plant colouration, they can guide feeding, and in the case of animal colouration, they can guide social interactions such as mating. In general, colouration affects visibility, and so is involved in both camouflage and many kinds of visual recognition, such as species recognition, sexual recognition, individual recognition, and recognition of motivational state (Baylis 1979; Rowland 1979). Categorical colour vision is crucial in these recognition contexts, for as Hardin notes, 'if the [colour] signal is not to be misidentified, there must be a gap between one [chromatic] equivalence class and the next' (Hardin 1992b: 380).

In pursuing an ecologically and evolutionarily based approach to the perceptual content of colour vision, then, one must be concerned just as much with animal colouration, indeed with the colouration of living things in general, as with animal colour vision (Hailman 1977; Lythgoe 1979; Burtt 1979; Burkhardt 1989; Neumeyer 1991). On this point, some remarks from a recent review by Neumeyer are worth quoting at length:

> That the coloration of animals must be of high selective value was already discussed by Darwin ... Protection against predators can be provided either by a cryptic coloration, in combination with patterns, spots or stripes, which break up the outline of the body, or by very obvious colours, mostly red or yellow, which are used as warning signals. Now, as we know so much more about the colour vision systems of mammals, birds, reptiles, fishes, and insects, it would be worthwhile to reinvestigate animal

coloration under the aspect of coevolution between body colour and the colour vision systems of potential predators. Is it a specific predator for which an animal wants to be invisible, or is it of higher selective advantage to be cryptic for as many as possible?

(Neumeyer 1991: 302)

The question now before us is whether Hardin's neurophysiological subjectivism can do justice to these ecological aspects of colour vision. Whereas computational objectivism is externalist about perceptual content, neurophysiological subjectivism is *internalist*: the perceptual content of colour vision is to be specified in terms of subjective visual qualities, and these are to be reductively identified with features of neural states. Thus neurophysiological subjectivism provides a *narrow*, that is, entirely intradermal, framework for perceptual content. But it is precisely the signal significance of the perceptual content of colour vision that becomes intractable in such a framework. The signal significance of chromatic perceptual content cannot be exhaustively explained in narrow (intradermal) terms because it is constituted by organism–environment pairs (where the environment of course includes other animals). In general, nothing is intrinsically a signal: something is a signal only in relation to both a sender and a receiver. So too the signal significance of colour is neither intrinsic to spectral reflectances nor intrinsic to neural states: it is a relational feature constituted by the animal as a whole as it interacts with its environment. What the relational nature of colour signals indicates, then, is that chromatic perceptual content must be construed *widely*, that is, in relation to the extradermal context of the environment.

The intractability of a purely internalist approach to chromatic perceptual content can be brought home by considering not simply the signal significance that colours have for animals, but also the cognitive significance they have for humans.[17] Discussion of this point, however, requires a digression to review a certain body of empirical research on human colour perception.[18]

Consider the numerous names that we have in English for colours – red, yellow, orange, green, blue, purple, violet, indigo, pink, turquoise, aquamarine, mauve, chartreuse, etc. Given these many names, as well as the numerous names in other languages, one might suppose that human colour categories are ultimately arbitrary, that is, that nothing compels us to categorize colours in one way rather than another. This was in fact the dominant view some time ago within the fields of linguistics and anthropology. For example, Gleason (1961) in his well-known introductory linguistics text wrote:

There is a continuous gradation of color from one end of the spectrum to the other. Yet an American describing it will list the hues as red, orange, yellow, green, blue, purple or something of the kind. There is nothing inherent either in the spectrum or the human perception of it which would compel its division in this way.

(Gleason 1961: 4)

This view was dramatically challenged in 1969 with the publication of the now classic work *Basic Color Terms: Their Universality and Evolution*, by Brent Berlin and Paul Kay (1969). In this work, Berlin and Kay specified a number of linguistic criteria for determining which colour names in a given language should be counted as 'basic' colour terms. Then, on the basis of an examination of over ninety languages, they argued that there are at most eleven basic colour terms (in English: black, white, red, yellow, green, blue, brown, purple, pink, orange, and grey), though not all languages contain all eleven. After establishing the set of basic colour terms for a given language, Berlin and Kay then presented speakers of that language with a standardized array of colour chips and asked them to specify both the boundaries and the best examples of the colours to which their basic terms refer. They found that although there was considerable variation among speakers over colour-category boundaries, individuals virtually always agreed on the best example of a colour category. Furthermore, they found that when several languages contained a common basic term, such as a basic term for blue, individuals virtually always agreed on the best example of the colour category no matter which language they spoke. Berlin and Kay argued therefore that the basic colour terms name basic colour categories whose structure is not uniform, for some members are central and so constitute 'foci'. Since these central members are universally agreed upon, Berlin and Kay concluded that 'the eleven basic color categories are pan-human perceptual universals' (1969: 109).

Although some languages do not encode all eleven basic colour categories, it should not be supposed that the colour domain is in some way impoverished for speakers of these languages. On the contrary, the set of basic colour terms in a given language always encompasses the entire phenomenal colour space. For example, the language of the Dani tribe of New Guinea has only two basic colour terms. In studies of the Dani, Rosch (then Heider) showed that these two terms, which had previously been translated as 'white' and 'black', were actually better translated as 'white-warm' and 'dark-cool', for the former term covered white plus all the warm colours (red, yellow, orange, reddish-purple, pink), whereas the latter covered black plus all the cool colours (blue, green) (Heider 1972).

Berlin and Kay's conclusion about the eleven basic colour categories being perceptual universals for the human species was strengthened by Rosch's studies of the Dani. She performed a series of four experiments to test the hypothesis that there are perceptually salient areas of colour space, which she called 'focal colors', and that this perceptual salience determines which colours are universally the most linguistically 'codeable' as well as the most easily remembered. Rosch found that focal colours (1) correspond to the most saturated colours within the Berlin and Kay 'foci' (Berlin and Kay had not mapped the location of their foci with respect to saturation); (2) are given shorter names and are learned more rapidly than nonfocal colours; (3) are more easily remembered than nonfocal colours, even by speakers of a language (Dani) that lacks basic hue terms; and (4) are more easily retained in long-term memory, again even by speakers of a language that lacks basic hue terms. From these experiments Rosch concluded:

> Given the attributes of focal colors – their occurrence as exemplars of basic color names, their linguistic codability across languages, and their superior retention in short- and long-term memory – it would seem most economical to suppose that these attributes are derived from the same underlying factors, most likely having to do with the physiology of primate colour vision. In short, far from

being a domain well suited to the study of the effects of language on thought, the color space would seem to be a prime example of the influence of underlying perceptual-cognitive factors on the formation and reference of linguistic categories.

(Heider 1972: 20)

Whereas Rosch suggests in this passage that the physiology of primate colour vision is responsible for the perceptual salience and universality of focal colours, Berlin and Kay had claimed that they could 'offer no physical or physiological explanation for the apparently greater perceptual salience of these particular color stimuli' (1969: 109). Ten years later, however, Kay and McDaniel (1978) tried to provide a model of how to derive the semantic universals of basic colour terms from properties of the visual system. They made use of the results of some physiological experiments conducted by DeValois and Jacobs (1968). The experiments identified four types of opponent-response cells in the lateral-geniculate nucleus of the macaque, a species of monkey that has trichromatic vision similar to ours. The cells are grouped into two pairs that DeValois and Jacobs labelled 'red–green' and 'yellow–blue'. Some red–green cells fire above their spontaneous rate when stimulated by 'red' (far long-wave) lights and below when stimulated by 'green' (near-short wave); others fire above their spontaneous rate when stimulated by 'green' and below when stimulated by 'red'. An analogous pattern holds for the yellow–blue cells. Kay and McDaniel applied fuzzy set theory to the responses of these cells to model the semantics of basic colour terms. Unlike standard set theory, fuzzy set theory operates with sets that admit degrees of membership. Degree of membership in a set is specified by a function that assigns to each member some value between 0 and 1. Thus for colour, focal colours have degree of membership 1 in their respective categories, whereas nonfocal colours have degrees of membership between 0 and 1. In Kay and McDaniel's model, the red–green and yellow–blue neuronal responses directly determine the basic categories red, green, yellow, and blue. Orange, purple, brown, and pink, however, are said to be generated by an additional type of operation on these neuronal responses that corresponds to fuzzy set intersection. Thus orange is the fuzzy set intersection of red and yellow, purple of red and blue, pink of white and red, and brown of black and yellow. (Black and white are directly determined in the model by achromatic response cells.) Since these categories require such a higher-level operation, Kay and McDaniel term them *derived* basic colour categories. Their conclusion is that 'the semantics of basic color terms in all languages directly reflect the existence of these pan-human neural response categories' (1978: 609).

At this point, one might suppose that the models and empirical findings of Berlin and Kay, Rosch, and Kay and McDaniel support neurophysiological subjectivism and internalism about chromatic perceptual content.[19] It should therefore be noted that Kay and McDaniel's model rests on highly problematic 'linking propositions' (Teller and Pugh 1983; Teller 1984, 1990) between the perceptual experience of red, green, yellow, and blue and the existence of chromatically opponent cells that are given the somewhat misleading labels 'red–green' and 'yellow–blue'. As discussed in Chapter 2, there are numerous issues that arise when one attempts to relate colour opponency at the perceptual and psychophysical levels to the physiological level; in particular, the analogy between the existence of opponent colours and the existence of chromatically opponent cells neglects many details of fit between the properties of colour perception and the properties of these cells (Hood and Finkelstein 1983; Teller 1990).

Additional findings indicate that colour categories, though experiential and embodied, are not simply a function of the neurophysiological constitution of the perceiver. First, as Lakoff (1987: 29) discusses, Kay and McDaniel's model predicts that the boundaries, as well as the focal colours, should be uniform across languages. Such uniformity is not the case, however. There are significant variations in the placement of non-primary focal colours, such as purple and brown. Lakoff reports that 'MacLaury has found cases where purple is entirely within the cool color range (a single color with focal points at blue and green) and other cases where purple is on the boundary between cool and red. He has also found cases where brown is subsumed by yellow and other cases where it is subsumed by black' (1987: 29). On the basis of these results, Lakoff argues that the cognitive operations that specify colour categories 'vary in their boundary conditions from culture to culture. They are thus at least partly a matter of convention, and not completely a matter of universal neurophysiology and cognition' (1987: 30).

Second, although the work of Berlin and Kay, and of Rosch, has shown the great extent to which colour perception affects colour language, some findings suggest that colour language can also affect perception. In a study designed to test the 'Sapir–Whorf' hypothesis, Kay and Kempton (1984) found that the lexical classification of colours can affect subjective judgements of similarity among colours. For example, English contains terms for both green and blue, whereas Tarahumara (a Uto-Aztecan language of northern Mexico) has a single term that means 'green or blue'. This linguistic difference does appear to correlate with a difference in subjective judgements of similarity among colours: English speakers tend to exaggerate the subjective distances of colours close to the green–blue boundary, whereas Tarahumara speakers do not. Kay and Kempton argue that this effect results from what they call the 'name strategy': 'the speaker who is confronted with a difficult task of classificatory judgement may use the lexical classification of the judged objects as if it were correlated with the required dimension of judgement even when it is not, so long as the structure of the task does not block this possibility' (1984: 75). Kay and Kempton argue that although this effect does not support the strong claims that Whorf (1956) made about language determining experience, it does support a more modest Whorfian view in which some differences in non-linguistic cognition (subjective judgements of similarity) can be correlated with differences in linguistic structure.

Finally, recent studies indicate that cultural conditions too can contribute to the neurophysiological and cognitive operations that are involved in the generation of colour categories. For example, MacLaury (1987) reports that many Native American languages of the Pacific North-West use one colour term to name both yellow and green, and so possess a yellow-with-green colour category. It does not seem possible to explain the development of this category in neurophysiological terms. As MacLaury remarks:

> There is no known physiological mechanism that would encourage the development of the yellow-with-green

category, and probably there is a mechanism that would discourage its development at the expense of displacing the cool category ...

The wide recurrence of the cool category suggests that speakers of most languages categorize color in compliance with physiology. But the rare emergence of the yellow-with-green category implies that a nonphysiological incentive can supersede neural constraints. At least, the implication counters what little we know of visual physiology.

(1987: 112, 116)

These three aspects of human colour categories – the variations in category boundaries from culture to culture, the modest Whorfian effects of colour language on colour perception, and the development of colour categories that cannot be predicted from neurophysiology – suggest that the perceptual content of human colour vision cannot be completely specified in purely internalist, neurophysiological terms. The categorical structure of human colour experience is constituted by a tangled hierarchy of perceptual and cognitive processes, some species-specific and others culture-specific. As Lakoff observes in his discussion of this material:

Color concepts are *embodied* in that focal colors are partly determined by human biology. Color categorization makes use of human biology, but color categories are more than merely a consequence of the nature of the world plus human biology. Color categories result from the world plus human biology plus a cognitive mechanism that has some of the characteristics of fuzzy set theory plus a culture-specific choice of which basic color categories there are.[20]

In conclusion, neurophysiological subjectivism is unsatisfactory on both philosophical and scientific grounds because it implies internalism about chromatic perceptual content. In both the nonhuman and human cases, however, certain central features of colour perception – the signal significance of colours as constituted by organic colouration (pigmentation) and categorical colour perceivers, and the experientially significant variations within the categorical structure of phenomenal colour space as constituted by language and culture – cannot be captured in intradermal (for example, neurophysiological) terms. Neurophysiological subjectivism is right when it insists, against computational objectivism, that a purely distal, externalist specification of chromatic perceptual content is fundamentally mistaken. But it is wrong both philosophically and scientifically in its conclusion that perceptual content must therefore be internal and reducible to features of neural processes. On the philosophical side, perceptual content is neither internal nor external because it is *relational*, constituted jointly by both the perceiver and the world. On the scientific side, perceptual content is neither physical (extradermal) nor neurophysiological (intradermal) because it is *ecological*, constituted jointly by both the animal and the environment. The task now before us is to say something more positive about colour and colour perception in ecological terms.

5

THE ECOLOGICAL VIEW

The mechanists have pieced together the sensory and motor organs of animals, like so many parts of a machine, ignoring their real functions of perceiving and acting ... But we who still hold that our sense organs serve our perceptions, and our motor organs our actions, see in animals as well not only the mechanical structure, but also the operator, who is built into their organs, as we are into our bodies. We no longer regard animals as mere machines, but as subjects whose essential activity consists of perceiving and acting. We thus unlock the gates that lead to other realms, for all that a subject perceives becomes his perceptual world and all that he does, his effector world. Perceptual and effector worlds together form a closed unit, the *Umwelt*. These different worlds, which are as manifold as the animals themselves, present to all nature lovers new lands of such wealth and beauty that a walk through them is well worth while, even though they unfold not to the physical but only to the spiritual eye.

(Jakob von Uexküll 1934/1957: 6)

Color is the 'place where our brain and the universe meet'.
(Paul Cézanne, as quoted by
Maurice Merleau-Ponty (1964: 180))

At the beginning and end of Chapter 3 I suggested that the concept of colour as it figures in visual science is inherently double-sided or Janus-faced (Mausfeld et al. 1992: 47) – one side

215

faces the world and the other side faces the perceiver – and I suggested that this feature be taken as the inspiration for a relational ontology of colour. If such an ontology is to be appropriately naturalistic, then the comparative argument pursued in Chapter 4 indicates that the proper descriptive and explanatory level is an ecological one.

THE ECOLOGICAL LEVEL

The term 'ecological' has been used in many different ways, and so it is best to begin by specifying more precisely what I mean by an ecological level of description and explanation. First, as just indicated, an ecological level is naturalistic, as opposed to purely conceptual or a priori. This does not mean that there is no place for conceptual analysis or a priori reflection, but it does mean that such investigations must be pursued in close collaboration with visual science.

Naturalism is not equivalent to reductionism, however. Thus a second crucial feature of the ecological level is its commitment to the view, well articulated by, for example, von Uexküll in the passage above, that the animal is not simply a collection of neuronal and psychophysical processes, but most properly also a perceiving and acting *subject*. The types of generalization that can be stated at the ecological level accordingly include not only generalizations about the psychophysical organization and physiological structure of the perceiving animal, but also ones about the behavioural interactions of the animal as a whole in its environment. In advocating his neurophysiological subjectivist approach to colour perception, Hardin (1988) relies heavily on the first type of generalization, often writing as if he supposed it were adequate to explain colour perception in its entirety, though he does not really believe this (see Hardin 1992a). But the two types of generalization require each other: on the one hand, the perceptually guided, behavioural inter-actions of the animal cannot be fully explained unless we understand how internal processes make them possible, but on the other hand, the role these internal processes play in generating behaviour cannot be fully understood unless we know how the animal as a whole normally behaves in its environment.

Someone sympathetic to neurophysiological subjectivism, or

to neuroscientific reductionism in general in cognitive science (for example, P. M. Churchland 1985, 1986; P. S. Churchland 1986), might wish to argue that the second type of generalization is actually reducible to, or replaceable by, the first. Without even considering the philosophical problems such a proposal would raise, there is evidence from neuroscience itself to speak against it. First, it is important to remember that the neuronal responses that are typically correlated with aspects of visual perception generally occur in anaesthetized animals in highly simplified, artificial, and hence unecological surroundings. For example, as discussed in Chapter 2, Zeki (1983a) found that he could correlate the responses of 'colour-coded' cells in area V4 of the monkey visual cortex with the hues of Mondrian images (as perceived by humans). Since his animals were anaesthetized, however, they were not seeing colours (in one sense of 'seeing') (Boynton 1988: 93). Second, it has been found in other experiments that when animals are awake and behaving in somewhat more normal sensory surroundings many kinds of neuronal response become highly dependent on other behavioural factors, such as the bodily tilt of the animal (Horn and Hill 1969) and auditory stimulation (Morell 1972; Fishman and Michael 1973), as well as attention and the relevance of a stimulus for a behavioural task (Moran and Desimone 1985; Haenny et al. 1988). These results suggest that neuronal responses depend in part on how the animal as a whole is motivated and behaving. It is therefore unlikely that generalizations stated over the animal as a whole interacting in its environment can be reduced to generalizations stated over collections of neural subsystems. This unlikelihood is one reason why an ecological level of explanation, in contrast to a purely neurophysiological one, insists on the importance of a twofold mode of description in which, to borrow Francisco Varela's words, 'we switch back and forth between an organism as a system in its own internal logic, and the organism as a unity in its interactions' (Varela 1984: 217). To make the point in relation to scientific methodology, one might say that, at the ecological level, the role neuronal processes play is revealed by neuroethology rather than neurophysiology per se (Heiligenberg 1991).

The third and final feature of the ecological level to which I wish to draw attention is one of the most important. Biologists have long emphasized that an organism cannot be understood apart from the world with which it interacts, nor can that part of the world with which it interacts – its niche or environment – be understood apart from the organism. For example, Jakob von Uexküll, in his classic work cited above, argued that the environment (*Umwelt*) of an animal is to be specified by referring to what an animal can perceive and can do as determined by its sensorimotor capacities. A more recent example is provided by Richard Lewontin, who, in the context of evolutionary theory, writes:

> The niche is a multidimensional description of all the relations entered into by an organism with the surrounding world ... the external world can be divided up in a noncountable infinity of ways so that there is a noncountable infinity of conceivable ecological niches. Unless there is a preferred and correct way in which to partition the world, the idea of an ecological niche without an organism filling it loses all meaning.
>
> (Lewontin 1980: 237)

Because of this mutual dependence between an animal and its environment, the two can be described as jointly composing a larger system – an animal–environment ecosystem. It is under such a description that, at the ecological level, the animal and its environment are most properly considered.

The environment, taken as a component in an animal–environment ecosystem, does not coincide with the physical world as it might be understood independent of animal life. Instead, the environment is the world so described that it implicates the sensorimotor capacities and evolutionary history of animal life. The idea that sensorimotor capacities are implicated is, of course, evident in the above passage from von Uexküll – the environment (*Umwelt*) corresponds to the co-ordinated perceptual and effector worlds of the animal. And, as I shall discuss later, the perceptual psychologist J. J. Gibson too emphasized a similar idea. He distinguished between the 'physical world', which is independent of the animal, and the 'animal environment', which consists of the 'surroundings of animals', and so is defined in relation to animals and their perceptual and motor activities (Gibson 1979: 7–9).

The implication of the evolutionary history of animal life in the world as an environment deserves special comment. In Neo-Darwinian evolutionary theory the notion of 'adaptation' plays a central role. Richard Levins and Richard Lewontin have challenged the adequacy of this notion, however, claiming that it should be replaced by one of 'construction' (Levins and Lewontin 1985). What is important for our purposes here is not the debate over adaptationism,[1] but rather the phenomena to which Levins and Lewontin draw our attention in their argument. Their main claim is that 'the environment and the organism actively codetermine each other', and consequently that 'The organism cannot be regarded as simply the passive object of autonomous internal and external forces; it is also the subject of its own evolution' (Levins and Lewontin 1985: 89). To show that the organism is subject as well as object, they draw attention to five ways in which a species 'constructs' its environment (99–102): (1) Organisms determine what in the physical world constitutes their environment ('Organisms determine what is relevant'). (2) Organisms alter the external world as they interact with it. (3) Organisms transduce the physical signals that reach them from the outside world, and so the significance the signals have depends on the structure of the organism. (4) Organisms transform the statistical pattern of environmental variation in the external world. (5) The organism–environment relationship defines the 'traits' selected. Each of these five kinds of phenomena involves circular and reciprocal (though not symmetrical) processes of interaction in which the structure of the environment constrains the activity of the organism, but the activity of the organism shapes the environment, and so contributes to the constitution of the environmental constraints (see also Odling-Smee 1988). It is on the basis of these interactive processes that Levins and Lewontin argue that organism and environment codetermine each other.

To summarize this section, the ecological level of description and explanation has three key features. First, it is naturalistic. Second, it involves a twofold mode of description that switches back and forth between, on the one hand, internal processes, and, on the other hand, the animal as a perceiving and acting subject. Third, it considers the animal and its environment as jointly constitutive of a larger animal–environment ecosystem.

Owing to these three features, generalizations at the ecological level can also be classified into three types – generalizations about the internal organization of the perceiver, generalizations about the behavioural interactions of the animal as a whole in its environment, and generalizations about the extra-dermal world as an animal-inhabited environment.

PERCEPTION AND THE ECOLOGICAL LEVEL

In the context of perceptual theory the term 'ecological' is associated with the so-called 'ecological approach' formulated by J. J. Gibson (1979) and developed by his followers (Turvey et al. 1981). The ecological view that I shall present in this chapter will build on Gibson's ecological approach, but will also depart in several significant respects from this theory. In particular, I think it is possible to construct a theoretical and empirical framework in visual science that integrates many of Gibson's insights with both neurophysiology and computational vision (see Bruce and Green 1990). I shall offer some remarks later about the general features such a framework would have. One of the central points of Gibson's approach is his rejection of the representationist framework for understanding visual perception. It is mainly this point on which I wish to build my own ecological view.

Representationism revisited

In Chapter 1 I indicated that by 'representationist' I meant any theory that considers perception to depend on an internal medium in which features of the external world are represented to the perceiver. I also emphasized two general features of representationism – its causal-explanatory order and its principled subjective/objective distinction. These two features are closely connected: the causal-explanatory order corresponds to the sequence physical world → stimulus → sensory transduction → neural processing → perception/experience → action. The objective comprises the physical world and the proximal stimulus; the subjective comprises perceptual experience; and sensory transduction plus neural processing somehow link the two.

In the classical representationism of Newton and Locke, the internal medium of representation consists of mental items called 'ideas' that are the immediate objects of perception. As I discussed briefly in Chapter 4, one way to state this representative theory, as it is usually called, is with reference to the notion of perceptual content. Perceptual states are about something or have objects, and they present what they are about in a certain manner. According to the representative theory, what is seen, the immediate object of a visual state, is a collection of sense-data or ideas, and this collection stands for or represents some physical object external to the perceiver. Thus in this view we do not see the world directly: we see the world only in virtue of seeing ideas.

Most philosophers today no longer subscribe to the representative theory (Jackson 1977 is an exception). But many continue to subscribe to representationism, in particular to representationism based on the computational theory of perception pioneered by Marr (1982). According to this contemporary form of representationism, the internal representations mediating visual perception are not the immediate objects of perception; rather, the object of visual perception is the distal physical world. Internal representations are what enable the perceptual state to be directed towards the world – they *re*present the world to the perceiver in a certain manner. Thus it is often said that we do not see our representations; rather, we 'see right through them', as it were, to the distal world (for example, Dretske 1981).

The computational theory nonetheless takes as fundamental the same question that motivates representationism about visual perception in general: how does one get from impoverished and meaningless (nonintentional) sensory stimuli to meaningful (intentional) percepts? And the answer, of course, is that internal representations mediate between sensory stimulation and perception. Consider again the inverse optics approach to early vision (Marr 1982; Poggio et al. 1985). According to inverse optics, the distal three-dimensional world is not directly presented in visual perception: what are directly presented are two-dimensional projections on the retinal surface. The task is to understand how the three-dimensional world can be 'recovered' from such two-dimensional projections. Given only the retinal image, the problem admits of no unique solution; it is underconstrained or ill-posed. The problem must therefore be regularized by introducing constraints that restrict the class of admissible solutions. The constraints involve assumptions about the physical world and operations internal to the perceiver that mediate between sensory stimuli and perception. The operations 'recover' the distal world from proximal projections and in so doing represent the world to the perceiver.

The problem with this contemporary form of representationism is that it does not do justice to the ecological relation between the perceiving animal and the world.[2] First, the animal and its environment are treated as fundamentally separate systems. The distal world is specified in advance and provides a source of input that is independent of the animal; the perceiving animal, on the other hand, is treated as an input-output system among whose functions is to solve the ill-posed problem of recovering the prespecified world. Second, perceptual and motor capacities are treated as fundamentally distinct subsystems of the animal. Since the outputs of perceptual systems are considered to be ultimately perceptual beliefs about the distal scene, perceptual systems form a mechanism for the fixation of belief. On the basis of its perceptual beliefs, the animal may adjust its activity, but the adjustment of activity per se is not treated as part of the perceptual process. Third, visual perception does not shape the environment: it merely recovers the physical world. And although it might be admitted that animal activity can modify or shape the world into an environment, visual perception per se, since it is fundamentally distinct from action, does not participate in this process. In other words, in visual perception there is no coupling back from the animal to the environment: such coupling is the result only of action.

If perception is considered to be fundamentally distinct from action, then the ecological relation between the perceiving animal and its environment will never be evident at the perceptual level. Consequently, any theory that wishes to understand visual perception within an ecological context must refuse to separate perception from action. This refusal has been most strenuously and consistently voiced by Gibson and his followers, and so I turn now to consider their theory.

Gibson's 'ecological approach'

In his book *The Ecological Approach to Visual Perception* (1979), Gibson argues against both the causal-explanatory order and the principled subjective/objective distinction of representationism. He begins by distinguishing between two levels of description and explanation, the physical and the ecological. The former includes the physical and physiological processes involved in sensory stimulation; the latter is composed by the animal as an active perceiving subject and the world as an animal environment. In taking the perceiving animal to be an active subject, Gibson criticizes the construal of visual perception as receptive and passive implicit in the representationist causal-explanatory order (stimulus → sensory transduction → neural processing → perception/experience → action). In an ecological context perception is always perceptually guided activity. Perception and action have evolved together, coupled to each other: perceptual systems serve to guide activity and motor systems serve to direct perception. Thus perception and action coordinate to form a basic functional unity (Kelso and Kay 1987). The processes that compose this unity have a causal order that is fundamentally circular: it is the perceptually guided bodily activity of the animal that typically brings about the stimulation and sensory response that in turn initiate perceptually guided activity. Turning now to the world as an animal environment, Gibson tries to sidestep the representationist problem of how to get from impoverished physical stimuli to meaningful and subjectively rich percepts by arguing that, at the ecological level, the environment is already significant for the animal. The environment, as discussed above, relationally implies the animal, and so is not an indifferent physical world. Consisting of 'textured surfaces which are themselves immersed in a medium (air)' (Bruce and Green 1990: 225), it serves as the ground on which and the air through which an animal lives and moves. Because it thus implicates the animal, the environment supports certain kinds of animal-significant properties that would not be revealed in a neutral physical description. In Gibson's terminology, these properties result from the 'mutuality of animal and environment' (Gibson 1979: 8), and so require an ecological level for their specification.

Gibson calls the most significant type of ecological property an *affordance* (1979: 127–43). An affordance is a relational property of something in the environment: it consists in a particular sort of opportunity for interaction that something in the environment has in relation to the animal. For example, trees, in relation to certain animals, afford climbing; they are climb-up-able and so fall within the extension of the affordance climb-up-able thing. An affordance is related to another kind of ecological-level property called by Turvey et al. (1981) *effectivities*. An effectivity is a relational property of an animal: it consists in a particular sort of opportunity for interaction that the animal has in relation to the environment. For example, lizards are things that climb, and so fall within the extension of the effectivity climber-thing. Since these two types of properties are relational, they are neither objective nor subjective in the representationist sense. As Gibson writes:

> an affordance is neither an objective property nor a subjective property; or it is both if you like. An affordance cuts across the dichotomy of subjective–objective and helps us to understand its inadequacy. It is equally a fact of the environment and a fact of behavior. It is both physical and psychical, yet neither.
>
> (1979: 129)

In the writings of other Gibsonian theorists, affordances and effectivities have been given a more positive characterization as emergent and systemic properties of animal–environment ecosystems or of what Gibsonians call the animal–environment mutuality (Prindle et al. 1980; Turvey et al. 1981: 260–7).

The main effort of Gibson's theory is devoted not to the specification of ecological properties, however, but rather to explaining how an environment containing such properties can be perceived. Gibson's theory of visual perception can be summarized in two main assertions: visual perception is intentional and it is direct. It is intentional in the familiar sense already discussed of being about or directed towards things. In the Gibsonian view the things to which visual perception is directed are simply 'the things that populate an environment' (Turvey et al. 1981: 242). Thus, contrary to the representative theory, perception is not directed towards any intermediate psychological item, such as sensations, sense-data, or mental images. This is one reason why Gibson claims that perception is direct. Another reason is that he denies visual perception depends on cognitive processes such as belief, memory, and inference. It is primarily this reason, I think, that has led both Gibson and his followers to argue that, for visual perception to be direct, it cannot depend on internal operations of the sort typically hypothesized in computational vision. Here the Gibsonian approach strikes me as much less persuasive, but the adjudication of this dispute is a complex matter, and so I shall postpone discussion of it until the next section.

How, then, is the environment perceived according to Gibson? His central hypothesis, which defines his ecological approach as a research programme in visual science, is that the topological structure of the ambient light directly specifies its environmental source. Gibson claims, in other words, that there are lawful correlations between properties of the ambient light and ecological properties such as affordances. It must be emphasized that these correlations are not supposed to hold for properties of the light reflected locally from some area in the scene. Rather, they hold for properties of the 'ambient optic array', which is defined as the pattern of light reaching a point in space from all directions, and the 'optic flow field', which is defined as the fluctuating pattern of light intensity reaching the perceiver as caused by any relative movement between the perceiver and the environment. The relevant optical properties are thus high-level, global properties of the light in a scene corresponding to 'invariant ratios and relations' (Gibson 1972: 255) in transformations of the optic array and optic flow field over time. This feature of Gibson's hypothesis is very important because it is well known that features such as wavelength and intensity as reflected locally by an area are not sufficient to specify their environmental source. Indeed, the tradition in perceptual psychology dating back to von Helmholtz has appealed to representation and unconscious inference largely on the basis of this insufficiency: since local intensity-values at the retina are insufficient to specify features of the environment, these must be inferred, but this type of inference would require internal representations to serve as premises; hence visual perception depends on inferences of which the perceiver is unaware. On the other hand, if there are high-level properties of the light in a scene that do unambiguously specify the environment, then visual perception would presumably not require inference, and so need not depend on internal representations. Thus Gibson rejects the idea that perception is mediated by inference, claiming instead that the perceptual system 'resonates' to invariants in the optic array and the optic flow field that directly inform the perceiver about both himself or herself and the environment. It is in this sense that Gibson claims information is simply 'picked up' or 'attended to', not 'processed'.

The extent to which there are such perceptually informative, lawful correlations between the environment and the optic array and optic flow field is an open empirical question. But Gibsonians have produced a significant body of experimental findings in support of their ecological approach to visual perception (for an overview see Bruce and Green 1990). To cite only one example, Lee (1980) has shown that there is a parameter of the optic flow field that specifies time-to-contact under constant closing velocity when an animal is moving towards a surface or an object is approaching. This parameter, which Lee calls τ (tau), is the ratio (at a given time) of the distance of any point from the centre of an expanding optic flow pattern to its velocity away from the centre. In what they describe as a 'paradigm of ecological optics', Lee and Reddish (1981) have shown that the gannet, a seabird that catches fish by plummeting into the water from heights of up to 30 metres and at speeds of up to 24 metres per second (54 m.p.h.), employs a strategy based on detecting values of this optical parameter in order to determine the optimum time to streamline its wings as it approaches the water.

Having outlined the main features of the Gibsonian approach, I wish now to turn to a somewhat more philosophical issue – the ontological status of the environment and of ecological-level properties such as affordances. Gibson's own writings are not clear on this matter. For example, although affordances are relational properties of the 'animal–environment mutuality', Gibson also sometimes describes them as independent of the perceiving animal:

The affordance of something does *not change* as the need

of the observer changes. The observer may or may not perceive or attend to the affordance, according to his needs, but the affordance, being invariant, is always there to be perceived. An affordance is not bestowed upon an object by a need of an observer and his act of perceiving it. The object offers what it does because it is the object it is.

(Gibson 1979: 138–9)

Gibson makes a similar point about invariance in the ambient optic array:

invariance comes from reality, not the other way round. Invariance in the ambient optic array is not constructed or deduced; it is there to be discovered.

(Gibson 1972: 293)

In the first remark Gibson's concern is to emphasize that affordances are not projected on to the environment by the perceiver; in the second, it is to emphasize that the optical invariances that specify affordances are not constructed from or inferred on the basis of internal representations. But there are several issues here that need to be disentangled. The first is whether internal representations play a role in the visual perception of affordances. Clearly they cannot, in Gibson's view, because his entire approach is nonrepresentationist. The second is whether affordances must be *specified* in relation to the perceiving animal. Clearly they must, because an affordance is defined as an opportunity for animal interaction possessed by something in the environment. The third is whether affordances depend for their existence on the perceiving animal, or to put the point the other way round, whether the perceiving animal plays a role in determining what an affordance is. Gibson does not consider this third idea with the precision it demands. He supposes that although affordances are relationally specified, they are not subjective because they are not projected on to the environment, and so they must exist independently of the perceiver. But this conclusion does not follow. Gibson has conflated subjectivism – the view that affordances depend on the animal because they are mentally or cognitively projected on to the environment – with the quite different idea that affordances are constituted in part by the animal because they are ecological-level properties of the animal–environment mutuality. Gibson has forgotten the implications of his own insight that affordances are neither objective nor subjective, that they are 'equally a fact of the environment and a fact of behavior'.

Several commentators have noticed the lack of clarity in Gibson's treatment of affordances and have tried to resolve the matter in various ways.[3] Heft (1989) argues that although affordances are relationally specified, they can be said to exist independently of the perceiver in two senses. First, affordances can be taken as dispositional properties whose grounds or bases are the physical properties of things in the environment. Whether something potentially affords, say, climbing (i.e., has the dispositional property of affording climbing) depends on its material constitution, which is independent of the perceiving animal, though the manifestation of the disposition depends on the presence of the animal. Second, an affordance is 'always there to be perceived' because, according to the Gibsonian hypothesis, there are lawful correlations between affordances and invariances in the ambient optic array and optic flow field.

Construing affordances as dispositional properties has also been suggested by Turvey et al. (1981). They present affordances and effectivities as emergent or systemic properties of the animal–environment mutuality. In this presentation, affordances and effectivities do depend in part on the animal for their existence because they are ecological-level dispositional properties, unlike physical-level dispositional properties, such as solubility or fragility:

> the dispositions of an organism-free world and the dispositions of an organism-populated world, *viz.*, affordances, are not of the same order. The latter are ontologically condensed out of the former, so to speak, by the presence of living things. As such dispositional properties exist whether there are living things or not; but affordances exist only in their mutuality with living things.
>
> (Turvey et al. 1981: 263)

228

Turvey et al. (1981) do uphold the second sense in which affordances are independent of the animal, however, namely, that they 'are always there to be perceived' because they are lawfully specified in the ambient light. They formulate this idea in the following way (where X stands for a thing, a for a property of that thing, and Z for an animal):

The perceiving of X-having-a by Z presupposes a law L: an ambient energy property e is nomically related to a in that it is unique and specific to a in Z's niche.

(1981: 283)[4]

Perhaps the most useful philosophical treatment of affordances is provided by Ben-Ze'ev (1984, 1988, 1989). He argues for two important and related distinctions. First, one must distinguish between actual and potential properties of the environment. Actual properties are those found in that part of the environment that actually existing animals encounter at a given time; potential properties are those that the animals have the capacities to encounter. As potential properties affordances are independent of actually existing animals, but they do depend on the animal when the animal and the environment are considered on the same level of modality (Ben Ze'ev 1984: 74–5). Second, one must distinguish between statements made within the framework of a given environment and statements made about the framework of a given environment: 'When we speak within the framework of the ecological reality ... the affordances ... may have a non-relational and independent existence. But when we discuss the very basis of the ecological reality ... or when we compare that reality to the physical world, we should realize the relational nature of affordances and their dependence on the animal' (Ben Ze'ev 1984: 77).

I think that Gibson and his followers have not fully embraced the animal-dependence of the environment because of their desire to uphold direct realism against idealism in perceptual theory. Ben-Ze'ev (1984: 76–7) cites Michaels and Carello (1981: 100) as asserting that in the ecological approach it is the existence of the animal that contributes to the constitution of the environment, rather than the perception of the animal as idealism claims. But, as Ben-Ze'ev rightly goes on to observe, this issue depends on how perception is characterized:

> If (following the traditional approach) perception is characterized as a production process at the end of which percepts are produced, then this process inevitably contributes to the perceptual reality. If however, perception – or better yet, perceiving – is characterized as a state of awareness of the ecological environment ... this state does not contribute anything to that environment. However, the very existence of this state presupposes contributions of both the perceiver and his surroundings.
>
> (Ben-Ze'ev 1984: 77)

Ben-Ze'ev's point can be further refined. For Gibson perception must always be understood as perceptually guided activity. Strictly speaking, then, Gibson must consider perception to be not simply awareness of the environment, but activity guided by awareness of the environment. In his words:

> Perceiving is an achievement of the individual, not an experience in the theatre of consciousness. It is a keeping-in-touch with the world, an experience of things rather than a having of experiences. It involves awareness-of instead of just awareness ... perception is not a mental act. Neither is it a bodily act. Perceiving is a psychosomatic act, not of mind or of body, but of a living observer.
>
> (Gibson 1979: 239–40)

Awareness considered simply as a state does not participate in the constitution of the environment. But considered more properly as a psychosomatic act (perceptually guided activity) it not only presupposes contributions of both the perceiving animal and its surroundings, but also participates in shaping the physical world into an environment.

So far I have considered only the status of the environment and ecological-level properties such as affordances, not the hypothesis that such properties are lawfully specified in the ambient light. But there are subtleties to this hypothesis too, ones which Gibsonians – again because of their desire to uphold direct realism against idealism – have largely neglected.

Gibsonians typically emphasize how the distal layout of the environment sculpts the light it reflects in such a way that higher-order invariances of the ambient optic array and the optic flow field lawfully specify environmental features. But just as significant are the ways in which the light is sculpted by an active moving perceiver. For example, consider a perceiver standing at the edge of a precipice. Movement by the perceiver will make the edge of the supporting surface shear the texture of the surface below (E. J. Gibson 1969). Here the transformations in the ambient light that inform the perceiver about 'falling-off places' are generated by the perceiver's movement in relation to the distal layout; the structure of the light is not waiting ready-made for the perceiver having been already fully sculpted by the environment.

The point can be generalized. Within an ecological context visual perception is in Gibson's words both 'ambient' and 'ambulatory': the perceiver moves his or her head to scan the layout visually while simultaneously moving through the environment. Thus visual perception occurs not as a series of snapshots or images at a point, but as a dynamic visual flow. Within the flow the perceptually informative parameters in the optic array and optic flow field depend on both the distal layout and the moving perceiver. It should be emphasized that this is not a subjectivist or idealist point – it is not being asserted that invariance in the ambient light is *mentally* imposed or constructed. Rather, the point is that the *body* of the animal, its sensorimotor organization and behaviour, *shapes the light in ways relevant to the animal's adaptive ecological needs*. Though not acknowledged as such, this point is in fact implicit in Turvey et al.'s (1981) formulation of the Gibsonian hypothesis cited above, for it relativizes the lawful correlations between the ambient light and the environment to a given animal niche, and it is well known that 'niche' is a relational concept that implicates a given animal's sensorimotor organization and behavioural repertoire (Lewontin 1980).

On the whole, Gibsonians have resisted this implication of their own hypothesis. Instead, they continue to place virtually exclusive emphasis on how the distal layout sculpts and is specified by the ambient light. Thus they attempt to build up perceptual theory entirely from the side of the environment, neglecting both the neuroethological and evolutionary processes that have brought forth that environment from the physical world and the complex internal processes that are required for the visual guidance of activity within that environment. By showing how the environment an animal encounters is already significant, though in an animal-dependent way, Gibson and his followers have taken a monumental step away from representationism and its problem-space of subjective-versus-objective. But their ecological approach needs to be aligned both with theories of the neuroethological and evolutionary processes involved in animal–environment 'mutuality' or 'codetermination' and with theories of the internal organization of the animal at the neurophysiological level as well as the algorithmic and task levels typical of computational research.[5]

The ecological approach and computational vision

In this chapter I have been arguing for the necessity of an ecological level of explanation in perceptual theory. Contrary to the Gibsonian tendency, however, I have also just emphasized the need for computational and neuroscientific levels as well. In this section I wish to consider in more detail how I see the relation between Gibson's ecological approach and the computational approach of Marr (1982) and his colleagues (Poggio et al. 1985).

In the first chapter of his posthumous book *Vision* Marr presents his own view of the relation between his work and Gibson's:

> Gibson's important contribution was to take the debate away from philosophical considerations of sense-data and the affective qualities of sensation and to note instead that the important thing about the senses is that they are channels for perception of the real world outside, or, in the case of vision, of the visible surfaces. He therefore asked the critically important question, How does one obtain constant perceptions in everyday life on the basis of continually changing sensations? This is exactly the right question, showing that Gibson correctly regarded the problem of perception as that of recovering from sensory information 'valid' properties of the external

world. His problem was that he had a much over-simplified view of how this should be done. His approach led him to consider higher-order variables – stimulus energy, ratios, proportions, and so on – as 'invariants' of the movement of an observer and of changes in stimulation intensity ... its major, and in my view, fatal shortcoming ... results from a failure to realize two things. First, the detection of physical invariants, like image surfaces, is exactly and precisely an information-processing problem, in modern terminology. And second, he vastly underrated the sheer difficulty of such detection.

(Marr 1982: 29–30)

Marr's view is basically that Gibson's ecological approach is nothing but an inadequate attempt to formulate a computational or information-processing level of explanation. But Marr has almost completely misunderstood Gibson in these passages. It is true that Gibson argued that the senses should be considered as systems for the perception of the world (Gibson 1966) or of the animal environment (Gibson 1979). But he then went on to argue that perception is not based at all on sensation (1966: 2, 1968–9) and consequently that 'The puzzle of constant perception despite varying sensation disappears' (1966: 320). What Marr claims is the 'critically important' and 'right question' about perception, and attributes to Gibson – how does one obtain constant perceptions in everyday life on the basis of continually changing sensations? – is precisely the question that Gibson and his followers *reject* as the starting point for perceptual theory (see Prindle et al. 1980; Reed 1980). Gibson strenuously denied that visual perception requires an internal medium of representation, and so he cannot consistently have regarded perception as the 'problem' of 'recovering' from impoverished sensations features of the external world.

Two key features of the Gibsonian ecological approach must be emphasized in this context. The first is its refusal to separate perception from action. In holding that perception is perceptually guided activity, the Gibsonian approach takes the 'result' or 'output' of a perceptual system to be not a perceptual judgement or belief that is relayed to some more central system, but rather a perceptuomotor adjustment in the activity of the whole animal as it explores its environment (see Shaw

233

and Todd 1980; Turvey et al. 1981: 241). As Gibson puts it: 'In my theory, perception is *not* supposed to occur in the brain but to arise in the retino-neuro-muscular system as an activity of the whole system ... Retinal inputs lead to ocular adjustments, and then to altered retinal inputs, and so on. It is an exploratory circular process, not a one-way delivery of messages to the brain' (1972: 217–18).

The second feature is implicit in the first. It is the level of generalization at which the Gibsonian theory primarily resides – the whole animal as a perceiving-acting subject. Perceiving is an act that is performed by the animal, not by its brain. Although the brain subserves the act of perceiving, it is not the subject of this act. Perception depends on the delivery of messages to and within the brain, but it is the animal that perceives, not the brain or some central system within the brain.

It is within the context of these two key features that Gibson's denial that visual perception is information-processing must be understood. Perceiving is not information-processing because the *animal*, the proper subject of perception, does not process information: it simply attends to the world. When Gibson says that the animal picks up or takes in information, but does not process it, the 'information' he has in mind is contained in the world or the environment that the animal itself sees. In contrast, when Marr says that visual perception is information-processing, the 'information' he has in mind is contained in the retinal images and regularization constraints that must be brought to bear on the images to derive or recover features of the world. But this sort of information-processing is not an act that the animal performs: rather it is something accomplished by the animal's visual system.

Marr claims that vision is information-processing because 'vision is the *process* of discovering from images what is present in the world, and where it is' (1982: 3). The images are patterns of light reflected on to the retinal array, and to discover what is present in the world and where it is, the content the images contain must be extracted and reconstructed by complex internal operations. At the level of the visual system this definition of vision provides a fertile scientific research programme, but when (mis)applied at the level of the animal it leads to conceptual confusions and category errors of the worst homuncular sort. Consider, for example, this statement of Marr's: 'The purpose of these representations [the primal sketch and 2½-D sketch involved in early vision] is to provide useful descriptions of aspects of the real world' (1982: 43). Who is reading the descriptions? The animal simply sees aspects of the world. Marr is of course right when he insists that, at the level of the visual system, complex internal operations are required for visual perception. Thus in one sense vision can be described as the process of discovering from images what is present in the world and where it is. But Gibson is also right when he insists that, at the level of the animal as a perceiving-acting subject, what is directly present in visual perception is simply the world. There is therefore another sense in which vision is not a process of *discovering from images* what is present in the world and where it is, but rather a process of *exploration* in which the perceiver *discovers through a perceptual system* what is present in the world and where it is. At the level of the animal, there are no images and representations in visual perception; there is rather a perception-action system that enables the animal to guide its activity visually and thereby visually explore its world.

Although Marr misunderstands Gibson, the criticisms he expresses at the end of the above-quoted passage are valid and point to one of the major shortcomings of the Gibsonian approach as a scientific theory of visual perception – its failure to try to explain *how* visual perception arises as an activity of the whole system and *how* perceptual systems accomplish their tasks. The hypothesis at the centre of the Gibsonian theory is that perceptual systems 'resonate' to invariants in the optic array and the optic flow field that directly inform the perceiving animal about both itself and the environment. But how exactly is this accomplished at the level of the animal's perceptual systems? The concept of 'resonance' is evocative, but without being embedded in some theory – now at the level not of the animal but of the internal organization of its perceptuomotor systems – it remains metaphorical. Thus once again we see the necessity of complementing the Gibsonian approach with neuroscientific and computational theories of the internal organization of the perceiver.

Integrating computational vision, neuroscience, and the ecological level: an action-based paradigm

Marr's computational theory is (among other things) one attempt to provide a framework for rigorously formulating the principles involved in visual perception at the level of the internal organization of the perceiver. I have concentrated on Marr up to now because he tries to appropriate Gibson as a forerunner to his own pioneering computational approach[6] and because his inverse optics conception of early vision has dominated the computational approach to colour vision. But there are, of course, many other theories and models of perceptual systems in the fields of computational and neural network research (see Zornetzer et al. 1990). And a significant number of these theories and models involve departing, in different ways and to varying degrees, from one or the other, and sometimes both, of the two main assumptions of representationism in its contemporary computational form – the prespecification of the world independently of the perceptuomotor organization and behavioural repertoires of the perceiving animal, and the separation of perception and action. In the field of neural networks, for example, Stephen Grossberg, Gail Carpenter, and their colleagues have worked for many years developing mathematical models of perception, adaptive pattern recognition, and motor control in environments that are nonstationary and not prespecified (Grossberg 1982, 1988; Carpenter and Grossberg 1990); another example is the work of George Reeke, Jr and Gerald Edelman on models for the adaptive perceptuomotor categorization of objects and events based on selectionist theories of brain function (Reeke and Edelman 1988; Reeke et al. 1990).[7] Even in the field of robotics, which answers to immediate and pragmatic engineering concerns, Rodney Brooks (1986, 1987, 1989, 1991) has argued that representations in the form of an internal symbolic model of the world should be replaced by 'layers' of 'activity-producing systems', each of which 'individually connects sensing to action' (Brooks 1986).

But perhaps the most interesting development in relation to the issues that concern us here is an area of research at the interface of computational vision, artificial intelligence, and robotics known as *animate vision* (Ballard 1991). In contrast to the view that the purpose of vision is to represent the physical world, 'animate vision argues that vision is more readily understood in the context of the visual behaviors that the system is engaged in, and that these behaviors may not require elaborate categorical representations of the 3-D world' (Ballard 1981: 57–8). Here the term 'behaviour' is being used to refer to visually guided activities, as in, for example, behaviours depending on hand–eye coordination. But as Ballard notes later in the article, in animate vision the term 'behaviour' is also 'used … in a very general sense to capture the self-motion of the animate system as well as the structure of the environment ("the behavior of the environment") in which the system operates' (69). The environment is of course dynamic, not static, and so animate vision depends on continual processes of motor-coupling back to the environment, thus making vision active and exploratory rather than passive and receptive. On the basis of a review of the computer vision literature, Ballard argues that situating vision within such an interactive behavioural context considerably simplifies and improves the computations involved in various visual tasks.

The central design feature in animate vision is 'gaze control' – a collection of processes that keep the fovea of the eye fixed on a given spatial target while the perceiver and/or things in the environment move. Thus the degrees of freedom of the eyes (or cameras) are controlled by the animal (or robot) itself as it interacts with its environment. As Ballard observes:

> Gaze control mechanisms fundamentally change computational models of vision. Without them the visual system must work in isolation, with the burden of solving difficult problems with many degrees of freedom. With them a new paradigm emerges in which the visual calculations are embedded in a sensory-motor behavioral repertoire. Rather than thinking of visual processing as separate from cognitive or motor processing, they are interlinked in terms of integral behaviors.
>
> (1991: 61)

One of the most interesting implications of gaze control is that, by enabling visual fixation on a spatial target, it also enables the visual system to choose a coordinate frame that is viewer-orientated but world-centred. Such a coordinate frame is called the 'frame of fixation' because it is centred on the point of viewer-fixation in the environment. Depending on the perceiver's goals, expectations, etc., the vision system actively selects a fixation frame through gaze control and then has the task of relating the information present in the frame to object-centred coordinate frames (Ballard 1991: 62, Figure 3). In contrast, a passive vision system is constrained to rely largely on the viewer-centred frame of reference provided by the optical properties of the eye (or camera),[8] a limitation making the computations involved in early vision considerably more difficult.

In Ballard's formulation the animate vision paradigm is explicitly anthropomorphic in the sense that it is based on the principles and design features of the human (or primate) visual system, and is 'geared towards hand–eye coordination behaviors' (1991: 58). But 'animate vision also has its roots in the study of vision of the lower animals' (ibid.), and so we might take the term more broadly to denote an action-based paradigm for investigating visual perception in general in natural and artificial systems.

Indeed, an action-based paradigm can be generalized beyond its anthropomorphic base in Ballard's programme of animate vision by considering the three features of the ecological level of explanation that I developed in the first section of this chapter. An action-based approach is clearly naturalistic, and so we can set aside this first feature and turn to the other two – the twofold mode of description that switches back and forth between internal processes and the animal as a perceiving-acting subject, and the animal and its environment considered as jointly constitutive of an animal–environment ecosystem. In an action-based approach, the animal, rather than some computational homunculus centrally lodged in the animal's brain, is explicitly acknowledged as the proper subject of perception, and this subject is moreover considered to be active and exploratory, not passive and receptive. Here the Gibsonian tradition must once more be recognized, for it has done more to recognize and develop this point than other traditions in perceptual psychology and psychophysics. But unlike the general trend of Gibsonian research the action-based paradigm clearly recognizes the need for algorithmic explanations at the level of the internal processes that subserve perception and action. These two levels of the animal and its internal processes are not insulated from each other, however. The behavioural repertoires of the animal are subserved by perceptuomotor systems that possess a variety of special-purpose algorithms, but the behavioural repertoires also constrain the algorithms. In Ballard's words: 'If these special-purpose algorithms [ones where including the behaviour simplifies the computation – shape from shading, time to adjacency, kinetic depth, colour homing, edge homing] were the rule rather than the exception, then it may be that the visuo-motor system is best thought of as a very large amount of distinct special-purpose algorithms where the results of a computation can only be interpreted if the behavioral state is known' (1991: 69). Finally, turning to the third feature of the ecological level, the action-based pro-gramme implicitly recognizes the animal and its environment as jointly constitutive of an ecosystem, for it explicitly situates visual perception in the context of animal–environment behaviour.

What distinguishes such an action-based paradigm from more traditional computational approaches, then, is that, rather than asking how a prespecified world is to be recovered from images, it asks how visual processes enable the animal to explore its environment. The key idea is to embed visual processes in the sensorimotor behavioural repertoires of the perceiver and in the structure of the perceiver's environment.[9] Thus, at the level of the algorithms involved in visual percep-tion, the reference point shifts from an animal-independent environment that must be recovered to the visuomotor behav-iour of the animal embedded in its environment.

This point can be appreciated by considering the non-anthropomorphic, indeed nonmammalian, visual system of birds, the most visual of animals. The avian retina has two regions of high neuronal density (foveas), which give rise to distinct frontal and lateral visual fields that in turn correspond roughly to further anatomical projections in the brain – the parallel thalamo-fugal and tecto-fugal pathways. Experiments reveal interesting differences between these two visual fields: frontal fixation is used for static and slow stimuli, and lateral fixation for fast-moving stimuli (Maldonado et al. 1988). There are also differences in accommodation, depth of focus (Bloch and Martinoya 1983), spectral sensitivity (Nuboer and Wortel 1987; Remy and Emmerton 1989), and probably colour vision (Varela et al. 1983). Thus, visual discrimination for birds is not a cyclopean image reconstruction, but a contextualized specification according to avian sensorimotor activity – a visuomotor world-to-the-front and a visuomotor world-to-the-side are specified by the animal. It is the visuomotor behaviour that actually reveals what is the relevant world for the animal, not a reconstruction of the world as it appears visually to us.

The action-based approach also has implications for the explanation of visual perception at neuroscientific levels. Consider the entire system of the animal plus its environment. The motor activity of the animal changes the arrangement and constitution of things in the environment, as well as the relative position and posture of the animal; these changes in both the animal and the environment modify the animal's sensory activity both internally and at receptor surfaces; in turn these changes in sensory activity modify motor activity, which again leads to changes in both the animal and the environment. In this continuing circular process, various kinds of sensorimotor patterns of activity are generated in the animal. The specific nature of the patterns depends on both the kinds of neural networks that couple the sensory and motor surfaces of the animal and on the local environmental context of activity. Thus at this neurophysiological level the perceptual guidance of activity is subserved by approximately invariant patterns of activity in the sensori-neuronal-motor linkages (Varela 1979, 1984; Maturana and Varela 1980, 1987). It bears repetition, especially in this neuroscientific context, however, that the subject of perception is the animal, and so the anatomical and physiological study of perceptual systems needs to be complemented by a neuroethological approach to the animal (Heiligenberg 1991).

By thus shifting the emphasis from an animal-independent world to the visuomotor behaviour of the animal in its environment the action-based paradigm brings both computational vision and neuroscience into alignment with what Levins and Lewontin (1985) call the 'codetermination' of animal and environment – the idea that during evolution animal and environment 'construct' each other. In arguing for this idea, Levins and Lewtontin point to a variety of ways in which animal activity shapes the physical world into an environment (see above). In the case of visually perceiving animals, action is constantly coupled to visual perception: visual perception guides action and action directs perception. For such animals visual perception – that is, visually guided activity – plays a central role in the 'construction' of the environment:

> our central nervous systems are not fitted to some absolute laws of nature, but to laws of nature operating within a framework created by our own sensuous activity. Our nervous system does not allow us to see the ultraviolet reflections from flowers, but a bee's central nervous system does. And bats 'see' what nighthawks do not. We do not further our understanding of evolution by general appeals to 'laws of nature' to which all life must bend. Rather, we must ask how, within the general constraints of the laws of nature, organisms have constructed environments that are the conditions for their further evolution and reconstruction of nature into new environments.
>
> (Levins and Lewontin 1985: 103–4)

The 'construction' and 'reconstruction' of environments to which Levins and Lewontin draw attention happens on an evolutionary time-scale. On the time-scale of ontogeny, however, the environment is comparatively constant and stable. Nevertheless, there is a sense of animal–environment 'co-determination' that applies to visual perception even on the time-scale of individual animal life, for it is the visuomotor behaviour of the animal that endows the purely physical world with ecological significance.

Colour vision provides one of the most vivid examples at both time-scales, and thus we return to the topic that motivates this discussion. On the time-scale of ontogeny, colour vision serves to detect and identify objects, to segment and group attributes in the visual scene, and to generate perceptual categories that have visuomotor significance for the animal in its ecological interactions. And on an evolutionary time-scale, colour-seeing animals shape the physical world into an environment by coevolving with fruit- and pollen-bearing plants. As Barth (1985) observes in his wonderful study of insects and flowers: 'The colorful field of flowers is an insect environment that reflects the insects themselves' (vii); 'the plants and their pollinators are environment and reflection of one another' (266). The same point is made by Humphrey in a more general way:

> the evolution of colour vision is intimately linked to the evolution of colour on the surface of the earth. It may go without saying that, in a world without colour, animals would have no use for colour vision; but it does need saying that in a world without animals that possessed colour vision there would be very little colour. The variegated colours which characterise the earth's surface (and make the earth perhaps the most colourful planet in the universe) are in the main *organic* colours, carried by the tissues of plants and animals – and most of these life-born colours have been designed in the course of evolution to be *seen* ... the most striking colours of nature, those of flowers and fruits, the plumage of birds, the gaudy fishes of a coral reef, are all 'deliberate' evolutionary creations which have been selected to act as visual *signals* carrying messages to those who have the eyes to see them. The pigments which impart visible colour to the petals of a dandelion or a robin's breast are there for no other purpose.
>
> (Humphrey 1984: 146–7)

WHERE IS COLOUR?

In Chapters 3 and 4 we determined that colours are dependent on the perceiver and so cannot be conceived as intrinsic properties of the perceiver-independent world. The temptation, given that psychophysics and neuroscience seem able to model the central phenomenal features of colour, is to take this dependence as implying that object colour is really an illusion, and that colour experience can be reductively identified with neural states of the visual system (Hardin 1988). The temptation should be resisted for at least two reasons. First, neurophysiological subjectivism is not logically entailed by colours being perceiver-dependent, for, even in conjunction with the fact that the visual system bears the main responsibility for the central phenomenal features of colour, it is still possible to hold that being coloured is a relational property (see the final section of Chapter 3). Second, neurophysiological subjectivism provides only a narrow account of the perceptual content of colour vision, but the ecological phenomena reviewed in Chapter 4 indicate that chromatic perceptual content should be taken widely in relation to the extradermal context of the environment. Together these reasons suggest that a proper account of the ontology of colour and of chromatic perceptual content should be relational and ecological.

An account of colour can be relational without being ecological, and so the ecological view I shall now present can be seen as a species of relational account. It is therefore the relational aspect that should be considered first. Recall the senses of 'colour' that I distinguished in Chapter 2.[10] 'Colour' can refer to the property of being coloured; it can refer to particular determinate colours or shades; and it can refer to categories of particular determinate colours or shades. Colour in all these senses is relational. First, being coloured is a relational property because something is coloured only in relation to a perceiver. Second, particular determinate colours are relational properties because something is coloured a particular determinate colour only in relation to some perceiver in specific viewing conditions. Finally, colour categories are relational because their members (particular determinate colours) are relational, and because the within-category and between-category similarity and difference relations are determined in relation to a perceiver.

Relational accounts of colour have a long philosophical heritage stretching back to Aristotle. In *De Anima* (III. 2) Aristotle says that being coloured (object colour) as an occurrence is the joint actualization of a capacity in the object and a capacity in the perceiver; thus the 'actuality' of object colour depends on the colour perceiver (McKeon 1941: 583–4). But the 'potentiality' of colour does not, because objects remain potentially coloured even in the absence of colour perceivers. The Lockian received view is also relational, for it holds that being coloured corresponds to the disposition to look coloured to a suitable perceiver. As we saw in Chapter 1, however, this received view is unstable: given representationism and the metaphysics of sensation, the dispositionalist and subjectivist components of the received view come apart, and colours become identified either with the physical basis of the disposition or with sensations. Thus the received view ultimately fails to give an adequate relational treatment of colour.

For a relational account to be philosophically satisfying and naturalistic it must be ecological. The world outside the perceiver must be considered as an environment, rather than a neutral material universe, and the perceiver must be considered as an active exploring animal, rather than a passive spectator that simply receives sensations from physical impressions.

Consider now the three senses of 'colour' in the context of the ecological framework outlined in the previous sections. First, being coloured is a relational property of the environment and is tied to what the environment affords in the Gibsonian sense. As a property of the surfaces on, around, and above which animals move, including especially the organic surfaces of plants and animals (colouration), being coloured corresponds to surface spectral reflectance as visually perceived by the animals; as a property of the ambient light in the aerial and aquatic media in which animals live and through which they move, it corresponds to the spectral characteristics of the illumination as visually perceived by the animals; and as a property of such ecologically significant light sources as the sun and bioluminescent organs, it corresponds to spectral emittance as visually perceived by the animals.

This ecological account of being coloured is superficially similar to the received view, according to which being coloured consists in having the disposition to look coloured to a suitable perceiver. There are two important differences, however. First, in the received view being coloured is considered as a physical-level dispositional property, whereas in the ecological view it can be considered as an ecological-level dispositional property. At the ecological level, colours – especially in their roles as biological signals and as perceptual categories that satisfy the perceiver's adaptive ecological needs – are tied to affordances and effectivities: they indicate what the environment affords for the animal and what the animal can effect in its environment. The difference between such ecological-level dispositions and dispositions at the physical level is well captured in the remark by Turvey et al. quoted earlier: 'the dispositions of an organism-free world and the dispositions of an organism-populated world

... are not of the same order. The latter are ontologically condensed out of the former, so to speak, by the presence of living things' (1981: 263). Second, in the received view the perceiver and the world are conceived as only extrinsically and accidentally related, whereas in the ecological view they are conceived as inherently interdependent. Thus, as Prindle et al. note, the ecological approach to perceptual and sensory qualities is actually more Aristotelian than Lockian:

> Consider the state of affairs termed 'sourness'. On the assumption of a logical independence of animal and environment, sourness might be ascribed to the object being tasted but, more likely, would be ascribed to the animal doing the tasting (probably to the activity of some of its neural fibers). Herein lies the perennially popular story of secondary qualities. Aristotle, assuming a logical dependence, told a quite different story: Object X has the 'potential' to taste sour to animal Z ... while animal Z has the 'potential' to taste, as sour, object X ... and in the mutuality of these two potentials, 'sourness' is actualized. The object-focused statement and the animal-focused statement refer, respectively, to affordance ... and to effectivity.
>
> (Prindle et al. 1980: 396)

We can now turn to the other two senses of 'colour', beginning with colour as a category. Chapter 4 considered colour in this sense in the context of issues about perceptual content. I argued that categorical colour perception serves to integrate a physically heterogeneous collection of distal properties into a small set of visually salient equivalence classes. Considered now as a relational property of things, being coloured a categorical colour is simply equivalent to having a spectral reflectance, illuminance, or emittance that is perceived as belonging to some specific colour category by a particular perceiver in specific viewing conditions. Being coloured a particular determinate colour or shade, on the other hand, is equivalent to having a particular spectral reflectance, illuminance, or emittance that looks that colour to a particular perceiver in specific viewing conditions.[11]

Two main consequences follow from this position. First,

apart from a specification of the perceiver and the viewing conditions there is no fact of the matter about what colours (in either the particular or categorical sense) things have. Second, because colours are perceiver-dependent and viewing-condition-dependent properties, the same thing can have different colours (again in either the particular or categorical sense). Although these two consequences might strike some as counterintuitive, they are for me much less counterintuitive than what follows from computational objectivism (a creature could see red, green, yellow, and blue, yet not have colour vision, and vice-versa) or from neurophysiological subjectivism (all object colour is an illusion).

The standard philosophical move for trying to get around these two consequences of my position is to invoke the notions of a 'normal observer' and 'standard conditions': to be coloured is to look coloured in standard conditions to a normal observer. But for the reasons already discussed in Chapter 3 this move will not work: within visual science there is no single 'normal observer-standard conditions' procedure for determining the colours of things (Hardin 1983, 1988: 67–82, 1990b). Visual science is replete with very precise ways of specifying viewing conditions, but the specifications are interest-relative, suited to the pragmatic demands of specific colour-matching tasks, not to the philosophical demand for a principled determination of the 'real' colours of things. Moreover, in the context of comparative colour vision the position becomes even more difficult to maintain. The comparative evidence requires, at the very least, that the 'normal observer-standard condition' formula be revised so that there would be different standard conditions for different normal observers.[12] Such a revision would certainly be a move in the right direction, but the comparative evidence demands even more: not only would there have to be different normal observers according to the species; there would also have to be different normal observers within the very same species – recall the sex-linked colour vision polymorphisms in New World monkeys – as well as different normal observers for the very same individual at different times – recall the visual pigment variations in fishes according to season and time of day, which probably change considerably the colours seen by the animal. Once we allow for such a plurality of normal observers – to say nothing of the plurality of conditions that are to count as standard – the normal observer-standard condition formula is doing very little of the work it was originally intended to do.

There are two further objections that could be made to my relational-ecological account that need to be considered. First, I have argued that being coloured is a relational property of the environment that depends on the colour perceiver. But what about the colours of afterimages? Here one sees something that has colour, but one does not see the colour as an attribute of anything in the environment. How, then, can my ecological account accommodate afterimage colours?

To accommodate the colours of afterimages it is necessary to distinguish between perception and sensation. Perception is the awareness of things in the world. Sensation, on the other hand, is the awareness of changes in one's own bodily state or condition. In perception, one is aware of things as stable and distinct entities in relation to an indeterminate background. In sensation, one is not aware of any stable and distinct entity different from oneself; rather, one *feels* one's bodily state or condition change along certain qualitative dimensions. In the case of afterimages we are dealing with a kind of visual experience that belongs in the category of sensation, not perception. Careful attention to the experiential character of afterimage phenomena in contrast to the experiential character of surface colour perception supports this way of classifying them (Westphal 1987: 86–7, 115). For example, in contrast to the colour of a surface, an afterimage colour seems self-illuminating, lacks texture, grain, and a sharp outline, changes gradually in hue, saturation, and brightness, as well as in shape, darts about as one moves one's eyes, and can be seen in the dark and with one's eyes closed. Unlike visual *perception*, then, the experience of having an afterimage is one of feeling one's bodily condition in vision change along certain qualitative dimensions; and the experiential character of these felt changes is relatively unstable and impermanent.[13]

My ecological view as stated so far is not meant as an account of the visual sensing of colour in this sense, though I shall take up some related issues in the next chapter. Instead, my ecological view is meant as an account of the property of *being coloured* and its relation to colour *perception*. Its aim is to explicate what it is for something in the world to be coloured and what it is to perceive something in the world as coloured. Afterimage colours do not fall within the purview of the ecological view thus understood, and so they do not present any special problem for the view.

In taking this route I do not mean to deny that the visual experience of afterimage colours deserves philosophical treatment. But I do mean to deny the premise that is typically presupposed by those who cite the afterimage phenomena as presenting a special problem for theories of perception. This premise is the sensationalist form of representationism, according to which perceptual experience is composed of sensations as basic constituent elements. If this doctrine were right, then colour perception would contain as proper parts colour sensations, and hence afterimage phenomena would present a problem for the ecological view of colour perception. But one of the distinctive features of the ecological view is that it *rejects* the sensationalist doctrine as well as representationism in general. As discussed in this chapter, perception, according to the ecological view, is to be understood as perceptually guided activity, and this kind of activity does not contain sensations as constituent elements.

Of course, in distinguishing between perception and sensation, I am clearly committed to the idea that there is such a thing as sensation. In my view, sensation is a mode of bodily awareness that can be distinguished from (and is probably evolutionarily more primitive than) perception, though I also think that the two are best understood as poles along a continuum rather than as absolutely distinct (Kelly 1986: 49). But, contrary to sensationalism, I would also argue that sensation as a distinct mode of bodily awareness too needs to be understood ecologically as a kind of embodied activity – as *sensing* or *feeling*, or, at the risk of straining a term, as 'sentiently' guided activity.[14] Thus, even in the case of sensation, the sensationalist doctrine should be rejected.[15]

Let me turn now to the second objection that could be made to my relational account. It is undeniable that we see colours as perceiver-independent properties of things. In holding that colours are relational, am I not then committed to holding that our colour experience is mistaken, that it misrepresents the nature of colour? And if I am so committed, then, ecological considerations aside, what really is the difference between my view and the Lockian view according to which colours as we experience them do not 'resemble' colours as dispositional properties of things?

This objection also rests on sensationalism and a representationist conception of perceptual content.[16] It is assumed that what we are directly aware of in colour perception is a sensation that stands at the end of a certain causal sequence. As the effect of this sequence the sensation is the immediate object of perception, and it mediates the perception of its distal cause, the physical object. If the sensation does not adequately or correctly represent ('resemble') the way the object is apart from the perceiver, then the perceptual experience misrepresents the object.

This conception of perceptual content is fundamentally mistaken. Perceptual content is object-directed and always presents its object under an aspect. But the aspect under which an object is presented in visual perception – for example, being coloured red – is not itself an inner object, such as a sensation or sense-datum; rather it is simply how the thing *looks* given its physical characteristics and the psychophysiological characteristics of the perceiver.[17] Now, how something looks is clearly a relational property because something looks as it does only in relation to a perceiver. But *this* relation is not something that it is possible for the subject to perceive. To suppose otherwise is to imagine that the perceiving subject is essentially a disembodied spectator who can watch the means by which he or she perceives (Kelly 1986: 107). It is to suppose not only that visual perception is a one-way delivery of messages to the brain, rather than an exploratory circular process (to use Gibson's formulation), but also that the subject can be aware of this transaction and observe the messages that arrive there. The perceiving subject is embedded within the relation, however, and partly constitutes it; it in turn constitutes the perceptual situation. It therefore makes no sense to suppose that visual appearances are deceptive simply because they depend on the perceiver. And this general point holds no less for the specific case of colour perception. As Kelly argues in his philosophical study of perception:

The common claim that this experience is deceptive assumes that there ought in the nature of the case to be some way for the subject to grasp that color is a relational property, dependent on his own nervous system. But that is not the way sense perception works. To be perceptually aware that color is relational, he would have to perceive the relation on which it depends. Then he would have to perceive this relation by some means, it would have to appear some way to him, raising the same questions all over again. So there is nothing deceptive about this experienced externality. On the contrary, color is the way he perceives something that *is* external and independent of him. Experiencing color as external is the only way he could experience the externality of the reflectance properties. Given the necessity of perceiving by specific means, he experiences color in just the right 'place' – the place of the attribute he is aware of by means of it.

(Kelly 1986: 109)

There is therefore nothing mistaken about our experience of colours as independent of the perceiver, even though colours are relational properties. Furthermore, the ecological framework gives this philosophical result the substantive empirical content it needs in a naturalistic investigation, for this framework enables us to appreciate how colours as relational properties of the environment emerge on both evolutionary and individual time-scales, as well as the adaptive ecological value of perceiving colours as external and independent properties.

6

VISUAL EXPERIENCE AND THE ECOLOGICAL VIEW

> Perceiving is an achievement of the individual, not an experi-
> ence in the theatre of consciousness. It is a keeping-in-touch with
> the world, an experience of things rather than a having of
> experiences. It involves awareness-of instead of just awareness
> ... perception is not a mental act. Neither is it a bodily act.
> Perceiving is a psychosomatic act, not of mind or of body, but of
> a living observer.
>
> (J. J. Gibson 1979: 239–40)

In the previous two chapters I argued for a relational and
ecological approach to colour and perceptual content: colours
are relational properties constituted by animal–environment
pairs. Although one of the terms in this relation is the
perceiving-acting subject, I have so far touched only briefly, at
the end of the previous chapter, on the topic of the nature of
perceptual experience and its relation to colour. It is this topic
that forms the subject of this final chapter.

Considering the nature of perceptual experience can rather
quickly lead one into the notorious philosophical thicket
known as the mind–body problem. My interest here, however,
is not in defending a position on the mind–body relation, and
so I do not intend to confront this problem directly. Instead,
what I am interested in exploring is the very nature of
perceptual experience itself and the extent to which a phenomenon of this nature is amenable to scientific investigation. The
latter issue about science has figured largely in recent philosophy of mind, but, in my estimation, not in a way conducive to
making any kind of deep philosophical progress. One cannot
determine what limits there might or might not be to scientific

explanations of perceptual experience without first gaining some understanding in conceptual and phenomenological terms of what perceptual experience is.[1] But those on both sides of the issue about science in recent philosophy of mind persist in misunderstanding the phenomenon of perception – or so I shall argue.

The approach that I am going to take in this chapter will be somewhat dialectical. I shall argue first that certain influential arguments that purport to establish a priori that there is a limit to what science can tell us about perceptual experience are not convincing (Nagel 1974, 1986; Jackson 1982). The problem with these arguments is that they presuppose a mistaken conception of the nature of perceptual experience and an inadequate conception of science – the former is largely sensationalist, while the latter is largely positivist. This response on my part will differ, however, from other influential counterarguments that deny that there is any coherent notion of the qualitative aspects of perceptual experience that poses a genuine problem for scientific accounts of the mind (Dennett 1990, 1991). The problem with these arguments is that they too rest on a mistaken conception of perceptual experience, though in this case the mistaken conception is a cognitivist or 'intellectualist' one. I shall argue to the contrary that there is indeed a legitimate – though nonsensationalist – conception of the qualitative content of visual perception and that providing an account of such content does constrain the scientific project considerably. Finally, given a more adequate conception of perceptual experience based on the ecological view presented in the previous chapter, I shall try both to enrich our sense of how the scientific project might proceed and to assess the kind of limits it might face.

SENSATIONALISM

Towards the end of Chapter 3, when discussing Hardin's neurophysiological subjectivism, I raised the question of whether it would be possible to give a neuroscientific explanation of the conscious visual experience of colour. Hardin's view is that problems about the relation between mind and body 'that are intractable at the extradermal physical level or at the phenomenal level promise to yield to analysis in neurological terms', but he also admits that 'at the present rudimentary state of our knowledge of the visual system, most of this is promise, program, and principle' (1988: 111). Some philosophers would challenge even this qualified claim, however, by arguing that any scientific explanation of the mind must, in principle, be incomplete because it will always leave out the qualitative aspects of conscious experience – what an experience is like for the subject who has it. The best-known arguments to this effect are due to Thomas Nagel (1974, 1986) and Frank Jackson (1982). Their arguments bear detailed examination, for they rest on a mistaken sensationalist conception of the nature of perceptual experience.

Nagel and the subjective character of perceptual experience

In English-speaking philosophy Thomas Nagel's now twenty-year-old article, 'What is it like to be a bat?' (Nagel 1974),[2] continues to set the agenda for contemporary discussions of consciousness, subjectivity, and the mind–body problem. The main point that Nagel tries to demonstrate in this article is a negative one: we do not have any conception of how there could be an explanation of the mind in physical terms, because we do not understand how there could be a physical explanation of consciousness. In Nagel's words: 'physicalism is a position we cannot understand because we do not at present have any conception of how it might be true' (176).

Nagel reaches this verdict from an argument that can be presented as having six main steps:

1   For an organism to have conscious experience means that there is something it is like to be that organism – something it is like *for* the organism. Call what it is like the subjective character of experience (166).
2   If physicalism is true, then there must be some physical account of the subjective character of experience (167).
3   But (a) every subjective phenomenon is essentially connected with a single point of view – that of the subject, and so (b) an adequate conception of subjective phenomena can be had only by 'adopting' or 'taking up' the subject's point of view (167–72).
4   An objective physical theory will abandon the subjective

point of view and will therefore be unable to give an account of the subjective character of experience (167).

Steps (1) to (4) purport to establish that it is impossible to give a physical account of consciousness. This conclusion bears on the mind–body problem, for if the facts about the subjective character of experience are accessible only from the subjective point of view of the organism, then:

5   It is a mystery how the subjective character of experience could be revealed in the physical operation of the organism (172).

And, finally, steps (1) to (5) have consequences for physicalism:

6   Physicalism is a position we cannot understand, because we do not at present have any conception of how it might be true (176).

On the surface this argument turns on considerations about subjectivity and objectivity, about the difference between subjective and objective 'points of view'. As Nagel puts it in another article: 'subjective aspects of the mental can be apprehended only from the point of view of the creature itself (perhaps taken up by someone else), whereas what is physical is simply there, and can be externally apprehended from more than one point of view' (1979a: 201). But buried within the argument there is also a particular conception of what the subjective aspects of the mental are in the case of perception. The conception is a sensationalist one: perceptual experience contains as proper parts items called *sensations* that have intrinsically a qualitative character but no intentional content. Qualitative characters are the essential properties of sensations; such properties are called *qualia* or the *sensational properties* of experience. What the qualification 'intrinsically' is supposed to mean when it is said that a sensation is intrinsically qualitative is difficult to specify precisely, but the general idea seems to be that the qualitative character of a perceptual state – its quale or sensational property – is not exhausted by the relations the state bears to other mental states or by how the state provides access to the world.

How is this sensationalist conception of perceptual experience to be found in steps (1)–(6)? Consider (1) first. One of the interesting (and attractive[3]) features of Nagel's argument is that, rather than beginning with a definition of consciousness, he begins by asking what it means for a creature to have conscious experience:

> Conscious experience is a widespread phenomenon. It occurs at many levels of animal life, though we cannot be sure of its presence in the simpler organisms, and it is very difficult to say in general what provides evidence of it ... But no matter how the form may vary, the fact that an organism has conscious experience *at all* means, basically, that there is something it is like to *be* that organism ... fundamentally an organism has conscious mental states if and only if there is something that it is like to *be* that organism – something it is like *for* the organism.
>
> We may call this the subjective character of experience.
>
> (Nagel 1974: 166)

The meaning of this answer to the question of what it is for a creature to have conscious experience is not obvious, however. It depends on how we are to understand the expression 'what it is like' (for the subject). What does this expression mean?

The expression has the grammatical form of a singular term, and so it is tempting to take it as a referring expression (see Nemirow 1990: 494–5). The question would then be, to what does the expression refer? Nagel uses it to refer to certain properties of experience – ones that are conceived as purely qualitative. And although he does not use the terms 'qualia' or 'sensational properties', it is clear that his conception of 'what it is like' for a subject to have a given experience is a sensationalist one. For example, in a later work he writes:

> If we try to understand experience from an objective viewpoint that is distinct from that of the subject of the experience, then even if we continue to credit its perspectival nature, we will not be able to grasp its *most specific qualities* [my italics] unless we can imagine them

subjectively. We will not know how scrambled eggs taste to a cockroach even if we develop a detailed objective phenomenology of the cockroach sense of taste.

(Nagel 1986: 25)

What it is like to be a cockroach is a matter of the most specific qualities of its experience – cockroach sensations. And since Nagel also uses the expression 'what it is like' as a synonym for what he calls 'the subjective character of experience', it is clear that he thinks that the sensational properties or qualia of experience are what constitute its subjective character.

Given this conception of experience, step (2) becomes the problem of how there can be a physical account of qualia. The novelty of Nagel's discussion is that it presents this problem within the larger philosophical context of the problematic relation between the subjective and objective perspectives (see especially Nagel 1979a, 1986), but the problem is nonetheless the same as the sensationalist one of sixteenth- and seventeenth-century natural philosophy as discussed in Chapter 1 – indeed, Nagel accepts this formulation of the problem (1986: 14, 75–6).

Turning now to step (3), the first part is, as Nagel puts it, 'a general observation about the subjective character of experience' – facts about what it is like to be a particular type of experiencing subject are facts that embody the point of view of that subject (1974: 171). This belief in the existence of irreducibly subjective facts does not by itself commit one to a sensationalist conception of subjective experience. But such a conception does emerge in the support that Nagel gives for the second part of step (3), which asserts that an adequate conception of subjective phenomena can be had only by 'taking up' the subject's point of view. The argument given on behalf of this claim rests on the familiar sensationalist assumption that, in the case of the sensational properties of experience, the way something seems or feels is the way it is. In expressing this assumption, Nagel aligns the subjective/objective distinction with the appearance/reality distinction, claiming that in the case of the subjective character of experience, the appearance is the reality. And this assumption in turn is used to support step (4):

It is difficult to understand what could be meant by the *objective* character of an experience, apart from the particular point of view from which its subject apprehends it.

(1974: 173)

The idea of moving from appearance to reality seems to make no sense here ... If the subjective character of experience is fully comprehensible only from one point of view, then any shift to greater objectivity – that is, less attachment to a specific viewpoint – does not take us nearer to the real nature of the phenomenon: it takes us farther away from it.

(1974: 174)

Thus, in the case of the subjective character of experience, the 'real nature of the phenomenon' or the 'true character' of the experience (172) is equated simply with how the experience seems or feels to the subject. This collapse of the distinction between appearance and reality for the qualitative features of experience is a familiar thesis of the sensationalist tradition going back to Descartes, for, according to the tradition, the most specific qualities of experience are given in sensation and their reality is entirely exhausted by their subjective appearances. As I discussed in Chapter 1 (see also Westphal 1987), once such a conception of experience is in place, it becomes virtually impossible to imagine how there could be a solution to the mind–body problem, for this would require being able to imagine how something that is purely qualitative and has no reality beyond its subjective appearance could be physically revealed.

I have gone into some of the details in Nagel's argument because, although I too believe in the philosophical importance of experience and subjectivity (see Varela et al. 1991), I do not believe that sensationalism – tacit though it be in Nagel's case – is adequate to them. My objection to Nagel's argument is straightforward: the intuitions that support the argument are not philosophically neutral, but are based on a phenomeno-logically misguided sensationalist theory of subjective experience. Moreover, it is precisely the phenomenological deficiency of sensationalism that prevents one from appreci-ating the positive role that science can play in helping us to understand the subjective point of view (Akins 1990).

Why, then, is sensationalism mistaken? According to the

sensationalist, perceptual experience contains as a real constituent the awareness of specific qualities that have no intentional content, but that determine what the experience is qualitatively like for the subject. Such a mode of awareness is called sensation. To say that sensation is the awareness of a specific quality means that it is the awareness of a particular colour, taste, odour, etc.; and to say that sensation has no intentional content means that it is not *of* or *about* anything (in the world, for example) in addition to its distinctive quality. The reason that sensationalism is mistaken is that there is no such fundamental distinction between the qualitative and the intentional aspects of perceptual experience.

The best argument against the sensationalist attempt to make this distinction is still to be found in the Introduction to Maurice Merleau-Ponty's *Phenomenology of Perception*, especially Chapter 1 (Merleau-Ponty 1945/1962).[4] This first chapter is entitled 'The "sensation" as a unit of experience', and its main point is to refute the sensationalist thesis that the basic unit of perceptual experience is the simple sensation of a quality. In criticizing this thesis Merleau-Ponty examines three different conceptions of sensation – sensation as impression, as quality, and as the immediate consequence of stimulation – arguing that all three are fundamentally confused because they rest on the mistaken idea that perceptual experience can be analysed into separate qualitative and intentional components.

According to the first conception, a sensation is an experience that has no world-directed content but is a pure subjective impression – it is 'the way in which I am affected and the experiencing of a state of myself' (1945/1962: 3). As examples of what pure sensation, so conceived, might be, Merleau-Ponty cites 'The greyness which, when I close my eyes, surrounds me, leaving no distance between me and it', and 'the sounds that encroach on my drowsiness and hum "in my head"' (3). But because what is sensed is supposed to coincide with an impression that is simple and completely internal to the subject, pure sensation, strictly speaking, 'will be the experience of an undifferentiated, instantaneous, dotlike impact' (3). Thus sensationalist theories based on this conception of sensation necessitate that there be a layer of such impressions within perceptual experience, even though we never discern any such thing in our everyday experience.

Merleau-Ponty's argument against this version of sensationalism employs a basic tenet of the Gestalt theory of perception, but it also deepens this tenet to make a philosophical point about the nature of perception. The tenet from Gestalt theory is that the simplest thing that can be given in perceptual experience is a figure on a background. In Merleau-Ponty's eyes, however, 'this is not a contingent characteristic of factual perception ... It is the very definition of the phenomenon of perception, that without which a phenomenon cannot be said to be a perception at all' (4). Thus a pure impression, being homogeneous and instantaneous, is precisely the type of thing that cannot be an element of perceptual experience, because the very nature of perception forbids it: 'The pure impression is, therefore, not only undiscoverable, but also imperceptible and so inconceivable as an instant of perception' (4).

If it were possible for perceptual experience to contain a layer of pure sense-impressions, then the qualitative and intentional aspects of perceptual experience would be fundamentally distinct: sense-impressions assembled together into a mosaic would constitute the qualitative aspects of experience, whereas the cognitive processes of attention, expectation, judgement, etc. would constitute the intentional aspects. In taking the Gestalt figure–ground organization to be essential to any perception, however, Merleau-Ponty is also holding that any perception, even the most minimal sense-perception conceivable, is essentially both qualitative and intentional, and that these two aspects are inseparable:

> Let us imagine a white patch on a homogeneous background. All the points in the patch have a certain 'function' in common, that of forming themselves into a 'shape'. The colour of the shape is more intense, and as it were more resistant than that of the background; the edges of the white patch 'belong' to it, and are not part of the background although they adjoin it: the patch appears to be placed on the background and does not break it up. Each part arouses the expectation of more than it contains, and this elementary perception is therefore already charged with a *meaning*.
>
> (4)

According to the second conception, a sensation is an experience of an isolated quality, such as a shade of colour or a tone, that is not necessarily sensed as the quality of an entity. Such qualities serve to individuate sensations, and sense-experience as a whole is thus conceived as the possession of qualities. Merleau-Ponty's argument against this version of sensationalism is that it makes qualities into elements of consciousness and so confuses sensation with what is sensed. Sense-experience is the awareness of qualities, but the qualities are experienced as properties of things, not elements of consciousness. Contrary to the sensationalist prejudice, a quality is never perceptually isolated, and indeed could not be given in pure isolation for the reasons advanced in the previous argument. Thus, rather than 'providing a simple means of delimiting sensations, if we consider it in the experience itself which evinces it, the quality is as rich and mysterious as the object, or indeed the whole spectacle perceived' (4).

If sense-experience were in part composed of isolated qualities that were not sensed as the qualities *of* anything, then there would again be a nonintentional and purely qualitative component of experience. But in saying that 'the quality is as rich and mysterious as the object', Merleau-Ponty is arguing that a purely qualitative component can never be found in perception:

> This red patch which I see on the carpet is red only in virtue of a shadow which lies across it, its quality is apparent only in relation to the play of light upon it, and hence as an element in a spatial configuration. Moreover the colour can be said to be there only if it occupies an area of a certain size, too small an area not being describable in these terms. Finally this red would literally not be the same if it were not the 'woolly' red of a carpet. Analysis, then, discovers in each quality meanings which reside in it.
>
> (4–5)

According to the third conception, a sensation is the immediate consequence of physical stimulation – it is a response produced by the sensory receptors. Receptor responses provide the initial qualitative data in perception and then intentional processes such as inference, judgement, and association integrate the data and derive meaningful percepts from them. This conception of sensation and of the role it plays in perception is meant to be explanatory, rather than phenomenological (descriptive), and so sensationalist theories based on it cannot be refuted simply by appealing to experience. In arguing against such theories Merleau-Ponty directs his criticisms rather to the representationism they imply: 'The objective world being given, it is assumed that it passes on to the sense-organs messages which must be registered, then deciphered in such a way as to reproduce in us the original text' (7). His objection is that the physical stimulus cannot provide an objective definition of sensation because, even at the physiological and behavioural levels, sense-experience is not initiated by the passive reception of an independently specifiable message; rather, sense-experience is based on an integrated sensorimotor activity in which 'the excitation is itself already a response, not an effect imported from outside the organism; it is the first act of its proper functioning' (1942/1963: 31). A passage from his first major work, *The Structure of Behavior*, makes this point in a way that connects naturally with the ecological view of perception I presented in the previous chapter:

> The organism cannot properly be compared to a keyboard on which the external stimuli would play and in which their proper form would be delineated for the simple reason that the organism contributes to the constitution of that form ... Since all the movements of the organism are always conditioned by external influences, one can, if one wishes, readily treat behavior as an effect of the milieu. But in the same way, since all the stimulations which the organism receives have in turn been possible only by its preceding movements which have culminated in exposing the receptor organ to the external influences, one could also say that the behavior is the first cause of the stimulations.
>
> Thus the form of the excitant is created by the organism itself, by its proper manner of offering itself to actions from the outside. Doubtless, in order to be able to subsist, it must encounter a certain number of physical and chemical agents in its surroundings. But it is the organism

itself – according to the proper nature of its receptors, the thresholds of its nerve centers and the movements of the organs – which chooses the stimuli in the physical world to which it will be sensitive.

(1942/1963: 13)

If sensation were the reception and transmission of qualitative data caused by receptor stimulation, then once again there would be a way to distinguish between purely qualitative and intentional components in perceptual experience. But in the real world, in contrast to the restricted and artificial conditions of the laboratory, there is no such thing as sensation as mere receptoral stimulation, for there is no such thing as mere stimulation, that is, stimulation that is not also a consequence of animal activity. Thus any stimulation is 'a formation already bound up with a larger whole, already endowed with a meaning, distinguishable only in degree from the more complex perceptions, and ... therefore gets us no further in our attempt to delimit pure sensation' (1945/1962: 9).

What bearing does this critique of sensationalism have on Nagel's position? Nagel presents himself as upholding the irreducibility of the subjective character of experience, but the critique of sensationalism shows that his argument presupposes a misguided phenomenology, for perceptual experience cannot be analysed into separate intentional and qualitative components. The specific qualitative aspects of our sensory and perceptual experience cannot be separated, even in principle, from the intentional framework in which we experience ourselves and the world. Therefore, whether there could be a scientific account of subjective experience is not a matter of whether science can explain the nonintentional, purely qualitative features of experience, because there are no such features. The issue of what science might, or might not, be able to tell us about our own subjectivity and experience, or those of other creatures such as the bat or the pigeon, is a very important one, but it is not properly addressed by advancing a priori conceptual arguments that presuppose misguided conceptions of experience such as sensationalism. Instead, the proper way to join the issue is to undertake both phenomenological and scientific investigations of the mind, using each to illuminate the other, thereby bringing the two into a kind of reflective alignment (Varela et al. 1991; Flanagan 1992). Only in this way can one prevent one's ability to imagine what the science of mind can accomplish from being held hostage to a mistaken phenomenology, on the one hand, and one's phenomenology from being held hostage to unconstrained, self-indulgent introspection, on the other.

Novel colours and Jackson's knowledge argument[5]

The other best-known argument for showing that any scientific explanation must, in principle, be incomplete because it will always leave out the qualitative features of conscious experience is due to Frank Jackson (1982) and is known as the *knowledge argument*. This argument is especially relevant to our discussion because, in one version, it depends on a philosophical thought experiment involving the idea of novel colours, that is, visual qualities having a hue that bears a resemblance relation to red, green, yellow, and blue, yet is neither reddish, nor greenish, nor yellowish, nor bluish. For this reason, I am going to consider Jackson's argument and the topic of novel colours at some length.

In his article 'Ephiphenomenal qualia', Jackson asks us to imagine a perceiver named Fred who is like us except that he has the ability to see a hue we cannot see. Jackson's question is: 'What is the new colour or colours like?'[6] He argues that all the physical information about Fred, including the physiology of his brain and visual system, and his dispositions to behaviour, would not enable us to answer this question. The totality of physical information would still leave out something about Fred's experience, namely, what the extra hue is like from the subjective perspective of Fred. And if at some point we became able to see this extra hue (perhaps by undergoing an operation that made our visual system like Fred's), we would learn something that we did not know as a result of having all the physical information about Fred: we would learn how the extra hue looks and thereby learn just what it was that made Fred's experience different from ours. Jackson concludes that physicalism is false because the complete physical account does not tell us everything there is to know.

Jackson also presents another thought experiment in support of the knowledge argument, one which has attracted most of the philosophical commentary, the example of Fred remaining to my knowledge undiscussed. We are asked to imagine a brilliant scientist named Mary who is confined to a black and white room and is forced to investigate the world through a black and white television. She specializes in visual science and comes to know everything physical that there is to know about visual perception. Jackson claims that, upon being released from her room, Mary will learn something she did not know before, namely, how the colours (hues) look. As a result, she will realize that there was something about the colour experiences of other people that all along she did not know in virtue of having all the physical information about them, something she learns only when she comes to have the same kind of experiences (see Jackson 1986). Consequently, the physical account again leaves something out.

This thought experiment, however, is poorly conceived. Mary's vision is supposed to be like ours except that she has been confined to an entirely black and white environment. But simply confining Mary in this way will not deprive her of colour experience: she will still see the colour of her own body. Moreover, she will see colours when she rubs her eyes and when she dreams, and she will see colour afterimages induced as a result of brightness and lightness perception. Perhaps we should suppose that Mary's ability to see hues atrophies as a result of her confinement. But then when Mary is released from her room she will still not be able to see any hues. In either case, Jackson's experiment as described cannot be performed. To remedy the defects we need to suppose, first, either that Mary's ability to see hues atrophies (and as a result she loses all memory of hue) or that she has been completely colour-blind (monochromatic) from birth; and second, that while completely unconscious she is released from her room and undergoes an operation that enables her to see hues.

Spelling out the thought experiment in this way shows more clearly how it is both related to and different from the example of Fred. Mary is unable to see any hues before her vision is corrected; therefore all of our hues are to her novel hues in the sense that they are new to her when she acquires the ability to see them. But they are not novel hues in the strong sense discussed in Chapter 4, for they are not novel to us. In the Fred example, however, the hue that Fred sees is a novel hue in this stronger sense, for it is (*ex hypothesi*) a hue that we cannot see. It is this version of the knowledge argument that I wish to examine here.

Jackson's thought experiments are made to bear considerable weight in the course of his argument. We have already seen that the Mary example is not described as it should be. The situation is in some ways worse with the example of Fred, for the very idea of a novel hue upon which it relies is not developed with the care and attention to detail that are needed. By exploring this idea in detail we can uncover some of the unstated intuitions that motivate Jackson's arguments, intuitions that are not at all philosophically neutral and uncontroversial – indeed, they are basically the same kind of sensationalist intuitions that lie behind Nagel's treatment of consciousness. In the end, I shall show that the idea of a novel hue when thought out with the care it demands actually undermines the sensationalist conception of the qualitative features of conscious experience.

In Chapter 4 I discussed novel colours in relation to the possibility that certain animals have phenomenal colour spaces of more than three dimensions – colour hyperspaces. But I did not discuss the very idea or *concept* of a novel hue, and so left myself open to the charge that this concept is incoherent, that it is conceptually impossible for there to be such a hue (and hence for there to be novel colours) because for something to be a hue it must have a location in the hue dimension of our colour space. Jackson too leaves himself open to precisely this accusation. Since the visual quality that Fred perceives has (*ex hypothesi*) no location in our colour space, what reason do we have for counting it as a hue at all? Perhaps what Fred perceives should rather be counted as, say, a certain sort of shimmer or a distinctive kind of lustre that some objects have, but which we are unable to see (see van Brakel 1992).

The idea that our main criterion for something to be a colour is that it have a location in our colour space can be found in Wittgenstein's *Remarks on Colour* (1977). At III-42 he writes:

> We will, therefore, have to ask ourselves: What would it be like if people knew colours which our people with normal vision do not know? In general this question will not admit of an unambiguous answer. For it is by no

265

means clear that we *must* say of this sort of abnormal people that they know other *colours*. There is, after all, no commonly accepted criterion for what is a colour, unless it is one of our colours.

And yet we could imagine circumstances under which we would say, 'These people see other colours in addition to ours.'

It should be noted that Wittgenstein does not in this passage assert unequivocally that something is a colour only if it is one of our colours, contrary to the interpretation of some commentators (for example, Ackermann 1989: 143). Rather, he says that there is no other 'commonly accepted criterion' for something to be a colour, but then goes on to say that we could imagine circumstances in which we would say that someone sees other colours in addition to ours. The problem, then, is to say what these circumstances would be.

Consider Jackson's example of the imaginary perceiver named Fred. Although Fred supposedly sees another hue in addition to ours, Jackson provides little to explain why the circumstances are such that we would say it is an extra *hue* that Fred perceives. He notes that people vary in their colour-discriminating abilities and then says that Fred 'makes every discrimination that anyone has ever made, and moreover he makes one that we cannot even begin to make.' Jackson spells out the example in a bit more detail by saying that Fred sorts a batch of ripe tomatoes 'into two roughly equal groups and does so with complete consistency'. Jackson explains that 'all ripe tomatoes do not look the same colour [hue] to Fred,' that 'he has in consequence developed for his own use two words "red$_1$" and "red$_2$" to mark the difference', and that 'his discriminatory behaviour bears this out: he sorts red$_1$ from red$_2$ tomatoes with the greatest of ease in a variety of viewing circumstances' (Jackson 1982: 128).

It seems clear from these remarks that Jackson is asking us to imagine not simply that Fred's colour vision has greater *sensitivity* than ours, but also that it is of a different *type* or *dimensionality*, though Jackson does not make this distinction. What Jackson wishes us to imagine, then, is that we stand in relation to Fred as a dichromat stands in relation to a trichromat. As he says: 'We are to Fred as a totally red–green colour-blind person is to us' (129). It follows that the additional quality Fred sees cannot be a particular determinate colour or *shade* that belongs to one of our hue categories but that we cannot discriminate, after the fashion of David Hume's missing shade of blue. The ability to see Hume's missing shade would not require (for colour-normal humans) having colour vision of a different type (though it would for true yellow–blue dichromats); it would simply require having greater sensitivity (discriminatory ability) in the blue region of the colours. Indeed, as Hume discusses, we can imagine the missing shade by working out how it would have to look on the basis of the shades with which we are familiar. But (*ex hypothesi*) we cannot do this with Fred's red_2, for as Jackson says, to see red_2 requires discriminations that 'we cannot even begin to make'. Despite the name, then, red_2 cannot be a missing shade of red; it must be an entirely novel hue.

In fact we can be even more precise. It must be remembered that our hue terms are categorical: they cover the numerous discriminable colours (specific hue-saturation-lightness values) that belong to a given hue category. In the same way, Jackson's red_2 must be a novel hue category that comprises numerous members corresponding to the specific hue–saturation–lightness values that fall within the category. Hence when Jackson says that Fred 'sees two colours where we see one', or 'that we should admit that Fred can see ... at least one more colour than we can', he is being imprecise, to put it mildly. Fred can see many more particular determinate colours than we can because he can see colours that (unlike Hume's missing shade of blue) belong to a hue category none of whose members we can see.[7]

The question raised above about the circumstances in which we would say that Fred sees additional colours can now be refined. It now becomes: does Fred, like us, have colour vision, but unlike us (colour-normal humans) have colour vision of a different type? More precisely, is the dimensionality of his colour vision of a higher order than our own such that he can see not only all our colours but also colours that belong to a hue category none of whose members we can see? In short, is Fred a tetrachromat?

It may seem that in filling in the details of Jackson's example I have answered Wittgenstein's question about the circumstances in which we would say that someone sees other colours in addition to ours. Indeed, in filling in these details I have simply followed what is known about variations in colour vision in visual science, as discussed in Chapters 2 and 4. Recall, for example, the hypothesis currently being tested by J. D. Mollon and his colleagues that a certain proportion of the female human population may be tetrachromatic and hence capable of discriminating a hue not found in the normal human trichromatic colour space (Mollon 1992; Jordan and Mollon 1993). But the philosophical matters are not so simple. Recall Wittgenstein's point that 'it is by no means clear that we *must* say of this sort of abnormal people that they know other *colours*'. We must still face the question of why the extra quality that Fred perceives is to count as a hue rather than some other type of visual quality that we cannot see. The problem can be refined still further by making use of another of Wittgenstein's remarks (III-86):

> Can't we imagine people having a geometry of colours different from our normal one? And that, of course, means: can we describe it, can we immediately respond to the request to describe it, that is, do we know *unambiguously* what is being demanded of us?
> The difficulty is obviously this: isn't it precisely the geometry of colours that shows us what we're talking about, i.e., that we are talking about colours?

As a step towards developing this remark of Wittgenstein's, let me first comment on the idea that there is a 'geometry' of colours.[8] In Chapter 2 I discussed how certain aspects of the phenomenal structure of colour can be considered in terms of the locations of colours in a space of relations known as colour space. There are many geometrical representations of the relations that compose colour space. The best known is the colour solid shown in Figure 2. Other three-dimensional representations depart from this model in various ways (see Hunt 1987; Kuehni 1983; Wasserman 1978). For example, Ebbinghaus's colour solid is a double cone, whereas Munsell's is more like an irregular tree; there are also non-Euclidean models of colour space (Judd and Wyszecki 1963: 274, 309–10). These models are based on various sorts of data and have different purposes, and so are not incompatible. What is important for our purposes is simply that the relations among colours can be perspicuously displayed in a geometrical model.

The term 'geometrical' as just used refers to the spatial representation of how the colours are related. This use is similar to Wittgenstein's, but is not the same. Wittgenstein appears to be drawing on this sense as a way of talking about the *logical*, or as he would call them, the *grammatical* relations among (propositions about) the colours. But we can approach closer to Wittgenstein's point about the geometry of colour by asking, what is the logical status of the relations that colours bear to each other as displayed in the geometrical representations of colour space? This is a vexing question, and I do not wish to attempt a systematic answer to it here. I raise the question because many philosophers hold the reasonable view that certain properties of colours are essential to them whereas others are accidental (Hardin 1988: 66, 126–7). And among the properties deemed essential many would include the resemblance relations among the hues; therefore, according to this view, the relations that the hues bear to each other are internal relations (see Harrison 1973, 1986).

To take some examples: it is essential to orange that it be a binary hue composed of red and yellow; a hue that did not contain red and yellow as components could not be orange. (It is thus impossible for there to be a unitary orange.) Attention to these essential properties makes it easy to see why orange resembles red and yellow more closely than it resembles blue and green; it also makes it easy to see that these resemblance relations are essential properties of orange – a hue could not be orange unless it resembled red and yellow more than it resembled blue and green. Analogous remarks could be made about all of the other binary hues, such as turquoise and purple. Turning to the unitary hues, many have argued that the mutual exclusivities or opponencies of red and green, and yellow and blue, are essential to these hues, though confidence in this idea has recently been shaken by psychophysical experiments that in certain highly abnormal viewing conditions seem to induce perceptions of colours described by some observers as reddish-greens and yellowish-blues (Crane and Piantanida 1983). Certain resemblance relations among the unitary hues also appear to be essential. For example, that blue and green more closely resemble each other than either resembles red or yellow seems essential to blue and green; and that red and yellow more closely resemble each other than either resembles blue or green seems essential to red and yellow.

Matters become more complicated, however, when we note that not all of the resemblance relations appear to be essential to the colours. First, as Hardin (1988: 126) argues, the *number* of just-noticeable hue differences between two colours does not appear to be essential to the colours: two colours might for one observer be separated by five just-noticeably-different hue steps, whereas for another observer they might be separated by seven just-noticeably-different hue steps. It is essential to the two colours that there be some hue-resemblance route between them, but the number of steps on the route does not seem to be essential. Second, although it seems essential (for the unitary hues) that blue and green resemble each other more than either resembles red or yellow, and that red and yellow resemble each other more than either resembles blue or green, the identity of blue does not appear to depend on its resemblance to green (and vice versa), and the identity of red does not appear to depend on its resemblance to yellow (and vice versa): true red–green dichromats presumably see yellows but no reds, and blues but no greens; whereas true yellow–blue dichromats presumably see reds but no yellows, and greens but no blues. (Or should we say that these perceivers are simply unable to appreciate visually some of the internal relations in colour space?) Hardin's suggestion is that essential to the colours are their constituents and the relations that hold among the colours in virtue of those constituents.[9] This view would make the relations that hold among the colours in virtue of features of their hue constituents (like those in the above examples) essential to the colours.

Of course, to say that colours are thus internally related (via the internal relations among their hue components) is philo-sophically informative only to the extent that we have some grasp of what an internal relation is. But it is notoriously difficult to say precisely what is involved in the distinction between internal and external relations. It is perhaps not surprising, then, that appeals to colour are often made as a way of conveying what internal relations are supposed to be. Thus in the *Tractatus*, 4.123, Wittgenstein says that 'A property is internal if it is unthinkable that its object should not possess it', and he then goes on to give as an example the relation between two colours of the same hue but different lightness: 'This shade of blue and that one stand, eo ipso, in the internal relation of lighter to darker. It is unthinkable that these two objects should not stand in this relation' (Wittgenstein 1921/1961: 27).[10] Similarly, in his lectures entitled 'Form and content', Moritz Schlick writes that the

> relations which hold between the elements of the systems of colours are, obviously, *internal* relations, for it is customary to call a relation internal if it relates two (or more) terms in such a way that the terms cannot possibly exist without the relation existing between them – in other words, if the relation is necessarily implied by the very nature of the terms.
>
> (Schlick 1979: 293–4)[11]

The distinction between internal and external relations to which Wittgenstein and Schlick appeal in these remarks is another difficult topic that I do not wish to pursue here. It suffices for my purposes to observe that if one holds that the relations colours bear to each other are internal, then one holds that propositions about these relations are either necessarily true or necessarily false (Hardin 1984a: 128). Thus the proposition 'Orange resembles red and yellow more than it resembles either blue or green' is necessarily true; whereas the proposition 'Purple resembles yellow more than it resembles red' is necessarily false. One might also argue that there are necessarily true propositions about the relations among the dimensions of colour space. For example, it is necessarily true that all hues must have some saturation value (since saturation is the proportion of hue content in relation to an achromatic point); and it is necessarily true that all saturated colours must have a hue (achromatic colours have zero saturation). That all hues must be of some lightness also seems to be necessarily true (how could there be a hue that did not have a lightness?).

It is important to remember that the necessary propositions here are ones about what Wittgenstein calls the 'geometry' of colours. In other words, they are not (in the first instance) about colours considered as properties of objects (being coloured);

they are about the properties that colours themselves exhibit as displayed in geometrical representations of colour space (see notes 10 and 11). Nevertheless, it is also important to remember that colours are typically perceived as properties of objects; thus the properties of colours as displayed in colour space can be considered as second-order properties of coloured things.

We can now return to the topic of novel colours and to the Wittgensteinian claim that it is the geometry of colours that shows us what we are talking about. We were considering whether there could be a perceiver like Jackson's Fred whose colour space resembled our own except that it contained an entirely novel hue. The first point to be made is that such a colour space would have to have a geometry different from that of our own colour space. To see why, consider the problem of trying to insert a novel hue into our colour space. The problem here is that colour space is a closed structure, as is immediately apparent from any of its geometrical representations,[12] and so there is no place for a novel hue to be inserted without altering the geometry of the space. As Westphal observes:

> It is possible ... to show that the insertion of a fictitious colour into our three dimensional colour space will disrupt the order and prevent us from conceiving some other colour or group of colours in the space, independently of the explanation of this fact in the generative basis of the space. For colours and the similarity colour space are inseparable. The positions of the colours on the hue circuit, for example, are determined by the positions of their intermediaries and vice-versa, and these together determine the geometry of the space.
>
> (Westphal 1987: 100–1)

Westphal's concern is mainly to explicate Wittgenstein's 'puzzle proposition' that 'there can be a bluish green but not a reddish green'. (It should be noted that reddish-green is not an example of a novel hue in the main sense that we have been considering, that is, a novel unitary hue; rather it is a novel binary hue.) The point is that if reddish-green is to be a possible hue, then some location must be found for it within the colour space. But since the colour space is a closed structure, a new hue such as reddish-green cannot be added to the space without fundamentally disrupting its structure in arbitrary and unprincipled ways. On the other hand, a new hue cannot be located outside colour space, for then it would lie outside the hue dimension, and so could not be a hue. It is a conceptual truth that something is a colour only if it has a location within colour space, and there is no room within the closed space for a novel hue.

Westphal is right that a novel hue such as reddish-green cannot be inserted into our *three-dimensional* colour space without altering the space in unprincipled ways. But it does not follow that our colour space could not contain such a novel binary hue. To see why, recall the experiment that I mentioned above by Crane and Piantanida (1983) that purports to establish perceptions of colours described by some observers as reddish-green and yellowish-blue. As Hardin notes, 'if this experiment is valid, no resemblance ordering of *all* experienceable hues is possible in a three-dimensional color space' (Hardin 1988: 126). The possibility of such novel binary hues would therefore imply that our colour space is actually not three-dimensional for all conditions of viewing.[13] Thus a home could be found for reddish-green and yellowish-blue in our colour space without the problem arising of trying to insert them into a closed space of only three dimensions.

What now of a fully fledged novel hue, that is, not a novel binary hue like reddish-green and yellowish-blue, but a novel unitary hue that is neither reddish, nor greenish, nor yellowish, nor bluish? It is again a conceptual truth that such a hue must have some location in colour space. But finding a place for a novel unitary hue in colour space requires more than finding a place for a novel binary hue such as reddish-green. To find a place for this latter hue involves establishing a resemblance route between the two already existing unitary hues red and green that does not involve travelling through yellow or blue, or the neutral achromatic point. (It is this requirement that cannot be met in the familiar three-dimensional representation of colour space.) To find a place for a novel unitary hue, however, would require that we establish a resemblance route between this hue and at least one of the already existing unitary hues. In other words, we need to find a resemblance route from either red, green, yellow, or blue to a hue that is neither reddish, nor greenish, nor yellowish, nor bluish. The point can also be made in terms of hue categories and the geometrical representation of colour space: we need to find a resemblance route from a region (volume) of our colour space corresponding to one of our hue categories to an entirely new region (volume) of colour space corresponding to the novel hue category. But our colour space is certainly closed with respect to this possibility: the space is completely filled and so there is no place for a new hue region. Consequently, there is no way to build a novel hue into the space without fundamentally altering its geometry (both in the familiar representational sense and in the Wittgensteinian sense of logical or grammatical structure).

Considerations of this kind have led some philosophers to conclude that the concept of a novel hue is simply incoherent. For example, Bernard Harrison writes: 'To be incapable of being placed on the colour array as we perceive it is simply to be not a colour, and thus not capable of standing as a term in colour relationships' (Harrison 1973: 133). But this conclusion is based on a misunderstanding about what is conceptually required for a quality to be a novel hue. The concept of a novel hue cannot be that of a new hue inserted into our colour space, for that is impossible. Nor can it be that of a new hue located outside colour space, for that is incoherent. The concept of a novel hue must rather be that of a new hue located in a *novel colour space*, that is, a colour space that has a fundamentally different geometry from our own, as discussed in Chapter 4. Thus it does not follow that a quality having no place on the colour array as we perceive it is not a hue, for the quality might have a home in a different colour space. Harrison is right to think that our colour space is closed to the possibility of a novel hue, but he is wrong to think that there cannot be different types of colour space (as indeed there are for people who have colour vision of different dimensionalities).

We still have not fully established the coherence of the idea of a novel hue, however, for we have yet to establish securely that the concept of a novel colour space is not itself incoherent. The problem that arises in this connection is the one suggested by Wittgenstein's remark that it is 'the geometry of colours that shows us what we're talking about, i.e., that we are talking about colours.' If the relations that the hues bear to each other are, as we have been supposing, internal relations (if true propositions about these relations and those that obtain in colour space in virtue of them are necessarily true), then these relations determine what the hues are. And since these relations constitute the geometry of colours, the geometry of colours constitutes what the colours are. Westphal has written that 'Colour space is Leibnizian. The place holders determine the geometry of the space' (1987: 47). On the view we are considering, however, the reverse is also true: the geometry of the space – defined in terms of the (internal) relations among the place holders – determines the place holders. As Harrison puts it: 'the relationships which unite colour presentations into an array can only be specified by reference to colour presentations themselves (i.e., to certain contents), while colour presentations in turn can only be specified by reference to the relationships in which they stand to one another' (1973: 127). It follows, then, that changing the geometry (the relations) will change the place holders (the colours). But if, as Wittgenstein says, it is the geometry of the space that indicates in the first place that the qualities with which we are concerned are *colours*, then how are we to draw the line between changing the geometry and changing the qualities? Some changes in the geometry are certainly allowable (for example, those having to do with the number of just-noticeably different hue steps between colours), but if we change the geometry too much, our conviction that the *kind* of quality with which we are dealing is colour will be undermined. Perhaps a colour space that had a radically different geometry wouldn't really be a *colour* space. (Cf. the first remark of Wittgenstein's quoted above: 'For it is by no means clear that we *must* say of this sort of abnormal people that they know other *colours*.')

The foregoing considerations already indicate how this problem should be approached. First, I have all along insisted that a novel hue must bear a resemblance relation to at least one of our hues. Second, the novel hue must itself be located in some closed space of hue–saturation–lightness relations (see Hardin 1984a: 128, 1988: 145). These two conditions imply that there must be a resemblance route from our colour space to the novel colour space. A region in our colour space corresponding to one of our hue categories (red, green, yellow, or blue) must stand at the beginning of the route, and a region in the novel colour space corresponding to the novel hue category must stand at the end of the route. For there to be such a resemblance route it is necessary that the hue region in our colour space also be a component region of the novel colour space. By thus containing that region of our colour space as a necessary constituent, the novel colour space will be internally related to it (the proposition that the novel colour space is related to that hue region of our colour space by the relation of containment will be necessarily true).

Must the novel colour space contain our colour space in its entirety? It seems likely that answers to this question will vary depending on the extent to which one holds that the relations the colours bear to one another are internal. If every relation among the colours (in colour space) is internal, then it would seem impossible for our colour space not to be carried over in its entirety into the novel space. We have seen reason to deny, however, that the identity of the colours depends on every relation in which they figure in colour space. Instead we have adopted Hardin's (tentative) proposal that essential to the colours are their constituents and the relations that obtain in virtue of them. On this proposal, then, only these constituents would have to be carried over to the novel space. This proposal has a further interesting implication: if we suppose that opponency is essential to the hues, then any novel hue will require its own opponent complement. It would follow that a novel colour space could not contain just one novel hue: it would have to contain *two* opponently related novel hues. Applied to Fred, this would mean that Fred's colour space would have three pairs of opponently related hues (our two plus his novel pair) and that he might therefore perceive ternary hue combinations in addition to our mere binary hues – in short, that Fred's colour space is a tetrachromatic colour hyperspace of the sort discussed in Chapter 4. The problem with this proposal, however, is that opponency might not after all be essential to the hues. If this were the case, then a novel hue would not necessarily require an opponent complement. Furthermore, not even all of the relations among the hue constituents of our colours would need to be carried over to the novel space.[14]

These issues are difficult, and I do not see how they can be answered short of a fully articulated and well-grounded theory of which features of the colours are essential and which accidental. In the case of Fred, however, we can say something more definite. Since, as Jackson says, we stand to Fred as a true red–green dichromat stands to us, we can suppose that the hue constituents of our colours must be carried over in their entirety to Fred's novel colour space. Just as our colour space contains the hues and the relations between them of a true red–green dichromat (as well as those of a true yellow–blue dichromat), so Fred's novel colour space contains our hues and the relations between them. Whereas we are trichromats and have a colour space of three dimensions, Fred is a tetrachromat and has a four-dimensional colour hyperspace.

I have now laid down some conditions for a quality space to count as a colour space, and so have provided an answer to the Wittgensteinian question about what is conceptually required for someone to be said to see a novel hue, though there are certainly many questions that remain. The conditions attempt to preserve the idea that the geometry of colour space is in some sense constitutive of the colours. Yet they allow there to be variations in the geometry within certain limits: variations are allowed as long as there is some resemblance route from our colour space to the novel colour space. On the other hand, if the envisaged variations in the geometry have the result that there is no longer any such resemblance route, then the conditions necessary to count the space as a colour space are lacking.

It is worth noting that this view meets certain requirements suggested by two other passages in Wittgenstein's *Remarks on Colour* – I-66 and III-154, which differ only slightly in wording. In these passages, Wittgenstein responds to the question about whether we can imagine people having a different geometry of colour from our own by saying (III-154):

> —That, of course, means: Can't we imagine people who have colour concepts which are other than ours; and that in turn means: Can't we imagine that people do *not* have our colour concepts and that they *have* concepts which are related to ours in such a way that we would also want to call them 'colour concepts'?

I have argued that a novel hue must reside in a novel colour space and that this novel space must contain as a component some region of our colour space corresponding to one of our hue categories. The colour concepts operating in the novel space would consequently cover some of our colours, though they would, of course, differ from our concepts in various ways. Furthermore, there seems no reason to suppose that these differences could not be revealed behaviourally (for example, in psychophysical experiments or everyday colour-sorting tasks) and linguistically in the repertoire of colour terms available to the speakers (for example, our 'red', and Fred's 'red$_1$' and 'red$_2$').

We can now return finally to the issue of what it would be like to perceive a novel hue. Jackson's claim is that the totality of physical information would still not tell us how the novel hue looks to Fred, and so would be silent about various properties of his perceptual experience, such as how his experience of seeing the novel hue differs from his experience of seeing red, green, yellow, and blue.

The first thing to be said is that, physical knowledge aside, we have already said a great deal about what it would be like to see a novel hue. In the case of Fred, we have determined that he is a tetrachromat and that his colour space is accordingly a four-dimensional colour hyperspace. Given the similarity of his visual system to ours, we can suppose that this colour space contains a novel opponent hue pair and ternary hue combinations. I see no reason not to count these as facts about what it is like for Fred to see his additional colours. Therefore, Jackson must be speaking loosely when he says that we do not know the 'kind of experience' Fred has when he sees red$_1$ and red$_2$. On the contrary, we do indeed know what *kind* of experience he is having in several respects: we know first and most generally that his experience is colour experience. Second, we know that the difference between red$_1$ and red$_2$ is not like the difference between one of the shades of blue we can see and Hume's missing shade of blue: as Jackson himself stipulates, red$_1$ and red$_2$ are not shades of the one colour red. The difference between them must therefore be a categorical difference in hue. Third, as a novel hue in an opponently organized colour space, red$_2$ must have a novel opponent hue complement. Finally, Fred's novel opponent hue pair in combination with our two opponent hue pairs enables Fred to see colours that are ternary combinations of hue.

Jackson might fairly reply that the foregoing misses the point of his argument. Just as someone who is a true red–green dichromat can know all the analogous facts about normal human colour vision (for example, that we have an additional opponent hue pair that enables us to see binary combinations of hue) while still not knowing everything there is to know about how red and green look to us, so in knowing the above facts about the kind of experience Fred enjoys we still do not know everything there is to know about how the additional colours look to Fred.

We can accept this point, yet two things should be noted. First, we have been forced to *exclude* certain things that are legitimately covered by the phrases 'what the colours are like for Fred' and 'how the colours look to Fred'. Thus these phrases do not immediately or unequivocally indicate which features of Fred's colour perception are the ones Jackson takes to be relevant to his argument; and Jackson provides no further description in addition to these phrases. Second, the analogy with colour-deficient perceivers not knowing everything there is to know about how red and green look is made in the context of our present state of knowledge. But if we attempt to extrapolate the analogy to the context Jackson wishes us to imagine in which we have 'all the physical information', then matters are not so clear. How can we be sure that Jackson is right in his presumption that we would not know how the colours look? Jackson does not provide *any* substantive argument for his claim; he just says 'it *seems* [my italics] that no amount of physical information ... tells us' (1982: 129).

The most glaring problem with this assertion, however, is not that it is unargued. It is rather that we simply have no idea a priori what would be included in 'all the physical information'. 'Physical' as Jackson uses the term includes the knowledge gained by the physical, chemical, and biological sciences. If we extrapolate to some science fictional future in which we know *everything* physical there is to know, then 'physical' will cover the knowledge gained by all future developments in physics, chemistry, and biology; it will include all the knowledge gained by the yet to be invented sciences studying the yet to be discovered levels of organization in the natural world; and it will include a theory of how all the levels are interrelated (including new concepts for relating the levels). That we have in advance no idea what all these developments would entail strikes me as intuitively obvious if anything is. Jackson thus requires us to imagine something that is actually unimaginable, with the result that his thought experiment is at worst defective at its very foundation and at best wildly unconstrained.

It is instructive nonetheless to try to imagine briefly what it would be like to have all the relevant physical information about Fred's colour perception, a task Jackson himself neglects to perform.[15] Again we can suppose that we determine that Fred's colour space has a novel opponent hue pair and novel ternary hue combinations. Let us also suppose that Fred is as interested as we are to learn all the facts about his unique colour perception and consequently that he is a willing experimental subject. To exercise our imaginations let us first consider some of the things Fred can simply *tell* us about his experience: he tells us that one of his novel hues is like red and yellow in that it can be described as 'warm', 'advancing', and 'light', whereas the other is like blue and green in that it can be described as 'cool', 'receding', and 'dark'. He tells us that the ternary hues he perceives are also arrayed in various ways along these polarities. He divulges to us the various other affective and emotional associations he has with his novel colours, including some intriguing novel intermodal and synaesthetic associations. Imagine now that we have collected all such phenomenological information about Fred.

Second, consider some of the things we can establish in standard psychophysical experiments: we determine whether Fred is able to perceive any unitary examples of his novel hues or whether he typically perceives them in combination with another hue (as spectral red for us always has a small amount of yellow). We determine the number of just-noticeably different hue steps between each of Fred's novel hues and red, green, yellow, and blue. We determine the various degrees of saturation and of lightness that his novel hues exhibit. Imagine now that we have collected all such psychophysical information about Fred so that we have a complete psychophysical specification of his novel colour space.

Third, consider some of the things we would know about Fred's physiology: we discover that Fred has a fourth type of receptor photopigment with a distinct spectral absorption profile, and we isolate and sequence the gene that specifies it. We discover that signals from cells containing this type of pigment are combined and compared with the other receptor signals by postreceptoral cells, thereby generating a third chromatically opponent channel. We also uncover the cortical processes involved in the generation of Fred's novel colour space. Imagine now that we have collected all such neurophysiological information and that we have a complete theory that shows us how to relate the psychophysical phenomena to their neuronal substrates. (Since this is science fiction, we can also imagine that we were able to carry out this research without any harm or serious discomfort to Fred.)

Fourth, consider some of the things we would know about the objects that Fred perceives to be categorically different in hue. We discover, for example, that the tomatoes Fred sorts into two different groups reflect light differently in the near-ultraviolet. One kind of tomato has a prominent rise in its surface spectral reflectance curve in the ultraviolet, whereas the other kind does not. Thus Fred's visual system is sensitive to physical characteristics of the tomatoes to which our visual system is not. Imagine now that we have collected all such environmental information about Fred's visual perception.

Finally, remember that, according to Jackson, what we know about Fred also includes everything physical about 'his behaviour and dispositions to behaviour ... and everything about his history and relation to others that can be given in physical accounts of persons' (1982: 129).

The question now before us is: what features of Fred's colour experience would this kind of account not include? Again it is no help to say that this kind of account would not tell us how the novel colours look to Fred. The account tells us quite a lot about how the colours look to Fred – after all, much of what we know Fred told us. And yet the temptation is still to insist that something is left out. What might this something be? How might we describe it?

The idea that inevitably suggests itself at this point is that we do not know what the 'intrinsic properties' of Fred's colours are. We learn many things as a result of the kind of account sketched above, but we do not learn the 'intrinsic qualitative characters' of Fred's novel hues, and so we do not know exactly how they differ from our hues. The problem now is to say what is meant by the term 'intrinsic qualitative character' as applied to the colours.

Although the term 'intrinsic' as applied to the qualitative aspects of experience has been charged with incoherence by some philosophers (Dennett 1990), I think that there is a coherent sense it can be given in this context. Consider the three-dimensional representations of colour space discussed above in which each colour is represented by a vector or a distinct point in the space. The size and shape of the colour solid will result from the coordinates we choose and the way they are oriented relative to one another. Yet as colour scientists Judd and Wyszecki observe, 'a mere organization of the manifold of colors does not give us any information on the intrinsic properties of the manifold besides the fact that it is three-dimensional' (1963: 308). Here the term 'intrinsic' is being used, as they go on to say, for 'those properties which are independent of the choice of coordinate system and thus independent of any transformation we might use to convert a given color solid into another of different size and shape'. In this context, then, intrinsic properties are simply ones that colours have *qua* colours, that is, ones they have regardless of which objects they happen to be the colour of. It is the representation of these properties that must be preserved in any geometrical colour space. The example that Judd and Wyszecki give as 'the most fundamental intrinsic property of the color space' is the difference between two colours as measured in terms of the number of just-noticeable hue differences between them. This property is clearly a relational one between the colours; it is therefore precisely not intrinsic in the sense typically meant by philosophers, namely, non-relational.[16]

The term 'intrinsic', then, is perfectly respectable when used to characterize the properties of colours *qua* colours.[17] But this sense still does not succeed in pinning down exactly what it is that we are supposed not to know about Fred's novel colours. (The just-noticeable difference relations among Fred's colours, for example, are features of his colour space that we imagined determining using typical psychophysical procedures.) Just what exactly is it that we mean to indicate, then, when we speak of the intrinsic qualitative features of colours?

It is at this precise moment that the term 'intrinsic' becomes invoked in its metaphysically dubious sensationalist sense. Colours are said to have qualitative features that are intrinsic in the sense that they are *purely phenomenal*: they have only a certain qualitative character but no intentional content. These purely phenomenal features are also *nonrelational*: they are features that each colour supposedly has on its own independently of its relations to the other colours (they belong to the colours intrinsically). Finally, the features are supposedly *simple* in the sense that they have no internal structure, and so do not admit of any analysis. We have, then, the circle of interlocking terms that within the sensationalist tradition has always been applied to colour qualities.

It is this sensationalist view that the intrinsic qualitative features of colour are not only features the colours have *qua* colours, but are also purely phenomenal, nonrelational, and simple properties accessible only from the first-person perspective that lies at the root of Jackson's conception of what is missing from our knowledge of Fred when we know everything physical about him. It is not simply that we lack Fred's kind of colour perception and so cannot see the colours as he sees them; it is rather that our inability to see his colours is conceived as an inability to be directly acquainted with certain simple, nonrelational, and purely phenomenal visual presentations – colour sensations. It is this conception that most probably lies behind Jackson's silence about just which features of the colours he means when he says that we do not know 'what the new colours are like', for Jackson treats this phrase as if it unproblematically picked out – as though by ostension – some simple and purely phenomenal visual sensation.

Jackson is certainly not alone in holding to this sensationalist conception of how visual experience is constituted. Appealing to such putative characteristics of colour has in fact become paradigmatic for discussions of the qualitative features of experience (qualia) in most English-speaking philosophy of mind. And since it is rather difficult to say more about what these mysterious intrinsic properties are – they are, after all, 'ineffable' according to the sensationalist tradition – almost all claims on their behalf involve appeals to intuition rather than argument. Terence Horgan provides a typical example when in a discussion of the so-called 'inverted spectrum' problem he writes:

I take the intrinsic, nonrelative nature of qualia to be a

self-evident fact, a fact which unavoidably impresses itself upon most of us who actually experience these states. The point is virtually impossible to *argue* for, however, because it depends on an individual's first-person perspective towards his own mental life.

(Horgan 1984: 459)

Horgan is right that the issue depends on the perspective one takes towards one's experience; the question, however, is whether the perspective that would appeal to nonrelational and purely phenomenal properties is philosophically cogent or whether it results from little more than prejudiced and unargued intuitions.

It might not be possible to demonstrate that there are no such intrinsic sensational properties, though philosophers in a variety of traditions have attempted to show that the very idea of this kind of property is incoherent, as we saw, for example, in Merleau-Ponty's critique of sensationalism. Our exploration of novel colours provides further support for this attempt because it shows how the intuition that there are such properties is misinformed and misguided in its treatment of colour. To show the coherence of the very concept upon which Jackson's thought experiment relies, the concept of a novel hue, we had to navigate the complexities of colour space as a system of internally related qualities. To make sense of the very idea of a novel hue we thus had to treat the colours as qualities whose features are not at all intrinsic in the sense of being nonrelational. The properties that colours exhibit depend on the internal relations that to a considerable (though still undetermined) extent compose the structure of colour space. We also had to treat the properties that colours exhibit as complex, not simple (see also Westphal 1984). To find a home for a novel hue we had to analyse colours along the dimensions of hue, saturation, and lightness; and we had to analyse the colours into their unitary, binary, and novel ternary hue constituents, as well as their constituent opponent relations. *Thus the conception of the qualitative features of experience upon which Jackson's knowledge argument relies is actually undermined by the very idea of a novel hue that he invokes.*

What about the intuition that colours have features that are purely qualitative and nonintentional? Although I have placed considerable emphasis on the properties that colours exhibit as displayed in geometrical representations of colour space, that is, on the properties of colours *qua* colours, we do not perceive these properties as floating freely, as it were. As I indicated at the outset, we typically perceive colours as properties of things in some visual context. This fact has two important implications. First, the properties of colour that we have been considering are actually best construed as second-order properties of coloured things. To get a handle on these second-order properties we abstract away from the coloured things that exemplify them and consider the properties directly in a space of colour relations. *But this space is not itself something perceived.* (Of course, representations of it are things perceived.) It is rather the logical structure that constitutes the (second-order) properties embedded in our perceptual experiences of coloured things. Second, when sensationalists make the phenomenological claim that the fundamental qualitative element of this perceptual experience is a *sensation* of colour, they are simply mistaken. The fundamental element is the *seeing of a coloured thing*. Strictly speaking, the qualitative character in any actual colour perception cannot be separated from the thing that is being perceived as coloured; as Merleau-Ponty puts it, 'this red would literally not be the same if it were not the "woolly" red of a carpet' (1945/1962: 4–5). The general point holds even in the most restricted aperture conditions of typical psychophysical experiments on colour and brightness perception, for there we still perceive *luminous coloured areas* at various levels of brightness. Colour and brightness perception always involve spatial perception; and both depend on the amount of light transmitted from the area in relation to other areas in the visual scene as well as on changes in intensity over time (Lockhead 1992). The qualitative features of colour are thus always perceived as contextually situated or embedded in some way, and such situatedness is not accidental to them; rather it constitutes how we experience them. Consequently, the qualitative features of colour always have some intentional content, and so are precisely not purely qualitative or phenomenal. I submit, then, that the claim made by many contemporary philosophers that the qualitative aspects of our experience include nonrelational and purely qualitative features is not even phenomenologically cogent.

This discussion has several morals for the knowledge argument. First, contrary to Jackson, the ability to see novel colours would not be a matter of one's visual experience having novel sensational properties. Rather, it would be a matter of having a novel perceptual system with novel qualitative *and* intentional capacities. Second, were we to acquire such capacities, there might be a sense in which we would learn something, even if we knew everything physical that there is to know, but such knowledge could not be a matter of 'knowledge *that*', where 'that' picks out some nonintentional and purely qualitative sensation or sensational property of experience with which one is immediately acquainted. Finally, the methodological moral to be drawn is that we should not pursue our investigations in the philosophy of mind by advancing completely a priori arguments about what science will and will not be able to tell us about our experiences and the experiences of other sentient creatures. Indeed, it may not be possible to know what science can (or cannot) tell us in advance of doing the science (Akins 1990; Hardin 1991, 1992c). Doing the science need not mean abandoning the philosophy, nor in this context need it mean abandoning the phenomenology (Varela et al. 1991; Flanagan 1992), but it does mean that our philosophical and phenomenological explorations should not involve unconstrained thought experiments and unargued appeals to misguided intuitions. Knowledge of the qualitative aspects of perceptual experience, whether scientific or otherwise, can never be had unless we begin from a more accurate and faithful portrayal than that found in Jackson's knowledge argument and many current discussions of qualia.

COGNITIVISM: DENNETT'S DISQUALIFICATION OF QUALIA

Readers familiar with Daniel C. Dennett's notorious attack on the very idea of qualia (Dennett 1990, 1991) may at this point be wondering how my approach to this issue differs from his. Do I agree with Dennett that there really are no such things as qualia, that qualia should be 'quined'?[18] My own position is easy to summarize: if qualia are identified (as they are by many contemporary philosophers[19]) as sensational properties of experience that are purely qualitative and devoid of any intentional content, then I deny that there are any such qualia. But if qualia are more carefully and less tendentiously identified as the qualitative features that we experience ourselves and things in the world as having, then there are indeed qualia, because we do indeed experience ourselves and the world in a qualitative manner. My point, which is taken directly from Merleau-Ponty, is that the qualitative aspects of our experience are also intentional – they are constituted by the kinds of situations in which we intentionally (in the phenomenological sense) experience ourselves and the world.

Dennett too denies the notion of qualia that I have portrayed as sensationalist, though he does not describe it with this term. But his strategy is to argue that the qualitative dimensions of experience are constituted entirely by the discriminative judgements and reactive behavioural dispositions of the subject. He thus denies that there is any such thing as genuine qualitative content in perceptual experience – content whose character is (as one might say in an older philosophical idiom) presentational but not judgemental. It is this thesis about the character of perceptual experience that I do not accept and that differentiates my position from Dennett's. The purpose of this section is to elaborate on these remarks.

Dennett likens the philosophical literature on qualia to a snarled kite string – better to go and get a new kite string than trying to unsnarl the old one (1991: 369). I agree with this estimation of the qualia literature, but I think that Dennett's treatment of qualia also manages to tangle up the issues in a number of ways.

First, there is the issue of just what should be understood by the term 'qualia' (see Flanagan 1992: 61). At the beginning of his article 'Quining qualia', Dennett says '"Qualia" is an unfamiliar term for something that could not be more familiar to each of us: the *ways things seem to us*' (Dennett 1990: 519). The ways things seem to us depend both on the ways things are – for example, their physical constitutions – and on the ways we are – for example, our perceptual systems. The way milk tastes to me, for example, depends on the physical and chemical constitution of milk (hence cow's milk tastes different from goat's milk) and on the physiological characteristics of my gustatory and olfactory systems. On this construal, then, qualia are most naturally understood as relational properties constituted by things in the world and characteristics of the perceiver.

It is not this conception of qualia that Dennett is primarily concerned to undermine. Instead, the main target of his attack is a particular philosophical account of the ways things seem to us. It is an account that depends on imputing certain properties to experience in virtue of which mental states have the experiential content they do. The properties are themselves defined by their possession of certain second-order properties – being *ineffable, intrinsic, private,* and *directly* or *immediately apprehensible in consciousness* (Dennett 1990). These second-order properties are exactly the ones that have always been applied to experience in the sensationalist tradition. We thus arrive at a second sense of the term 'qualia' as applying to the (imputed) sensational properties of experience.

Although many philosophers have responded to Dennett by claiming that this conception of qualia is a strawman, Dennett thinks that it is nonetheless implicit in the standard assumption of the qualia literature, which is that the qualitative character of an experience at any given time can be isolated from everything else that is going on in the subject, such as sensory stimulation, motor activity, memory, belief, desire, expectation, various dispositions to believe and to behave, etc. (1990: 521).[20] Dennett tags this assumption as 'the big mistake' because it gives us the idea of a quale as a residual qualitative property or qualitative residue that can in principle be isolated from everything else in the subject. Indeed, once this idea is in place it is easy to see how qualia are supposed to pose an intractable problem for any scientific theory of the mind. To use Nagel's formulation, how could there be a scientific account of the 'most specific qualities' in the subjective character of experience? Or to use another common formulation, how could science ever bridge the 'explanatory gap' (Levine 1983, 1991) between physiology and the intrinsic qualitative character of a mental state? We thus once again arrive at essentially the same sensationalist problem that was presented in Chapter 1 and that reappeared in our discussion of Jackson's knowledge argument: how can one imagine there to be any nonarbitrary connection between the qualitative and the physical, where the former is conceived as ultimately logically simple, nonintentional, and nonrelational? Therefore, the conception of qualia that Dennett scrutinizes cannot be dismissed as a strawman, for its basic core – the idea of a qualitative residue that is isolable from everything else in the subject – is pervasive in the qualia literature, tacit though it may be.

Disentangling these two conceptions of qualia is only the first step towards untying the various issues bound together in Dennett's treatment of the qualia-debate. The next step is to disentangle the issue about the relation between perceptual experience and judgement. One of the reasons why Dennett claims that the 'traditional' (i.e., sensationalist) concept of qualia is 'so thoroughly confused' (1990: 520) is that perceptual qualities are actually relational, not intrinsic, and so cannot be isolated from everything else in the subject and in the world (533–4). It would seem, then, that Dennett should embrace a relational approach to qualia that does not construe them as intrinsic sensational properties of experience. But although Dennett (1991: 375–83) does sketch an evolutionary and relational account of colour that is similar in some ways to the account I have defended in this book, nonetheless his account of perceptual qualities remains a dismissive one. The reason is that Dennett does not allow the perceiver side of the relation to include anything presentational: he allows it to include only discriminative judgements and reactive dispositions available from the third-person point of view.

This issue about the nature of perception in relation to judgement is different from the debate about the sensationalist conception of qualia, though the two are completely tied together in Dennett's discussion. One can perfectly well (and indeed should) reject the sensationalist conception of qualia that Dennett very effectively undermines. But denying sensationalism does not entail that the content of perceptual experience is constituted entirely by judgement. The issue about perception and judgement is the issue of whether perceptual experience contains as a proper component a kind of content that is not judgemental. One can hold that it does without holding that the nonjudgemental component is constituted by sensations or sensational properties.

The way that Dennett links the issue about perceptual experience and judgement to the issue about qualia emerges in his argument against the core idea in the sensationalist conception of qualia – the assumption that a perceptual experience has an intrinsic qualitative character that can be isolated from everything else going on in the perceptual situation. What Dennett tries to show is that the qualitative character of a perceptual experience is not intrinsic to the experience, but rather extrinsic and relational, and this moreover in the particular sense that it is constituted entirely by the judgements and reactive dispositions of the subject.

One of Dennett's best examples is the case of beer as a so-called 'acquired taste' (1990: 533–4; 1991: 395–6). Does this expression mean that a liking for the taste of beer is acquired, that is, a liking for the flavour of the very first sip? Or does it mean rather that the taste of beer changes because one gradually comes to enjoy it? Most people, it seems, would opt for the latter construal, in which case the qualitative character of one's experience turns out to be an extrinsic and relational property, because it depends, at least in part, on one's attitudes and discriminative reactions. Suppose, on the other hand, some people were to insist that beer has always tasted the same to them, but that they have gradually trained themselves to like that very taste. Dennett writes:

> Is there a real difference [between these two cases]? ... It *could* be that the different convictions spring from genuine differences in discriminative capacity of the following sort: in the first sort of beer drinker the 'training' has changed the 'shape' of the quality space for tasting, while in the second sort the quality space remains roughly the same, but the 'evaluative function' over that space has been revised. Or it *could* be that some or even all of the beer drinkers are kidding themselves ... We have to look ... to the actual happenings in the head to see whether there is a truth-preserving interpretation of the beer drinkers' claims, and *if* there is, it will only be because we decide to *reduce* 'the way it tastes' to one complex of reactive dispositions or another ... We would have to 'destroy' qualia in order to 'save' them.
>
> (1991: 396)

Dennett is thus led to the view that the qualitative character of experience is in reality nothing other than the intentional content of the judgements that a subject makes, or has the disposition to make, given various patterns of stimulation. The 'qualitative' character of experience turns out to be, on this view, merely intentional, and so like other merely intentional objects (for example, Pegasus), strictly speaking fictional, not real. The lived world of the subject is to be treated as a fictional world, in which there are certain fictional items in good standing, such as qualia. But in reality there are no such items; there are only brain-based dispositions to react and to judge that such and such is the case. In Dennett's formulation, 'the way it is with me' is to be identified 'with the sum total of all the idiosyncratic reactive dispositions inherent in my nervous system as a result of my being confronted with a certain pattern of stimulation' (1991: 387).

The problem with Dennett's view is that, in assimilating perceptual experience to judgement, it gets the nature of perceptual content wrong; in particular, it neglects what is distinctive about *perceptual* content, in contrast to other kinds of content. In more phenomenological parlance, Dennett's view neglects the distinctive features of the intentionality of perception. One traditional way to mark the difference between perception and judgement is to appeal to the difference in mode of presentation that each involves (for example, Brentano 1874/1973: 201–34). Perception involves certain distinctive modes of presentation that depend on the characteristics of the particular sense modality, whereas judgement does not. For example, to see something in front of one is to have something visually appear to be present before one, whereas to judge that it is there is to make a claim (based perhaps on one's visual experience) about the thing's existence and location, a claim one can seek to support and justify by offering reasons. Assimilating perception to judgement is thus to commit the cognitivist error of intellectualizing perception – it is to succumb to what Merleau-Ponty calls the 'intellectualist' extreme in relation to sensationalism ('empiricism'):

> Ordinary experience draws a clear distinction between sense experience and judgement. It sees judgement as the taking of a stand, as an effort to know something which shall be valid for myself at every moment of my life, and equally for other actual or potential minds; sense experience, on the contrary, is taking appearance at its face value, without trying to possess it and learn its truth. This

distinction disappears in intellectualism, because judgement is everywhere where pure sensation is not – that is,
absolutely everywhere.

(1945/1962: 34)

In contemporary Anglo–American philosophy, an account of
what is distinctive to the intentionality of perception in
contrast to belief (the paradigm case of judgement) can be
found in John Searle's theory of intentionality (Searle 1983). In
a view rather reminiscent of Husserl's, Searle holds that belief
and visual perception differ in the formal features of their
intentionality. Both can be identified and described in terms of
their intentional content, but there are crucial differences in the
nature of the content in each case. For example, in the case of
visual perception, but not in the case of belief, the intentional
content is said to be causally self-referential, in the sense that
its satisfaction conditions require that the visual experience be
caused by what it is about (1983: 47–50). But the difference that
is even more relevant to our concerns here is that the intentional content in visual perception is said to be *presentational*,
whereas in belief it is *representational*:

> If, for example, I see a yellow station wagon in front of me,
> the experience I have is directly of the object. It doesn't
> just 'represent' the object, it provides direct access to it.
> The experience has a kind of directness, immediacy and
> involuntariness which is not shared by a belief I might
> have about the object in its absence. It seems therefore
> unnatural to describe visual experiences as representa-
> tions, indeed if we talk that way it is almost bound to lead
> to the representative theory of perception. Rather,
> because of the special features of perceptual experiences I
> propose to call them 'presentations'. The visual experi-
> ence does not just represent the state of affairs perceived;
> rather, when satisfied, it gives us direct access to it, and in
> that sense it is a presentation of that state of affairs.
>
> (1983: 45–6)

It is just this sort of distinction between presentation and
representation or judgement that Dennett is at pains to deny. In
his view there simply are no real presentations or 'real

292

seemings', as he calls them, in perceptual experience: 'There is no such phenomenon as really seeming – over and above the phenomenon of judging in one way or another that something is the case' (1991: 364).

In advancing this claim, however, Dennett conflates several importantly distinct philosophical issues. First, he again runs together the position that perception, unlike judgement, involves certain sense-modality based and qualitatively specific modes of presentation – qualitatively specific ways that things can appear to be to one – with the sensationalist position that such modes of presentation are composed of internal and purely phenomenal mental items ('real seemings' in the mind). But, as argued above, to deny the latter does not in any way commit one to denying the former.

Second, Dennett conflates the level of the *animal* as the proper subject of perception and action with the level of the animal's *brain*:[21] he supposes that the only way perceptual experience could be presentational is if there were some 'Witness' in an inner theatre of consciousness in the brain – a 'Cartesian Theater' (1991: 322). As he says: 'Perhaps the Cartesian Theater is popular because it is the place where the seemings can happen in addition to the judgings' (134). The thought here is that, if there were such an inner theatre, then one could, at least in principle, isolate the qualitative contents of experience from other mental activities, such as judgements and discriminative reactions made either prior to or after the onset of some moment of consciousness. On such a view consciousness would consist in a series of presentations made to an inner witness, and these presentations would constitute the material upon which the witness's judgements would be based. Dennett rightly castigates this view, which he calls 'Cartesian materialism'[22] (see also Dennett and Kinsbourne 1992). But the denial of Cartesian materialism does not entail that perception is judgemental and not presentational in the relevant sense. To suppose otherwise is to neglect the fundamental difference in level between, on the one hand, the brain as a component system of the animal and, on the other hand, the whole embodied animal interacting in its environment. It is the latter that is the proper subject of perception and action, not the former. Indeed, Dennett himself has in other writings drawn attention to this difference in level by distinguishing between what he calls the 'sub-personal level' and the 'personal level' (Dennett 1978: 153–4). The distinction is crucial in this context because when one claims, as, for example, Searle does in the passage above, that perceptual experience, unlike belief, is presentational, not representational, one is describing perception and belief at the personal level, the level of the perceiving-acting subject, not at the subpersonal level, the level of the subject's brain.[23] But Cartesian materialism – the view that there is a consciousness system centrally located within the subject's brain – is a subpersonal theory of the functional architecture of the brain, and the denial of this theory has no immediate bearing on whether the subject-level character of perceptual experience is presentational or judgemental.

The way that Dennett presents his own positive account of perceptual experience being constituted by judgement also slides back-and-forth between the personal and subpersonal levels. On the one hand, Dennett says that it is 'the phenomenon of judging in one way or another that something is the case' that constitutes how something seems to be to the subject in perception (1991: 364). On the other hand, he says that acts of judgement correspond to 'various events of content-fixation occurring in various places at various times in the brain', and consequently that the intentional content of a judgement 'doesn't have to be expressible in a "propositional" form – that's a mistake, a case of misprojecting the categories of language back onto the activities of the brain too enthusiastically' (365). Sometimes Dennett seems sensitive to this difference in level between subject-level judgement and brain-level judgement, for he will often, when talking at the brain level, place the term 'judgement' in scare-quotes:

Visual stimuli evoke trains of events in the cortex that gradually yield discriminations of greater and greater specificity. At different times and different places, various 'decisions' or 'judgements' are made; more literally, parts of the brain are caused to go into states that discriminate different features ... These localized discriminative states transmit effects to other places, contributing to further discriminations, and so forth ... The natural but naïve question to ask is: Where does it all come together? The answer is: Nowhere ... there is no one place in the brain through which all these causal trains must pass in order to deposit their content 'in consciousness'.

(1991: 134–5)

It turns out, then, that the term 'judgement' as Dennett uses it is something of a metaphor for brain-level discriminations. And, as the above passage makes plain, Dennett thinks the position that perceptual experience is nothing but a certain sort of spontaneous judgement – or, to cite another term he favours, a certain sort of 'presentiment' – follows from the fact that there is no central system in the brain to which discriminations must travel for the content they contain to become conscious. But it is hard to see how the former position is supposed to follow from that fact. The main questions in the presentation-versus-judgement debate are: what is the subject-level phenomenon of perception? What experiential character and formal intentional features does it have in contrast to other mental phenomena, such as belief, desire, memory, etc.? And (part of) the answer is that, at the subject level, perceptual experience is fundamentally different from judgement because it gives the subject – *not* the subject's brain – direct and qualitatively specific access to the world. Whereas Cartesian materialism and its rivals are competing theories at the sub-personal level of how the brain contributes to the production of perceptual experience in the animal, the presentation-versus-judgement debate is a philosophical one at the subject level about how to *understand* the phenomenon of perception, the very phenomenon that one is trying to explain scientifically by descending to the brain level.

The distinction between the subject level and the brain level must be kept clear in this context for at least two reasons. First, we have no reason to assume that the presentational character of perceptual experience at the subject level is either logically or empirically incompatible with decentralized, multitrack processes at the brain level. Indeed, since we have good reasons for believing in both, we should suppose that the latter subserves the former in the embodied perceiving-acting subject. Second, there is nothing that is given or *presented* to the brain in the subject-level sense. All the brain does is to modulate its own activity in response to internally and externally generated perturbation. Hence it is a philosophical mistake to look inside the brain, rather than to the whole embodied perceiving-acting animal, for the subject of perceptual experience. To eliminate the subject-level phenomenon of qualitatively specific presentation in perception because one can find no such mode of presentation in the brain is therefore fundamentally confused and misguided. Although Dennett portrays himself as the champion of science and the 'third-person' perspective, his approach actually impoverishes the scientific project because he takes away its very subject-matter, thus forcing science into the essentially self-defeating predicament of having to *explain away* or *expunge* perceptual experience from our conception of the world, rather than trying to explain its presence empirically.[24]

Where, then, does this leave the issue of the status of the qualitative aspects of perceptual experience? Dennett takes the denial of the core idea in the sensationalist conception of experience to imply that it is impossible, even in principle, to separate *quality* and *content*. This inference is correct and is borne out by other critiques of sensationalism, such as Merleau-Ponty's. Dennett then goes on to infer that, although there seems to be quality, there is really no such thing: there is only judgement. This further inference is mistaken. Quality and content cannot be separated, because there can be no such thing in perception as contentless quality and qualityless content. Perception is always intentional – it is always directed towards an object – and it is always qualitative – it always presents its objects in a qualitative manner. The two cannot be separated, nor can the one be reduced to the other. Thus instead of speaking (as is usually done in contemporary philosophy of mind) of qualitative (or phenomenal) *properties*, where these are meant in contrast to intentional content, we should speak simply of the *qualitative content* of perceptual experience. The reason why perception has qualitative content is not that quality is constituted by judgement, but rather that perception is always *embodied* (Varela et al. 1991: Chapter 8). It is embodiment, rather than judgement, that invests quality with content and content with quality:

Vision is already inhabited by a meaning (*sens*) which gives it a function in the spectacle of the world and in our existence. The pure *quale* would be given to us only if the world were a spectacle and one's own body a mechanism with which some impartial mind made itself acquainted. Sense experience, on the other hand, invests the quality with vital value, grasping it first in its meaning for us, for that heavy mass which is our body, whence it comes about that it always involves a reference to the body ... Sense experience is that vital communication with the world which makes it present as a familiar setting of our life.

(Merleau-Ponty 1945/1962: 52–3)

Dennett says that there seem to be qualia, but in reality there are no qualia (1991: 372). This way of looking at the matter is mistaken on two counts. First, if by 'qualia' we mean sensational properties, then not only are there no such properties, but there do not even *seem* to be any such properties (in any experientially significant sense of 'seem'). Qualia or sensational properties are theoretical *posits* made by certain philosophers, and the intuitions they cite to support them are philosophical intuitions. Such posits and their supposedly intuitive basis have virtually nothing to do with how we actually understand our perceptual experience in everyday life. It is therefore hardly surprising that some of the best arguments against this type of posit – for example, the first two of the three given by Merleau-Ponty reviewed above – are *phenomenological*. Second, if by 'qualia' we mean the qualitatively specific ways in which we as perceiving-acting subjects experience ourselves and the world, then there are qualia, and they are best construed as relational properties constituted by the environment and the perceiving-acting subject. On the side of the environment, they correspond to various physical, chemical, and biological properties; on the side of the perceiving subject, they correspond to modes of presentation in perceptual experience. Such modes of presentation do not require any inner witness in a Cartesian Theatre: they require only an embodied perceiving-acting animal embedded in an environment. We thus arrive in another context and by another route at the main theses of the ecological view defended in the previous chapter – that perceptual qualities such as colour should be given a relational treatment, and that neuroscientific and computational approaches to visual perception need to be integrated with an ecological approach to the embodied animal as the proper subject of perception and action.

VISUAL EXPERIENCE, SCIENCE, AND THE ECOLOGICAL VIEW

How do the issues about the qualitative content of visual experience look from the vantage point of the ecological view presented in the previous chapter? There are two features of the ecological view that are especially relevant. The first is the explicit recognition of the animal as the proper subject of perception, rather than the animal's brain; the second is the refusal to separate perception from action. Together these two imply that perception – or rather *perceiving* – is a particular sort of activity in which the subject engages – embodied activity guided by a form of awareness that is object-directed and that presents its objects in various qualitative ways depending on the sense-modality.

From this vantage point the qualitative content of visual perception is equivalent to how things look (to be) to the subject in its visually guided activity. Visual qualities determine how things look, but such qualities are not elements *of* consciousness – qualia in the usual (sensationalist) sense; they are attributes of things *for* consciousness (Merleau-Ponty 1945/1962: 5). In visually guided activity it is the object itself that is seen, and the object is seen by way of how it looks. How it looks is in part determined by the visual system, and so its look cannot be an intrinsic property of the object. But it is fallacious to infer that the look of an object is any kind of mental item inside the head, whether this be a composite of visual qualia or merely the intentional content of a visual judgement. The look of an object is constituted by the interaction of the object and the perceiving-acting subject, and so is essentially relational: viewed from the side of the world, it is a relational feature of the object; viewed from the side of the perceiving-acting subject, it is the mode in which the object is presented or alternatively the aspect in which the subject sees the object.[25]

It is worth reconsidering for a moment from this perspective Dennett's assertion that there is no such phenomenon in perception as 'really seeming' over and above really judging. On the contrary, there is a perfectly legitimate sense in which the look of an object, when considered at the right level, can be understood as just such a presentational phenomenon. The right level is the one proper to the phenomenon of perception *per se*, the ecological level. At this level, the perceiving subject cannot be removed from our conception of the world, and so the world itself must be understood as containing appearances. In one sense, corresponding to the distinction between appearance and reality, such appearances are not real simply because they are appearances. But in another sense, corresponding to the distinction between what is fictional (or merely intentional) and what is real, such appearances are real precisely because they are not fictional. The leaves of the maple tree in late autumn appear to be fiery red, but it is at best confused and at worst perverse to suggest that this colourful appearance is fictional in the sense of being merely the intentional content of a judgement inside my head. The best way to describe the status of such an appearance might be to say that the appearance is a *genuine* one, for although it is certainly not fictional, it is also not 'real' in the literal sense in which this term applies mainly to things. The appearance is not a thing; it is an ecologically constituted relation. Dennett misses this way of understanding what a perceptual appearance is because he ignores perception at its own proper level, the ecological level. He assumes that the only way to vindicate subject-level phenomena is by projecting them on to the brain, and when this projection fails, as it must in the case of essentially subject-level phenomena, such as how things appear to us in our visual experience of the world, he takes the failure to show that there really are no such phenomena; there only seem to be as a result of our judgements. It is exactly this route that leads him to make the mistake of collapsing the appearance/reality distinction into the fictional/real distinction when considering the qualitative content of visual perception.

Earlier when I was discussing Nagel I mentioned that believing in the existence of irreducibly subjective facts does not by itself commit one to sensationalism. The ecological view provides a case in point, for, according to this view, the look of an object is a fact that is in a certain sense irreducibly subjective. It is irreducibly subjective not in the sense of being a mental fact that only the subject can discern introspectively, but rather in the sense of being a fact that is constituted in part by the whole embodied perceiving-acting subject. The subject is thus included as an essential component of the fact, and so cannot be eliminated from it.

The essential inclusion of the subject in this way also explains why the subject's relation to the aspect in which he or she sees an object is different from anyone else's relation to that same aspect (Kelly 1986: 89–90). Both the subject and someone else – say, a scientist studying the subject – can know that the subject is seeing the object in a given aspect. But the subject has a distinctive kind of access to the aspect because he or she stands inside the relation that determines it. In contrast, everyone else, in particular the scientist, stands outside the relation and so has only an indirect access to the aspect in which the subject sees the object, indirect in the sense of having to be mediated by verbal reports or other behavioural responses on the part of the subject. On the other hand, the subject's access is direct in the relevant sense, for it is not (in the typical case) mediated by anyone else's experience, verbal report, or behavioural response.[26]

In fact, this way of putting the point remains unsatisfactory because it is still too close to the philosophical idea of 'privileged access' – the idea that the subject has a unique epistemic relation to the contents of his or her own mind through introspection. The problem with this idea is not just that it has often gone hand in hand with a sensationalist conception of the mind. The deeper mistake is to construe the relation that the subject has to his or her own perceptual experience of the world as being primarily epistemic. It is possible to adopt an introspective attitude towards one's perceiving, and such an attitude does have an epistemic dimension, but it is also an attitude that is fundamentally different from one's usual mode of worldly involvement in perceiving. Our perceiving is not in the first instance something to which we are epistemically related; it is rather that by which we are epistemically related to the world. (Indeed, this point warrants generalization: our whole embodied experiential life is not something to which we are epistemically related, for it is that by which we can be epistemically related to anything at all (Thornton 1989: 38).) In visual perception (visually guided activity), we relate to things by means of how they look, but their looks are not separate objects of awareness to which we have privileged access. The only privileged access that I as subject have in visual perceiving is to how the world looks as seen by me from here.

We can now return to the question that I raised at the beginning of this chapter about the possible limits that science might face in trying to explain the phenomenon of perceptual experience. So far we have managed to canvass only extreme responses to the question. On one side there is Nagel, who asserts that it is a mystery how the subjective character of experience could ever be revealed in anything objective, such as the physiology of the perceiver. On the other side there is Dennett, who tries to defend the prospects of science by eliminating what is distinctive about perceptual experience. In the debate between the two, Nagel is right to believe that there are subjective facts in the world. Such facts come into existence with the presence of perceiving-acting animals. But in arguing that it seems impossible to imagine how the experiential character of these facts could ever be anything but mysterious from a scientific perspective, Nagel typifies the sort of philosopher who believes that one could come to understand the relation between mind and nature by simply staring hard at examples of the two while pursuing an entirely conceptual investigation. Dennett, on the other hand, is one of the few genuine natural philosophers of the mind, and so he would never make this kind of mistake. What leads Dennett astray is his neglect of the subject-level character of perception and his a priori commitment to what one commentator has aptly called 'third-person absolutism' – the idea that the only warrant one can have for beliefs about one's own experience is derived from an observational theory about one's behaviour (Siewert 1993). Given this idea, there can be no epistemologically legitimate first-person way of investigating experience. Dennett's only defence of third-person absolutism, however, is a dogmatic one: 'my epistemological position ... is not a rare one. It is, in fact, the more or less standard or default epistemology assumed by scientists and other "naturalists" when dealing with other phenomena, and for good reason' (Dennett 1993: 153). But this reply merely dismisses out of hand the idea that experience might be ontologically different from other natural phenomena, and so might require something else besides a third-person observational theory for its characterization and investigation.

It thus becomes impossible to separate the issue about the

limits of the scientific study of perceptual experience (or indeed of any experiential phenomenon at all) from issues about the very nature of science itself. My own view, which I do not propose to defend here, having already done so in part elsewhere (Varela et al. 1991), is that in cognitive science we need to pursue both genuinely phenomenological investigations of experience – phenomenological psychology in the tradition of Brentano, James, Husserl, and Merleau-Ponty[27] – and scientific investigations of the mind, circulating back and forth between the two, thus bringing both into a kind of mutual accommodation or reflective equilibrium (see also Flanagan 1992). The limits that *this* kind of endeavour might face, however, cannot, as far as I can see, be determined a priori: they will be known only after we have taken the endeavour as far as we can.

On the scientific side, however, I think that the ecological view has a contribution to make. Consider once more Nagel's argument that because every subjective phenomenon is essentially connected with the point of view of the subject, it is a mystery how the subjective character of experience could be revealed in anything objective, such as the 'physical operation' of the subject. I think that one of the main sources of mystery here is not so much the difference between the subjective and objective points of view, but rather the disparity in level between subjective phenomena and brain-level phenomena. Once again, brain-level phenomena are 'subpersonal', to use Dennett's term, and so there is nothing particularly subjective to be found in them per se. As Dennett himself has written: 'You enter the brain through the eye, march up the optic nerve, round and round the cortex, looking behind every neuron, and then before you know it, you emerge into daylight on the spike of a motor nerve impulse, scratching your head and wondering where the self is' (Dennett 1984: 74–5). As I argued above, however, it is a mistake to think that the subject is to be found in the brain in this way in the first place. Although the brain and nervous system subserve the act of perceiving, they do not form the subject of that act. It is the animal that is the proper subject of perception, and the animal is always embedded in an environment. Hence there is no perceiving subject to be found in the brain, but there is one to be found in the world, in particular in the ecosystem formed by the animal and the environment. One contribution the ecological view can make is thus to correct the disparity in level in contemporary discussions of mind and nature by introducing a naturalistic approach to perceptual phenomena at their own proper level. Of course, in advocating this kind of naturalistic approach, my intention is not to replace or supersede the neuroscientific, psychophysical, and computational approaches to perception: rather, it is to provide a framework for connecting the specialized research of these approaches to a more general understanding of the animal as the proper subject of perception and action.

I believe that pursuing such an approach might go some way towards lessening the mystery that philosophers discern when they contemplate the relation between mind and nature. Many contemporary philosophers continue to treat the topic of the mind and its place in nature as if nothing had happened since Descartes, Newton, and Locke, as if on one side there is matter and on the other side mind, with no conceptual intermediaries between them. But as R. G. Collingwood observed earlier this century, there is a third term and it is introduced by biology, namely, *life* (Collingwood 1945: 133). Once the concept of life is (re)introduced, the form of the mind–body problem can no longer be the same: where once the body was conceived as little more than a particular accumulation of externally related bits of matter, now it must be conceived as an *organism*. One of the best hopes for an ecological cognitive science is that it might be able to introduce analogous sorts of intermediate concepts into our thinking about the mind and its relation to various forms of organic existence. Indeed, in regard to our thinking about visual perception, I think that neuroscience, computational vision, and ecological psychology have already begun to provide us with such concepts, though on a less grand scale.

NOTES

1 THE RECEIVED VIEW

1 See Meyering (1989) for a detailed study of how thoroughly philosophical and empirical developments interact in the history of optics and perception theory.

2 These laws were based on the law of sines discovered by Snell. As several scholars have noted, Newton's presentation here is misleading. The laws of optics at the time did in fact predict an oblong or elongated image, except for one position of the prism with respect to the beam of light, that of minimum deviation. Newton indicates that this was indeed the position of the prism only later in the letter. Furthermore, although the received laws did predict a circular image for the position of minimum deviation, this implication was not immediately obvious, but required a long geometrical demonstration. Newton's surprise would be shared, then, only by readers who were mathematically sophisticated or familiar with the demonstration. See Sabra (1967/1981: Chapter 9, especially 235–7). See also the extensive discussion of Newton's letter in Sepper (1988: Chapter 3, especially 107–9).

3 My summary and criticism of Newton's argument are based on Sabra (1967/1981: 249–50, 295).

4 One of the reasons for Newton's insistence was that he had specific views on the nature of hypotheses in science. A hypothesis was a proposition that was not rigorously deduced from experiments, but was merely supposed in order to explain experiments. A hypothesis had therefore only an approximate degree of truth, and so was strictly speaking false. Differential refrangibility according to colour was not a hypothesis for Newton because he claimed that it followed rigorously from his crucial experiment. See Sabra (1967/1981: 274–6).

5 Sabra (1967/1981: 250) warned against this way of speaking, but his warning seems to have gone unheard. Thus Henry Guerlac writes: 'Having established this fact [of differential refrangibility], Newton then set forth in thirteen numbered paragraphs his "doctrine"

of the origin of colors' (Guerlac 1986: 3). Similarly, Hilbert writes that 'As a result of his discovery of the heterogeneity of white light, Newton was able to supplement a dispositional account of color with an account of some of the physics involved' (Hilbert 1987: 8).

6   My discussion of these consequences is greatly indebted to Sepper (1988: 10–12).

7   For example, at higher light levels spectral stimuli become bluer or yellower, whereas at lower light levels they become redder or greener. This phenomenon is known as the Bezold–Brücke phenomenon. See Hurvich (1981: 72).

8   See Hilbert's discussion of what he calls 'the wavelength conception of colour' (Hilbert 1987: 7–8, 46–9).

9   This qualification is important because it is also possible to contest argument (a)–(c) by denying (b). In other words, one could claim not only that (c) does not follow from (a) and (b), but that (b) is false. Indeed, as we shall see in some detail in the next chapter, there simply is no one-to-one correspondence between perceived colour and locally reflected light. Therefore (a)–(c) is not only invalid, but has a false premise.

10   See Vision (1982: 157–8) for a similar point.

11   This distinction has been nicely criticized by Putnam (1987).

12   See also Jackson (1968: 3–77) and Mackie (1976: 20–1).

13   These two construals of secondary qualities seem to be related to Locke's distinction between 'nominal' and 'real' essences. In Bennett's (1971:123) words: 'The nominal essence of a red thing (*qua* red) is just the meaning of "red" or the idea we associate with that word. The real essence of a red thing (*qua* red) is that primary-quality texture of it which causes it to look as it does and thus qualify for the description "red".'

14   The following discussion of the Lockian and Newtonian model of perception is inspired by the final chapter of Jonathan Westphal (1987: 109–12), which is entitled 'Simple sensations, science and the subject'.

15   Arguments for this kind of claim, though not voiced often in English philosophy, are common to the phenomenological tradition, where they can be traced back to Husserl (1954/1970). Putnam (1987) has recently made a similar point. See also the extensive historical and philosophical reconstruction in Meyering (1989).

16   The dispositionalist analysis should not be taken to imply that there is a one-to-one correspondence between stimulus and sensation, or between properties of the external world and perceptual experience. The point, rather, is that a given objectively specifiable stimulus has the power to cause a particular subjective perceptual response, though some other, different stimulus might also have the power to cause the same response.

17   For two attempts to defend and extend this type of analysis, see Bennett (1971) and Mackie (1977).

18 See my discussion of the 'Helson–Judd effect' at the end of Chapter 2.
19 This point was the basis for many of Goethe's (1840/1970) criticisms of Newton. See Sepper (1988: 61, 123–30, 145–6). My discussion in the following paragraphs is based on Sepper.

2 COLOUR VISION: RECENT THEORIES AND RESULTS

1 In their formal model of 'the process of vision as a composite mapping', Teller and Pugh (1983) call the neural structure that 'forms the immediate substrate of visual perception' the *bridge locus*. They write:

> The occurrence of a particular activity pattern in these bridge locus neurons is necessary for the occurrence of a particular perceptual state; neural activity elsewhere in the visual system is not necessary. The physical location of these neurons in the brain is of course unknown. However, we feel that most visual scientists would agree that they are certainly *not* in the retina. For if one could set up conditions for properly stimulating them in the absence of the retina, the correlated perceptual state presumably would occur.
> (Teller and Pugh 1983: 581. See also Teller 1984, 1990)

2 Marr's conception of the computational level of explanation should be distinguished from what is called 'the computational theory of mind' in cognitive science. This theory makes a principled distinction between perception and cognition, and holds that cognition consists in operations on mental representations that have the form of a symbolic code (Fodor 1975, 1981, 1983; Pylyshyn 1984). Although the computational theory of mind invokes Marr to support its perception/cognition distinction (see especially Fodor 1983), one could accept Marr's claim that an abstract, information-processing level of explanation is required for vision (or perception in general) and yet disagree with the claim that cognition consists in the manipulation of symbolic expressions. See Kitcher (1988) for further discussion of various senses of 'computational' in relation to Marr.

3 When I use the phrase 'looks *F*' I shall generally mean 'looks to be *F*'. Hence in the above phrase the apple does not merely look red; it looks to be red, i.e., as if it really is red. The application of the distinction between 'looks' and 'looks to be' is conceptually rather complex, but it need not concern us here. See Sellars (1956); Chisholm (1957); and Anscombe (1965).

4 'Approximate colour constancy' refers to the *relative* independence of apparent colour from changes in the ambient light. Human colour vision exhibits only approximate constancy. Computational theories, however, assume that a system could

exhibit ideal or perfect colour constancy. Here apparent colour would be entirely independent of variations in the ambient light. I shall return to this issue in the final section of this chapter. For now, I shall simply use the term 'colour constancy'.

5   A notable exception is Buchsbaum and Gottschalk (1983), which I discuss below. It should be noted, however, that Buchsbaum and Gottschalk's analysis corresponds more to the algorithm level in Marr's framework than to the computational level.

6   Physiologists and psychophysicists have been concerned with colour constancy, but many of their investigations, especially the more recent, have been prompted by the computational formulation of colour constancy as an information-processing problem. On the whole, physiologists and psychophysicists have concentrated not on surface colour perception, where constancy phenomena are most apparent, but rather on the appearance of colours in the aperture mode or in a restricted surface mode, where the effects of context are eliminated. For example, two of the most detailed textbooks (Boynton 1979; Hurvich 1981) are concerned almost entirely with aperture colours. Boynton (1978) provides an example of the study of surface colours in a simplified visual context. See also Beck (1972) for a study of surface colour perception.

7   See Merleau-Ponty (1945/1962: Chapter 1); Ryle (1956); Kelly (1986); and Westphal (1987) for philosophical treatments; and Gibson (1968–9, 1979) and Davidoff (1991) for treatments in perception theory.

8   'Red', 'green', etc. are often said to be determinates of the determinable 'colour'. But as colour-category names, they are themselves determinables that cover what I am calling 'particular determinate colours' or 'shades'. Hence the hierarchy is: particular determinate colour (shade) → colour category (red, green, etc.) → colour (as a kind of quality).

9   Strictly speaking hue, chroma, and value are technical terms in the Munsell system and so do not correspond precisely to hue, saturation, and lightness as these are commonly used.

10 In visual science there is actually confusion and some disagreement over the terms 'brightness' ('luminosity' in Britain) and 'lightness'. According to Wyszecki and Stiles (1982: 493–500), *brightness* is the 'attribute of a visual sensation according to which a given visual stimulus appears to be more or less intense' (493), whereas *lightness* is the 'attribute of a visual sensation according to which the area in which the visual stimulus is presented appears to emit more or less light in proportion to that emitted by a similarly illuminated area perceived as a "white" stimulus' (494). Hence strictly speaking 'brightness' refers to the dim-to-dazzling scale, whereas 'lightness' refers to the grey scale of black-to-white. Nevertheless, many visual scientists, a large number of whom I cite throughout this book, use 'brightness' to refer to the black-to-white dimension. Furthermore, 'lightness' has been used in a

related, but nonetheless different, sense by researchers in computational colour vision to mean the psychophysical correlate of average relative reflectance (Land 1977, 1983; McCann et al. 1976; Hurlbert 1986). For this sense, see my discussion below in the section entitled 'Computational colour vision'.

11   The nature of brown is actually a matter of some dispute. See Bartelson (1976), Fuld et al. (1983), and Hurvich (1985). For a philosophical discussion see Westphal (1987: Chapter 3).

12   For a general case against modularity for colour perception see Davidoff (1991).

13   For an introductory discussion of additive colour mixture see Hurvich (1981: Chapters 8–9).

14   Wasserman (1978: 37–8) argues that since the theory is based more on ideas due to Newton and Maxwell, it should be called the Newton–Maxwell theory of colour vision.

15   The study by Dartnall et al. places the absorption peaks at 419 nm, 531 nm, 559 nm, and 556 nm (the last two being the alternative long-wave pigment values).

16   The absorption values determined by this study are 426 nm, 530 nm, 552 nm and 557 nm.

17   In additive colour mixture, the intensity, or more precisely, the *luminance*, of a light mixture is the psychophysical correlate of brightness, whereas the *dominant wavelength* of the mixture is the psychophysical correlate of hue. The dominant wavelength of a colour stimulus is the wavelength that when suitably combined with an achromatic light stimulus provides a match to the colour stimulus. Purples cannot be specified in terms of dominant wavelength; they are specified rather in terms of *complementary wavelengths*. The complementary wavelength of a monochromatic stimulus is the wavelength that when suitably combined with the colour stimulus provides a match with the achromatic stimulus.

18   As I shall discuss in Chapter 4, there is actually evidence of colour contrast and colour constancy in bee colour vision (Neumeyer 1980, 1981; Werner et al. 1988).

19   The following discussion of retinal physiology is based on Gouras (1991a). See Daw (1984) for a short review of the physiology of colour vision.

20   Figure 3 presents the standard 'textbook' model of the postreceptoral channels. There are, however, many modifications to the model that have been presented in the literature, and rival models have been proposed. Some of the issues are discussed and further references are provided below.

21   Readers interested in the details of the experimental procedure should consult Hurvich (1981: Chapter 5).

22   The representation of blue and green as negative, and yellow and red as positive, is arbitrary. The important point is that the two hue pairs are opponent.

23   The issues concerning the receptor–channel linkage in colour vision can also be approached from the point of view of a

frequency analysis of the signals for colour vision and of the postreceptoral channels. See Barlow (1982); Bowmaker (1983); and Bonnardel and Varela (1991). A brief presentation is also given in Thompson et al. (1992: Appendix B).

24 Hood and Finkelstein (1983) use this term to refer to assumptions meant to relate the channel signals to behaviour.

25 This axis lies close to the so-called *tritanopic confusion line.* Tritanopia is a colour vision deficiency involving reduced or absent yellow–blue response. The confusion line links the chromaticities of stimuli plotted on the CIE (Commission Inter-nationale de l'Eclairage) chromaticity diagram that are confused by an observer with a colour-vision deficiency (see Hurvich 1981: Chapter 20).

26 See Livingstone and Hubel (1987, 1988); Zeki and Shipp (1988); DeYoe and Van Essen (1988); Martin (1988); Lennie et al. (1990); and Schiller and Logothetis (1990).

27 The discussion in this section draws heavily from Gouras (1991b). See also the references in the previous note.

28 Computational colour vision is a highly technical and mathe-matical field, but I have written this section to be accessible to readers who have little background in visual science or advanced mathematics. Readers who would like a short but more formal introduction to computational colour vision should consult Thompson et al. (1992). This article, as well as my presentation here, is based on the much more extensive treatments by Maloney (1985), Maloney and Wandell (1986), Gershon (1987), and Hurlbert (1989).

29 See Goethe (1840/1970: Part I, Section VI) and the excellent historical and philosophical study by Sepper (1988). The debates surrounding Land's work are briefly reviewed by Hardin (1988: Appendix).

30 See Zeki (1980, 1983a, 1983b, 1985), Livingstone and Hubel (1984), and Ingle (1985).

31 See Campbell (1982), McGilvray (1983), Churchland (1985, 1986), and Matthen (1988).

32 See Horn (1974) and Blake (1985) for other models of lightness computation.

33 In an earlier study lightness is correlated with 'scaled integrated reflectance' (McCann et al. 1976). I discuss this study in Chapter 3.

34 This point does not of course invalidate the contributions made by retinex theory in attempting to construct artificial systems of more limited capacities.

35 The sets comprised, respectively, 462 Munsell colour chips sam-pled at 10-nm intervals between 400 and 700 nm inclusive, and the surface reflectances of 337 'natural formations' as measured by Krinov (1947) sampled at 10-nm intervals from 400 to 650 nm. Using a different method of analysis from Maloney's, Danne-miller (1992) finds that three to four basis functions suffice to represent the surface spectral reflectances of Krinov's natural formations.

36 As D'Zmura and Lennie note , their model also assumes several conditions that need not be true of the real world. The illuminant is spatio-temporally homogeneous, whereas in the real world the illuminant is often heterogeneous, for objects may be illuminated by more than one source, for example, daylight and tungsten light. Their model also takes scenes to be shadowless, and assumes little interreflectance among surfaces. When these conditions do not hold, the tasks of both colour constancy and segmentation will be more difficult.

3 NATURALISTIC ONTOLOGIES

1 Classifications of these views vary. For example, Armstrong (1968b) distinguishes among Realist, Lockian, and Subjectivist views, but most authors classify the Lockian position as a form of subjectivism (for example, Smart 1961; Campbell 1969; McGinn 1983).

2 It should be noted that the objectivist could hold that colours are mind-independent properties of objects without holding either that they are identical with or supervenient upon some set of physical properties. Such a view seems to have been held by James Cornman (1974, 1975). On the other hand, the subjectivist could hold not only that colours are subjective, but that the proper bearers of colour properties are irreducibly mental items that constitute the immediate objects of perception, namely, sense-data. This view has been espoused by Frank Jackson (1977, 1982), though recently he has retracted the claim that sense-data are the bearers of colour properties while continuing to uphold a sense-data theory of perception (Jackson and Pargetter 1987). Because my concern is the ontology of colour in relation to levels of explanation in visual science, I shall not discuss either of these views in this chapter. For criticism of the views of Cornman and of Jackson, see Hardin (1988). I discuss Jackson's views on colour 'qualia' in Chapter 6.

3 Campbell (1969) explicates this distinction as one between 'transitory colours' and 'standing colours'.

4 Note that it is the *plausibility* of the view that is being examined, not its conceptual coherence or logical possibility. Since Armstrong is a self-advertised scientific materialist, and since I too am committed to a naturalistic approach (though not Armstrong's), it is the plausibility of various colour ontologies in the light of the conceptual structure of visual science, rather than their a priori conceptual coherence or logical possibility, that should be taken as the main evaluative criterion.

5 For another perspective on the evolution of colour vision see Mollon (1989). I discuss evolutionary considerations about colour vision in Chapter 4.

6 Hilbert and Hardin published their books within months of each

other, and so they do not discuss each other's views. But see Hardin (1989) for a short review of Hilbert (1987).

7 By 'structure-preserving in a robust sense' I mean that the mapping should preserve not only the dimensionality of the phenomenal colour space, but also the salient features of colour displayed there, such as the unique/binary structure of hue.

8 For nonobjectivist interpretations of retinex theory, see Campbell (1982) and McGilvray (1983).

9 Hardin does not indicate whether it is the type-identity of chromatic visual states and neural states that is implied by the reduction he envisages, or whether it is only weaker token-identities.

4 THE COMPARATIVE ARGUMENT

1 See Gouras (1985: 386).

2 This discussion of the wavelength-discrimination function is based on Neumeyer (1991: 289). See also Backhaus and Menzel (1992).

3 For additional studies and discussions of near-ultraviolet sensitivity in bird vision, see Wright (1979); Delius and Emmerton (1979); Bowmaker (1980a); Emmerton (1983); Burkhardt (1982, 1989); and Burkhardt and Maier (1989). Cones with peak sensitivity in the near-ultraviolet have also been found in fishes; see the references in the discussion below.

4 The approach taken here is greatly indebted to Neumeyer (1988), Burkhardt (1989), and especially to Goldsmith (1990). See also Thompson et al. (1992).

5 For an extensive psychophysical treatment of the colour space of the bee, see Backhaus (1991).

6 I am grateful to Adrian Palacios and Justin Broackes for (independently) bringing this point to my attention.

7 In this study Jordan and Mollon draw a useful distinction between two possible forms of tetrachromacy called 'weak' and 'strong' tetrachromacy. Weak tetrachromacy would occur in carriers who possessed four different types of cone photoreceptors but only three independent postreceptoral channels. Here the receptoral-level colour space spanned by all possible cone quadruplets would be transformed at the postreceptoral level into a colour space of only three dimensions. Thus, at the postreceptoral level, only three independent signals would be preserved, and so trichromatic matches would be made. On the other hand, strong tetrachromacy would occur if the carriers possessed four independent postreceptoral channels, because then the cone quadruplets would be recoded in a four-dimensional postreceptoral colour space, and so tetrachromatic matches would be made. It is of course strong tetrachromacy that is required for the kinds of novel phenomenal colours discussed in the previous section.

8 Lythgoe (1979: 191) provides a photograph with an ultraviolet pass-filter, which enables one to see the contrasting pattern. How such patterns look to the bee, however, is another matter (see the discussion above).

9 The discussion in this section is based on Thompson (in press).

10 There are of course other differences between the representative and computational theories. For example, computational theories do not allow that there could be some causally effective aspect of perceptual content that is not physical; in contrast, the sense-data of the representative theory are typically (though not always) held to be irreducibly mental items.

11 Matthen holds that the function is to detect *particular* spectral reflectances, but this is an empirical claim that is not logically required by his theory. For example, Hilbert (1987: Chapters 5 and 6) holds that the biological function of human colour vision is to detect spectral reflectances as members of a *class* or *category* of reflectances. On this account, metameric matches do not count as misperceptions.

12 Hilbert (1987) argues that Land's retinex theory can generate these categories and the resemblance and difference relations among the colours. See Chapter 3 for a discussion of why this attempt will not work.

13 For colour contrast and colour constancy in the honeybee, see Neumeyer (1980, 1981) and Werner et al. (1988). For colour constancy in fish, see Ingle (1985). For a report of some preliminary data about colour constancy in birds, see Varela et al. (1993). For categorical colour perception in pigeons, see Wright and Cummings (1971).

14 There is a problem with this hypothesis, however: once something is lost in evolution it is very difficult to regain or reachieve it later. It therefore seems unrealistic to suppose that trichromacy could have been reachieved in Old World primates after having been lost earlier in mammalian evolutionary history. I am grateful to Sahotra Sarkar for bringing this problem to my attention. As far as I have been able to determine, the literature on the evolution of colour vision to date has not addressed it.

15 The reflecting properties of surfaces are clearly important for all three of these perceptual tasks. But whereas computational objectivism takes the biological function of colour vision to be simply the detection or recovery of reflectance, Mollon's framework situates the abilities colour vision affords within the biological and ecological context of visual behaviour. In doing so, he provides a natural route to the categorical aspects of colour vision I go on to discuss. These are the reasons why I think Mollon's framework provides a broader and more satisfying perspective on natural colour vision than computational objectivism.

16 For evidence in favour of a broadly adaptationist story about colour vision, see Goldsmith (1990). For a theoretical framework that lends itself to adaptationism, see Snyder and Barlow (1988). For some

remarks that cast doubt on an adaptationist story about the visual system, see Ramachandran (1985). See also Hatfield's (1992: 499–501) discussion of evolution, optimization, and trichromacy.

17 I do not mean to imply by this remark that colours do not have cognitive significance for certain nonhuman animals. Whether they do is something that needs further investigation.

18 The discussion of the following material is indebted to conversations with Eleanor Rosch and is based in part on the discussion of colour categorization in our jointly authored book, *The Embodied Mind: Cognitive Science and Human Experience* (Varela et al. 1991: 167–71). I am also indebted to conversations with Don Dedrick on this topic. Unfortunately, his philosophical treatment of colour categories and colour language (Dedrick 1993) was completed only at the very latest stage of this book, and so I have not been able to make use of it in this discussion.

19 For other attempts to provide neurophysiological explanations of Berlin and Kay's findings, see Bornstein (1973) and Ratliff (1976).

20 For more recent findings and a new model of how perceptual, cognitive, and cultural factors interact in colour-category evolution, see MacLaury (1991a, 1991b, 1992). I am grateful to MacLaury for making these articles available to me; unfortunately, I became aware of them too late to incorporate them into the discussion here.

5 THE ECOLOGICAL VIEW

1 For some of my views on this debate, see Varela et al. (1991: Chapter 9).

2 Contrary to Gibson and his followers, however, I think that much of computational vision can be freed from its representationist assumptions and be rearticulated within an ecological framework. This is one of the ways in which my own ecological view departs from the Gibsonian. I take up this point in more detail below.

3 See Noble (1981), Ben-Ze'ev (1984, 1988, 1989), Heft (1989), and Stroll (1986).

4 It should not be allowed to escape the reader just how strong a claim this is, especially for human visual perception. Consider, for example, the visual perception of a mailbox's having the property of affording mailing letters. The above claim would imply that this presupposes a law linking some property of the ambient light with this property of mailboxes. There is no reason to believe that there is any such law, however. One way to deal with this situation would be to distinguish between visual perception in its most basic form as visually guided activity and a more complex form of visual perception involving concepts and visual understanding. Gibson (1979) resists this distinction, however. In any case, the above claim does not appear to be sufficiently

constrained, a point made at length by Fodor and Pylyshyn (1981) in their critical review of the Gibsonian programme. For further discussion, see Bruce and Green (1990: 375–92).

5   An excellent example of this latter alignment is provided by Bruce and Green (1990).

6   Marr writes: 'In perception, perhaps the nearest anyone came to the level of computational theory was Gibson (1966)' (1982: 29).

7   In their review article on colour constancy Jameson and Hurvich, after criticizing certain assumptions about colour vision implicit in computational models, write: 'In the long run, the kind of widely encompassing approach that seems to us to offer the most promise for modeling of perceptual effects is exemplified by Edelman's *neuronal group selection* theory (Reeke and Edelman 1988)' (Jameson and Hurvich 1989: 19).

8   As in Marr's inverse optics approach to early vision, where viewer-centred coordinates are used in the construction of the 'primal sketch', which extracts intensity changes and their geometrical structure from the retinal image, and in the construction of the '2½-D sketch', which represents the depth and orientation of the visible surfaces.

9   In Varela et al. (1991) and Thompson et al. (1992) we use the term 'enactive' for what I am here calling an action-based paradigm.

10 Throughout the following discussion the term 'colour' includes the achromatic (white–black) dimension.

11 The term 'viewing conditions' covers not only the extradermal circumstances of viewing, for example, the level and quality of the illumination, the surfaces present in the scene, etc., but also the position and state of the perceiver, for example, the degree of photoreceptor adaptation.

12 I am grateful to Mark Thornton for this formulation. His intention in making it, however, was to defend the normal observer-standard condition procedure.

13 As Westphal (1987: 86–7) observes, these differences between surface colour perception and the visual experience of after-images show why J. J. C. Smart's so-called 'topic-neutral' analyses of sentences reporting visual experiences are unacceptable. Smart proposes to analyse a sentence such as 'I am having a yellowish-orange afterimage' as meaning 'What is going on in me is like what is going in me when my eyes are open, the lighting is normal, etc., etc., and there really is a yellowish-orange patch on the wall' (Smart 1963: 94). Another example of careless phenomenology and hence mistaken philosophy in this regard (though of completely different motivation from Smart's) is provided by Michael Lockwood, who claims that 'as regards its conscious aspect, what I am experiencing in the two cases [of a patch of surface colour and a patch of afterimage colour] is the same' (Lockwood 1989: 141). Finally, although I agree completely with Harding (1991) that 'careful characterization of some aspects of our conscious experience, that is, some phenomenology' (290) is

needed to make philosophical progress on the question of whether the qualitative content of perceptual experience presents a major obstacle to physicalist theories of mind, I disagree that 'typical afterimages are helpful examples in the initial stage of inquiry into the nature of color perception' (291). On the contrary and for the reasons given above, afterimages are unhelpful examples when inquiring into the nature of colour *perception*, though they might be helpful when inquiring into the nature of the (much more unusual) case of visual *sensation*.

14 An intriguing example along these lines is provided by Humphrey (1992). Although he begins with a distinction between perception and sensation along sensationalist lines, the positive theory of sensation he advocates construes sensation as a kind of bodily activity that is biologically based and ecologically embedded.

15 See Westphal (1987: 115): 'Why should sensation, or perception, be composed of sensations? If someone argued that digestion must be composed of digestings or digestions, we would need to be persuaded of some very definite advantages to this way of looking at the facts.'

16 Kelly (1986) considers the same objection in defending his own relational view of colour. In his view the objection rests on what he calls the 'diaphanous model of awareness', which 'can be expressed as the thesis that if the means by which perceive affect the way things appear in perception, then we cannot perceive things as they are, but only their effects on us' (104). My discussion of this objection is greatly indebted to Kelly's treatment.

17 Michael Lockwood provides a splendid example of the mistaken sensationalist view to the contrary when he writes: 'By "phenomenal qualities" I mean, for example, the red that is, so to speak, *in me* when I look at that tomato – what, for a Hobbesian brand of materialist, might be dubbed "the red in the head"' (Lockwood 1989: 6).

6 VISUAL EXPERIENCE AND THE ECOLOGICAL VIEW

1 There is no reason not to allow, however, that such prior conceptual and phenomenological understanding can be tentative and provisional, subject to revision and enhancement as investigations in other areas – for example, psychophysics, cognitive psychology, and neuroscience – proceed. And, by the same token, investigations in these areas too can be subject to revision and enhancement in the light of the conceptual and phenomenological investigations. See Varela et al. (1991) and Flanagan (1992).

2 Page references to this article will be to the reprinted version in Nagel (1979b).

3 I say 'attractive' because the proper subject of consciousness is the

creature itself, not its brain. When one begins by trying to define consciousness as a property, and then asks how this property might be evident in brain activity, one is easily led to the mistaken idea that it is the brain that is the subject of conscious experience. Unfortunately, Nagel does not take advantage of this feature of his argument and in fact has succumbed to the mistaken idea in his more recent writings (1986: 40–1).

4   Another excellent critique of sensationalism can be found in Kelly (1986).

5   The discussion in this section is based on Thompson (1992).

6   Jackson uses the term 'colour' to refer to the visual quality that Fred can see, but that we cannot. As I shall show in detail, use of the term in this way is imprecise and invites confusion. The term 'hue' is preferable because what Jackson's example actually involves is a perceiver who has the ability to see particular determinate colours (shades) that belong to a hue category none of whose members we can see. It is therefore the hue that is in the first instance the novel quality.

7   Note, however, that I do not say that Fred can see *all* the colours that belong to his novel hue category. Just as there is Hume's missing shade of blue, perhaps there is a missing shade in Fred's novel hue category, that is, a shade in this category that Fred cannot discriminate.

8   My main concern here is not Wittgenstein exegesis. It is rather to develop a certain line of argument about colours and their relations, elements of which seem attributable to Wittgenstein.

9   Hardin goes on to observe that even this view is flawed, for the opponencies of red and green, and yellow and blue, might not be essential to them, as the experiment by Crane and Piantanida (1983) suggests. In Hardin's view, 'the characteristics and relationships of colors depend on their biological substrate, and we delude ourselves if we suppose it possible systematically to understand the relations colors bear to each other in isolation from that substrate' (1988: 127).

10 Similar examples can be found throughout the *Remarks on Colour*. For example, at I-1, the first passage of the work, Wittgenstein distinguishes between two 'language-games,' one which involves 'reporting whether a certain body is lighter or darker than another', and another which involves stating 'the relationship between the lightness of certain shades of colour.' He then says: 'The form of the propositions in both language-games is the same: "X is lighter than Y". But in the first it is an external relation and the proposition is temporal, in the second it is an internal relation and the proposition is timeless.'

11 Schlick goes on to say that 'the relation of similarity between two coloured objects is external, but the relation of similarity between the particular colours as such is internal.' This remark should be compared with Wittgenstein's quoted in the previous note.

12 It might be thought that the Munsell colour space which has the

structure of a branching tree is a counterexample to this claim. One of the virtues of the Munsell space is that whenever some new pigment is made it can be incorporated into the space by extending some existing branch. But these extensions are always in one of the already existing hue families and typically involve creating a more saturated or lighter or darker shade. In this sense, extending a branch of the tree is like creating one of Hume's missing shades. The extensions do not involve adding an entirely new kind of hue not found in the space.

13 It should be noted that the viewing conditions in the experiment are highly abnormal, involving the stabilization of images on the retina, and so for normal conditions our colour space might still be three-dimensional. The point is that the colour space comprising all the hues we can experience regardless of viewing conditions would not be three-dimensional.

14 I must confess that I find it very difficult to *imagine* how opponency could be inessential to the hues. But the persuasiveness of the (still to my knowledge unreplicated) experiments by Crane and Piantanida (1983) is undeniable, and as Hardin notes, 'to agree that this is a matter to be settled by experiment is of course to agree that it is conceptually possible that something could look red and green all over' (1988: 125).

15 Here I follow the lead of Dennett (1991: 398–401), who does the same for Jackson's Mary example. My point in attempting to spell out the thought experiment, however, is not to show that physicalism is true. It is rather to uncover the mistaken sensationalist intuitions that motivate Jackson's views about the qualitative features of conscious experience.

16 If one were to hold that the difference relation as specified in terms of the number of just-noticeably different hue-steps were essential to the *colours* (though not the *hues* of which the colours are composed), then the relation would be internal to the colours, and so would be intrinsic in the sense of being essential to them, but not in the sense of being nonrelational.

17 This is the sense in which Harrison (1986) seems to use the term: 'Moreover, speakers agree, for the most part, about the intrinsic properties of colors. They agree, for the most part, about what color samples satisfy identifying descriptions such as "a dark, purplish red," "the color midway blue and green," and so on' (108). And on the next page, he says: 'we identify turquoise as "the color midway between between blue and green," or burgundy as a "dark, purplish red." Such a characterization identifies a color *intrinsically – qua* color, that is – by characterizing its bare *quale*, without reference to any contingent fact about its empirical circumstances of manifestation (as that boiled lobsters happen to be red, the unclouded sky blue, and so on)' (109).

18 The term 'to quine' is defined in *The Philosophical Lexicon* (Dennett 1987) as 'to deny resolutely the existence or importance of something real or significant.'

19 In addition to the writings by Nagel and Jackson already discussed, see Levine (1983, 1991); Horgan (1984); McGinn (1983); Peacocke (1983, 1984); and Lockwood (1989).

20 It is this idea that lies behind the philosophical thought experiments involving 'inverted qualia,' such as the 'inverted spectrum' (see Shoemaker 1984; Hardin 1988: 134–45).

21 The following line of criticism owes much to McDowell (1991) and to Sedivy (1992).

22 Let's call the idea of such a centered locus in the brain *Cartesian materialism,* since it's the view you arrive at when you discard Descartes's dualism but fail to discard the imagery of a central (but material) Theater where "it all comes together" ... Cartesian materialism is the view that there is a crucial finish line or boundary somewhere in the brain, marking a place where the order of arrival equals the order of "presentation" in experience because *what happens there* is what you are conscious of.

(Dennett 1991: 107)

23 Unfortunately, as McDowell (1991) points out, Searle is unable to hold on to this fundamentally important point, for later in his book, when discussing the issue of whether meanings are in the head, he mistakenly identifies the subject with its brain (1983: 230). See also note 3 above.

24 See Siewert (1993: 94): '[Dennett] does not so much *explain* consciousness as illustrate how one might try to *expunge* it from one's conception of the world. Its fault lies not so much in its failure to add to our knowledge as in its potential to impoverish our understanding.' Dennett's response is in Dennett (1993).

25 What I am here calling the mode in which the object is presented or the aspect in which the subject sees the object is similar to what Kelly (1986: 83–95) calls the *form* in which a subject perceives the object. My discussion in this and subsequent paragraphs is indebted to Kelly.

26 I describe the directness of the subject's access in this way because there are familiar situations in which one does not know how something seems to one prior to or apart from what one says and does (as in the oft-quoted remark by E. M. Forster: 'How can I tell what I think until I see what I say?'). But deciding how things seem to one in this way is itself a first-person phenomenon with its own experiential characteristics.

27 In both Husserl and Merleau-Ponty, however, phenomenological psychology is meant as a stepping stone towards transcendental phenomenology. The relation between phenomenology as a transcendental project and cognitive science as a naturalistic project is too complex to be considered here.

REFERENCES

Abeles, M. (1984) *Local Circuits*, New York: Springer.

Ackermann, R. J. (1989) *Wittgenstein's City*, Amherst, Mass.: University of Massachusetts Press.

Akins, K. (1990) 'Science and our inner lives: birds of prey, bats, and the common (featherless) bi-ped', in M. Bekoff and D. Jamieson (eds) *Interpretation and Explanation in the Study of Animal Behavior*, Boulder, Colo.: Westview Press.

Albright, T. D. (1991) 'Color and the integration of motion signals', *Trends in Neurosciences* 14: 266–9.

Anscombe, G. E. M. (1965) 'The intentionality of sensation: a grammatical feature', in R. J. Butler (ed.) *Analytical Philosophy* (second series), Oxford: Oxford University Press.

Applebury, M. L. and Hargrave, P. A. (1986) 'Molecular biology of visual pigments', *Vision Research* 26: 1881–95.

Arend, L. E. and Reeves, A. (1986) 'Simultaneous color constancy', *Journal of the Optical Society of America A* 3: 1743–51.

Armstrong, D. M. (1968a) *A Materialist Theory of the Mind*, London: Routledge & Kegan Paul.

—— (1968b) 'The secondary qualities: an essay in the classification of theories', *Australasian Journal of Philosophy* 46: 225–41.

—— (1969) 'Colour-realism and the argument from microscopes', in R. Brown and C. D. Rollins (eds) *Contemporary Philosophy in Australia*, London: Allen & Unwin.

Arnold, K. and Neumeyer, C. (1987) 'Wavelength discrimination in the turtle *Pseudemys scripta elegans*', *Vision Research* 27: 1501–11.

Averill, E. (1985) 'Color and the anthropocentric problem', *Journal of Philosophy* 82: 281–304.

Avery, J. A., Bowmaker, J. K., Djagmoz, M. B. A., and Downing, J. E. G. (1983) 'Ultraviolet sensitive receptors in a freshwater fish', *Journal of Physiology* 334: 23.

Backhaus, W. (1991) 'Color opponent coding in the visual system of the honeybee', *Vision Research* 31: 1381–97.

Backhaus, W. and Menzel, R. (1992) 'Conclusions from color vision of insects' (Open Peer Commentary on E. Thompson et al., 'Ways of coloring: comparative color vision as a case study for cognitive science', *Behavioral and Brain Sciences* 15: 1–74), *Behavioral and Brain Sciences* 15(1): 28–30.

Ballard, D. H. (1991) 'Animate vision', *Artificial Intelligence* 48: 57–86.

Barlow, H. B. (1982) 'What causes trichromacy? A theoretical analysis using comb-filtered spectra', *Vision Research* 22: 635–43.

Barlow, H. B. and Foldiak, P. (1989) 'Adaptation and decorrelation in the cortex', in R. M. Dubin, C. Miall, and G. J. Mitchinson (eds) *The Computing Neuron*, Wokingham: Addison-Wesley.

Barrett, P. H. (1974) 'Darwin's early and unpublished notebooks', in H. E. Gruber (ed.) *Darwin on Man*, New York: Dutton.

Bartelson, J. C. (1976) 'Brown', *Colour Research and Application* 1: 181–91.

Barth, F. G. (1985) *Insects and Flowers: The Biology of a Partnership*, trans. M. A. Biederman-Thorson, Princeton: Princeton University Press.

Baylis, J. R. (1979) 'Optical signals and interspecific communication', in E. H. Burtt Jr (ed.) *The Behavioural Significance of Color*, New York and London: Garland STPM Press.

Beatty, D. D. (1969) 'Visual pigments of the burdot (*Lota lota*) and seasonal changes in their relative proportions', *Vision Research* 9: 635–43.

—— (1984) 'Visual pigments and the labile scotopic visual system of fish', *Vision Research* 24: 1173–83.

Beck, J. (1972) *Surface Color Perception*, Ithaca: Cornell University Press.

Bennett, J. (1971) *Locke, Berkeley, Hume: Central Themes*, Oxford: Oxford University Press.

Benzschawel, T., Brill, M. H., and Cohen, T. E. (1986) 'Analysis of human color mechanisms using sinusoidal spectral power distributions', *Journal of the Optical Society of America A* 3: 1713–25.

Ben-Ze'ev, A. (1984) 'The Kantian revolution in perception', *Journal for the Theory of Social Behaviour* 14: 69–84.

—— (1987) 'A critique of the inferential paradigm in perception', *Journal for the Theory of Social Behaviour* 17: 243–63.

—— (1988) 'Can non-pure perception be direct?', *Philosophical Quarterly* 38: 315–25.

—— (1989) 'Explaining the subject–object relation in perception', *Social Research* 56: 511–42.

Berkeley, G. (1710/1965) *A Treatise Concerning the Principles of Human Knowledge*, in *Berkeley's Philosophical Writings*, ed. D. M. Armstrong, New York: Macmillan.

Berlin, B. and Kay, P. (1969) *Basic Color Terms: Their Universality and Evolution*, Berkeley and Los Angeles: University of California Press.

Blake, A. (1985) 'On lightness computation in the mondrian world', in D. Ottoson and S. Zeki (eds) *Central and Peripheral Mechanisms of Colour Vision*, London: Macmillan.

Bloch, S. and Martinoya, C. (1983) 'Specialization of the visual functions for the different retinal areas of the pigeon', in P. Ewert, R. Capranica, and D. Ingle (eds) *Advances in Behavioral Neuroethology*, New York: Plenum Press.

Boghossian, P. A. and Velleman, J. D. (1989) 'Colour as a secondary quality', *Mind* 1989: 81–103.

Bonnardel, V. and Varela, F. J. (1991) 'A frequency view of colour: measuring the human sensitivity to square-wave spectral power distributions', *Proceedings of the Royal Society of London B* 245: 165–71.

Bornstein, M. (1973) 'Color vision and color naming: a psychophysiological hypothesis of color difference', *Psychological Bulletin* 80: 257–85.

—— (1987) 'Perceptual categories in vision and audition', in S. Harnad (ed.) *Categorical Perception: The Groundwork of Cognition*, Cambridge: Cambridge University Press.

Bowmaker, J. K. (1977) 'The visual pigments, oil droplets and spectral sensitivity of the pigeon', *Vision Research* 17: 1129–38.

—— (1980a) 'Birds see ultraviolet light', *Nature* 284: 306.

—— (1980b) 'Colour vision in birds and the role of oil droplets', *Trends in Neurosciences* 3: 196–9.

—— (1983) 'Trichromatic colour vision: why only three receptor channels?', *Trends in Neurosciences* 6: 41–3.

—— (1991) 'Visual pigments, oil droplets and photoreceptors', in P. Gouras (ed.) *The Perception of Colour: Vision and Visual Dysfunction*, vol. 6, London: Macmillan Press.

Bowmaker, J. K., Dartnall, H. J., and Herring, P. J. (1988) 'Longwave-sensitive visual pigments in some deep-sea fishes: segregation of "paired" rhodopsine and porphyropsins', *Journal of Comparative Physiology A* 163: 685–98.

Bowmaker, J. K., Jacobs, G. H., and Mollon, J. D. (1987) 'Polymorphism of photopigments in the squirrel monkey: a sixth phenotype', *Proceedings of the Royal Society of London B* 231: 383–90.

Bowmaker, J. K. and Kunz, Y. W. (1987) 'Ultraviolet receptors, tetrachromatic colour vision and retinal mosaics in the brown trout (*Salmo Trutta*): age dependent changes', *Vision Research* 27: 2101–8.

Bowmaker, J. K. and Martin, G. R. (1985) 'Visual pigments and oil droplets in the penguin, *Spheniscus humboldti*', *Journal of Comparative Physiology A* 156: 71–7.

Boyle, R. (1666/1979) 'The origin of forms and qualities according to the corpuscular philosophy', in M. A. Steward (ed.) *Selected Philosophical Papers of Robert Boyle*, Manchester: Manchester University Press.

Boynton, R. M. (1978) 'Color in contour and object perception', in E. C. Carterette and M. P. Friedman (eds) *Handbook of Perception*, vol. 8, New York: Academic Press.

—— (1979) *Human Color Vision*, New York: Holt, Rinehart & Winston.

—— (1988) 'Color vision', *Annual Review of Psychology* 39: 69–100.

Brainard, D. H. and Wandell, B. A. (1986) 'An analysis of the retinex theory of color vision', *Journal of the Optical Society of America A* 3: 1651–61.

Brakel, J. van (1992) 'The ethnocentricity of colour' (Open Peer Commentary on E. Thompson et al., 'Ways of coloring: comparative color vision as a case study for cognitive science', *Behavioral and*

Brain Sciences 15: 1–74), *Behavioral and Brain Sciences* 15: 53–4.

Brentano, F. (1874/1973) *Psychology from an Empirical Standpoint*, ed. Oskar Kraus and Linda L. McAlister, trans. Antos C. Rancurello, D. B. Terrell, and Linda L. McAlister, London: Routledge & Kegan Paul.

Bridges, C. D. (1972) 'The rhodopsin-porphyropsin visual system', in H. J. Dartnall (ed.) *Handbook of Sensory Physiology*, vol. VII/1, Berlin: Springer.

Brill, M. H. (1990) 'Image segmentation by object color: a unifying framework and connection to color constancy', *Journal of the Optical Society of America A* 7: 2041–7.

Brooks, R. (1986) 'Achieving artificial intelligence through building robots', *AI Memo 899*, MIT Artificial Intelligence Laboratory.

—— (1987) 'Autonomous mobile robots', in W. E. L. Grimson and R. S. Patil (ed.) *AI in the 1980s and Beyond*, Cambridge, Mass.: MIT Press.

—— (1989) 'A robot that walks: emergent behaviors from a carefully evolved network', *AI Memo 1091*, MIT Artificial Intelligence Laboratory.

—— (1991) 'Intelligence without representation', *Artificial Intelligence* 47: 139–59.

Brou, P., Sciascia, T. R., Linden, L., and Lettvin, J. Y. (1986) 'The colors of things', *Scientific American* 255 (3): 84–91.

Brown, P. K. and Wald, G. (1964) 'Visual pigments in single rods and cones of the human retina', *Science* 144: 45–52.

Bruce, V. and Green, P. R. (1990) *Visual Perception: Physiology, Psychology and Ecology*, Hove and London: Lawrence Erlbaum.

Brusatin, M. (1986) *Histoires des couleurs*, translated from the Italian edition of 1983, Paris: Flammarion.

Brush, A. H. (1990) 'Metabolism of carotenoid pigments in birds', *FASEB* 4: 2969–79.

Buchsbaum, G. and Gottschalk, A. (1983) 'Trichromacy, opponent colours coding, and optimum colour information transmission in the retina', *Proceedings of the Royal Society of London B* 220: 89–113.

Budnik, V., Mpodozis, J., Varela, F. J., and Maturana, H. R. (1984) 'Regional specialization of the quail retina: ganglion cell density and oil droplet distribution', *Neurosciences Letters* 51: 145–50.

Burkhardt, D. (1982) 'Birds, berries and UV: a note on some consequences of UV vision in birds', *Naturwissenschaften* 69: 153–7.

—— (1989) 'UV vision: a bird's eye view of feathers', *Journal of Comparative Physiology* 164: 787–96.

Burkhardt, D. and Maier, E. (1989) 'The spectral sensitivity of a passerine bird is highest in the UV', *Naturwissenschaften* 76: 82–3.

Burnham, R. W., Hanes, R. M., and Bartelson, C. J. (1963) *Color: A Guide to Basic Facts and Concepts*, New York: Wiley.

Burt, E. A. (1954) *The Metaphysical Foundations of Modern Science*, Garden City, N.Y.: Doubleday.

Burtt, E. H. Jr (ed.) (1979) *The Behavioral Significance of Color*, New York and London: Garland STPM Press.

Campbell, K. (1969) 'Colours', in R. Brown and C. D. Rollins (eds)

REFERENCES

Contemporary Philosophy in Australia, London: Allen & Unwin.
—— (1982) 'The implications of Land's theory of colour vision', in L. J. Cohen (ed.) *Logic, Methodology and Philosophy of Science*, Amsterdam: North Holland.
Carpenter, G. A. and Grossberg, S. (1990) 'Self-organizing neural network architectures for real-time adaptive pattern recognition', in S. F. Zornetzer et al. (eds) *An Introduction to Neural and Electronic Networks*, San Diego: Academic Press.
Chen, D. M., Collins, J. S. and Goldsmith, T. H. (1984) 'The ultraviolet receptor of bird retinas', *Science* 225: 337–40.
Chen, D. M. and Goldsmith, T. H. (1986) 'Four spectral classes of cones in the retinas of birds', *Journal of Comparative Physiology A* 159: 473–9.
Chisholm, R. (1957) *Perceiving: A Philosophical Study*, Ithaca: Cornell University Press.
Churchland, P. M. (1979) *Scientific Realism and the Plasticity of Mind*, Cambridge: Cambridge University Press.
—— (1985) 'Reduction, qualia, and the direct introspection of brain states', *Journal of Philosophy* 82: 8–28.
—— (1986) 'Some reductive strategies in cognitive neurobiology', *Mind* 1986: 279–309.
—— (1988) *Matter and Consciousness*, revised edition, Cambridge, Mass.: MIT Press.
Churchland, P. S. (1986) *Neurophilosophy*, Cambridge, Mass.: MIT Press.
Churchland, P. S. and Sejnowski, T. J. (1988) 'Perspectives on cognitive neuroscience', *Science* 242: 741–5.
Collingwood, R. G. (1945) *The Idea of Nature*, Oxford: Clarendon Press.
Cornman, J. (1974) 'Can Eddington's "two tables" be identical?', *Australasian Journal of Philosophy* 52: 22–38.
—— (1975) *Perception, Common Sense and Science*, New Haven: Yale University Press.
Cowey, A. and Stoerig, P. (1991) 'The neurobiology of blindsight', *Trends in Neurosciences* 14: 140–5.
Crane, H. D. and Piantanida, T. P. (1983) 'On seeing reddish green and yellowish blue', *Science* 221: 1078–80.
Crawford, M. L. J., Anderson, R. A., Blake, R., Jacobs, G. H., and Neumeyer, C. (1990) 'Interspecies comparisons in the understanding of human visual perception', in L. Spillman and J. S. Werner (eds) *Visual Perception: The Neurophysiological Foundations*, San Diego: Academic Press.
Crescitelli, F., McFall-Ngai, M., and Horowitz, J. (1985) 'The visual pigment sensitivity hypothesis: further evidence from fishes of varying habitats', *Journal of Comparative Physiology A* 157: 323–33.
Creutzfeldt, O., Lange-Malecki, B., and Wortmann, K. (1987) 'Darkness induction, retinex and cooperative mechanisms in vision', *Experimental Brain Research* 67: 270–83.
Crick, F. and Koch, C. (1990) 'Towards a neurobiological theory of consciousness', *Seminars in the Neurosciences* 2: 263–75.
Dannemiller, J. (1989) 'Computational approaches to color constancy:

adaptive and ontogenetic considerations', *Psychological Review* 96: 255–66.

—— (1990) 'Lightness is not illuminant invariant: reply to Troost and de Weert (1990)', *Psychological Review* 98: 146–8.

—— (1992) 'Spectral reflectance of natural objects: how many basis functions are necessary?', *Journal of the Optical Society of America A* 9: 507–15.

Dartnall, H. J. A., Bowmaker, J. K. and Mollon, J. D. (1983) 'Human visual pigments: microspectrophotometric results from the eyes of seven persons', *Proceedings of the Royal Society of London B* 220: 115–30.

Davidoff, J. (1991) *Cognition through Color*, Cambridge, Mass.: MIT Press.

—— (1992) 'What is a colour space?' (Open Peer Commentary on E. Thompson et al., 'Ways of coloring: comparative color vision as a case study for cognitive science', *Behavioral and Brain Sciences* 15: 1–74), *Behaviour and Brain Sciences* 15(1): 34–5.

Daw, N. W. (1968) 'Colour-coded ganglion cells in the goldfish retina: extension of their receptive fields by means of new stimuli', *Journal of Physiology* 197: 567–92.

—— (1984) 'The psychology and physiology of colour vision', *Trends in Neuroscience* 7: 330–5.

Dedrick, D. (1993)'Color language, cultures, and color science', doctoral dissertation, Department of Philosophy, University of Toronto.

Delius, J. D. and Emmerton, J. (1979) 'Visual performance of pigeons', in A. M. Granda and J. H. Maxwell, *Neural Mechanisms of Behaviour in the Pigeon*, New York and London: Plenum Press.

Dennett, D. C. (1978) 'Toward a cognitive theory of consciousness', in Daniel C. Dennett, *Brainstorms: Philosophical Essays on Mind and Psychology*, Cambridge, Mass.: MIT Press.

—— (1984) *Elbow Room. The Varieties of Free Will Worth Wanting*, Cambridge, Mass.: MIT Press.

—— (ed.) (1987) *The Philosophical Lexicon*, Delaware: American Philosophical Association.

—— (1990) 'Quining qualia', in W. G. Lycan (ed.) *Mind and Cognition: A Reader*, Oxford: Basil Blackwell.

—— (1991) *Consciousness Explained*, Boston: Little Brown.

—— (1993) 'Living on the edge', *Inquiry* 36: 135–59.

Dennett, D. C. and Kinsbourne, M. (1992) 'Time and the observer: the where and when of consciousness in the brain', *Behavioral and Brain Sciences* 15: 183–247.

Derrington, A. M., Krauskopf, J. and Lennie, P. (1984) 'Chromatic mechanisms in lateral geniculate nucleus of macaque', *Journal of Physiology* 357: 241–65.

Descartes, R. (1985) *Descartes, Philosophical Writings*, ed. E. Anscombe and P. T. Geach, New York: Macmillan.

Desimone, R. and Schein, S. J. (1987) 'Visual properties of neurons in area V4 of the macaque: sensitivity to stimulus form', *Journal of Neurophysiology* 57: 835–68.

Desimone, R., Schein, S. J., Moran, J., and Ungerleider, L. G. (1985) 'Contour, color and shape analysis beyond the striate cortex', *Vision Research* 25: 441–52.

DeValois, R. L. and DeValois, K. (1975) 'Neural coding of color', in E. C. Carterette and M. P. Friedman (eds) *Handbook of Perception. Volume V: Seeing,* New York: Academic Press.

DeValois, R. L. and Jacobs, G. H. (1968) 'Primate color vision', *Science* 162: 533–40.

DeYoe, E. A. and Van Essen, D. C. (1988) 'Concurrent processing streams in monkey visual cortex', *Trends in Neuroscience* 11: 219–26.

Dretske, F. (1981) *Knowledge and the Flow of Information,* Cambridge, Mass.: MIT Press.

Durrer, H. (1986) 'Coloration', in J. Breiter-Hahn, A. G. Matolsky and K. S. Richards (eds) *Biology of the Integument: The Skin of Birds,* Berlin: Springer.

D'Zmura, M. and Lennie, P. (1986) 'Mechanisms of color constancy', *Journal of the Optical Society of America A* 3: 1662–72.

Edelman, G. M. (1989) *The Remembered Present: A Biological Theory of Consciousness,* New York: Basic Books.

Egeth, H. E. and Pachellea, R. (1969) 'Multidimensional stimulus identification', *Perception and Psychophysics* 5: 341–6.

Emmerton, J. (1983) 'Pattern discrimination in the near-ultraviolet by pigeons', *Perception and Psychophysics* 34: 555–9.

Emmerton, J. and Delius, J. D. (1980) 'Wavelength discrimination in the "visible" and ultraviolet spectrum by pigeons', *Journal of Comparative Physiology A* 141: 47–52.

Engel, A. K., König, P., Kreiter, A., Schillen, T. B., and Singer, W. (1992) 'Temporal coding in the visual cortex: new vistas on integration in the nervous system', *Trends in Neurosciences* 15: 218–26.

Felfoldy, G. L. and Garner, W. R. (1971) 'The effects on speeded classification of implicit and explicit instructions regarding stimulus dimensions', *Perception and Psychophysics* 9: 289–92.

Finkelstein, M. A. (1992) 'Psychophysical modeling: the link between objectivism and subjectivism' (Open Peer Commentary on E. Thompson et al., 'Ways of coloring: comparative color vision as a case study for cognitive science', *Behavioral and Brain Sciences* 15: 1–74), *Behavioral and Brain Sciences* 15(1): 36–7.

Finkelstein, M. A. and Hood, D. C. (1984) 'Detection and discrimination of small, brief lights: variable tuning of opponent channels', *Vision Research* 24: 175–81.

Fishman, M. C. and Michael, C. R. (1973) 'Integration of auditory information in the cat's visual cortex', *Vision Research* 13: 1415.

Flanagan, O. (1992) *Consciousness Reconsidered,* Cambridge, Mass.: MIT Press.

Flanagan, P., Cavanagh, P., and Favreau, O. E. (1990) 'Independent orientation-selective mechanisms for the cardinal directions of colour space', *Vision Research* 30: 769–78.

Fodor, J. A. (1975) *The Language of Thought,* Cambridge, Mass.: Harvard University Press.

REFERENCES

—— (1981) *Representations: Philosophical Essays on the Foundations of Cognitive Science*, Cambridge, Mass.: MIT Press.

—— (1983) *The Modularity of Mind*, Cambridge, Mass.: MIT Press.

Fodor, J. A. and Pylyshyn Z. W. (1981) 'How direct is visual perception? Some reflections on Gibson's "ecological approach"', *Cognition* 9: 139–96.

Fuld, K., Werner, J. S., and Wooten, B. R. (1983) 'The possible elemental nature of brown', *Vision Research* 23: 631–7.

Funt, B. V. and Drew, M. S. (1988) 'Color constancy computation in near-Mondrian scenes using a finite dimensional linear model', IEEE Conference on Computer Vision and Pattern Recognition, Ann Arbor, Mich., 5–9 June.

Galileo, G. (1623/1957) *The Assayer*, in Stillman Drake (ed. and trans.) *Discoveries and Opinions of Galileo*, Garden City, N.Y.: Doubleday.

Garner, W. R. (1974) *The Processing of Information and Structure*, New York: Wiley.

Garner, W. R. and Felfoldy, G. L. (1970) 'Integrality of stimulus dimensions in various types of information processing', *Cognitive Psychology* 1: 225–41.

Gautier-Hion, A., Duplantier, J. M., Quris, R., Feer, F., Sourd, C., Decoux, J. P., Dubost, G., Emmons, L., Erard, C., Hecketsweiler, P., Moungazi, A., Roussilhon, C., and Thiollay, J-M. (1985) 'Fruit characteristics as a basis of fruit choice and seed dispersal in a tropical forest vertebrate community', *Oecologia* 65: 324–37.

Gershon, R. (1982) *Survey on Color: Aspects of Perception and Computation*, Technical Reports on Research in Biological and Computational Vision: RBCV–84–4. Department of Computer Science, University of Toronto.

—— (1987) *The Use of Color in Computational Vision*, Technical Reports on Research in Biological and Computational Vision: RBCV–TV–87–15. Department of Computer Science, University of Toronto.

Gershon, R., Jepson, A. D., and Tsotsos, J. K. (1986) 'Ambient illumination and the determination of material changes', *Journal of the Optical Society of America A* 3: 1700–7.

Gibson, E. J. (1969) *Principles of Perceptual Learning and Development*, New York: Appleton-Century-Crofts.

Gibson, J. J. (1966) *The Senses Considered as Perceptual Systems*, Boston: Houghton Mifflin.

—— (1967) 'New reasons for realism', *Synthese* 17: 162–72.

—— (1968–9) 'Are there sensory qualities of objects?', *Synthese* 19: 408–9.

—— (1972) 'A theory of direct visual perception', in J. R. Royce and W. W. Rozeboom, *The Psychology of Knowing*, New York: Gordon & Breach.

—— (1979) *The Ecological Approach to Visual Perception*, Boston: Houghton Mifflin.

Glas, H. W. van der (1980) 'Orientation of bees, *Apis mellifera*, to unpolarized colour patterns, simulating the polarized skylight pattern', *Journal of Comparative Physiology A* 139: 224–41.

Goethe, J. W. (1840/1970) *Theory of Colours*, trans. Charles Lock Eastlake, Cambridge, Mass.: MIT Press.

Goldsmith, T. H. (1980) 'Hummingbirds see near ultraviolet light', *Science* 207: 786–8.

—— (1990) 'Optimization, constraint, and history in the evolution of eyes', *Quarterly Review of Biology* 65: 281–322.

—— (in press) 'Ultraviolet receptors and color vision: evolutionary implications and a dissonance of paradigms', *Vision Research*.

Goldsmith, T. H., Collins, J. S., and Licht, S. (1984) 'The cone oil droplets of avian retinas', *Vision Research* 24: 1661–71.

Gould, S. J. and Lewontin, R. (1979) 'The spandrels of San Marco and the Panglossian paradigm: a critique of the adaptationist programme', *Proceedings of the Royal Society B* 205: 591–8.

Gouras, P. (1985) 'Visual system IV: color vision', in E. R. Kandel and J. H. Schwartz, *Principles of Neural Science*, second edition, New York: Elsevier North Holland.

—— (1991a) 'Precortical physiology of colour vision', in P. Gouras (ed.) *The Perception of Colour: Vision and Visual Dysfunction*, vol 6, London: Macmillan Press.

—— (1991b) 'Cortical mechanisms of colour vision', in P. Gouras (ed.) *The Perception of Colour: Vision and Visual Dysfunction*, vol. 6, London: Macmillan Press.

—— (ed.) (1991c) *The Perception of Colour: Vision and Visual Dysfunction*, vol. 6, London: Macmillan Press.

Gouras, P. and Krüger, J. (1979) 'Responses of cells in foveal visual cortex of the monkey to pure color contrast', *Journal of Neurophysiology* 42: 850–60.

Gouras, P. and Zrenner, E. (1981) 'Color vision: a review from a neurophysiological perspective', *Progress in Sensory Physiology* 1: 139–79.

Granda, A. M. and Maxwell, J. H. (1979) *Neural Mechanisms of Behavior in the Pigeon*, New York and London: Plenum Press.

Grossberg, S. (1982) *Studies in Mind and Brain*, Boston Studies in the Philosophy of Science, vol. 70, Boston: D. Reidel.

—— (ed.) (1988) *Neural Networks and Natural Intelligence*, Cambridge, Mass.: MIT Press.

Guerlac, H. (1986) 'Can there be colors in the dark? Physical color theory before Newton', *Journal of the History of Ideas* 47: 3–20.

Haenny, P. E., Maunsell, J. H. R., and Schiller, P. H. (1988) 'State dependent activity in monkey visual cortex', *Experimental Brain Research* 69: 245–59.

Hahm, D. E. (1978) 'Early Hellenistic theories of vision and the perception of color', in P. Machamer and R. Turnbull (eds) *Studies in Perception*, Columbus, Ohio.

Hahmann, O. and Güntürkün, O. (1993) 'The visual acuity for the lateral visual field of the pigeon (*Columba livia*)', *Vision Research* 33: 1659–64.

Hailman, J. P. (1977) *Optical Signals: Animal Communication and Light*,

Bloomington and London: Indiana University Press.

Hardin, C. L. (1983) 'Colors, normal observers, and standard conditions', *Journal of Philosophy* 80: 806–13.

—— (1984a) 'A new look at color', *American Philosophical Quarterly* 21: 125–33.

—— (1984b) 'Are "scientific" objects coloured?', *Mind* 93: 491–500.

—— (1988) *Color for Philosophers. Unweaving the Rainbow,* Cambridge, Mass.: Hackett.

—— (1989) 'Review of David Hilbert, *Color and Color Perception: A Study in Anthropocentric Realism*', *Canadian Philosophical Reviews* 9: 47–9.

—— (1990a) 'Why color?', in M. Brill (ed.) *Perceiving, Measuring, and Using Color,* Proceedings of the SPIE/SPSE Symposium on Electronic Imaging: Science and Technology 1250: 293–300.

—— (1990b) 'Color and illusion', in W. G. Lycan (ed.) *Mind and Cognition: A Reader,* Oxford: Basil Blackwell.

—— (1991) 'Reply to Levine', *Philosophical Psychology* 4: 41–50.

—— (1992a) 'Color for pigeons and philosophers' (Open Peer Commentary on E. Thompson et al., 'Ways of coloring: comparative color vision as a case study for cognitive science', *Behavioral and Brain Sciences* 15: 1–74), *Behavioral and Brain Sciences* 15: 37–8.

—— (1992b) 'The virtues of illusion', *Philosophical Studies* 68: 371–82.

—— (1992c) 'Physiology, phenomenology, and Spinoza's true colors', in Ansgar Beckermann, Hans Flohr, and Jaegwon Kim (eds) *Emergence or Reduction? Essays on the Prospects of Nonreductive Physicalism,* New York: Walter de Gruyter.

Harding, G. (1991) 'Color and the mind–body problem', *Review of Metaphysics* 45: 289–307.

Harosi, F. I. and Hashimoto, Y. (1983) 'Ultraviolet visual pigment in a vertebrate: a tetrachromatic cone system in the dace', *Science* 222: 1021–3.

Harrison, B. (1973) *Form and Content,* Oxford: Basil Blackwell.

—— (1986) 'Identity, predication and color', *American Philosophical Quarterly* 23: 105–14.

Hatfield, G. (1992) 'Color perception and neural encoding: does metameric matching entail a loss of information?', *PSA 1992* 1: 492–504.

Heft, H. (1989) 'Affordances and the body: an intentional analysis of Gibson's ecological approach to visual perception', *Journal for the Theory of Social Behaviour* 19: 1–30.

Heider, E. R. (1972) 'Universals in color naming and memory', *Journal of Experimental Psychology* 93: 10–20.

Heiligenberg, W. (1991) 'The neural basis of behavior: a neuroethological view', *Annual Review of Neuroscience* 14: 247–67.

Helson, H. (1938) 'Fundamental problems in color vision. I. The principles governing changes in hue, saturation, and lightness of nonselective samples in chromatic illumination', *Journal of Experimental Psychology* 23: 439–76.

Helson, H. and Jeffers, J. B. (1940) 'Fundamental problems in color vision. II. Hue, lightness, and saturation of selective samples in chromatic illumination', *Journal of Experimental Psychology* 25: 1–27.

Helverson, O. v. (1972) 'Zur spektralen Unterschiedsempfindlichkeit der Honigbiene', *Journal of Comparative Physiology* 80: 439–72.

Hering, E. (1920/1964) *Outlines of a Theory of the Light Sense*, trans. L. Hurvich and D. Jameson, Cambridge, Mass.: Harvard University Press.

Heywood, C. A. and Cowey, A. (1987) 'On the role of cortical area V4 in the discrimination of hue and pattern in macaque monkeys', *Journal of Neuroscience* 7: 2601–17.

Hilbert, D. R. (1987) *Color and Color Perception: A Study in Anthropocentric Realism*, Stanford University: Center for the Study of Language and Information.

—— (1992a) 'Comparative color vision and the objectivity of color' (Open Peer Commentary on E. Thompson et al., 'Ways of coloring: comparative color vision as a case study for cognitive science', *Behavioral and Brain Sciences* 15: 1–74), *Behavioral and Brain Sciences* 15: 38–9.

—— (1992b) 'What is color vision?', *Philosophical Studies* 68: 351–70.

Hood, D. C. and Finkelstein, M. A. (1983) 'A case for the revision of textbook models of colour vision: the detection and appearance of small brief lights', in J. D. Mollon and L. T. Sharpe (eds) *Color Vision*, London: Academic Press.

Horgan, T. (1984) 'Functionalism, qualia, and the inverted spectra', *Philosophy and Phenomenological Research* 44: 453–69.

Horn, B. K. P. (1974) 'Determining lightness from an image', *Computer Graphics and Image Processing* 3: 277–99.

Horn, G. and Hill, R. M. (1969) 'Modifications of the receptive field of cells in the visual cortex occurring spontaneously and associated with bodily tilt', *Nature* 221: 185–7.

Hubel, D. H., and Wiesel, T. N. (1960) 'Receptive fields of optic nerve fiber in the spider monkey' *Journal of Physiology* 337: 183–200.

Hudon, J. and Brush, A. H. (1989) 'Probable dietary basis of a color variant of the cedar waxwing', *Journal of Field Ornithology* 60: 361–8.

Humphrey, N. (1984) *Consciousness Regained: Chapters in the Development of Mind*, Oxford: Oxford University Press.

—— (1992) *A History of the Mind: Evolution and the Birth of Consciousness*, New York: Simon & Schuster.

Humphrey, N. and Keeble, G. (1978) 'Effects of red light and loud noise on the rates at which monkeys sample the sensory environment', *Perception* 7: 343.

Hunt, R. W. G. (1987) *Measuring Color*, West Sussex: Ellis Horwood.

Hurlbert, A. (1986) 'Formal connections between lightness algorithms', *Journal of the Optical Society of America A* 3: 1684–93.

—— (1989) *The Computation of Color*, MIT AI Lab Technical Report 1154, Cambridge, Mass.

—— (1991) 'Deciphering the colour code', *Nature* 349: 191–3.

Hurlbert, A. and Poggio, T. (1988) 'Making machines (and artificial intelligence) see', *Daedelus* 117(1): 213–39.

Hurvich, L. M. (1981) *Color Vision*, Sunderland, Mass.: Sinnauer Associates.

—— (1985) 'Opponent-colours theory', in D. Ottoson and S. Zeki (eds) *Central and Peripheral Mechanisms of Colour Vision*, London: Macmillan.

Hurvich, L. M. and Jameson, D. (1957) 'An opponent process theory of color vision', *Psychological Review* 64: 384–404.

Husserl, E. (1954/1970) *The Crisis of European Sciences and Transcendental Phenomenology*, trans. David Carr, Evanston: Northwestern University Press.

Huygens, C. (1897) *Œuvres complètes de Christiaan Huygens, VII, Correspondence*, The Hague: Martinus Nijhoff.

Ingle, D. J. (1985) 'The goldfish as a retinex animal', *Science* 225: 651–3.

Ingling, C. R. and Tsou, B. H.-P. (1977) 'Orthoganal combination of the three visual channels', *Vision Research* 17: 1075–82.

Jackson, F. (1977) *Perception*, Cambridge: Cambridge University Press.

—— (1982) 'Epiphenomenal qualia', *Philosophical Quarterly* 32: 127–36. Reprinted in W. G. Lycan (ed.) *Mind and Cognition: A Reader*, Oxford: Basil Blackwell.

—— (1986) 'What Mary didn't know', *Journal of Philosophy* 83: 291–5.

Jackson, F. and Pargetter, R. (1987) 'An objectivist's guide to subjectivism about colour', *Revue Internationale de Philosophie* 160: 129–41.

Jackson, R. (1968) 'Locke's distinction between primary and secondary qualities', reprinted in C. B. Martin and D. M. Armstrong (eds) *Locke and Berkeley*, University of Notre Dame Press.

Jacobs, G. H. (1981) *Comparative Color Vision*, New York: Academic Press.

—— (1983) 'Colour vision in animals', *Trends in Neurosciences* 7: 137–40.

—— (1985) 'Within-species variation in visual capacity among squirrel monkeys (*Saimiri sciureus*): color vision', *Vision Research* 24: 1267–77.

—— (1986) 'Color vision variations in non-human primates', *Trends in Neurosciences* 12: 320–3.

—— (1990) 'Evolution of mechanisms for color vision', in Michael Brill (ed.) *SPIE Volume 1250: Perceiving, Measuring, and Using Color*, 287–91.

—— (1992) 'Ultraviolet vision in vertebrates', *American Zoologist* 32: 544–54.

Jacobs, G. H. and Neitz, J. (1985) 'Color vision in squirrel monkeys: sex related differences suggest the mode of inheritance', *Vision Research* 25: 141–3.

—— (1987) 'Color vision polymorphism and its photopigment basis in a callitrichid monkey (*Saguinus fuscicollis*)', *Vision Research* 27: 2089–2100.

Jacobs, G. H., Neitz, J., and Deegan, J. F. H. (1991) 'Retinal receptors in rodents maximally sensitive to ultraviolet light', *Nature* 353: 655–66.

Jameson, D. (1985) 'Opponent-colours theory in the light of physiological findings', in D. Ottoson and S. Zeki (eds) *Central and Peripheral Mechanisms of Colour Vision*, London: Macmillan.

Jameson, D. and Hurvich, L. M. (1955) 'Some quantitative aspects of an opponent-colors theory: I. Chromatic responses and spectral saturation', *Journal of the Optical Society of America* 45: 546–52.

—— (1989) 'Essay concerning color constancy', *Annual Review of Psychology* 40: 1–22.

Jane, S. D. and Bowmaker, J. K. (1988) 'Tetrachromatic colour vision in the duck (*Anas platyrhynchos* L.): microspectrophotometry of visual pigments and oil droplets', *Journal of Comparative Physiology* 162: 225–35.

Jassik-Gerschenfeld, D., Lange, R. V., and Ropert, N. (1977) 'Response of movement detecting cells in the optic tectum of pigeons to change of wavelength', *Vision Research* 17: 1139–46.

Jitsumori, M. (1976) 'Anomaloscope experiment for a study of color mixture in the pigeon', *Japanese Psychological Research* 18: 126–35.

Jordan, G. and Mollon, J. D. (1993) 'A study of women heterozygous for colour deficiencies', *Vision Research* 33: 1495–1508.

Judd, D. B. (1940) 'Hue, saturation, and lightness of surface colors with chromatic illumination', *Journal of the Optical Society of America* 30: 2–32.

Judd, D. B., McAdam, D. L., and Wyszecki, G. (1964) 'Spectral distribution of typical daylight as a function of correlated color temperature', *Journal of the Optical Society of America* A 54: 1031–40.

Judd, D. B. and Wyszecki, G. (1963) *Colour in Business, Science and Industry*, second edition, New York: Wiley.

Kandel, E. R. and Schwartz, J. H. (1985) *Principles of Neural Science*, second edition, New York: North Holland.

Katz, D. (1935) *The World of Colour*, London: Kegan Paul.

Kay, P. and Kempton, W. (1984) 'What is the Sapir–Whorf hypothesis?', *American Anthropologist* 86: 65–79.

Kay, P. and McDaniel, C. K. (1978) 'The linguistic significance of the meaning of basic color terms', *Language* 54: 610–46.

Kelly, D. (1986) *The Evidence of the Senses*, Baton Rouge: Louisiana State University Press.

Kelso, J. A. S. and Kay, B. A. (1987) 'Information and control: a macroscopic analysis of perception-action coupling', in H. Heuer and A. F. Sanders (eds) *Perspectives on Perception and Action*, Hillsdale, N.J.: Lawrence Erlbaum Associates.

Kitcher, P. (1988) 'Marr's computational theory of vision', *Philosophy of Science* 55: 1–25.

Kondrashev, S. (1992) 'Ethological and ecological aspects of color vision' (Open Peer Commentary on E. Thompson et al., 'Ways of coloring: comparative color vision as a case study for cognitive science', *Behavioral and Brain Sciences* 15: 1–74), *Behavioral and Brain Sciences* 15: 42.

Krauskopf, J. and Farrell, B. (1990) 'Influence of colour on the perception of coherent motion', *Nature* 348: 328–31.

Krauskopf, J., Williams, D. R., and Heeley, D. W. (1982) 'Cardinal directions in color space', *Vision Research* 22: 1123–31.

Krauskopf, J., Williams, D. R., Mandler, M. B., and Brown, A. M. (1986)

'Higher order color mechanisms', *Vision Research* 26: 22–32.

Krinov, E. L. (1947) 'Spectral reflectance properties of natural formations', Technical Translation TT–439, National Research Council of Canada.

Krüger, J. and Fischer, B. (1983) 'Colour columns and colour areas', in J. D. Mollon and L. T. Sharpe (eds) *Colour Vision*, London: Academic Press.

Krüger, J. and Gouras, P. (1980) 'Spectral selectivity of cells and its dependence on slit length in monkey visual cortex', *Journal of Neurophysiology* 43: 1055–69.

Kuehni, R. G. (1983) *Color: Essence and Logic*, New York: Van Nostrand.

Kulli, J. and Koch, C. (1991) 'Does anesthesia cause loss of consciousness?', *Trends in Neurosciences* 14: 6–10.

Ladd-Franklin, C. (1929) *Colour Vision and Colour Theories*, New York: Harcourt Brace.

Lakoff, G. (1987) *Women, Fire, and Dangerous Things: What Categories Reveal about the Mind*, Chicago and London: University of Chicago Press.

Land, E. H. (1959) 'Experiments in color vision', *Scientific American* 200(5): 84–99.

—— (1977) 'The retinex theory of color vision', *Scientific American* 237(6): 108–28.

—— (1978) 'Our "polar partnership" with the world around us', *Harvard Magazine* 80: 23–6.

—— (1983) 'Recent advances in retinex theory and some implications for cortical computations: color vision and the natural image', *Proceedings of the National Academy of Sciences U.S.A.* 80: 5163–9.

—— (1985) 'Recent advances in retinex theory', in D. Ottoson and S. Zeki (eds) *Central and Peripheral Mechanisms of Colour Vision*, London: Macmillan. Also printed in *Vision Research* 26 (1986): 7–21.

—— (1986) 'An alternative technique for the computation of the designator in the retinex theory of color vision', *Proceedings of the National Academy of Sciences U.S.A.* 83: 3078–80.

Land, E. H., Hubel, D. H., Livingstone, M. S., Perry, S. H., and Burns, M. M. (1983) 'Colour-generating interactions across the corpus callosum', *Nature* 303: 616–18.

Land, E. H. and McCann, J. J. (1971) 'Lightness and retinex theory', *Journal of the Optical Society of America* 61: 1–11.

Landesman, C. (1989) *Color and Consciousness: An Essay in Metaphysics*, Philadelphia: Temple University Press.

Lee, D. N. (1980) 'The optic flow field: the foundation of vision', *Philosophical Transactions of the Royal Society of London, Series B* 290: 169–79.

Lee, D. N. and Reddish, P. E. (1981) 'Plummeting gannets: a paradigm of ecological optics', *Nature* 293: 293–4.

Lehky, S. R. and Sejnowski, T. J. (1988) 'Network model of shape from shading: neural function arises from both receptive and projective fields', *Nature* 333: 452–4.

Lennie, P. (1984) 'Recent developments in the physiology of color vision', *Trends in Neurosciences* 7: 243–8.

Lennie, P., Trevarthen, C., Van Essen, D., and Wässel, H. (1990) 'Parallel processing of visual information', in L. Spillman and J. S. Werner (eds) *Visual Perception: The Neurophysiological Foundations*, San Diego: Academic Press.

Levine, J. (1983) 'Materialism and qualia: the explanatory gap', *Pacific Philosophical Quarterly* 64: 354–61.

—— (1991) 'Cool red', *Philosophical Psychology* 4: 27–40.

Levine, J. S. and MacNichol, E. F., Jr (1979) 'Visual pigments in teleost fishes: effect of habitat, microhabitat and behavior on visual system evolution', *Sensory Processes* 3: 95–131.

—— (1982) 'Color vision in fishes', *Scientific American* 246: 140–9.

Levins, R. and Lewontin, R. (1985) 'The organism as the subject and object of evolution', in R. Levins and R. Lewontin, *The Dialectical Biologist*, Cambridge, Mass.: Harvard University Press.

Lewontin, R. (1980) 'Adaptation', reprinted in Eliot Sober (ed.) *Conceptual Issues in Evolutionary Biology*, Cambridge, Mass.: MIT Press.

Livingstone, M. S. and Hubel, D. H. (1984) 'Anatomy and physiology of a color system in the primate visual cortex', *Journal of Neuroscience* 4: 309–56.

—— (1987) 'Psychophysical evidence for separate channels for the perception of form, color, movement, and depth', *Journal of Neuroscience* 7: 3416–68.

—— (1988) 'Segregation of color, movement, and depth: anatomy, physiology, and perception', *Science* 240: 740–9.

Locke, J. (1690/1975) *An Essay Concerning Human Understanding*, ed. P. H. Nidditch, Oxford: Oxford University Press.

Lockhead, G. R. (1992) 'Psychophysical scaling: judgements of attributes or objects?', *Behavioral and Brain Sciences* 15(3): 543–601.

Lockwood, M. (1989) *Mind, Brain, and the Quantum. The Compound 'I'*, Oxford: Basil Blackwell.

Loew, E. R. and Lythgoe, J. N. (1978) 'The ecology of cone pigments in teleost fishes', *Vision Research* 18: 715–22.

Logothetis, N. K., Schiller, P. H., Charles, E. R., and Hurlbert, A. C. (1990) 'Perceptual deficits and the activity of the color-opponent and broad-band pathways at isoluminance', *Science* 247: 214–17.

Lycan, W. G. (ed.) (1990) *Mind and Cognition: A Reader*, Oxford: Basil Blackwell.

Lythgoe, J. N. (1972) 'The adaptation of visual pigments to their photic environment', in H. J. A. Dartnall (ed.) *Handbook of Sensory Physiology*, vol. VII, Berlin: Springer.

—— (1979) *The Ecology of Vision*, Oxford: Oxford University Press.

McCann, J. J., McKee, S. P., and Taylor, T. H. (1976) 'Quantitative studies in retinex theory', *Vision Research* 16: 445–58.

McDowell, J. (1991) 'The content of perceptual experience', paper given at a Conference on the Nature of Perception, Scarborough College, University of Toronto, 1 November 1991.

McGilvray, J. A. (1983) 'To color', *Synthese* 54: 37–70.

McGinn, C. (1983) *The Subjective View: Secondary Qualities and Indexical*

Thoughts, Oxford: Clarendon Press.

McKeon, R. (ed. and trans.) (1941) *The Basic Works of Aristotle*, New York: Random House.

Mackie, J. L. (1976) *Problems from Locke*, Oxford: Oxford University Press.

MacLaury, R. E. (1987) 'Color-category evolution and Shuswap yellow-with-green', *American Anthropologist* 89: 107–24.

—— (1991a) 'Exotic color categories: linguistic relativity to what extent?', *Journal of Linguistic Anthropology* 1: 26–51.

—— (1991b) 'Social and cognitive motivations of change: measuring variability in color semantics', *Language* 67: 34–62.

—— (1992) 'From brightness to hue: An explanatory model of color-category evolution', *Current Anthropology* 33: 137–86.

Maier, E. and Burkhardt, D. (1992) 'In search of common features of animals' color vision systems and the constraints of environment' (Open Peer Commentary on E. Thompson et al., 'Ways of coloring: comparative color vision as a case study for cognitive science', *Behavioral and Brain Sciences* 15: 1–74), *Behavioral and Brain Sciences* 15: 44–5.

Maldonado, P. E., Maturana, H., and Varela, F. J. (1988) 'Frontal and lateral visual system in birds', *Brain, Behavior and Evolution* 32: 57–62.

Maloney, L. T. (1985) *Computational Approaches to Color Constancy*, Stanford University: Applied Psychological Laboratory Technical Report 1985–01.

—— (1986) 'Evaluation of linear models of surface spectral reflectance with small numbers of parameters', *Journal of the Optical Society of America A* 3: 1673–83.

—— (1992) 'A mathematical framework for biological color vision' (Open Peer Commentary on E. Thompson et al., 'Ways of coloring: comparative color vision as a case study for cognitive science', *Behavioral and Brain Sciences* 15: 1–74), *Behavioral and Brain Sciences* 15: 45–6.

Maloney, L. T. and Wandell, B. A. (1986) 'Color constancy: a method for recovering surface spectral reflectance', *Journal of the Optical Society of America A* 3: 29–33.

Marks, W. B., Dobelle, W. H., and MacNichol, E. F., Jr (1964) 'Visual pigments of single primate cones', *Science* 143: 1181–3.

Marr, D. (1982) *Vision: A Computational Investigation into the Human Representation and Processing of Visual Information*, New York: W. H. Freeman.

Martin, G. R. (1986) 'The eye of a passeriform bird, the European starling (*Sturnus vulgaris*): eye movement amplitude, visual fields and schematic optics', *Journal of Comparative Physiology A* 159: 545–57.

Martin, G. R. and Gordon, I. E. (1974) 'Increment-threshold spectral sensitivity in the tawny owl (*Strix aluco*)', *Vision Research* 14: 615–21.

Martin, G. R. and Lett, B. T. (1985) 'Formation of associations of coloured and flavoured food with induced sickness in five avian species', *Behavioral Neural Biology* 43: 223–37.

Martin, K. A. C. (1988) 'From enzymes to visual perception: a bridge too far?', *Trends in Neurosciences* 9: 380–4.

Matthen, M. (1988) 'Biological functions and perceptual content', *Journal of Philosophy* 85: 5–27.

—— (1989) 'Intensionality and perception: a reply to Rosenberg', *Journal of Philosophy* 86: 727–33.

—— (1992) 'Color vision: content versus experience' (Open Peer Commentary on E. Thompson et al., 'Ways of coloring: comparative color vision as a case study for cognitive science', *Behavioral and Brain Sciences* 15: 1–74), *Behavioral and Brain Sciences* 15: 46–7.

Maturana, H. R. and Varela, F. J. (1980) *Autopoiesis and Cognition: The Realization of the Living*, Boston Studies in the Philosophy of Science, vol. 42, Dordrecht: D. Reidel.

—— (1982) 'Colour-opponent responses in the avian lateral geniculate: a case study in the quail', *Brain Research* 247: 227–41.

—— (1987) *The Tree of Knowledge: The Biological Roots of Human Understanding*, Boston: New Science Library.

Maund, J. B. (1981) 'Colour – a case for conceptual fission', *Australasian Journal of Philosophy* 59: 308–22.

Mausfeld, R. J., Neiderée, R. M., and Heyer, K. D. (1992) 'On possible perceptual worlds and how they shape their environments' (Open Peer Commentary on E. Thompson et al., 'Ways of coloring: comparative color vision as a case study for cognitive science', *Behavioral and Brain Sciences* 15: 1–74), *Behavioral and Brain Sciences* 15: 47–8.

Maxwell, J. C. (1890/1970) 'On colour vision', in D. L. MacAdam (ed.) *Sources of Color Science*, Cambridge, Mass.: MIT Press.

Menaud-Buteau, C. and Cavanagh, P. (1984) 'Localisation de l'interférence forme/couleur au niveau perceptuel dans une tache de type Stroop avec des stimuli-dessins', *Canadian Journal of Psychology* 38: 421–39.

Menzel, R. (1979) 'Spectral sensitivity and color vision in invertebrates', in H. Autrum (ed.) *Handbook of Sensory Physiology Volume VII/6A: Comparative Physiology and Evolution of Vision in Invertebrates*, Berlin: Springer.

—— (1985) 'Colour pathways and colour vision in the honey bee', in D. Ottoson and S. Zeki (eds) *Central and Peripheral Mechanisms of Colour Vision*, London: Macmillan.

Menzel, R. and Backhaus, W. (1991) 'Color vision in insects', in P. Gouras (ed.) *The Perception of Colour: Vision and Visual Dysfunction*, vol. 6, London: Macmillan Press.

Merbs, S. L. and Nathans, J. (1992) 'Absorption spectra of human cone pigments', *Nature* 356: 433–5.

Merleau-Ponty, M. (1942/1963) *The Structure of Behavior*, trans. Alden Fisher, Pittsburgh: Dusquesne University Press.

—— (1945/1962) *The Phenomenology of Perception*, trans. Colin Smith, London: Routledge & Kegan Paul.

—— (1964) 'Eye and mind', in Maurice Merleau-Ponty, *The Primacy of Perception*, ed. James M. Edie, Evanston: Northwestern University Press.

Meyering, T. C. (1989) *Historical Roots of Cognitive Science: The Rise of a Cognitive Theory of Perception from Antiquity to the Nineteenth Century.* Synthese Library, vol. 208, Dordrecht, Boston, and London: Kluwer Academic Publishers.

Michael, C. R. (1987a) 'Color vision mechanisms in monkey striate cortex: dual opponent cells with concentric receptive fields', *Journal of Neurophysiology* 41: 572–88.

—— (1987b) 'Color vision mechanisms in monkey striate cortex: simple cells with dual opponent color receptive fields', *Journal of Neurophysiology* 41: 1233–49.

—— (1987c) 'Color-sensitive comple cells in monkey striate cortex', *Journal of Neurophysiology* 41: 1250–66.

Michaels, C. F. and Carello, C. (1981) *Direct Perception*, Englewood Cliffs, N.J.: Prentice-Hall.

Mishkin, M., Ungerleider, L. G., and Macko, K. A. (1983) 'Object vision and spatial vision: two cortical pathways', *Trends in Neurosciences* 6: 414–17.

Mollon, J. D. (1989) '"Tho' she kneel'd in that place where they grew ... " The uses and origins of primate colour vision', *Journal of Experimental Biology* 146: 21–38.

—— (1990) 'Neurobiology: the club sandwich mystery', *Nature* 343: 16–17.

—— (1992) 'Worlds of difference', *Nature* 356: 378–9.

Mollon, J. D., Bowmaker, J. K., and Jacobs, G. H. (1984) 'Variations of colour vision in a New World primate can be explained by polymorphism of retinal pigments', *Proceedings of the Royal Society B* 222: 373–99.

Mollon, J. D. and Sharpe, L. T. (eds) (1983) *Color Vision*, London: Academic Press.

Moran, J. and Desimone, R. (1985) 'Selective attention gates visual processing in the extrastriate cortex', *Science* 229: 782–4.

Morell, F. (1972) 'Visual system's view of acoustic space', *Nature* 238: 44–6.

Mundle, C. W. K. (1971) *Perception: Facts and Theories*, Oxford: Oxford University Press.

Munsell, A. H. (1905) *A Color Notation*, Baltimore, Maryland: Munsell Color Company.

Muntz, W. R. (1975) 'Behavioral studies of vision in a fish and possible relationships to the environment', in M. A. Ali (ed.) *Vision in Fish*, Plenum Press.

Muntz, W. R. and Mouat, G. S. (1984) 'Annual variation in the visual pigments of brown trout inhabiting lochs providing different light environments', *Vision Research* 24: 1575–80.

Munz, F. W., and McFarland, F. N. (1977) 'Evolutionary adaptations of fishes to the photopic environment', in F. Crescitelli (ed.) *Handbook of Sensory Physiology Volume VII/5. The Visual System in Vertebrates*, Berlin: Springer.

Nagel, T. (1974) 'What is it like to be a bat?', *Philosophical Review* 83: 435–50. Page references in the text are to the reprinted version in T.

Nagel, *Mortal Questions*, Cambridge: Cambridge University Press, 1979.

—— (1979a) 'Subjective and objective', in T. Nagel, *Mortal Questions*, Cambridge: Cambridge University Press, 1979.

—— (1979b) *Mortal Questions*, Cambridge: Cambridge University Press.

—— (1986) *The View from Nowhere*, New York: Oxford University Press.

Nassau, K. (1983) 'The causes of color', *Scientific American* 242(10): 124–54.

Nathans, J. (1987) 'Molecular biology of visual pigments', *Annual Review of Neuroscience* 10: 163–94.

—— (1989) 'The genes for color vision', *Scientific American* 260: 28–35.

Nathans, J., Piantanida, T. P., Eddy, R. L., Shows, T. B., and Hogness, D. S. (1986b) 'Molecular genetics of inherited variation in human colour vision', *Science* 232: 203–10.

Nathans, J., Thomas, D., and Hogness, D. S. (1986a) 'Molecular genetics of human color vision: the genes encoding blue, green, and red pigments', *Science* 232: 193–202.

Neitz, J. and Jacobs, G. H. (1986) 'Polymorphism of the long-wavelength cone in normal human color vision', *Nature* 323: 623–35.

Nemirow, L. (1990) 'Physicalism and the cognitive role of acquaintance', in W. G. Lycan, *Mind and Cognition: A Reader*, Oxford: Basil Blackwell.

Neumeyer, C. (1980) 'Simultaneous color contrast in the honeybee', *Journal of Comparative Physiology A* 139: 165–76.

—— (1981) 'Chromatic adaptation in the honeybee: successive color contrast and color constancy', *Journal of Comparative Physiology A* 144: 543–53.

—— (1985) 'An ultraviolet receptor as a fourth receptor type in goldfish color vision', *Naturwissenschaften* 72: 162–3.

—— (1986) 'Wavelength discrimination in the goldfish', *Journal of Comparative Physiology* 158: 203–13.

—— (1988) *Das Farbensehen des Goldfisches: Eine verhaltensphysiologische Analyse*, Stuttgart: Thieme.

—— (1991) 'Evolution of colour vision', in John R. Cronly-Dillon and Richard L. Gregory (eds) *Evolution of the Eye and Visual System: Vision and Visual Dysfunction*, vol. 2, London: Macmillan Press.

—— (1992a) 'On perceived colors' (Open Peer Commentary on E. Thompson et al., 'Ways of coloring: comparative color vision as a case study for cognitive science', *Behavioral and Brain Sciences* 15: 1–74), *Behavioral and Brain Sciences* 15: 49.

—— (1992b) 'Tetrachromatic color vision in goldfish: evidence from color mixture experiments', *Journal of Comparative Physiology A* 171: 639–49.

Neumeyer, C. and Arnold, K. (1989) 'Tetrachromatic color vision in the goldfish becomes trichromatic under white adaptation light of moderate intensity', *Vision Research* 29: 1719–27.

Newton, I. (1730/1952) *Opticks, Or a Treatise of the Reflections, Refractions, Inflections and Colours of Light*, based on the fourth edition of

1730, New York: Dover Publications.

—— (1671/1953) 'The new theory about light and colors', in H. S. Thayer (ed.) *Newton's Philosophy of Nature: Selections from his Writings*, New York and London: Hafner Publishing Company.

Noble, W. G. (1981) 'Gibsonian theory and the pragmatist perspective', *Journal for the Theory of Social Behaviour* 11: 65–85.

Nuboer, J. F. W. (1986) 'A comparative view on colour vision', *Netherlands Journal of Zoology* 36: 344–80.

Nuboer, J. F. W. and Wortel, J. (1987) 'Colour vision via the pigeon's red and yellow retinal fields', in J. J. Kulkowski (ed.) *Seeing Contour and Colour*, Cambridge: Cambridge University Press.

Odling-Smee, F. J. (1988) 'Niche-constructing phenotypes', in H. C. Plotkin (ed.) *The Role of Behavior in Evolution*, Cambridge, Mass.: MIT Press.

Ottoson, D. and Zeki, S. (eds) (1985) *Central and Peripheral Mechanisms of Colour Vision*, London: Macmillan.

Overmeyer, S. P. and Simon, J. R. (1985) 'The effect of irrelevant cues on "same–different" judgements in a sequential information processing task', *Acta Psychologia* 58: 237–49.

Palacios, A. (1991) 'La Vision chromatique chez l'oiseaux: étude comportamentale', thèse de doctorat, Université de Paris VI.

Palacios, A., Bonnardel, V., and Varela, F. J. (1990a) 'L'"autoshaping": méthode psychophysique pour la discrimination chromatique chez les oiseaux. An autoshaping method for wavelength discrimination in birds', *Comptes Rendues à l'Académie des Sciences* (Paris) 311: Série III: 213–18.

Palacios, A., Gioanni, H., and Varela, F. J. (1991) 'Etude psychophysique de la discrimination chromatique du pigeon après lésion des noyaux thalamiques Rotundus (RT) et Geniculatus Lateralis ventralis (GLv). Chromatic discrimination in pigeons after thalamic lesions of nuclei Rotundus (Rt) and Geniculatus Lateralis ventralis (GLv): a psychophysical study', *Comptes Rendues à l'Académie des Sciences* (Paris) 312: Série III: 113–16.

Palacios, A., Martinoya, C., Bloch, S., and Varela, F. J. (1990b) 'Color mixing in the pigeon: a psychophysical determination in the longwave spectral range', *Vision Research* 30: 587–96.

Palacios, A. and Varela, F. J. (1988) 'Color vision in the pigeon: an anomaloscope experiment', *Proceedings of the Physiological Society* (1–2 July 1988), *Journal of Physiology* 406: 23P.

—— (1992) 'Color mixing in the pigeon (*Columba livia*) II: a psychophysical determination in the middle, short and near-UV range', *Vision Research* 32: 1947–53.

Partridge, J. C. (1989) 'The visual ecology of avian cone oil droplets', *Journal of Comparative Physiology A* 165: 415–26.

Partridge, J. C., Shand, J., Archer, S. N., Lythgoe, J. N., and Groningen-Luyben, W. A. (1989) 'Interspecific variation in the visual pigments of the deep-sea fishes', *Journal of Comparative Physiology A* 165: 513–29.

Peacocke, C. (1983) *Sense and Content: Experience, Thought, and their*

Relations, Oxford: Clarendon Press.

—— (1984) 'Colour concepts and colour experiences', *Synthese* 58: 365–81.

Poggio, T., Torre, V., and Koch, C. (1985) 'Computational vision and regularization theory', *Nature* 317: 314–19.

Polyak, S. (1957) *The Vertebrate Visual System,* Chicago: Chicago University Press.

Pöppel, E. (1986) 'Long-range color generating interactions across the retina', *Nature* 320: 523–5.

Prindle, S. S., Carello, C., and Turvey, M. T. (1980) 'Animal–environment mutuality and direct perception', *Behavioral and Brain Sciences* 3: 395–7.

Putnam, H. (1973) 'Reductionism and the nature of psychology', reprinted in John Haugeland (ed.) *Mind Design,* Cambridge, Mass.: MIT Press.

—— (1975) 'Philosophy and our mental life', in Hilary Putnam, *Mind, Language and Reality: Philosophical Papers,* vol. 2, Cambridge: Cambridge University Press.

—— (1987) *The Many Faces of Realism,* La Salle, Illinois: Open Court.

Pylyshyn, Z. W. (1984) *Computation and Cognition: Towards a Foundation for Cognitive Science,* Cambridge, Mass.: MIT Press.

Ramachandran, V. S. (1985) 'The neurobiology of perception', *Perception* 14: 97–103.

Ratliff, F. (1976) 'On the psychophysiological basis of universal color terms', *Proceedings of the American Philosophical Society* 120: 311–30.

Reed, E. S. (1980) 'Information pick-up is the activity of perceiving', *Behavioral and Brain Sciences* 3: 397–8.

Reeke, G. N., Jr and Edelman, G. M. (1988) 'Real brains and artificial intelligence', *Daedelus* 117(1): 143–73.

Reeke, G. N., Jr, Finkel, L. H., and Edelman, G. M. 'Selective recognition automata', in S. F. Zornetzer et al. (eds) *An Introduction to Neural and Electronic Networks,* San Diego: Academic Press.

Reeves, A. (1992) 'Areas of ignorance and confusion in color science' (Open Peer Commentary on E. Thompson et al., 'Ways of coloring: comparative color vision as a case study for cognitive science', *Behavioral and Brain Sciences* 15: 1–74), *Behavioral and Brain Sciences* 15: 49–50.

Reitner, A., Sharpe, L. T., and Zrenner, E. (1992) "Is colour vision possible with only rods and blue-sensitive cones?', *Nature* 352: 798–800.

Remy, M. and Emmerton, J. (1989) 'Behavioral spectral sensitivities of different retinal areas in pigeons', *Behavioral Neuroethology* 103: 170–7.

Robson, J. (1983) 'The morphology of cortico-fugal axons to the dorsal lateral geniculate nucleus', *Journal of Comparative Neurology* 216: 89–103.

Rowland, W. J. (1979) 'The use of color in interspecific communication', in E. H. Burtt Jr (ed.) *The Behavioral Significance of Color,* New York and London: Garland STPM Press.

Rubin, J. M. and Richards, W. A. (1982) 'Color vision and image intensities: when are changes material?', *Biological Cybernetics* 45: 215–26.

—— (1984) 'Color vision: representing material categories', MIT AI Lab. Memo 764, reprinted in W. Richards (ed.) *Natural Computation*, Cambridge, Mass.: MIT Press.

Ryle, G. (1956) 'Sensation', in Gilbert Ryle, *Collected Papers*, vol. 2, London: Hutchinson, 1971.

Sabra, A. I. (1967/1981) *Theories of Light from Descartes to Newton*, Cambridge: Cambridge University Press.

Sacks, O. and Wasserman, R. (1987) 'The case of the colorblind painter', *New York Review of Books*, 19 November: 25–34.

Schein, S. J., Marocco, R. T., and DeMonasterio, F. M. (1982) 'Is there a high concentration of color-selective cells in area V4 of monkey visual cortex?', *Journal of Neurophysiology* 47: 193–213.

Schiller, P. H. and Logothetis, N. K. (1990) 'The color-opponent and broad-band channels of the primate visual system', *Trends in Neurosciences* 13: 392–8.

Schiller, P. H., Logethetis, N. K., and Charles, E. R. (1990) 'Functions of the colour-opponent and broad-band channels of the visual system', *Nature* 343: 68–70.

Schlick, M. (1979) 'Form and content: an introduction to philosophical thinking', in Henk L. Mulder and Barbara Vele-Schlick (eds), *Moritz Schlick: Philosophical Papers (Volume II: 1925-1936)*, Dordrecht: D. Reidel.

Searle, J. (1983) *Intentionality: An Essay in the Philosophy of Mind*, Cambridge: Cambridge University Press.

Sedivy, S. (1992) 'The determinate character of perceptual experience', doctoral dissertation, Department of Philosophy, University of Pittsburgh.

Sekuler, R. and Blake, R. (1985) *Perception*, New York: Alfred A. Knopf.

Sellars, W. (1956) 'Empiricism and the philosophy of mind', in H. Feigl and M. Scriven (eds) *Minnesota Studies in the Philosophy of Science*, vol. 1, Minneapolis: University of Minnesota Press.

Sepper, D. L. (1988) *Goethe contra Newton: Polemics and the Project for a New Science of Color*, Cambridge: Cambridge University Press.

Shapley, R. (1986) 'The importance of contrast for the activity of single neurons, the VEP and perception', *Vision Research* 26: 45–61.

Shapley, R., Caelli, T., Grossberg, S., Morgan, M., and Rentschler, I. (1990) 'Computational theories of visual perception', in L. Spillman and J. S. Werner (eds) *Visual Perception: The Neurophysiological Foundations*, San Diego: Academic Press.

Shaw, R. and Todd, J. (1980) 'Abstract machine theory and direct perception', *Behavioral and Brain Sciences* 3: 400–1.

Shepard, R. N. (1987) 'Evolution of a mesh between principles of the mind and regularities of the world', in John Dupré (ed.) *Beyond the Best: Essays on Evolution and Optimality*, Cambridge, Mass.: MIT Press.

—— (1990) 'A possible evolutionary basis for trichromacy', in Michael

Brill (ed.) *Perceiving, Measuring, and Using Color. Proceedings of the SPIE/SPSE Symposium on Electronic Imaging: Science and Technology* 1250: 301–9.

—— (1992) 'What in the world determines the structure of color space?' (Open Peer Commentary on E. Thompson et al., 'Ways of coloring: comparative color vision as a case study for cognitive science', *Behavioral and Brain Sciences* 15: 1–74), *Behavioral and Brain Sciences* 15: 50–1.

Shoemaker, S. (1984) 'The inverted spectrum', in Sidney Shoemaker, *Identity, Cause, and Mind: Philosophical Essays*, Cambridge: Cambridge University Press, 1984.

Siewert, C. (1993) 'What Dennett can't imagine and why', *Inquiry* 36: 93–112.

Smart, J. J. C. (1961) 'Colours', *Philosophy* 36: 128–42.

—— (1963) *Philosophy and Scientific Realism*, London: Routledge & Kegan Paul.

—— (1975) 'On some criticisms of a physicalist theory of colors', in Chung-ying Chung (ed.) *Philosophical Aspects of the Mind–Body Problem*, Honolulu: University of Hawaii Press.

Snodderly, D. M. (1979) 'Visual discrimination encountered in food foraging by a neotropical primate: implications for the evolution of color vision', in E. H. Burtt Jr (ed.) *The Behavioral Significance of Color*, New York and London: Garland STPM Press.

Snow, D. W. (1971) 'Evolutionary aspects of fruit eating by birds', *Ibis* 113: 194–202.

Snyder, A. W. and Barlow, H. B. (1988) 'Revealing the artist's touch', *Nature* 331: 117–18.

Sober, E. (ed.) (1984) *Conceptual Issues in Evolutionary Biology*, Cambridge, Mass.: MIT Press.

Spillman, L. and Werner, J. S. (eds) (1990) *Visual Perception: The Neurophysiological Foundations*, San Diego: Academic Press.

Steriade, M. and Deschenes, M. (1985) 'The thalamus as a neuronal oscillator', *Brain Research Reviews* 18: 165–70.

Stoerig, P. and Cowey, A. (1989) 'Wavelength sensitivity in blindsight', *Nature* 342: 916–18.

—— (1992a) 'Wavelength processing and colour experience' (Open Peer Commentary on E. Thompson et al., 'Ways of coloring: comparative color vision as a case study for cognitive science', *Behavioral and Brain Sciences* 15: 1–74), *Behavioral and Brain Sciences* 15: 52–3.

—— (1992b) 'Wavelength discrimination in blindsight', *Brain* 115: 425–44.

Stroll, A. (1986) 'The role of surfaces in an ecological theory of perception', *Philosophy and Phenomenological Research* 46: 437–53.

Stroud, B. (1989) 'The study of human nature and the subjectivity of value', in *The Tanner Lectures on Human Values*, X, Salt Lake City: University of Utah Press.

Svaetichin, G. and MacNichol, E. F. (1958) 'Retinal mechanisms for chromatic and achromatic vision', *Annals of the New York Academy of Sciences* 74: 385–404.

Teller, D. Y. (1984) 'Linking propositions', *Vision Research* 24: 1233–46.

—— (1990) 'The domain of visual science', in L. Spillman and J. S. Werner (eds) *Visual Perception: The Neurophysiological Foundations*, San Diego: Academic Press.

Teller, D. Y. and Pugh, E. N., Jr (1983) 'Linking propositions in color vision', in J. D. Mollon and L. T. Sharpe (eds) *Color Vision*, London: Academic Press.

Thompson, E. (1992) 'Novel colours', *Philosophical Studies* 67: 105–33.

—— (in press) 'Colour vision, evolution, and perceptual content', *Synthese*.

Thompson, E., Palacios, A., and Varela, F. J. (1992) 'Ways of coloring: comparative color vision as a case study for cognitive science', *Behavioral and Brain Sciences* 15: 1–74.

Thornton, M. (1972) 'Ostensive terms and materialism', *Monist* 56: 193–214.

—— (1989) *Folk Psychology: An Introduction*, Canadian Philosophical Monographs, Toronto: University of Toronto Press.

Tovée, M. J., Bowmaker, J. K., and Mollon, J. D. (1992) 'The relationship between cone pigments and behavioural sensitivity in a New World monkey (*Callithrix jacchus jacchus*)', *Vision Research* 32: 867–78.

Troost, J. M. and de Weert, C. M. M. (1990) 'Surface reflectances and human color constancy: comment on Dannemiller (1989)', *Psychological Review* 98: 143–5.

Turvey, M. T., Shaw, R. E., Reed, E. S., and Mace, W. M. (1981) 'Ecological laws of perceiving and acting: in reply to Fodor and Pylyshyn (1981)', *Cognition* 9: 237–304.

Uexküll, J. von (1934/1957) 'A stroll through the world of animals and men', in Claire H. Schiller and Karl S. Lashley (trans. and ed.) *Instinctive Behavior: The Development of a Modern Concept*, New York: International Universities Press.

Ungerleider, L. G. and Mishkin, M. (1982) 'Two cortical visual systems', in D. J. Ingle, M. A. Goodale, and R. J. W. Mansfield (eds) *Analysis of Visual Behavior*, Cambridge, Mass.: MIT Press.

Varela, F. J. (1979) *Principles of Biological Autonomy*, New York: Elsevier North Holland.

—— (1984) 'Living ways of sense-making: a middle path for neuroscience', in Paisley Livingston (ed.) *Disorder and Order: Proceedings of the Stanford International Symposium*, Stanford Literature Series, vol. 1, Anma Libri.

Varela, F. J., Letelier, J. C., Marin, G., and Maturana, H. R. (1983) 'The neurophysiology of avian color vision', *Archivos de Biologia y Medicina Experimentales* 16: 291–303.

Varela, F. J., Palacios, A., and Goldsmith, T. H. (1993) 'Color vision of birds', in H. P. Zeigler and H. J. Bischof (eds) *Vision, Brain, and Behavior of Birds*, Cambridge, Mass.: MIT Press.

Varela, F. J. and Singer, W. (1987) 'Neuronal dynamics in the visual cortico-thalamic pathway as revealed through binocular rivalry', *Experimental Brain Research* 66: 10–20.

Varela, F. J., Thompson, E., and Rosch, E. (1991) *The Embodied Mind: Cognitive Science and Human Experience*, Cambridge, Mass.: MIT Press.

Vision, G. (1982) 'Primary and secondary qualities: an essay in epistemology', *Erkenntnis* 17: 135–69.

Walls, G. L. (1960) 'Land! Land!', *Psychological Bulletin* 57: 29–48.

Wasserman, G. S. (1978) *Color Vision: An Historical Introduction*, New York: John Wiley.

Webster, M. A. and Mollon, J. D. (1991) 'Changes in colour appearance following post-receptoral adaptation', *Nature* 349: 235–8.

Weedon, B. C. (1963) 'Occurrence', in O. Isler (ed.) *Carotenoids*, Birkhauser.

Weiskrantz, L. (1986) *Blindsight: A Case Study and Implications*, Oxford: Oxford University Press.

Werner, A., Menzel, R., and Wehrhahn, C. (1988) 'Color constancy in the honeybee', *Journal of Neuroscience* 8: 156–9.

Westphal, J. (1984) 'The complexity of quality', *Philosophy* 59: 457–71.

—— (1987) *Colour: Some Philosophical Problems from Wittgenstein*, Oxford: Basil Blackwell.

Whitmore, A. V. and Bowmaker, J. K. (1989) 'Seasonal variation in cone sensitivity and short-wave absorbing visual pigments in the rudd, *Scardinius erythrophthalmus*', *Journal of Comparative Physiology A* 166: 103–15.

Whorf, B. L. (1956) *Language, Thought and Reality*, Cambridge, Mass.: MIT Press.

Wilczek, F. and Devine, B. (1988) *Longing for the Harmonies: Themes and Variations from Modern Physics*, New York: Norton.

Williams, C. (1974) 'The effect of an irrelevant dimension on "same–different" judgements of multi-dimensional stimuli', *Quarterly Journal of Experimental Psychology* 26: 26–31.

Winderickx, J., Lindsey, D. T., Sanocki, E., Teller, D. Y., Motulsky, A. G., and Deeb, S. S. (1992) 'Polymorphism in red photopigment underlies variation in colour matching', *Nature* 356: 431–3.

Wittgenstein, L. (1921/1961) *Tractatus Logico-Philosophicus*, trans. D. F. Pears and Brian McGuinness, London: Routledge & Kegan Paul.

—— (1977) *Remarks on Colour*, ed. G. E. M. Anscombe, trans. Linda L. McAlister and Margarete Schättle, Berkeley: University of California Press.

Worthey, J. A. (1985) 'Limitations of color constancy', *Journal of the Optical Society of America A* 2: 1014–26.

Wright, A. (1972) 'The influence of ultraviolet radiation on the pigeon's color discrimination', *Journal of the Experimental Analysis of Behavior* 17: 325–37.

—— (1979) 'Color-vision psychophysics: a comparison of pigeon and human', in A. M. Granda and J. H. Maxwell, *Neural Mechanisms of Behavior in the Pigeon*, New York and London: Plenum Press.

Wright, A. and Cummings, W. W. (1971) 'Color naming functions for the pigeon', *Journal of the Experimental Analysis of Behavior* 15: 7–17.

Wright, W. D. and Pitts, F. G. H. (1934) 'Hue discrimination in normal colour vision', *Proceedings of the Physical Society of London* 46: 459.

Wyszecki, G. and Stiles, W. S. (1982) *Color Science: Concepts and Methods, Quantitative Data and Formulae,* second edition, New York: Wiley.

Yilmaz, H. (1962) 'Color vision and a new general approach to perception', in E. E. Bernard and M. R. Kare (eds) *Biological Prototypes and Synthetic Systems,* New York: Plenum Press.

Zeki, S. (1980) 'The representation of colours in the cerebral cortex', *Nature* 284: 412–18.

—— (1983a) 'Colour coding in the cerebral cortex: the reaction of cells in monkey visual cortex to wavelengths and colours', *Neuroscience* 9: 741–65.

—— (1983b) 'Colour coding in the cerebral cortex: the responses of wavelength-selective cells in monkey visual cortex to changes in wavelength composition', *Neuroscience* 9: 767–81.

—— (1985) 'Colour pathways and hierarchies in the cerebral cortex', in D. Ottoson and S. Zeki (eds) *Central and Peripheral Mechanisms of Colour Vision,* London: Macmillan.

Zeki, S. and Shipp, S. (1988) 'The functional logic of cortical connections', *Nature* 335: 311–17.

Zornetzer, S. F., Davis, J. L., and Lau, C. (eds) (1990) *An Introduction to Neural and Electronic Networks,* San Diego: Academic Press.

Zrenner, E., Abramov, I., Akita, M., Cowey, A., Livingstone, M., and Valberg, A. (1990) 'Color perception: retina to cortex', in L. Spillman and J. S. Werner, *Visual Perception: The Neurophysiological Foundations,* San Diego: Academic Press.

INDEX